Guns of the Cape Fear

The Civil War Defenses of Wilmington, NC

Volume One: The First Nineteen Months

H. J. Keith

Copyright © 2007, 2008, 2009, 2010, 2011 by H. J. Keith

First Paperback Edition 2011

Published by
CONFEDERATE IMPRINTS
597 E. Riverchase Way
Eagle, ID 83616

All rights reserved, including the right to reproduce this book or portions thereof in any form or by any means, electronic or mechanical, including recording, photographing or by any other storage and retrieval system, without permission in writing from the publisher. All inquiries should be electronically addressed to the publisher at: info@confederateimprints.com

Published in the United States of America

10 9 8 7 6 5 4 3 2

FIRST EDITION

ISBN 978-0-578-08983-6

Front Cover: Engineer's rendering of the two elevations of Fort Caswell's citadel. This is the only known rendering to exist of both front and side elevations of the "home to the garrison," and the fort's last line of defense. (National Archives and Records Administration, Cartographic Division)

Back Cover: Courtesy of Fort Macon State Park, North Carolina Division of Parks and Recreation. Photography approved by Paul R. Branch, Jr., Fort Macon State Park Ranger/Historian. Image courtesy of Jim McKee, Historic Site Interpreter, Brunswick Town/Fort Anderson State Historic Site.

Cover designed by Patricia C. Schweikert

For Nathaniel and Matthew

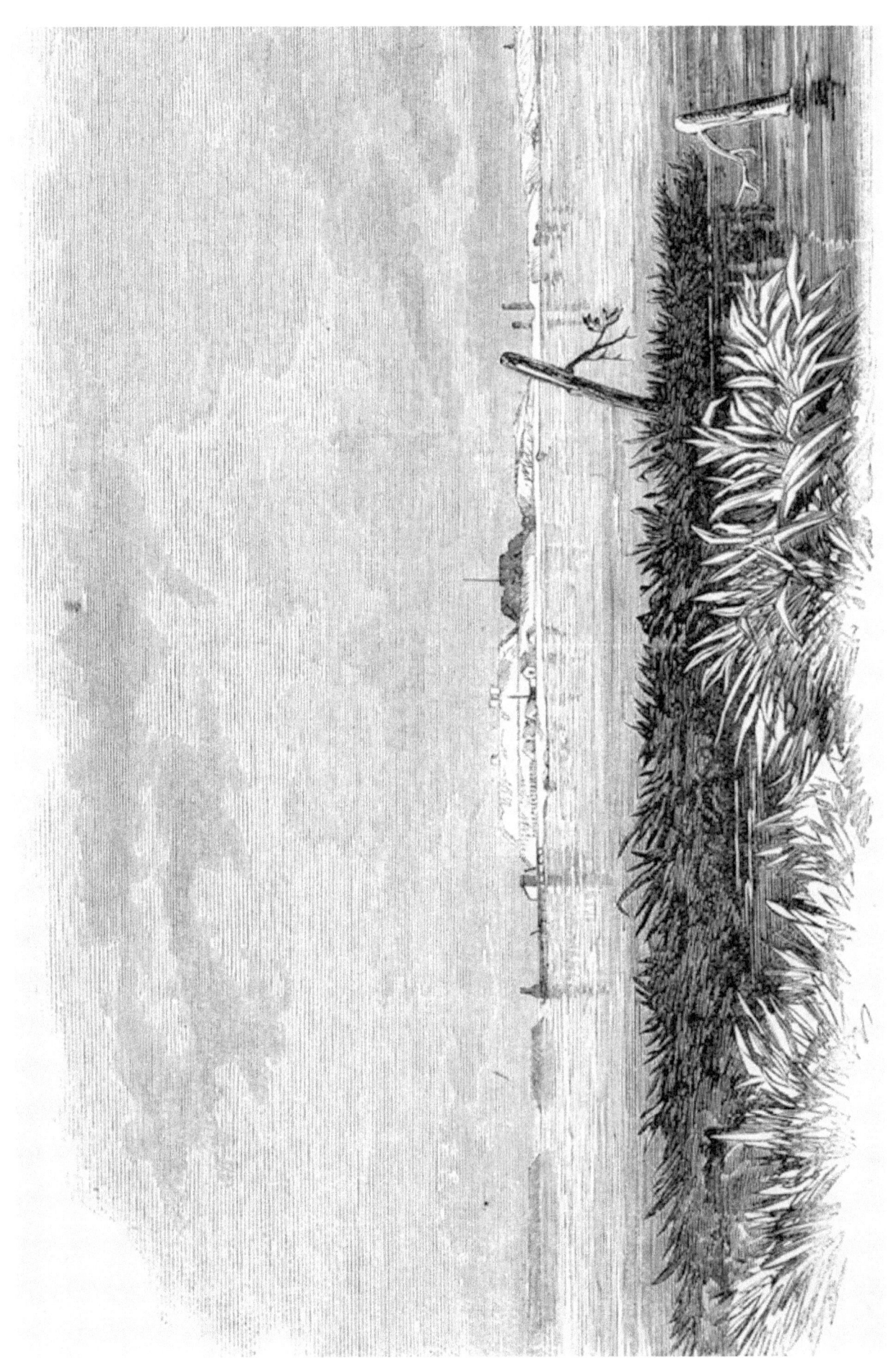

Artist's sketch of the west side of the Cape Fear River, depicting the formidable Fort Caswell, with the chimneys of the citadel visible above the works. (*Frank Leslie's Illustrated Newspaper*, Courtesy of the University of North Carolina at Chapel Hill, North Carolina Collection)

Table of Contents

Preface   *i*

Acknowledgements   *iii*

One   *1*
Fort Johnston

Two   *13*
Fort Caswell

Three   *49*
Siege Pieces

Four   *65*
Inspector General Whiting

Five   *77*
General Gatlin

Six   *93*
General Anderson

Seven   *117*
General French

Eight   *131*
Colonel Lamb

Nine   *145*
Brigadier General Whiting

Glossary   *153*

Notes   *163*

Bibliography   *187*

Index   *195*

Compendium   *209*
Commanders of the Cape Fear

Images and Renderings

Fort Caswell   Frontis
Lieutenant Joseph Gardner Swift   4
Cape Fear Light Artillery Co. Military Notice   5
6-pounder Field Gun Patterns   7
Surviving 6-pounder Iron Field Guns at Fort Branch, NC   8
Wilmington Rifle Guards Military Notice   18
German Volunteers Military Notice   18
Examples of Fort Caswell's Features   33 – 37
Example of a Caponiere Casemate Embrasure   41
Confederate 6-pounder Field Guns   48
24-pounder Gun of Unknown Pattern   49, 50
U.S. Pattern 1819 Siege and Garrison Gun   51
U.S. Pattern 1839 8-inch Seacoast Howitzer   53
U.S. Pattern 1844 8-inch Columbiad   53
U.S. Pattern 1857 8-inch New Columbiad   53
Confederate Fort Sumter and its Cannon – 1861   54
Artillery Ammunition   55 – 57
U.S. Pattern 1819 Siege and Garrison Gun Captured by Confederates   58
U.S. Pattern 1839 8-inch Seacoast Howitzer   59
U.S. Pattern 1844 8-inch Columbiad   61
Artillery Ammunition and Implements   63, 64
Major William Henry Chase Whiting, ACSA   66
Colonel Theophilus Hunter Holmes, ACSA   67
Classified Advertisement, Hart & Bailey   67
Artillery Implements   68
Wilmington Light Infantry Military Notice   70
8-inch Columbiad Chassis and Carriage   74
Columbiad Traverse Circle and Chassis   75
24-pounder Gun and Front Pintle Barbette Carriage   76
Captain Richard Caswell Gatlin, USA   77
Wilmington Light Artillery Military Notice   78
Wilmington Horse Artillery Military Notice   79
U.S. Navy Four-Truck Carriage   80
U.S. Navy 32-pounder Unchambered Cannon of 42 Hundredweight   82
U.S. Navy 8-inch Chambered Shell Gun of 63 Hundredweight   83
U.S. Navy 32-pounder Carronade of 17 or 18 Hundredweight   89

(Images and Renderings continued on page following)

(Images and Renderings continued from page preceding)

U.S. Navy 32-pounder Chambered Cannon of 27 Hundredweight   89
U. S. Navy 32-pounder (Round Shot) Gun of 57 Hundredweight   90
U. S. Navy Heavy (Round Shot) Gun of 61 Hundredweight   90
U.S. Navy 8-inch Chambered Shell Gun of 63 Hundredweight   91
Confederate Ordnance Department Circular – Artillery Propellant Charges   92
Brigadier General Joseph Reid Anderson   93
C.S. Bronze 12-pounder Howitzer   96
Banding of C.S. Rifled Cannon   97
Rifling of the Gosport Rifle   98
Rifling Patterns   108
C.S. 8-inch Columbiads, Carriages, and Center Pintle Chassis   109
U.S. Unchambered Navy Cannon of 57 Hundredweight, Banded and Rifled   110
C.S. Bronze 12-pounder Howitzer   111
U.S. or C.S. Pattern 1841 12-pounder Heavy Field Gun   113
Confederate Artillery Projectiles   115
Tredegar Iron Works and Foundry   116
Brigadier General Samuel Gibbs French   120
C.S. Rifled 10-inch Columbiad   123
C.S. 4.62-inch Siege Rifle   124
C.S. 8-inch Siege Howitzer   124
C.S. 4.62-inch Siege Rifle   130
Colonel William Lamb   133
Whitworth 12-pounder Breechloading Rifle   137
Colonel Collett Leventhorpe   138
Brigadier General Thomas Lanier Clingman   139
Brigadier General Gabriel James Rains   140
U.S. Navy 24-pounder Medium Gun of 31 Hundredweight   147, 150
U.S. Navy 32-pounder Chambered Cannon of 41 Hundredweight, 1st Pattern   151
U.S. Navy 32-pounder Chambered Cannon of 41 Hundredweight, 2nd Pattern   152
U.S. Navy 32-pounder, Rifled and Banded, with Renewed Trunnions   186

Maps and Plans

Forts Johnston and Caswell in the Lower Cape Fear River Defenses – 1861   2
Plan of a 6-pounder Field Gun   6
Forts Johnston and Caswell in the U.S. Coast Survey Map of 1856   9
Fort Johnston – 1835   10
Fort Johnston – 1856   11
Plan of an Early Blockhouse   12
Plot Plan of Fort Caswell   20
Profiles and Sections of Fort Caswell   21
Profiles and Sections of Fort Caswell – Enlargement   22
Plan of Fort Caswell and Description of its Principal Features   23
Site Plan of Fort Caswell   24
Plan Showing Progress of Fort Caswell's Construction in 1829   25
Elevations Showing Progress of Fort Caswell's Construction in 1829   26
Plan Showing Progress of Fort Caswell's Construction in 1830   27
Elevations Showing Progress of Fort Caswell's Construction in 1830   28, 29
Plan Showing Progress of Fort Caswell's Construction in 1831   30
Plan for Repairs to Two of Fort Caswell's Caponieres   31, 32
Plan and Cross Section of One of Fort Caswell's Six Caponieres   38
Plan and Elevations of a Caponiere Casemate Embrasure and Loopholes   39, 40
Plan of Fort Caswell's Citadel   42
Elevations of Fort Caswell's Citadel   43 – 47
Plan of a Pattern 1807 U.S. Navy 24-pounder Gun   50
Plan of Fort Sumter, SC   54
Plan of a U.S. Pattern 1839 8-inch Seacoast Howitzer   60
Plan of a U.S. Pattern 1844 8-inch Columbiad   62
Plan of Front Pintle Barbette Platform for Fort Caswell   72
Bolles Battery   73
Camp Davis   87
Lieutenant Galloway's Camp West of Fort Caswell   87
Cape Fear Defenses – August, 1861   88
Camp Heath   104
Camp Grant   105
Camp Hopkins   106
Cape Fear Defenses – December, 1861   107
Plan of Field 12-pounder Howitzer   112
Plan and Profiles of U.S. or C.S. Pattern 1841 12-pounder Heavy Field Gun   114

(Maps and Plans continued on page following)

(Maps and Plans continued from page preceding)

Cape Fear Defenses – April, 1862   126
Site of Fort St. Philip   127
Camp Davis   128
Camp Holmes   128
Light House Battery, Fort French, Lazaretto Battery   129
Camp Holmes Landing   142
Camp Jones   142
Land Defenses of Wilmington   143
Cape Fear Defenses – November, 1862   144
Entrenched Camp   149
Batteries in the Land Defenses of Wilmington   149
Camp Lamb   149

Preface

Much has been written of the history of Civil War Wilmington and the defenses of the Cape Fear River, all of which has done justice to the service of the Confederate soldiers who served there. The literary works to which I refer are masterpieces of research and presentation that have provided a comprehensive view of particular fortifications and the battles that were fought there, as well as the campaigns of which those engagements were a part.

Reading works of history provokes thought and thought gives rise to questions, not of accuracy or truthfulness in the literary works themselves, but from the natural inclination to know more. It is one thing to know that a soldier served at a particular fort or battery, but it is an entirely different matter to know how the fortification was built and what artillery served there. Unable to cope with so many unanswered questions, it occurred to me to try to resolve the conflicts, if only for my own satisfaction. In so doing, the massive amount of information that came to hand begged to be reduced to writing, the result of which is this work.

In a very basic sense, this book has as its subject matter the men, the guns, and the fortifications of the defenses of the Cape Fear River and Wilmington, North Carolina. It is a chronological presentation of the enlistments, assignments, and transfers of every unit and commander to serve in the Cape Fear during the early months of the Civil War. It is an analysis of the chronological evolution of the Cape Fear fortifications, as well as the technical aspects of their construction. Moreover, it is an attempt to present the struggle by the Confederacy to maintain parity with Union artillery. The types of cannon that served in the Cape Fear from the first day of the war to the last are outlined and discussed, as are their capabilities and shortcomings. The evolution of smoothbore to rifled cannon in the river and land defenses is traced, as are the many and varied sources of supply of artillery pieces.

Since 1860, artillery practice had been taught at the U.S. Military Academy using John Gibbon's *The Artillerist's Manual*. Written in 1859 and published in 1860, Gibbon's work merged the principles contained in the 1850 *Ordnance Manual for the Use of the Officers of the United States Army* with every new artillery practice adopted by the U.S. Army since then. In so doing, it became the *de facto* standard for artillery practice until the more formal 1862 Ordnance Manual was issued, which occupies perhaps as much time as the first year of the war. For those reasons, *The Artillerist's Manual* is the reference used herein to provide the details of ordnance, ammunition and artillery practice so necessary to understanding the early Civil War defenses of the Cape Fear River. The manual will be referenced only until the 2nd Confederate Edition of the *Ordnance Manual for the Use of the Officers of the Confederate States Army* was published in 1863. The 1st Confederate Edition of 1861, unfortunately, was merely a reprint of the 1850 U.S. Ordnance Manual, and, as such, was far outdated in comparison to *The Artillerist's Manual*.

Details of the battles and campaigns in the region will not be found in these pages. Others have done so well describing them, there is no room for improvement there. What is offered here, however, is the before and after of the battles, as they affected both men and materiel. The chess game that is war is presented in detail, even the many and varied movements of units within the Cape Fear. Those movements, however, are summarized and reflected in returns of troop organization at the various batteries and forts, properly cited in the notes to better preserve the chronology.

The movement of artillery within the Cape Fear is followed to the extent possible, given the paucity of such information in official and unofficial records. When such movement is reported here, it will sometimes be based upon inspections or eyewitness reports from far in the future, together with logical interpretation of enough facts to advance a supportable conclusion. Thus the presence or absence of a particular piece of artillery from one inspection or report to another may be proof of its transfer between fortifications. It is important to note that once a piece of artillery came into the defenses of the Cape Fear, it rarely, if ever, left. The same, of course, held true for other forts and batteries in the south, which very much needed every piece they had for their own defense. After the supply obtained at the Gosport Navy Yard was exhausted, the last sources of resort were the few foundries in the south capable of producing heavy artillery, as well as the all too limited importation from foreign suppliers.

No effort has been made to present biographical or genealogical information, except for that of the primary leaders of the Cape Fear district. All others are introduced as they enter or leave the region or a fortification, but their life details are left to other, more comprehensive works that the reader is encouraged to consult. Leadership changes outside the Cape Fear have been dealt with only to the extent of their impact on the region, in the interest of maintaining the focus of the work.

All maps found in the pages that follow are of the period or slightly before, and were altered by adding the locations of the various fortifications to assist the reader in following the sequence of events. Plans of fortifications from the National Archives were similarly altered to reflect the construction techniques and to guide the reader through the completely unfamiliar engineering jargon of the time.

Most of all, the chronological aspect was strictly adhered to, with obligatory breaks to step back in time to explain a technical point, as required. Some time periods were compressed more than others, due mainly to a lack of significant occurrences within them. If, however, a period manifested significant activity and the analysis required substantial treatment, no effort was spared to that end.

The struggle to build the defensive system of the Cape Fear was a war within a war. For one defensive point on the Confederate map to be more aggressive than another usually resulted in more resources being channeled there. But the exception became the rule, wherein no matter how squeaky the wheel, not enough grease was available to silence it, so battery after battery and fort after fort in North Carolina fell to the Union hordes until there was only one defensive stronghold left untested – the Cape Fear defenses. To this, the last bastion of blockade running, more artillery was funneled than to all other defenses in North Carolina combined. Cannon of every size and description were sent from every source imaginable, until there were simply not enough men to man the guns and the breastworks at the same time. The defenses of the Cape Fear were endemic to North Carolina soldiery, for when the river defenses had to be abandoned, every company save the Staunton Hill Artillery from Virginia called the Old North State home. And, in the end, the failing did not rest with them. Prophetic was Major General William Henry Chase Whiting's analysis of the Cape Fear defenses on 15 January 1863: "Their value, incomplete as they still are (necessarily from want of time, implements, and material), must shortly be tested. If they succeed, these officers and men should have great praise; if they fail, it is not their fault."

Acknowledgements

It's difficult to acknowledge every single person with whom one comes into contact over the course of writing a book. It's even more difficult to put into words the impact some have had on this, the finished product. But, every author owes it to those that have helped him to try to do them justice and honor them for their participation.

There are two classes of participants that deserve recognition. First are those that serve the many universities, libraries, and historical societies. These very knowledgeable and dedicated individuals provide the lifeblood of manuscript copies that are the very foundation of every research work. My special thanks go out to all of them.

Elizabeth Dunn and Janie Morris of the Rare Book, Manuscript, and Special Collections Library at Duke University were especially helpful in providing copies of the many manuscripts needed to attach a human element to an otherwise fact-based work. The same holds true for Martha Elmore and Dale Sauter of the Joyner Library at East Carolina University, who cheerfully steered me in the right direction and promptly fulfilled my every request for documentation.

Janet Costley of the University of North Carolina Wilmington is another of those informed individuals that I met along the way. She allowed me to take up some of her valuable time to show me the way to the treasures the William Madison Randall Library holds for the researcher. Robert Anthony and Linda Jacobson of the North Carolina Collection of the Louis Round Wilson Library at the University of North Carolina at Chapel Hill were very helpful in acquiring copies of prints and permissions to use them in the book, one of which occupies an important position as its frontispiece.

The Library of Virginia, the august repository of the Old Dominion's history, supplied copies of the records of Joseph Reid Anderson's Tredegar Iron Works, incalculably valuable to the supply of cannon to the Old North State in general, and to the defenses of the Cape Fear in particular. Thanks are due to Minor Weisiger, whose copies of those records permitted a reasonably accurate determination of the armament of the Wilmington district, whereas only guesswork would have been possible otherwise.

The City of Southport graciously supplied copies of a pair of maps of Fort Johnston that provided insight into its evolution from an ancient pre-Revolutionary War British outpost to the one that was seized by North Carolina forces in early 1861. My thanks to the officials of that hospitable city.

Then there is the second class of assistance to the author. That group is made up of those that are more than sources of information, rather, they are sources of inspiration and guidance. To that group belongs Dr. Chris E. Fonvielle of the University of North Carolina Wilmington, whose books and tracts on the history of the region inspired me to try my hand at the penman's trade. He has been the source of books, copies of manuscripts, and, most of all, an attentive ear to questions, of which there has been no shortage from my end. He has answered them all, much to his credit, and has influenced me to be thorough in my search for knowledge of the Civil War era Cape Fear. Thanks again, Chris.

Last, and by no means least, is a man to whom I am deeply indebted for, above all, conversation. Jim

McKee, Historic Site Interpreter of North Carolina's Brunswick Town/Fort Anderson State Historic Site, has not only been a wealth of knowledge on area history, but a model of research tenacity in my personal pursuit of historical truth. In truth, I missed more than a few historical facts along the way, but they still appear in the book in spite of my inattention to detail, thanks to Jim. Every discovery begets questions, and it has been my good fortune to have the benefit of his inquisitive nature. He has been kind enough to share copies of manuscripts, cartography and photographs, some of which appear in this work, and most of which have contributed to its textual content. I have never met Jim in person, but I will count it a distinct honor if and when I am ever privileged to do so. I am certain that Fort Anderson will be the better for his presence there in the years to come.

Without the invaluable assistance of these and others whose names I may have inadvertently omitted, this work would not have been possible and it is my sincere hope that they all meet with success in their individual areas of endeavor. History will benefit from their careful stewardship.

One

"Fort Johnston was . . . in the possession of the insurgents . . ."
Captain John G. Foster, U.S. Engineers

In the late afternoon of April 16, 1861, as the steamer *W. W. Harllee* plowed through the cool waters of the Cape Fear River with the transport schooner *Dolphin* in tow, Colonel John Lucas Paul Cantwell of the 30th North Carolina State Militia had time to reflect on the Governor's mandate. "Take Forts Caswell and Johnston without delay, and hold them until further orders against all comers." [1]

A simple enough directive by itself, it was a later order from Governor John Willis Ellis that was worrisome. "Observe strictly a peaceful policy and act only on the defensive." It may have seemed to the Colonel that the word *take* was contradictory to pursuing a peaceful policy, but he must have known that sheer numbers favored his success. At 4:00 P.M., the vessels docked at the Smithville wharf, landing Colonel Cantwell and his four companies of citizen soldiers. After discovering Ordnance Sergeant James Reilly's whereabouts, Cantwell demanded the surrender of Fort Johnston. Hopelessly outmanned, Reilly knew what he had to do. After all, he'd been in this predicament before. [2]

The state of mind in the Cape Fear region in the last months of 1860 bordered on paranoia, but nowhere more so than in the port town of Wilmington. Secession sentiments held by most southern states were not necessarily shared by the leadership of the State of North Carolina, and the citizens of the coastal counties were not very happy about it. Wilmingtonians were keenly aware that the U. S. garrison at Fort Sumter in the harbor of Charleston, South Carolina could seal that port at any time, and the situational similarity was not lost on them. That realization kindled fears that the United States Government would seek to protect its interests in the region by garrisoning the two forts on the Cape Fear River, thereby controlling Wilmington's access to foreign trade. The mere thought of losing the ability to decide their own fate was simply not acceptable to most residents. Many of the city's more influential citizens, led by Robert George Rankin, began to speak out in favor of overt preemptive action to prevent a perceived threat from becoming reality. [3]

A meeting of the citizenry of Wilmington was held at the Courthouse in the very early days of January, 1861, during which a Committee of Safety was constituted and a call made for able-bodied men to volunteer for service in the "Cape Fear Minute Men." Volunteers turned out as anticipated, and organization of the local militia unit was completed with the election of Major John Jackson Hedrick as its commander. With the mandate given by the citizens of Wilmington in mind, Hedrick and his troops set sail for the lower Cape Fear in the late afternoon of January 8, 1861. At 4:00 A.M. the following morning, the local Militia officer demanded and received the surrender of Fort Johnston from U.S. Army Ordnance Sergeant James Reilly. [4]

Forts Caswell and Johnston at the mouth of the Cape Fear River are visible on this map created by J. H. Colton in 1861. (Library of Congress, Geography and Map Division)

Reinforced by Captain Stephen D. Thurston's "Smithville Guards," Hedrick left one small detachment to garrison the fort before boarding a vessel bound for Oak Island. Once there, with his men brandishing shotguns brought from their homes, the Major demanded the surrender of Fort Caswell from Army Ordnance Sergeant Frederick Dardingkiller. He reluctantly complied at 7:00 P.M. on 10 January 1861. [5]

When the unilateral action of the Wilmington militiamen came to his attention, the Governor directed his Acting Adjutant General to reverse the seizure forthwith. In his 11 January dispatch to Colonel Cantwell, Graham Daves asserted, "There is no authority of law under exisiting circumstances for the occupation of U. S. forts situated in this State." He then concluded his communiqué by directing Cantwell to proceed to Smithville and order the withdrawal of troops from Fort Caswell. [6]

The Governor obviously intended for both forts to be returned to U.S. control, but Daves seemingly didn't know that Fort Caswell wasn't in Smithville, thereby creating an unnecessary stop for Cantwell in his search for Hedrick. In strict obedience to his orders, Colonel Cantwell and his entourage sailed for Smithville on the 12th, only to have their vessel becalmed four miles from the town. The captain then grounded the sloop, compelling the militia contingent to wade ashore and walk to Fort Johnston. After securing a pilot boat in Smithville and traversing the three miles to Oak Island, Cantwell informed Major John J. Hedrick of the Governor's order directing him to return Fort Caswell to Federal control. The next day, the Major replied, "I have to inform you that we as North Carolinians will obey his command." True to his word, Hedrick relinquished possession of both forts to their respective Ordnance Sergeants at 9:00 A.M. on the morning of January 14 and then returned to Wilmington. The opening of hostilities against Fort Sumter by South Carolina forces on April 12, in and of itself contrary to established law, led to its surrender two days later, an event that would change everything. [7]

As early as 1731, the British Crown conceded the need to protect the Cape Fear region and authorized George Burrington to build a fort on the lower river. Burrington was the latterly-appointed first Royal Governor of the colony, but his term lasted only until 1734, by which time the work still hadn't been commenced. His successor wasn't immediately successful either.

Governor Gabriel Johnston was unable to obtain the necessary legislative levy of 2,000 pounds to build the fort until 1745. The funds to repay the appropriation were to come from a tax levied on all ships entering provincial waters. The last of several Spanish incursions along the coast of North Carolina between 1741 and 1748 resulted in the repulse of the raiders at Brunswick in September of 1748. [8]

Apprehensive of a return engagement with the Spaniards, work on the hitherto leisurely-built fort was hastened forward, culminating with its substantial completion the following year. The *ramparts* and *epaulements* were built of *tapia*, an unusual term for a primitive type of concrete made from a mixture of sand, lime, and water. Imperfect proportions of ingredients, however, only resulted in part of the fort's walls crumbling at each discharge of the big guns. In 1750, there was a quarantine garrison of just two men and one officer, and it wasn't until 1755 that Captain John Dalrymple was named Johnston's first commander by the eminent British General, Edward Braddock. Prior to Dalrymple's arrival, the fort had neither cannon nor ammunition, despite a plea to the Crown from Governor Arthur Dobbs in 1753. [9]

In fact, it was not until Captain James Moore assumed command of the fort in 1757 that the *ordnance* and ammunition finally arrived from England. The Captain's command duties at Fort Johnston ended in 1758, which began a period of little known activity at the ancient post. This condition persisted until 1766, when Captain Robert Howe assumed command, only to relinquish it the following year to Captain John Abraham Collet. Apparently, the garrison during those years was quite small, housing only ten soldiers as late as 1761, and it wasn't until 1764 that repairs to Fort Johnston, contracted for eight years earlier, were accepted as complete by the North Carolina General Assembly. [10]

In May of 1775, an outpouring of rebellious sentiment in New Berne prompted Josiah Martin, the Royal Governor of North Carolina, to abandon his offices and seek refuge in Fort Johnston, under the guns of the British Man-of-War *HMS Cruizer*. That July, as the insurgent fervor in the Cape Fear increasingly portended an attack on Fort Johnston, Martin ordered its commander, Captain John Collett, to dismount the *cannon* and remove them to the seawall, whereupon he removed himself to safety aboard *Cruizer*. That action alone hastened the patriots' resolve to secure the ordnance for their own purposes. When he received an angry letter from the colonists indicating their intention to seize the fort, Martin testily responded that such an act would be resisted by all means at hand. Just a few hours later he was awakened to news that Fort Johnston was ablaze and suffering wanton destruction of everything that wouldn't burn. It seems the irascible Captain Collett, of his own volition and without orders, had applied the torch to his own fort. [11]

The patriot Robert Howe led more than a few determined attempts to secure the cannon lying at the seawall, but the guns of *Cruizer* kept his men at bay until November, when the redcoats began to transfer them to the transport ship *HMS Palliser*, destination Boston. The guns wouldn't leave the Cape Fear without a struggle, however. On at least two occasions over a period of four days, the overmatched patriots attempted to wrest them from British working parties, but grapeshot fired from the decks of *Cruizer* caused them to withdraw without achieving their objective. The remnants of Fort Johnston passed to the State of North Carolina in 1776 and remained in its possession until 1794, when it was given to the young United States of America with the stipulation that a fort would be erected there. Realization of that precondition couldn't begin until ten years later. [12]

In 1804, a contract was signed by the Federal Government for the construction of a *battery* on the site of old Fort Johnston. Once again, the makeshift concrete known as tapia would be employed in the erection of the fort's walls, but this time the work would be performed for the government under contract with Benjamin Smith, a future governor of North Carolina. [13]

The officer selected to be the superintending engineer was Second Lieutenant Joseph Gardner

Swift, the first cadet to graduate from the United States Military Academy at West Point in 1802. Swift arrived in Wilmington on June 17, 1804, and immediately set sail for Smithville. After settling into quarters at Mrs. Ann McDonald's, the Lieutenant began his new assignment by sounding the river entrances at Old and New Inlets with the purpose of validating conclusions drawn in Washington long before his assignment to the Cape Fear.

Joseph Gardner Swift. (Courtesy United States Army Corps of Engineers)

On July 26, Swift reported to the Secretary of War, confirming the need "to cover an anchorage in the harbor and to command its entrance by a small enclosed work on Oak Island, and an enclosed battery at Federal Point, at New Inlet, and also to complete the battery of tapia at the site of old Fort Johnston." The young Lieutenant passed a pleasant summer at Smithville, where he met his future wife, Louisa Margaret Walker, the daughter of Captain James Walker. They exchanged wedding vows on June 5, 1805 and Swift was promoted to First Lieutenant just six days later. [14]

In an attempt to improve the strength of the ramparts, the tapia was created by a different method than the one employed previously. First, thousands of oysters were harvested from the region's abundant oyster beds and then burned alive in lime pens constructed of pitch pine. This use of a natural accelerant created a very hot fire, "much to the annoyance of the neighborhood by the smoke and vapor of burning shellfish," confessed the Lieutenant. In this manner, the hard shells were reduced to ash in about one day. The ashes were then combined with traditional lime, sand, and water to create a paste that was then poured into forms six feet high by five to seven feet thick, which in turn hardened into the ramparts and protective epaulements for the guns that would serve there. [15]

On October 30, 1806, Joseph G. Swift was promoted to Captain and the rapidly rising star of the Corps of Engineers was reassigned to the Military Academy sometime in 1807. In spite of Swift's removal from the region, construction continued until 1809, shortly after which the fort boasted a *blockhouse*; a 15' by 20' brick powder *magazine*; a 103' long brick *barrack* for officers and enlisted men, the center portion of which measured 34 feet square and stood two stories high; a 20' by 22' brick guard house; and a 27' by 22' storehouse of wood construction. Johnston mounted just four heavy guns at the end of the year, all of which were likely of Revolutionary War vintage. [16]

The work itself was pentagonal in shape and was designed to mount twelve big guns, but Fort Johnston was not in reality a fort at all. The 140 foot long rampart and its protective *epaulements* were substantially built, but the rest of the battery was enclosed only by wood planks that were *loopholed* for infantry, therefore providing no protection from *artillery* fire. The battery's *terreplein* was less than a hundred yards from the buildings on the parade, and about ten feet lower in elevation. [17]

The *parapet* of the battery was pierced with *embrasures* for artillery as well as loopholes for muskets. The fortified blockhouse was thirty-three feet square and provided a sanctuary to which a beleaguered garrison could retreat to escape the pursuit of enemy troops. Based on military principles of the time, it was a two-story affair with a cantilevered upper story to provide protected plunging fire on attacking forces below, somewhat similar to the *machicoulis* defense presented by a medieval castle. The works thereby created were more closely akin to a wooden *stockade* from the Indian Wars period than they were to the more substantial forts of the early 1800's and beyond.[18]

In 1811, the ancient fort was issued eight long anticipated 24-pounder *siege guns* and its chief engineer, the returned Captain Joseph Gardner Swift, "replaced the old guns by mounting the battery with the eight new ones." Johnston still mounted eight *battering cannon* as late as 1818, but four years later, there were 28 24-pounders and fifteen 18-pounders of that class of cannon mounted there.[19]

The next year, Johnston's 24-pounders totaled only 14, with the same fifteen 18-pounders in place, but four 12-pounder iron guns had been added, presumably also of the battering class of cannon. Fast forward to 1834 and the count had changed again. At that time there were eighteen 24-pounders, 12-pounders to the number of six, fifteen 18-pounders, and an assortment of light artillery pieces.[20]

In 1826, construction of Fort Caswell was begun, which would turn out to be much more than the "small enclosed work on Oak Island" envisioned by Captain Swift and his superiors. As production at Fort Caswell intensified, the ancient Fort Johnston became increasingly less important, but it still inventoried 39 heavy guns and ten light artillery pieces in late 1834. The largest of those big guns were 24-pounders to the number of eighteen and, of the iron 6-pounder artillery pieces on hand at that time, four were serviceable and two were not.[21]

As a result of the military buildup for the second Seminole War, Fort Johnston's garrison and most of its armament were redeployed by 1836, and in May of 1840 only ten 24-pounders remained. By 1851, however, Fort Johnston was not counted among the armed forts in the United States. In spite of its relative inactivity in the twenty years between 1836 and 1856, Fort Johnston still managed to gain not only a new enlisted barrack, but a new hospital as well, suggestive of greater activity than recorded history indicates.[22]

The older buildings needed repair from time to time, and the U. S. government spent almost $70,000 for maintenance of both forts over the years. The paltry sum of about $3,500 per year for maintenance of two forts wasn't much, particularly for the ancient Fort Johnston, which ran a poor second to Fort Caswell in terms of its importance to the U. S. military. By early 1861, the Smithville fort wasn't in any condition for defense, mounting no heavy artillery at all. Fort Caswell was, on the other hand, "in good repair, having been quite thoroughly repaired" in fiscal 1859.[23]

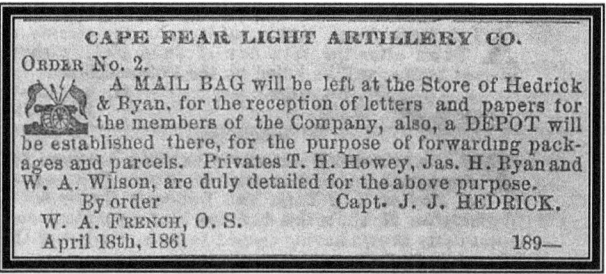

Military Notice posted by Captain John J. Hedrick two days after the second seizure of the forts. (*The Daily Journal*, May 31, 1861)

First Lieutenant James Martin Stevenson, commanding 24 men of the "Cape Fear Light Artillery," was left in control of Fort Johnston, leaving the main body of Colonel Cantwell's command free to descend upon Fort Caswell. Captain Stevenson's men uncovered four bronze and four iron 6-pounder guns in storage at the fort and immediately set about mounting them, but found one of the *carriages* to be broken and unserviceable. All seven guns were mounted in battery behind Johnston's parapets of tapia by 18 April.[24]

Just which patterns of 6-pounder Field Guns were in residence at Fort Johnston is purely conjectural. The puzzling thing is the fort's complete lack of *field guns* in the years 1840 and 1851, followed by their inexplicable appearance in 1861. Doubtless the bronze guns were from one or more of the patterns introduced in 1835, 1838, 1840, and 1841, all of which displayed a similar profile, varying only in girth at the breech or overall length. Pattern 1835 and 1841 cannon were 65.6 inches long, but the latter was thicker at the breech and therefore weighed almost 150 pounds more. Pattern 1838 and 1840 guns were only 59.3 inches long, but once again, the greater girth of the latter pattern's breech caused it to weigh over 125 pounds more. Iron guns present an entirely different case, though. There were simply far too many variants, whether identified or unidentified, marked or unmarked, State Militia or U.S. Government, to hazard even the wildest guess as to just which might have been represented in Fort Johnston. [25]

With five degrees of *muzzle* elevation and using a 1.25 pound powder charge, a 6-pounder field gun could fire a 3.58-inch solid shot weighing 6.1 pounds a distance of only about 1,523 yards. Firing case shot diminished that range by 323 yards, rendering the guns useless against attacking gunboats. Only as a defense against infantry assault could the little guns be of value to the defenders of the Cape Fear. While *smoothbore* field pieces were present early in the regional *fortifications*, most of them left the area with light artillery batteries just as soon as their service was needed on fields of battle far away, especially those of bronze manufacture. Besides, not until land warfare came to the Cape Fear would any of the little guns be employed in its defenses. [26]

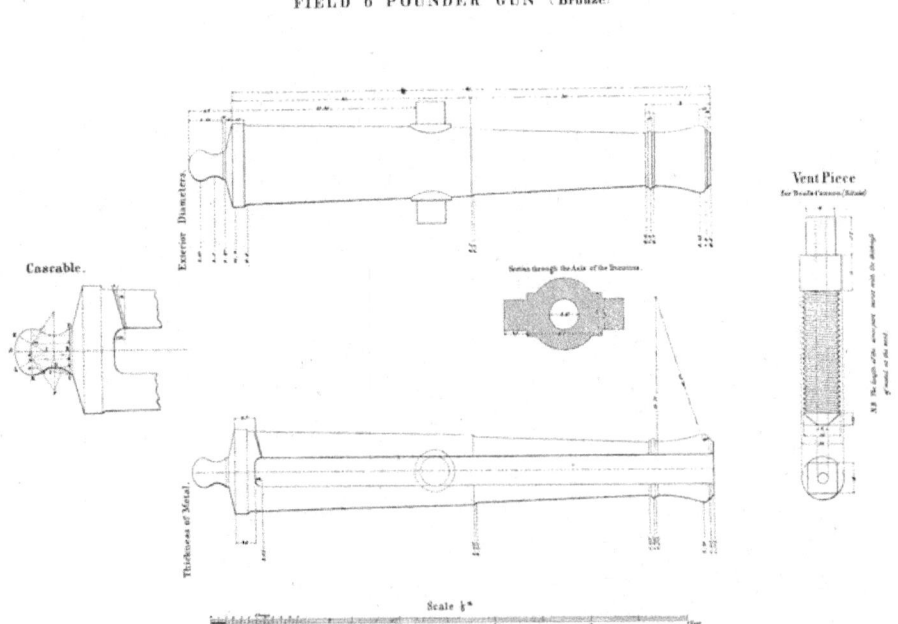

U. S. or C. S. Pattern 1841 6-pounder Gun. Note the lack of chamber, thereby defining this piece as a true gun. U.S. Patterns 1835, 1838, 1840 and 1841 bronze guns and the U.S. Pattern 1836 iron gun all had this exact design, varying only in length and/or thickness. Manufacturing profiles of this pattern were, for the most part, identical for both sides in the conflict, and virtually all 6-pounders in the hands of the Army of Northern Virginia were melted down and recast into Napoleons in early 1863. They would, however continue to serve the Confederate cause in every other theater of the war. (Courtesy Harpers Ferry Center, U. S. National Park Service)

U.S. Pattern 1841 bronze 6-pounder Field Gun. Total length, 65.6 inches; total weight, about 880 pounds. The U.S. Pattern 1835 bronze 6-pounder Field Gun is the same length as this mainstay of the early Civil War, but slimmer, and weighs about 740 pounds. (Courtesy of Geoff Walden)

U.S. Pattern 1838 bronze 6-pounder Field Gun. Total length, 59.3 inches; total weight, about 690 pounds. The U.S. Pattern 1840 bronze 6-pounder Field Gun is the same length, but bulkier, and weighs about 812 pounds. (Courtesy of Chris Christner under Creative Commons license)

6-pounder iron Field Gun. With two reinforces, this cannon bears a strong resemblance to the U.S. Pattern 1834 iron Field Gun, but this one is just a little shorter. (Courtesy of Perryville Battlefield State Historic Site, Perryville, KY, photography by Kurt Holman)

6-pounder Field Gun. Manufactured in a profile similar to the U.S. Pattern 1834, this gun provides an excellent example of several unmarked patterns that were pressed into service in the Civil War South. (Courtesy of Corinth Civil War Relics)

6-pounder iron Field Gun. Upper and lower images are different views of the same gun. This piece served in Fort Branch, North Carolina, and provides another example of an unmarked pattern that is highly similar to the U.S. Pattern 1834 Field Gun. There is no fitting on the breech for a pendulum-hausse sight. (Courtesy of Fort Branch, photography by Don Torrance)

6-pounder iron Field Gun. Again, upper and lower images are different views of another unknown pattern field gun surviving from Fort Branch, North Carolina. This one has a fitting for a pendulum-hausse rear sight and a front sight that is not at all similar to the sight on the other 6-pounder that served there. (Courtesy of Fort Branch, photography by Don Torrance)

Fort Johnston | 9

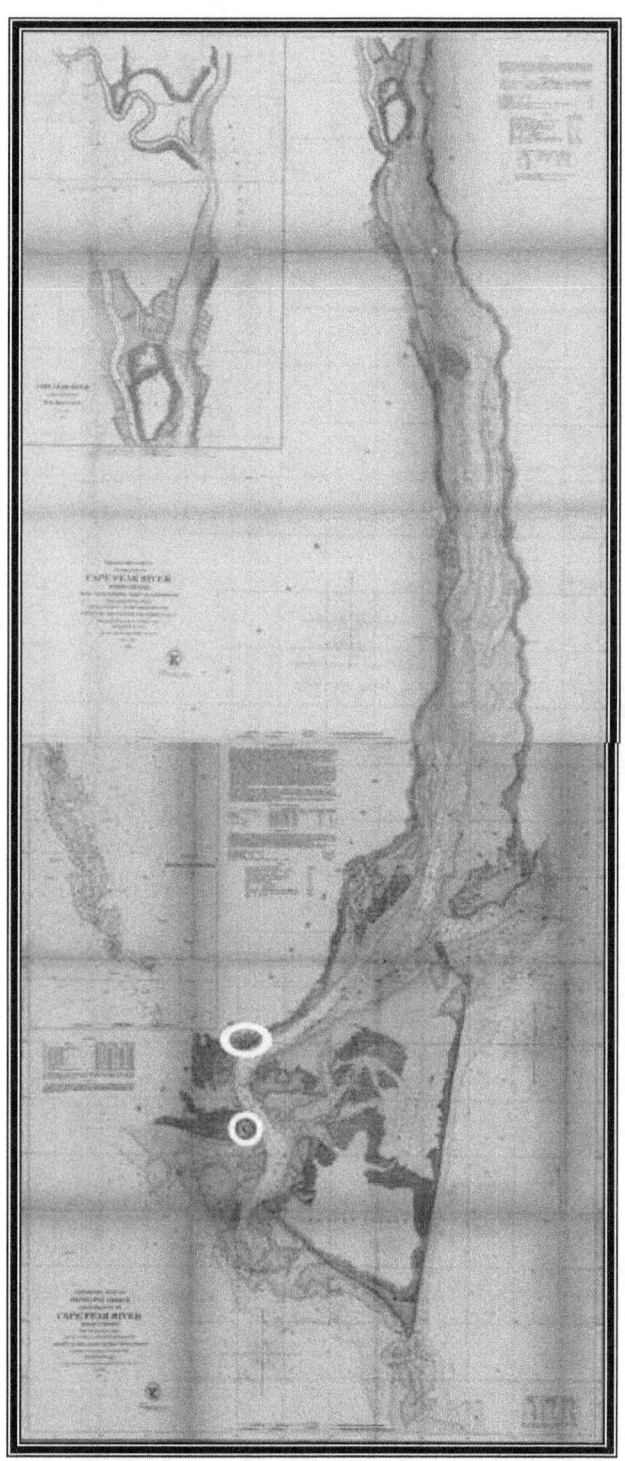

Coast Survey map from 1856 by Charles P. Bolles and Lieutenant John Newland Maffitt, U.S.N., showing the mouth of the Cape Fear River and the proximity of Fort Johnston in Smithville (oval) to Fort Caswell on Oak Island (circle). (National Oceanic and Atmospheric Administration)

Close-up of Smithville and Fort Johnston.

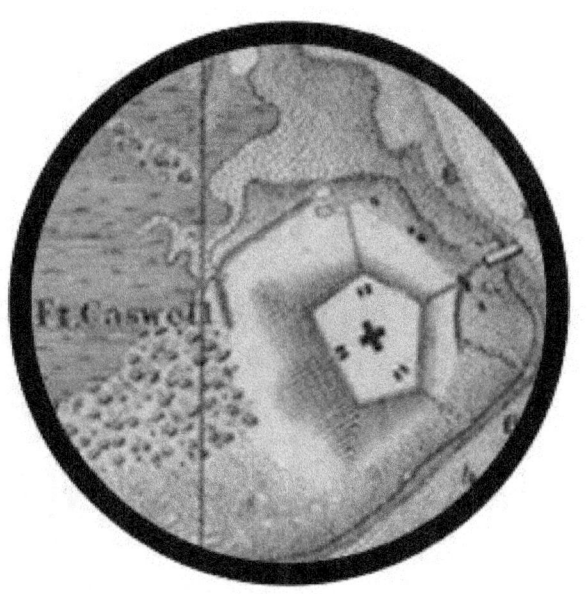

Close-up of Fort Caswell on Oak Island.

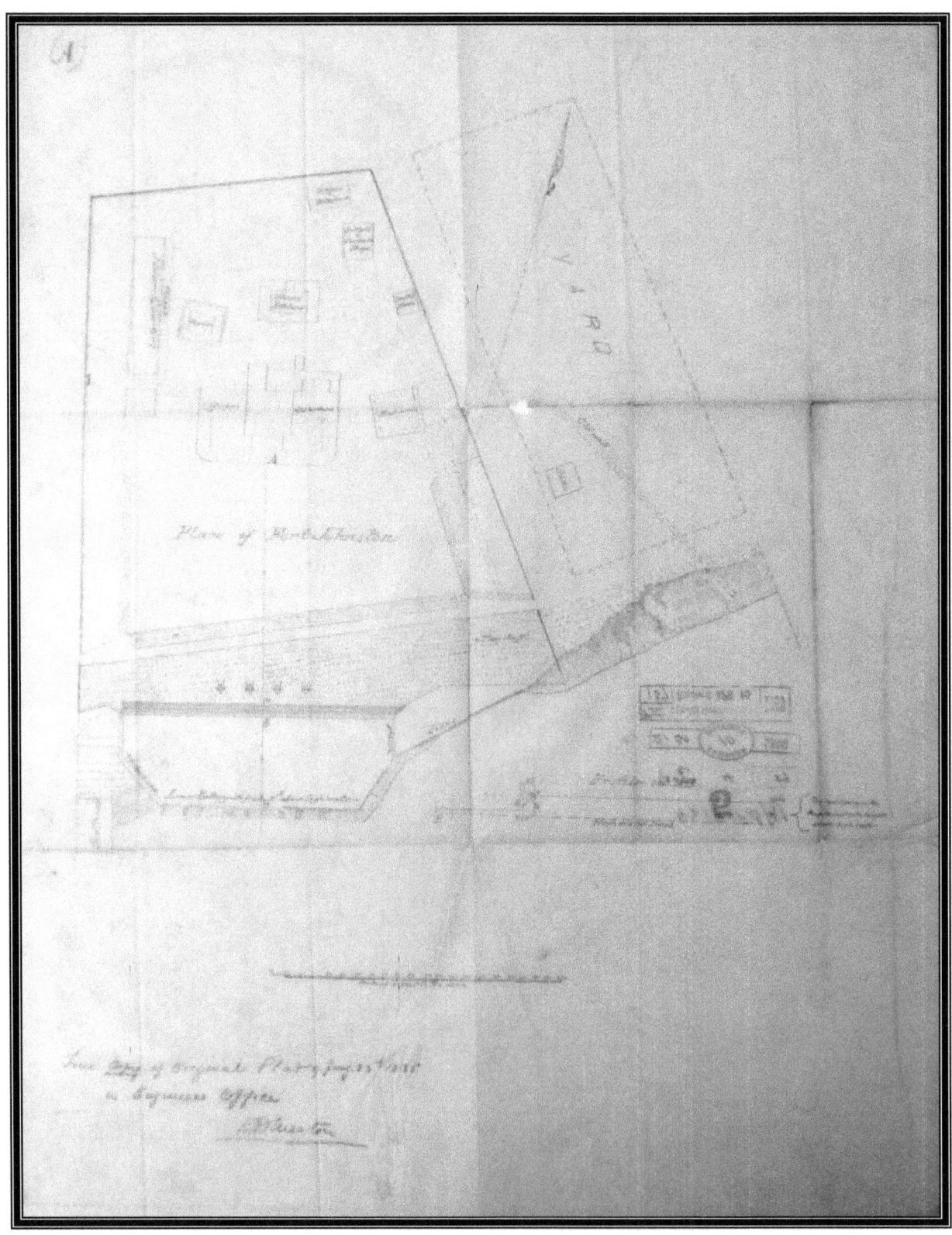

Fort Johnston as it appeared in January of 1835. (Courtesy of the City of Southport, North Carolina)

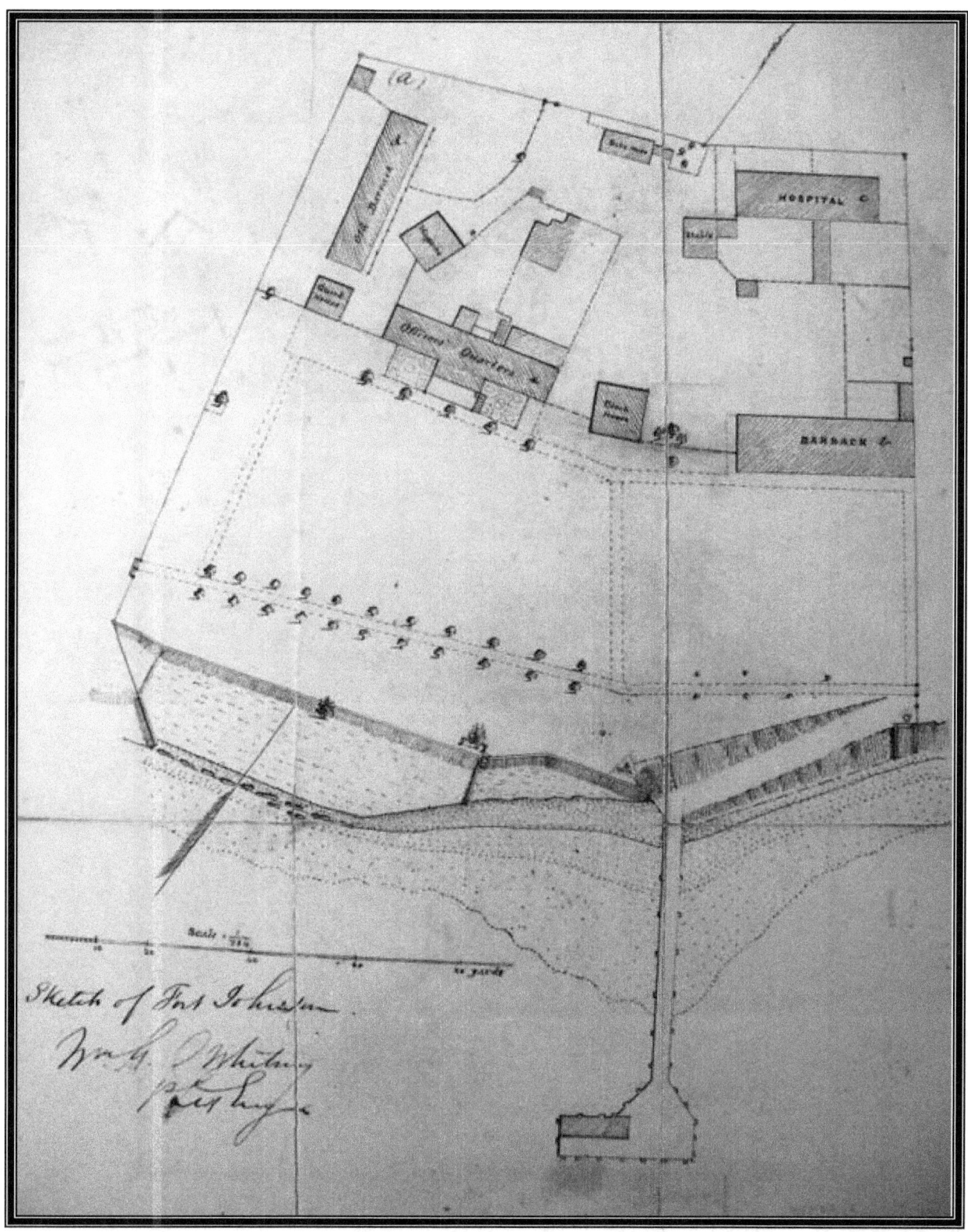

Plat of Fort Johnston drawn in 1856 by William Henry Chase Whiting, then a 1st Lieutenant of Engineers in the U.S. Army. It is very likely that the fort appears here substantially as it was found by Colonel Cantwell's men in April, 1861. (Courtesy of the City of Southport, North Carolina)

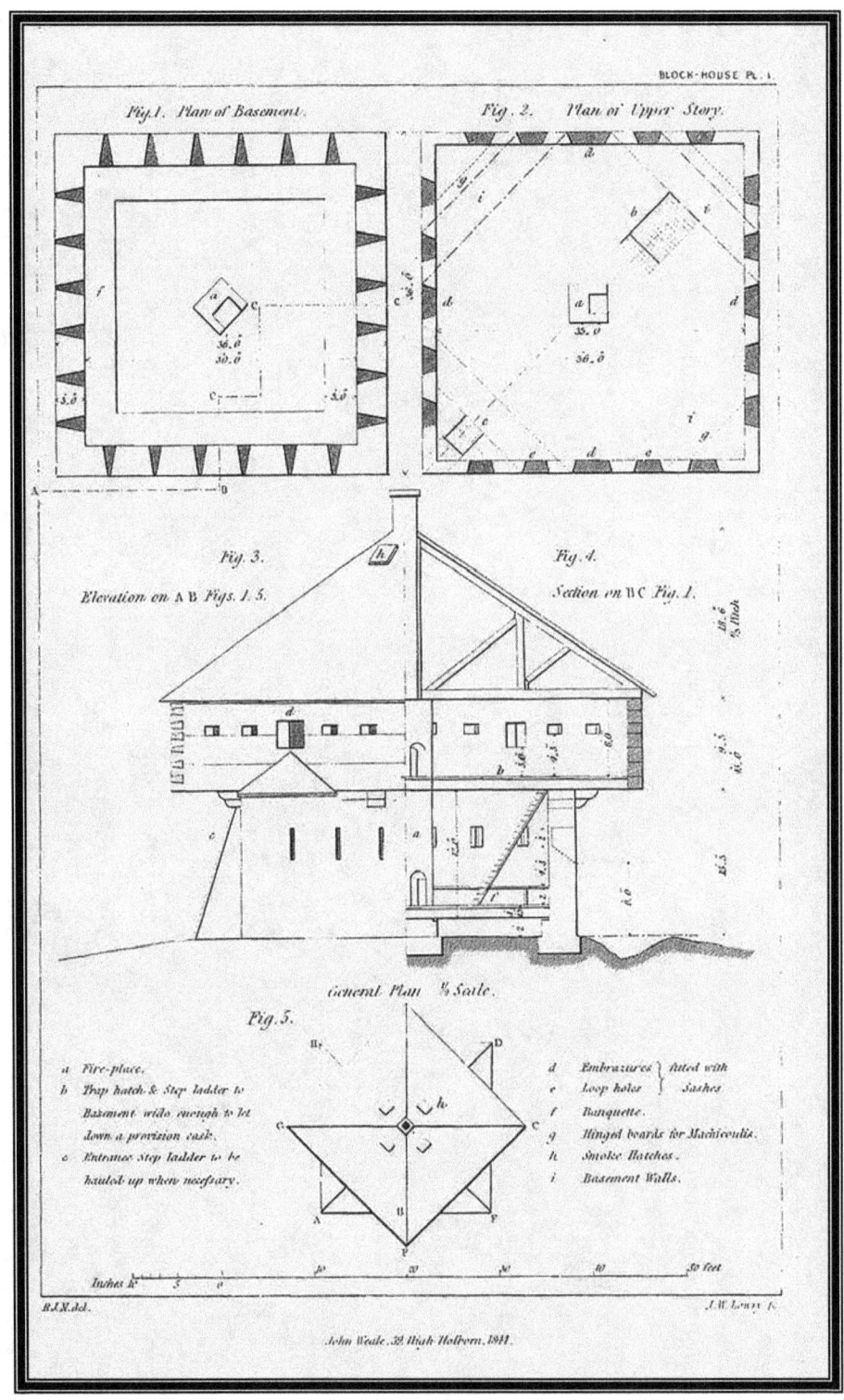

Typical blockhouse of the period. Offset second story allowed plunging fire on attackers below. (*Aide-Mémoire to the Military Sciences. Framed From Contributions Of Officers Of The Different Services, And Edited By A Committee Of The Corps Of Royal Engineers In Dublin, 1845. Part A. B. C. Sketch Of The Art And Science Of War. Abattis – Contours. With Eighty-Nine Plates And Numerous Woodcuts.* Volume I, Part I. London: John Weale, High Holborn, 1845. Printed By W. Hughes, King's Head Court, Gough Square, Plate I following p. 162)

Two

"Fort Caswell... was at once a pleasure and a mystery to me."
James Eastus Price

For some, memories from childhood never fade. James Eastus Price, son of Smithville pilot John B. Price, carried with him into maturity this vivid boyhood image of Fort Caswell:

> Across the bay, on the north side of the river's mouth, was old Fort Caswell, built many years before I was born. My grandfather had assisted in superintending its construction; and the old place, with its *citadel*, long brick galleries, *drawbridge*, and *moat*, was at once a pleasure and a mystery to me. A deep structure of brick formed a hollow square in which were buildings whose tall chimneys towered above the works; from the square a wide passage opened on a drawbridge which spanned the moat when down, and was to be raised from within when the enemy had carried the outer works. When the drawbridge was up, huge doors studded with spikes, were closed by a *portcullis*, like those of an ancient castle. Long galleries ran through the outer brick wall which *flanked* the moat; and in the sides of the galleries were openings, commanding all approaches, where the soldiers, with crossed guns, could shoot the opposers while they were trying to cross the water. A high earthwork surrounded the inner structure . . . [1]

The use of terms such as moat, portcullis, and drawbridge is common in descriptions of castles in medieval Europe, but unexpected when used in connection with American fortifications. The simple truth is that fortification terminology in the United States followed precisely that which was devised and employed by leading French military engineers, dating from the middle of the seventeenth century. Even though James Eastus Price used everyday English to describe Fort Caswell, it may not be easily understood, and the true lexicon of fortification is even less so, given its distinctly French origins. Had Price been a military engineer, his description might have looked something like this:

> The masonry *scarp* of the enceinte surrounded the *parade* in which was the citadel whose tall chimneys towered above the works; from the parade the *sally port* opened on a drawbridge that spanned the moat when down, and was to be raised from within when the enemy had crested the *glacis* and occupied the *covered way*. When the drawbridge was up, the portcullis was closed, like that of an ancient castle. *Caponieres* ran through the scarp and into the moat; and in their sides were loopholes commanding all approaches, where the fort's

defenders, employing a crossfire, could shoot the enemy while they were trying to cross the water. The glacis surrounded the entirety of the *outworks* and the *enceinte*. [2]

♦ ♦ ♦ ♦ ♦

For many years prior to the Civil War, the United States military had recognized three systems of fortifications, based primarily on the time frame during which they were built and the formidability of defense they presented. So-called First System forts were either those that the United States inherited from the British and French at the close of the American Revolution or those authorized to be built by Congress in 1794, of which Fort Johnston provides the clearest example. Constructed principally of earth or wood, the older defensive works would require substantial refitting to be minimally functional, while the new fortifications would be plagued by funding shortages and cessation of construction prior to their completion. Although a few substantial forts were produced under this system, many more would suffer from the ravages of time and significant neglect before they would be needed in 1812. [3]

Beginning in 1807, Second System forts were built as an outgrowth of concern that Britain's smoldering belligerence would lead to hostilities. Those fears were realized with the outbreak of the War of 1812, during which Washington, D.C. was captured and the Capitol torched, at least in part due to the insufficiency and frailty of the earth and masonry fortifications built during this period and before. [4]

Determined to better protect the coastline of the United States, Congress set a course for the country that envisioned the construction of some 200 forts to guard the approaches to every major port city. Teetering on the brink of bankruptcy from this massive project, the United States managed to begin construction on just forty-two forts between 1816 and 1855. Even then there were no surplus funds with which to purchase the heavy artillery pieces or to pay the garrisons required to serve them. By late 1860, the great majority of the Third System forts had precious few guns and were usually maintained by a single Ordnance Sergeant or even a civilian fort keeper, hardly the deterrent hoped for by the politicians in Washington. [5]

♦ ♦ ♦ ♦ ♦

It is sufficient to say, then, that Fort Caswell was a Third System pentagonal masonry work similar to many other forts built in America in the early to mid-1800's. All of them consisted of three principal components:

- ❖ The enceinte, which encompassed everything within the masonry wall. The masonry wall's outer face is termed the scarp.
- ❖ The outworks, which included every defensive structure outside the enceinte and within musket range of it, including the drawbridge, moat, covered way and its parapet, as well as the *places of arms* and caponieres.
- ❖ The glacis, a long, sloping blanket of sand or earth that protected the scarp from distant artillery fire. [6]

In spite of the many similarities shared by all Third System forts, there were three significant features that differentiated Fort Caswell from the others. First and not unusually, the masonry scarp was four feet thick, but there were no embrasures in it for *casemated* cannon, as was normally the standard in Third System forts. Next, Caswell had three sally ports, whereas nearly all of her sister forts had but one. The main sally port at Caswell exited the main work at the *gorge*, or rear of the fortified pentagon, and the other two provided access to the places of arms in the outwork known as the covered way. The last and most unique feature built into Caswell was the use of caponieres to defend the bridges and sweep the moat, instead of the customary *bastions* protruding from the angles of the work. All three sally ports and their bridges were located between a pair of double caponieres immersed in the moat, which by itself presented a formidable obstacle at five feet deep and twenty feet wide. [7]

The French word *caponiere* may be literally translated as a cage for fattening capons, and therefore a place of refuge. The caponieres at Fort Caswell were in truth the most inhospitable of places, particularly for an enemy. Not only was each of the three pairs capable of directing fire from forty muskets directly on each sally port bridge, every one of the six could enfilade the ditch and scarp with fire from twenty-one muskets and two cannon. Standing in water, Caswell's caponieres were damp and unpleasant places for defenders to be sure, but that small discomfiture pales in comparison to the distress felt by the infantryman who came under the firepower of musketry and cannonade while wading through water five feet deep. [8]

While the unique elements built into Fort Caswell contributed greatly to its formidability, it was a simple feature common to most masonry forts of the era that made it a stronghold to be reckoned with. Caswell's masonry walls were protected from distant artillery fire by a long, sloping sand and earth glacis. That which could not be seen, could not be hit with a projectile. Conversely, forts with exposed masonry walls would be quickly reduced early in the war. The glacis also would have forced infantry assaults to pursue a long uphill course under cannon and musket fire, only then to be confronted by the moat and the very deadly caponieres. [9]

The appropriation to build Fort Caswell was approved by the U.S. Congress in 1825, but its construction began slowly for lack of an engineer to oversee the work. Near the end of the year, Captain George Blaney of the U.S. Corps of Engineers was selected for the job. Formerly the superintendent of construction at Fort Hamilton in New York, he was no stranger to building Third System forts. The initial assignment for the March 4, 1815 graduate of West Point was that of Assistant Engineer at Fortress Monroe in Virginia. That posting gave way to one as the superintending engineer of construction at Fort Delaware, followed soon thereafter by a similar job at Fort Hamilton. With work at the latter project only barely begun, the Cape Fear River beckoned and Blaney seemed eager to prove himself equal to the task. [10]

This advertisement appeared in the National Intelligencer beginning in January and running through March 15, 1826:

> Bricks wanted. Sealed proposals will be received at Wilmington and Smithville, North Carolina, until the 15th of March next, for the delivery at Oak Island, near the mouth of the Cape Fear river [sic], of six millions of bricks, as follows, viz:
> 2,000,000 to be delivered prior to the 1st July, 1826.
> 2,000,000 to be delivered prior to the 1st October, 1826.
> 2,000,000 to be delivered prior to the 1st December, 1826.
> The bricks must be hard-burned and of the best quality, and it is desirable that they should be of the size of the Philadelphia or New York bricks, the former being 8½, 4½, and 2½, and the latter 8, 4, and 2 inches. Proposals will state which of these two sizes it is intended to deliver. Proposals will be accepted for a part of the above, say 100,000. It must be distinctly understood, by those who send proposals, that the contract will be so made, that the bricks will be liable to rejection if they do not pass the inspection of an officer of engineers or some other person who will be appointed for the purpose. A wharf will be in readiness previous to the 1st of April, where vessels can lie drawing nine feet at low water.
> GEORGE BLANEY,
> Captain Corps of Engineers.

Despite advertising for proposals to supply six million bricks, Captain Blaney later specified a slightly different number to the apparent low bidder:

> SMITHVILLE, N. C.,
> March 16, 1826.
> Mr. THOMAS CROWN,
> Washington City.
> SIR: Your proposal for the delivery of from one to six millions of bricks for the fortifications to be erected at Oak Island has been

examined and is hereby accepted. In consequence of previous arrangements having been made, three millions is the number wanted, provided I can procure stone for the foundations. If that material cannot be procured, four and a half millions will be required.

I am, very respectfully, your most obedient servant,

G. BLANEY,
Captain Corps of Engineers. [11]

The contract between Blaney and Thomas Crown was in fact executed on March 16, 1826, calling for three million bricks to be delivered at the rate of one million on or before each of three dates: October 1, November 30, and December 31, 1826. In addition, the contract stipulated that the contractor was to be paid $7.75 for each 1,000 bricks delivered on time and accepted by the government after inspection. Specifications also called for the brick to be "hard-burned" of 9⅛ inches in length by 4⅝ inches wide and 2⅝ inches thick, according to the standards then operative in the city of Washington. [12]

It appeared that Blaney had chosen wisely. Major William Wade was the superintending engineer of construction at the U. S. Allegheny Arsenal in Pittsburgh, Pennsylvania from 1814 to 1816, where he had the opportunity to observe Thomas Crown's abilities as a master bricklayer. "He performed nearly all the brick work of that extensive establishment by contract; and the work was executed in a satisfactory manner as respects both its quality and the promptness of performance." [13]

The Major's opinion was heartily endorsed by Colonel Abram R. Woolley, Wade's superior and first commanding officer of the Allegheny Arsenal. "I know of no instance of Mr. Crown's delinquency, unskilfulness, negligence, or want of promptitude; on the contrary, he always manifested great energy, skill, and diligence." Lieutenant Colonel George Bomford, Chief of the U. S. Army Ordnance Department, later reminded Crown that he was "one of the persons who recommended you for the employment [on Oak Island] . . . which was at the time supported by several persons of the most respectable character." Moreover, Bomford was joined in his enthusiasm for Crown's abilities by none less than Brevet Brigadier General and Chief of the U. S. Army Corps of Engineers Charles Gratiot and esteemed President of the Board of Naval Commissioners, Commodore John Rodgers. [14]

As always seems to be the case, though, the contract was subject to bureaucratic scrutiny at the Department of Engineering in Washington. Declaring the document "a nullity" for being "decidedly objectionable," Captain John L. Smith went on to question the lack of language for addressing financial assurances and penalties for non-performance by the contractor. As might be expected from any negative communication, paranoia set in and Blaney resolved that it would be in his best interest to remove Thomas Crown from the picture altogether. [15]

Instead of seizing the opportunity offered in Smith's letter to rewrite the Crown contract, Blaney allied himself with the wealthy Samuel Potter, who was coincidentally the Captain's landlord in Smithville. Thomas Crown, to his detriment, was indebted to Potter for furnishing slaves, firewood and clay to his open-air brick factory bordering Walden Creek, the land under which was, by no accident, also owned by the moneyed entrepreneur. [16]

Crown, however, had very quickly completed almost a half million bricks and asked Captain Blaney to take delivery of them so he could pay off his indebtedness. James H. Henry, a brick moulder doing double duty as Crown's foreman, knew the situation well. "The amount of brick tendered to Captain Blaney in the first instance was about four hundred and fifty thousand hard-burned brick, which Captain Blaney then refused to receive, and did not receive except about five thousand only." Z. H. Hawkins, a bricklayer that was also present, recalled the desperation of the situation. "Crown pressed hard on Blaney to receive his brick and enter into a new contract, as Crown informed him that he was deficient of means to proceed further." Had the bricks been delivered and paid for, things might have turned out differently. Mr. Henry continued, "I am under the impression that if Captain Blaney had received the brick made by Mr. Crown, he would have completed the contract without the least difficulty." [17]

Using Crown's mounting financial difficulties as leverage, Potter and Blaney approached the near-destitute contractor. Alfred Emerson, then clerking for Thomas Crown, witnessed the event. "Potter and Blaney came to the brick yard, and the said Potter said to the said Crown, that if he would not receive him as a partner, he would call the negroes and put him (the said Crown) across the creek." Mr. Henry was again present on this occasion and had a recollection of his own. "Captain Blaney and Mr. Potter came to Mr. Crown's brick-yards together, and he (Potter) said, in the presence of Captain Blaney, that if said Crown did not consider him as a partner in the business, he would call his negroes together and put him across the creek." Such threats didn't sit too well with Crown, and the coerced partnership failed to materialize. [18]

Unable to repay Potter the estimated $600.00 indebtedness or to continue manufacturing bricks without being paid for those already completed, the hapless Crown sold the finished bricks to Potter for $600.00, less than $1.50 per thousand. Potter in turn sold the bricks to the government for $7.50 to 8.50 per thousand. [19]

Including Thomas Crown's 500,000 bricks, Samuel Potter went on to furnish a total of 2,375,264 bricks to Fort Caswell between July 31, 1826 and July 31, 1827, of which 111,760 were soft, of 2nd quality, or salmon-colored. About 115,068 bricks were made by J. Seawell of Fayetteville; 88,000 came from Thomas Davis of Charleston, South Carolina; and another 40,120 were furnished by Dudley & Dickinson of New York. Ever resourceful, Thomas Crown returned to Washington, where he entered into another important contract with the Government, his administration of which A. B. McLean remembered favorably. "In 1829 and 1830, he delivered bricks at Fort Monroe, Virginia, which were approved of as bricks of good quality, and suitable for permanent building." [20]

By the end of 1826, and in spite of the brick fiasco, some work was done to advance the work at Fort Caswell. True to his promise, Captain Blaney built a temporary wharf to receive the building materials that were subsequently stored on the site. Storehouses, shops, and lodging for the workmen were also built, but yet another major problem confronted the superintending engineer. Local artisans with good and sufficient competence to effect the erection of the masonry walls were in short supply, requiring their importation from the more populous northern states. By November 18, 1826 only some of the workmen had arrived, so construction of the main work could not begin. [21]

One year later, the citadel was well underway, as was part of the masonry on the main work. The excavation of the moat was progressing, but still far from complete. In August of 1827 the improvements then in place sustained massive storm damage, the repair expenditures of which exhausted the original appropriation and brought work on Fort Caswell to a standstill. Congress would have to approve additional funding before construction could be resumed. [22]

Funds would eventually be secured, but not before the first half of 1828 had passed. By July, the masons had been reassembled and in only four months they were able to lay 115 cubic yards of stone and just short of 900,000 bricks. The anticipation was that the citadel would be completed by year's end. Indeed, by November 18, 1829, much of the masonry work of Fort Caswell had been finished, but more time would pass before the shot furnaces, traverse circles, and the works necessary to preserve the site from the encroaching waters of the Cape Fear River would be done. [23]

As it happened, the necessity for an all-out effort to stem the ravages of the storm-swollen river created the need for another engineer in the Cape Fear. The top graduate of the U.S. Military Academy in 1830, 2nd Lieutenant Alexander J. Swift, was assigned to the post of Assistant Engineer, reporting to Captain George Blaney. He was the son of none other than the engineer superintending the construction of Fort Johnston from 1804 to 1807, Brigadier General Joseph Gardner Swift. It became a two-man effort to complete the construction of Fort Caswell and simultaneously protect its site from further erosion. For two years they made great progress, until Swift was transferred to Fort Adams as an Assistant Engineer in 1832, leaving Captain Blaney with the lower Cape Fear's unfinished business to accomplish alone. [24]

In November of 1833 and again in 1834, Fort Caswell was reported ready to receive a garrison, but no such assignment was given to any unit of the United States Army. Having been appointed Brevet Major for faithful service on June 30, 1834, George Blaney died on May 15, 1835 at Fort Johnston in Smithville. [25]

That same year, storms were responsible for serious damage to the walls of the fort, creating breaches in the arches of two caponieres and their adjacent crenallated scarp galleries, not to mention erosion of the seaside dikes that again threatened compromise of the works. Moreover, the parapets and shot furnaces were still in an unfinished state due to a lack of funds, for which the all too familiar supplemental Congressional appropriation was once again necessary. The allocation was approved by Congress and the needed repairs to the dikes were completed by November of 1836. Additionally, the furnaces were finished and the locks to regulate the flow of water into the moat were begun. Repairs to the caponieres and the adjacent scarp gallery walls couldn't begin until the following year due to an insufficiency of brick. [26]

Over the next year, almost a million bricks were used in the construction of the counter-forts and relieving arches to salvage the damaged scarp walls, as well as to complete the tide lock for the moat and finish the breastwork parapets of the covered way and main work. Further compounding the problems created by the storm of 1835, an even more severe storm on August 18 and 19 of 1837 eroded much of the shoreline on the point of Oak Island, taking with it about a quarter of the glacis of Fort Caswell. The threat of additional damage necessitated the request of still another Congressional appropriation to build stone jetties and replace the eroded glacis of the fort with sand surmounted by mud. The repairs and Fort Caswell itself were almost done by October of 1838, but not before the total cost had reached $473,402.00. [27]

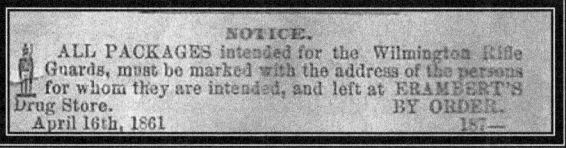

Captain Meares' Company.
(*The Daily Journal*, May 31, 1861)

At 6' 3½" tall, Ordnance Sergeant Frederick Dardingkiller was an imposing figure, despite all of his 43 years of age. But physical stature alone wouldn't dictate the events about to befall the German-born custodian of Fort Caswell. Shock and disbelief might best describe his realization that armed men from Wilmington had landed on Oak Island for the second time in three months. But it was true. They were back, and the career soldier must have known why they were there. This time, though, the men filing through the main sally port appeared more resolute, more determined. And there were more of them than before. Even with the presence of U. S. Army Sergeant Walker and civilian fort keeper John Russell, the Union men were still outnumbered thirty to one. Sergeant Dardingkiller's state of mind can only marginally be divined as Colonel Cantwell and his staff approached in the fading light of day. At 6:20 P.M. on April 16, 1861, the Regular Army Sergeant dutifully stood before the militia commander to receive the expected demand for the surrender of Fort Caswell in the name of the Governor of North Carolina. The outcome was never in doubt. "The fortification property was surrendered by Fort Keeper Russell and Ordnance Sergeant Dardingkiller," noted Cantwell. [28]

Captain Cornehlsen's Company.
(*The Daily Journal*, May 31, 1861)

With no more formality than that, military control of Fort Caswell passed from the United States of America to the State of North Carolina. More than 35 years after it was conceived, the fort at the mouth of the Cape Fear River stood ready to defend the gateway to Wilmington, with Colonel John Lucas Paul Cantwell commanding. The garrison at Caswell on April 17, however, consisted of only three very small companies: Captain William Lord DeRosset's "Wilmington Light Infantry," thirty strong; thirty-four troops belonging to Captain Christian Cornehlson's "German Volunteers;" and the "Wilmington Rifle Guards" numbering thirty citizen soldiers, under Captain Oliver Pendleton Meares. Just a short time after the takeover, the meager garrison was supplemented, if only until April 23, by eighty enlistees of Captain Lewis S. Williams' "Hornet's Nest Riflemen" from Charlotte.[29]

Surveying his new surroundings, Cantwell knew instinctively that an attack on Fort Caswell at this time would go badly for his command, "the present garrison being totally inadequate to the defense of the post." The Old North State took the Colonel's observation seriously and U.S. Representative Warren Winslow, military secretary to Governor John W. Ellis, wrote to President Jefferson Davis:

> Fort Caswell was taken yesterday . . . the guns there are not mounted, and it is absolutely necessary that an engineer officer should be there. It occurred to me that if you had such a person to spare he would be heartily welcome to the people of Wilmington. I wrote to the Governor to-day informing him I would write to you, and suggested that he would telegraph you to the same effect.

On April 19, the Governor wired Jefferson Davis. "I am in need of an engineer and artillery officers. Send them to me immediately at Raleigh." Sensing the urgency in Ellis' terse message, Davis immediately telegraphed his reply. "Have ordered a distinguished engineer and two artillery officers to report to you."[30]

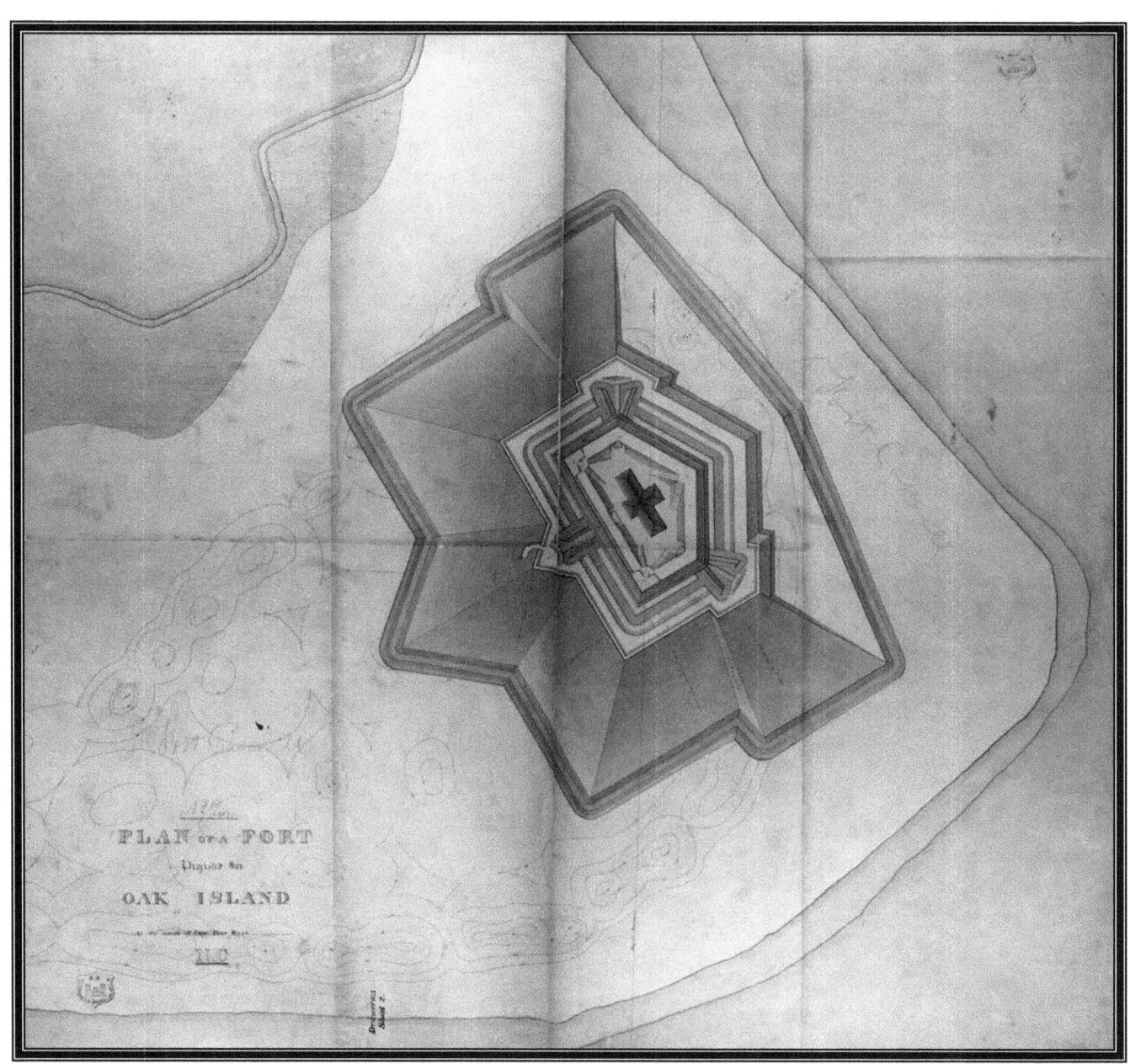

Plat of Fort Caswell as proposed by the U.S. Corps of Engineers in 1824.
(National Archives and Records Administration, Cartographic Division)

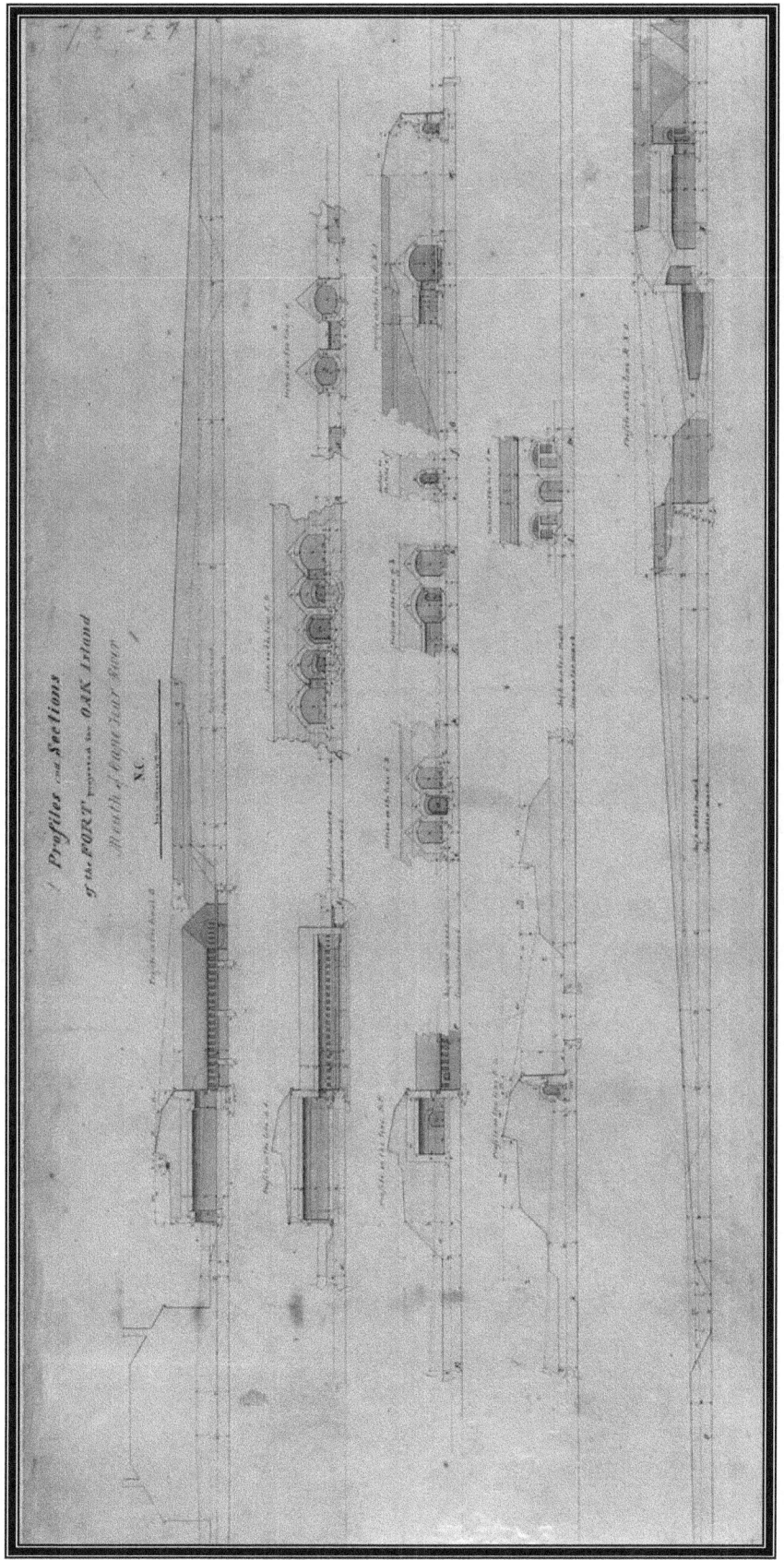

The profiles and cross-sections shown here portray the construction principles and techniques used in the erection of Fort Caswell. Unique among Third System forts built in America in the first half of the nineteenth century, Caswell's strength kept Union forces from its walls during the Civil War. (National Archives and Records Administration, Cartographic Division)

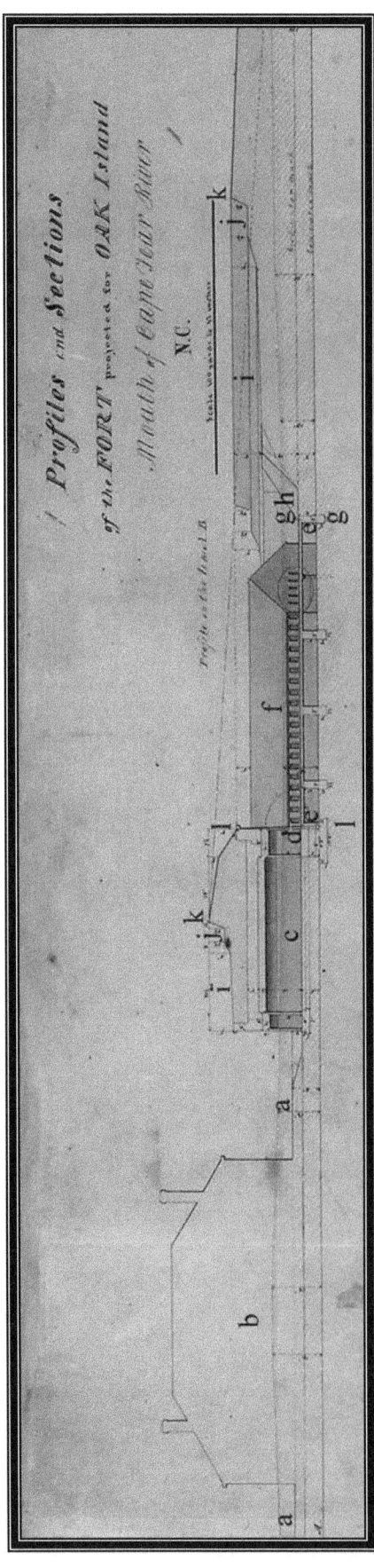

Together with the overall plan of Fort Caswell and the glossary, the profiles and sections shown here provide an understanding of most of the fort's components and how they were integrated with one another. (a) Parade; (b) Citadel; (c) Sally Port Gallery; (d) Sally Port; (e-e) Drawbridge; (f) Caponiere; (g-g) Counterscarp; (h) Crest of the Counterscarp; (i) Covered Way - there are two: The covered way normally referred to is the one exterior to the enceinte, and there is also a covered way within the enceinte, which is one by definition only, and not normally referred to as such; (j) Terreplein - there are two: The terreplein of the barbette tier on the main work and the terreplein of the covered way outside the main work; (k) Parapet - there are two: One parapet protects the gunners on the barbette tier and the other protects the infantry defending the covered way outside the main work; (l-l) Scarp Wall. (National Archives and Records Administration, Cartographic Division)

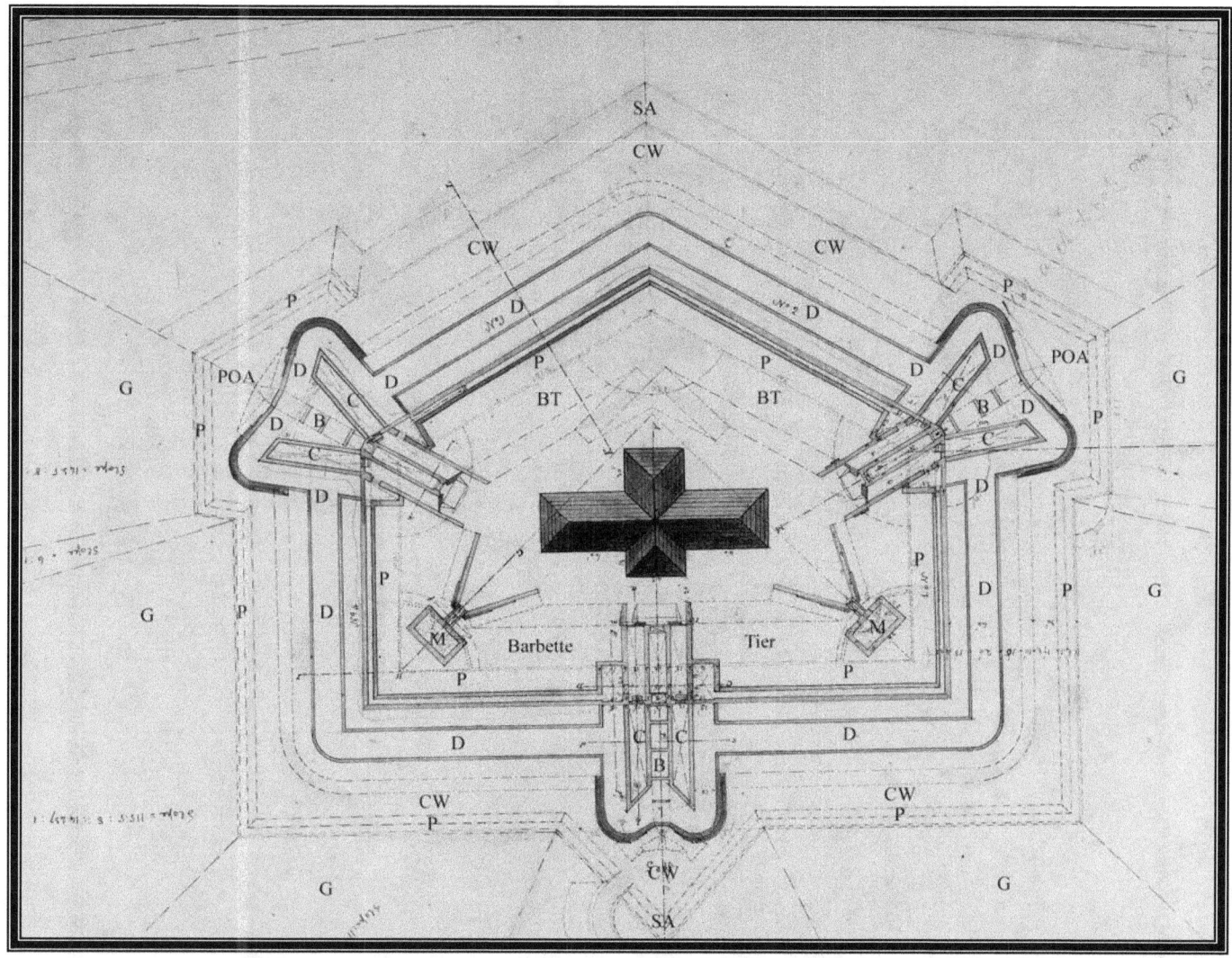

Plan of Fort Caswell. Most elements of this formidable fortress are visible here. The *citadel* is shown in the center of the *parade*. On the upper level are the *barbette tier* (BT) and the *parapet* (P). The *powder magazines* (M) are on the level of the *parade* and enclosed in masonry. The *enceinte* is defined by the double lines outside the parapet that form an exact pentagon, the base of which is termed the *gorge*, or rear of the fort, through which the main *sally port* is seen to exit. The *caponieres* (C) are shown standing in the *ditch* (D), with the drawbridge (B) between them. Beyond the *ditch* is the *covered way* (CW) and the two *places of arms* (POA), with the *parapet* (P) covered by the *glacis* (G). The fort's two *salient angles* (SA) are seen at the forward and rear angles of the *outworks*, which included every defensive feature outside of the *enceinte*. The rearmost *salient angle* protected the main *sally port*. (National Archives and Records Administration, Cartographic Division)

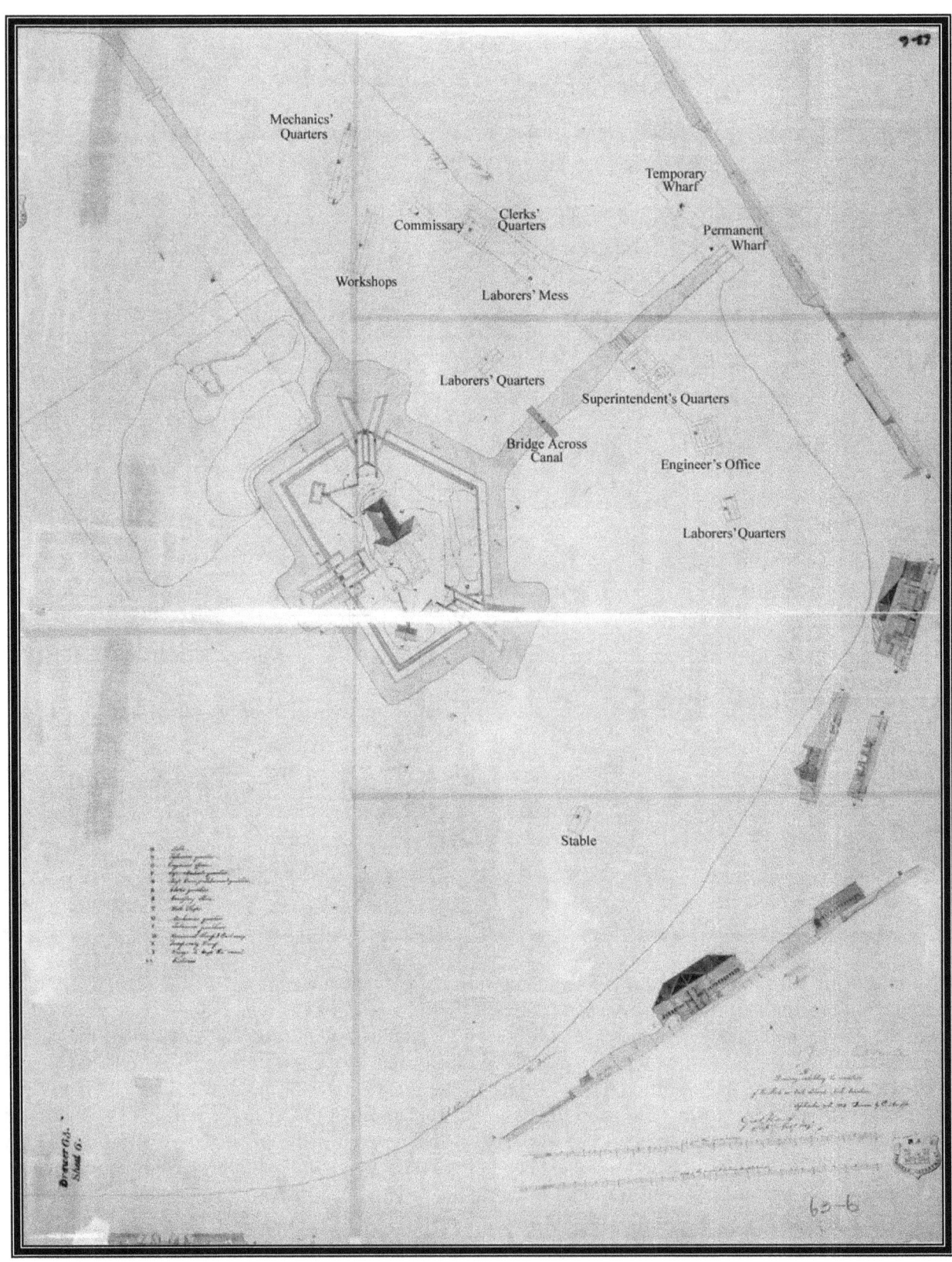

September 30, 1829 progress plan of Fort Caswell and location of support facilities for workmen.
(National Archives and Records Administration, Cartographic Division)

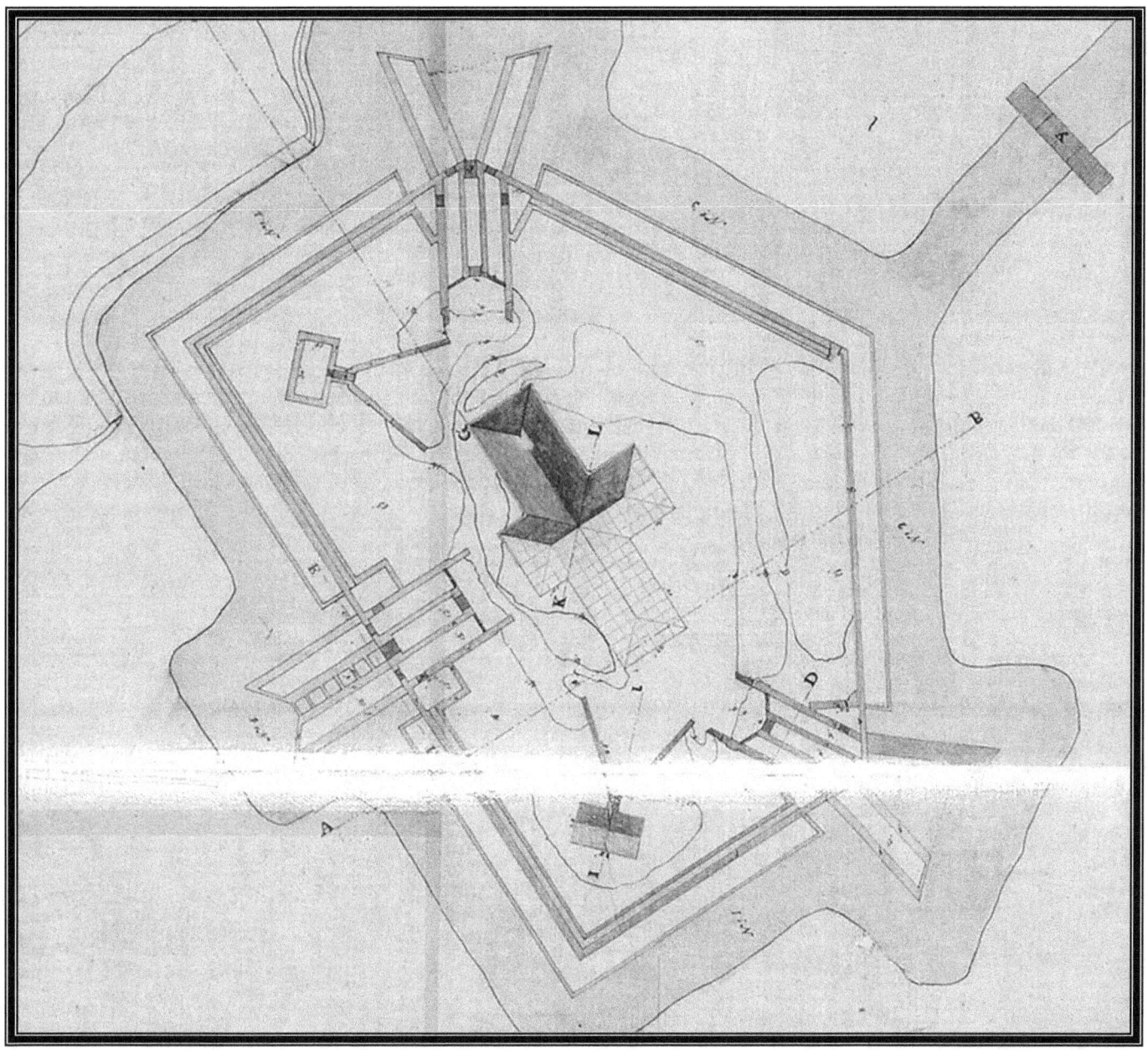

September 30, 1829 plan of Fort Caswell showing progress of its construction to date. Easily understood, the construction completed as shown on this plan is shaded. Briefly explained, the citadel was about 1/3 complete. One magazine and one caponiere were very nearly finished. The light red lines represent the footings for virtually all of the masonry walls that were to be constructed within the enceinte and caponieres. One magazine and the walls for its adjacent ramps to the barbette tier had been completed. The magazine was accessed by a door between those walls, which are seen here as a V pointing toward the magazine. Additionally, the canal from the river had been excavated, which served to fill the completed ditch. (National Archives and Records Administration, Cartographic Division)

Profile A-B provides more detail as to the progress of Fort Caswell as of September 30, 1829. The citadel is the large structure in the middle and to its right a portion of the completed scarp and one caponiere are apparent. On the left of the citadel, the very beginnings of the scarp and one ditch revetment may be seen. In fact, all of the footings for the masonry walls within the enceinte were in place and ready to receive the bricks that were yet to come. The water shown in the ditch is evidence of the completion of the feeder canal from the Cape Fear River. (National Archives and Records Administration, Cartographic Division)

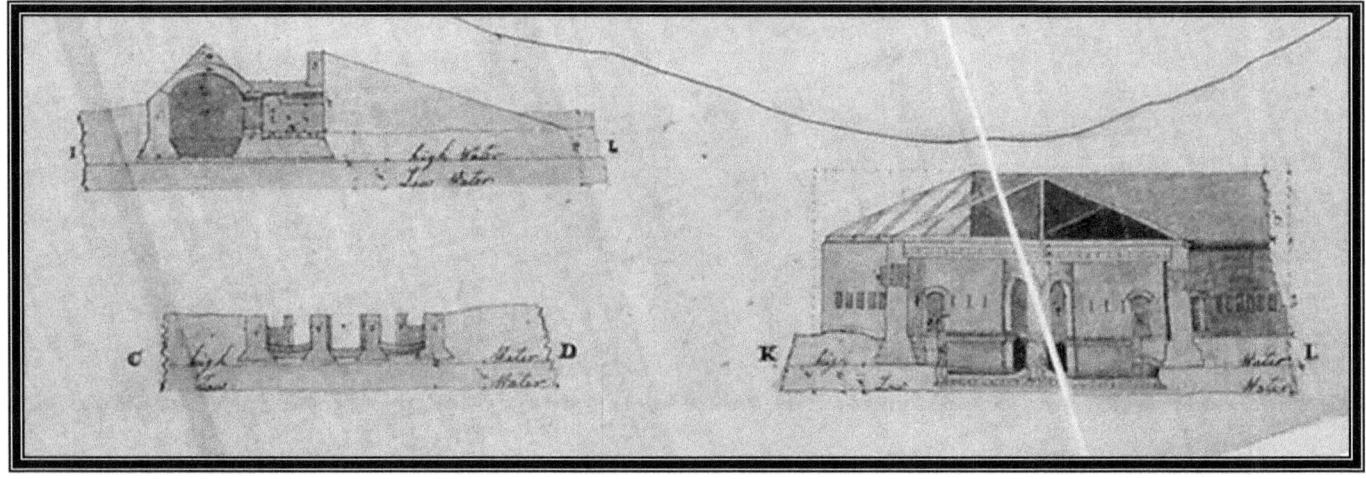

Additional profiles of the progress of Fort Caswell in 1829. Profile I-J shows one completed magazine and the two ramps adjacent to it that led to the barbette tier. Entry to the magazine was gained through the door shown between the ramps. Profile K-L indicates the relative progress of the citadel with roof covering on a portion and just the framing on the rest. Section C-D looks back toward the citadel and depicts partial construction of the dividing walls between the sally port gallery and the postern galleries on either side of it. (National Archives and Records Administration, Cartographic Division)

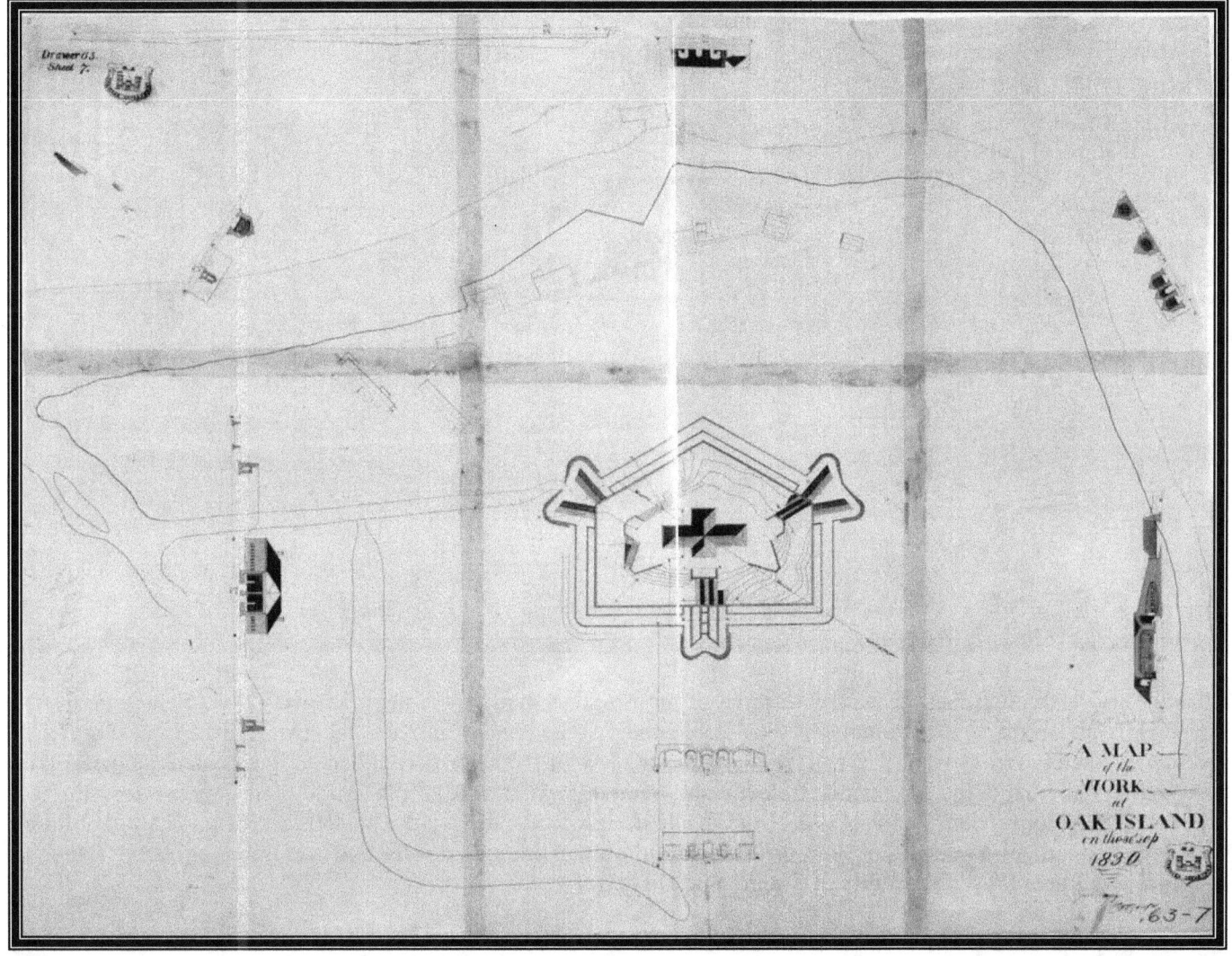

Map by Captain George Blaney from September 30, 1830 showing progress of the construction on Fort Caswell. The citadel was complete, as were the scarps and galleries, and work had begun on the interior walls that would carry the barbette tier. Two caponieres were finished and the other four lacked only their roof structures. The canal that was excavated prior to 1829 to transport water to the ditch had since been filled in and a new one dug from a small creek northwest of the fort. (National Archives and Records Administration, Cartographic Division)

Above: Section through the citadel is indicative of the progress made from September, 1829 to September, 1830. To the left and right of the completed citadel are the 2/3 height scarp, then the two finished masonry ditch revetments. Below left: Section L-M shows the interior view of the sally port gallery in the center, flanked by the two postern galleries to the caponieres. Below right: Section V-W is taken from inside the caponiere looking back toward the postern; section T-U also looks from inside the caponiere toward the postern and details its interior arch. Four of the caponieres were complete at this time, but the two at the main sally port were not yet begun. (National Archives and Records Administration, Cartographic Division)

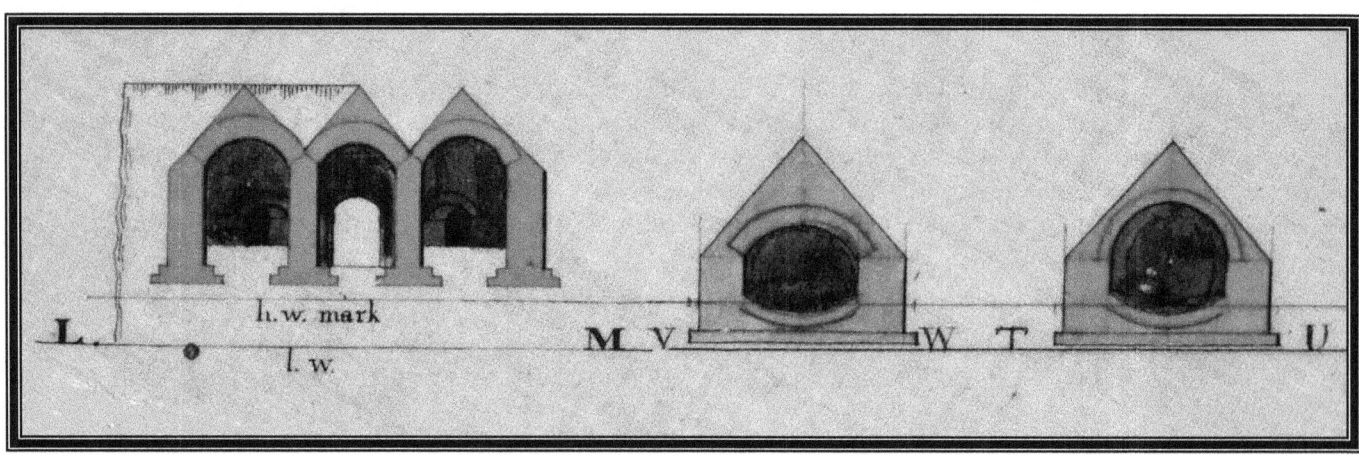

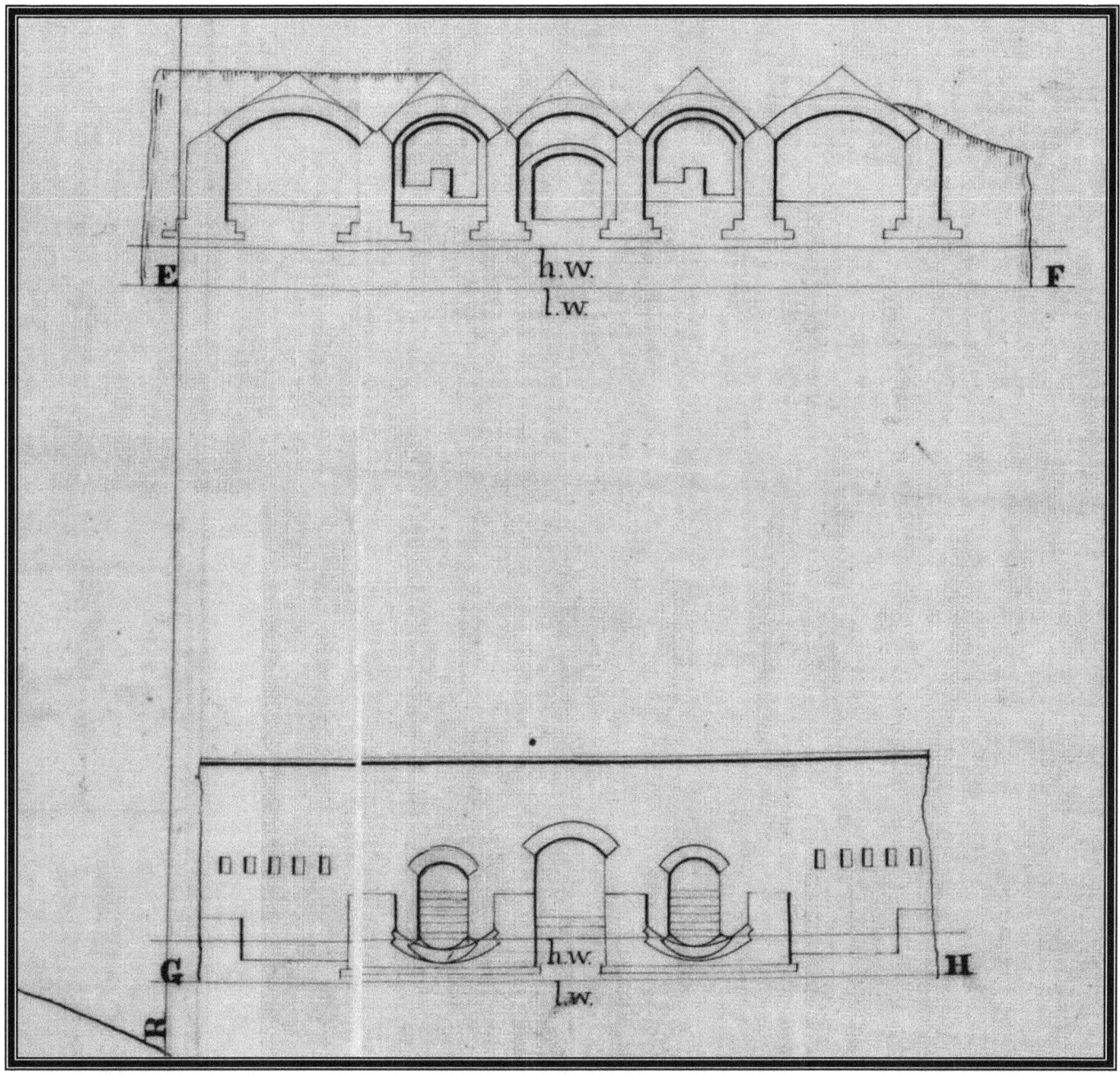

Cross section of main sally port. Above: Section E-F looks from the main sally port in the center toward the citadel. Flanking the main sally port are the postern galleries leading from the caponieres, and flanking those are galleries leading from the scarp. Below: Section G-H looks toward the scarp of the gorge from outside the works. In the center is the main sally port, flanked by the posterns of the caponieres, which were not yet begun at this location. Flanking the posterns may be seen the five loopholes of the scarp gallery that defended the outside walls of the caponieres. (National Archives and Records Administration, Cartographic Division)

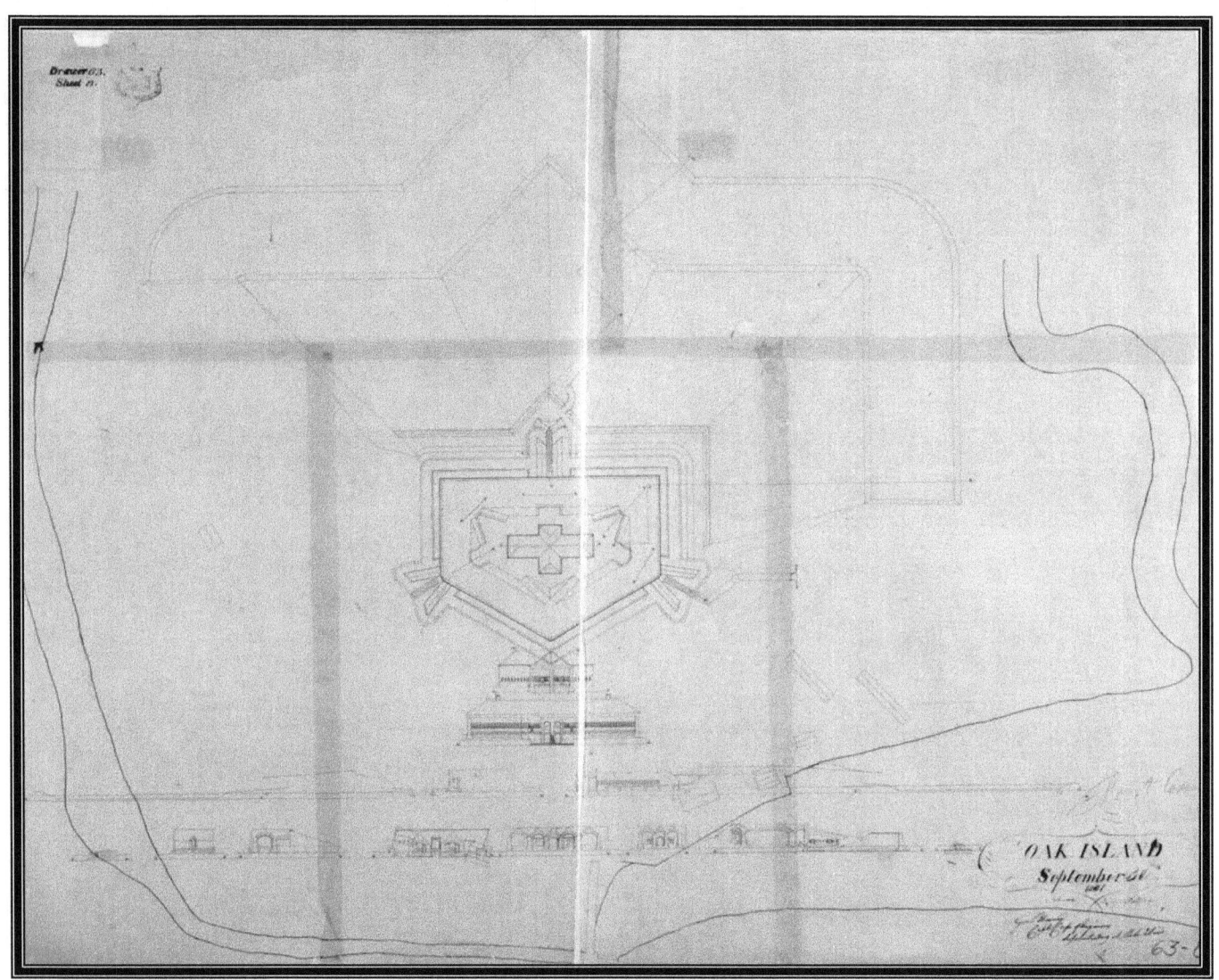

Another interim plan drawn by Lieutenant Alexander J. Swift and approved by Captain George Blaney dated 30 September, 1831. This plan shows substantial progress, except that only about one-half of the glacis had been completed. The citadel was finished and the masonry of the fortified pentagon and its outworks were almost complete. (National Archives and Records Administration, Cartographic Division)

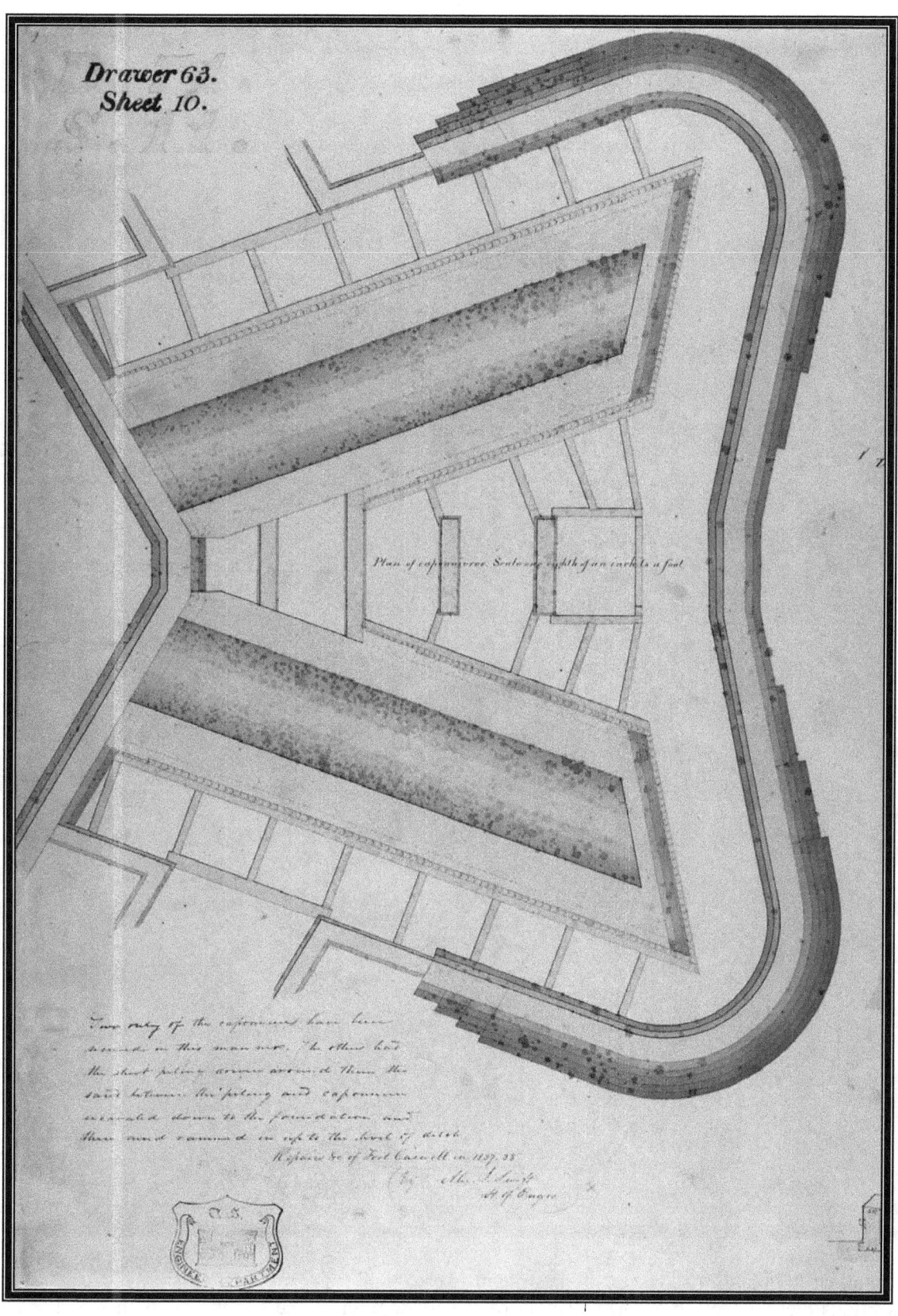

Plan for the repairs of two of the caponieres damaged in a storm in 1835, using wood timbers and sheet pilings. (NARA, Cartographic Division)

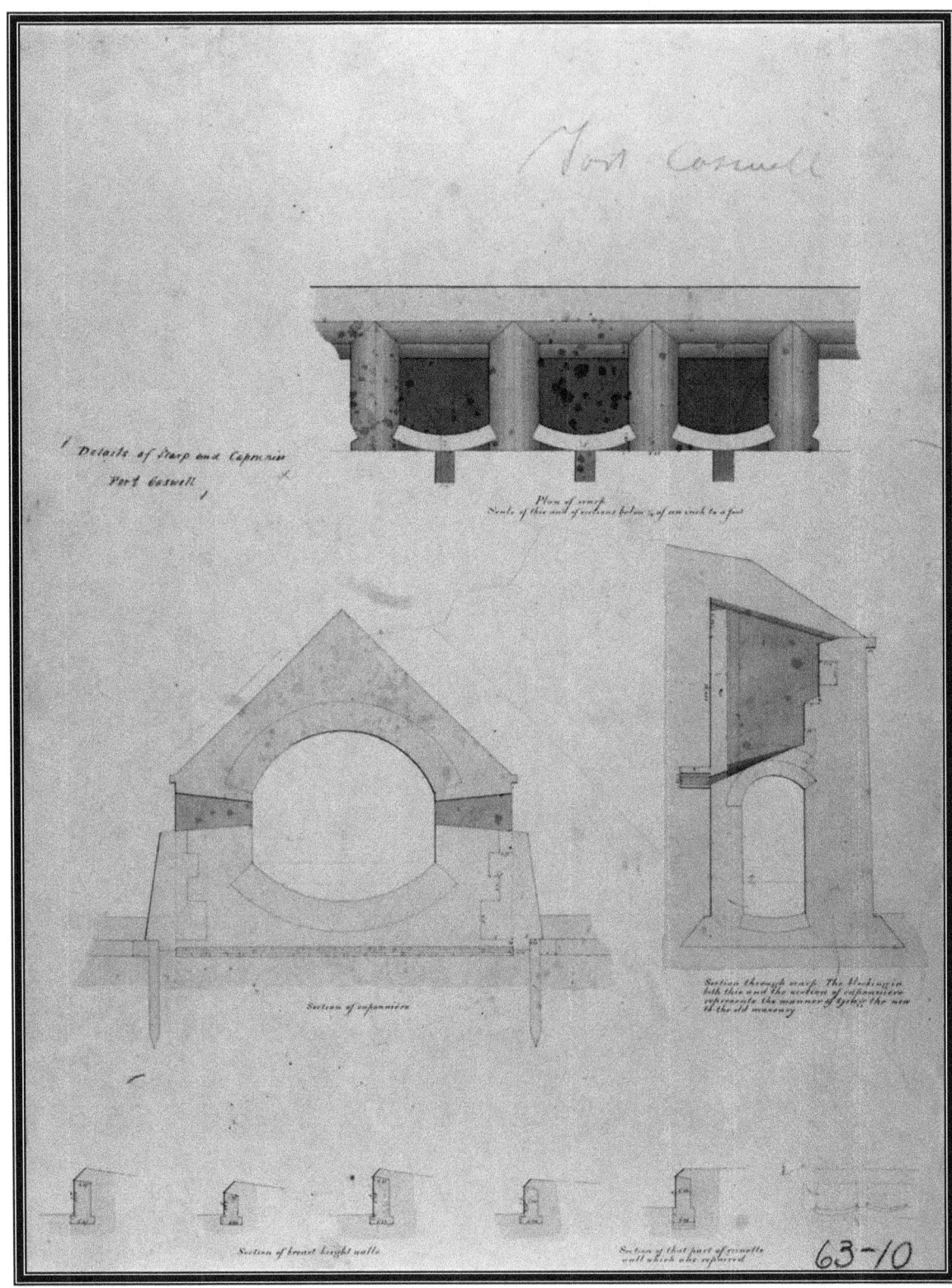

Detail of the plan for repair of the scarp and two caponieres damaged in a storm in 1835. The sections clearly show the reinforcement of the foundation of the caponieres with wood sheet piles as well as the keyed concrete reinforcement of the scarp at the crenallated galleries. (NARA, Cartographic Division)

Drawbridge, moat, sally port and portcullis. Those four features in this image are very similar to Fort Caswell's. In lieu of caponieres, however, this ditch and scarp was defended by flanking cannon and musket fire from the bastion at the far end of the ditch. The revetted masonry counterscarp upon which the bridge is seen to terminate is very likely similar to the one at Caswell. The masonry parapet at the crest of the scarp is, however, completely unlike Caswell's, which was earthen. (Library of Congress, Prints and Photographs Division)

Sally port and drawbridge. Another image depicting features similar to those employed by engineers in the design and construction of Fort Caswell. The bridge, drawbridge, moat, portcullis and sally port seen here probably resemble the components built into Fort Caswell better than any other surviving image of a Third System fort. The only missing features are the caponieres on either side of the bridge, since the engineers chose to defend this bridge and scarp with protruding bastions at the angles. (Library of Congress, Prints and Photographs Division)

Barbette tier. While this terreplein is of earth surmounted by grass and the gun emplacements are laid out for front pintle barbette carriages and 180 degree traverse circles like Fort Caswell's, the similarity ends there. Caswell's parapet was protected by earth, but this one is merely an extension of the masonry scarp, rendering it vulnerable to battering by artillery fire. Pintles and pintle plates are embedded in masonry next to the parapet and the iron traverse circles are shown embedded in the masonry arc behind them. This terreplein is made up of earth on a masonry floor, as was Fort Caswell's. Many of the traverse circles were missing at Caswell in the beginning, and would have to be manufactured before all its guns could be mounted on the barbette tier. (Library of Congress, Prints and Photographs Division)

Crenallated scarp gallery with loopholes and ventilation ports shown at right. Fort Caswell also had scarp galleries, but they consisted of six rooms pierced with five musket loopholes in each to protect the outside wall of each double caponiere. The unpierced corridors were used only to access the galleries, and therefore might be best described as scarp corridors. (Library of Congress, Prints and Photographs Division)

Compartmentalized crenallated scarp gallery with loopholes for musketry. While this gallery has just two loopholes, Fort Caswell was configured with five in each of six galleries, positioned to defend the outside wall of each caponiere and deliver reverse fire on the covered way. (Library of Congress, Prints and Photographs Division)

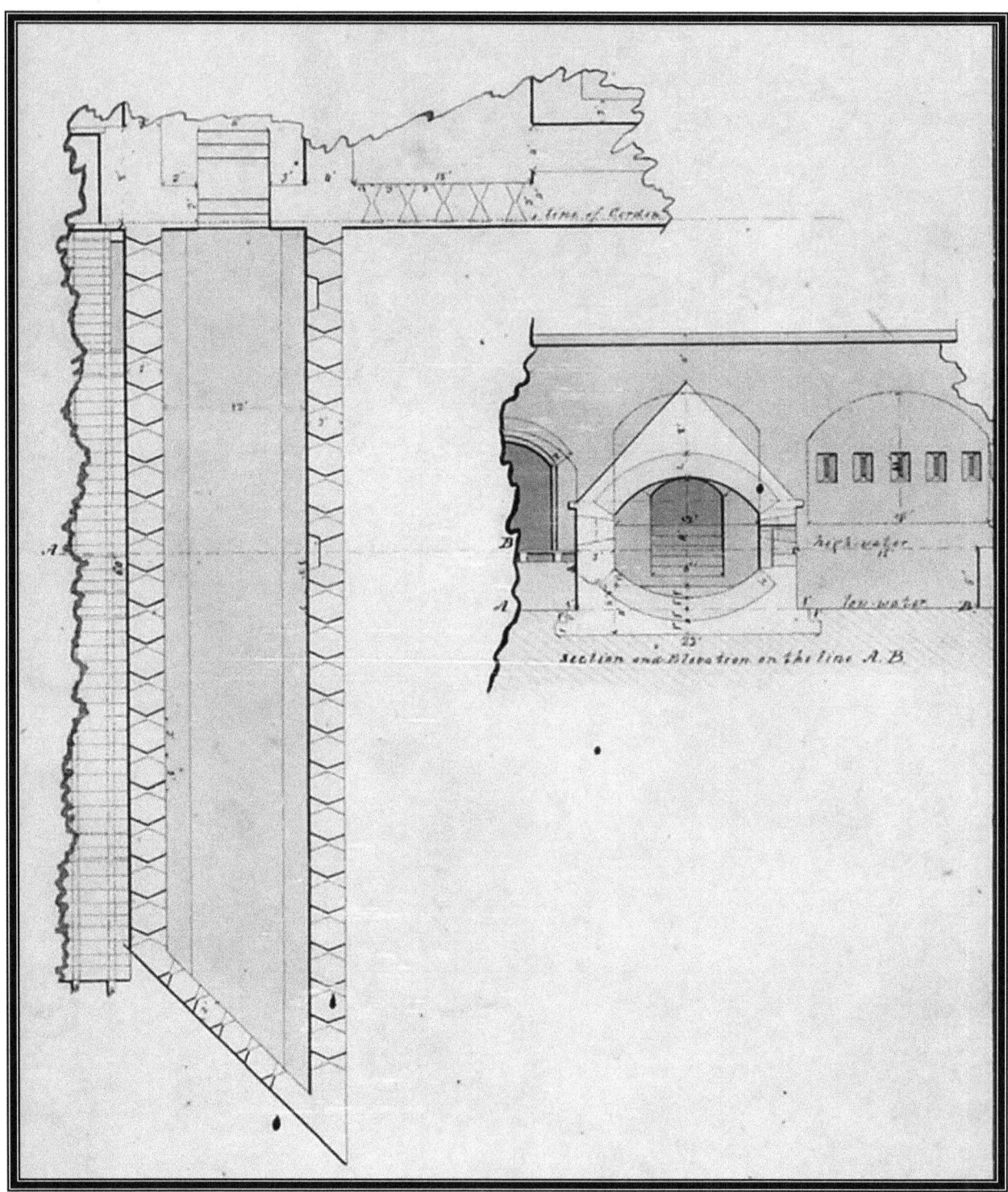

Left: Plan of one of Fort Caswell's six caponieres. Each sally port bridge was flanked by two caponieres with twenty musket loopholes in the short wall and twenty-one in the long wall, which also contained two casemates for cannon to enfilade the ditch. Five loopholes commanded the covered way from the angled end wall and five more in the loopholed scarp gallery covered the outer wall of each caponiere. Right: Exterior section of the caponiere through its length. Unquestionably unique to American Third System forts, there were no casemate embrasures for cannon in the scarp of Fort Caswell. (National Archives and Records Administration, Cartographic Division)

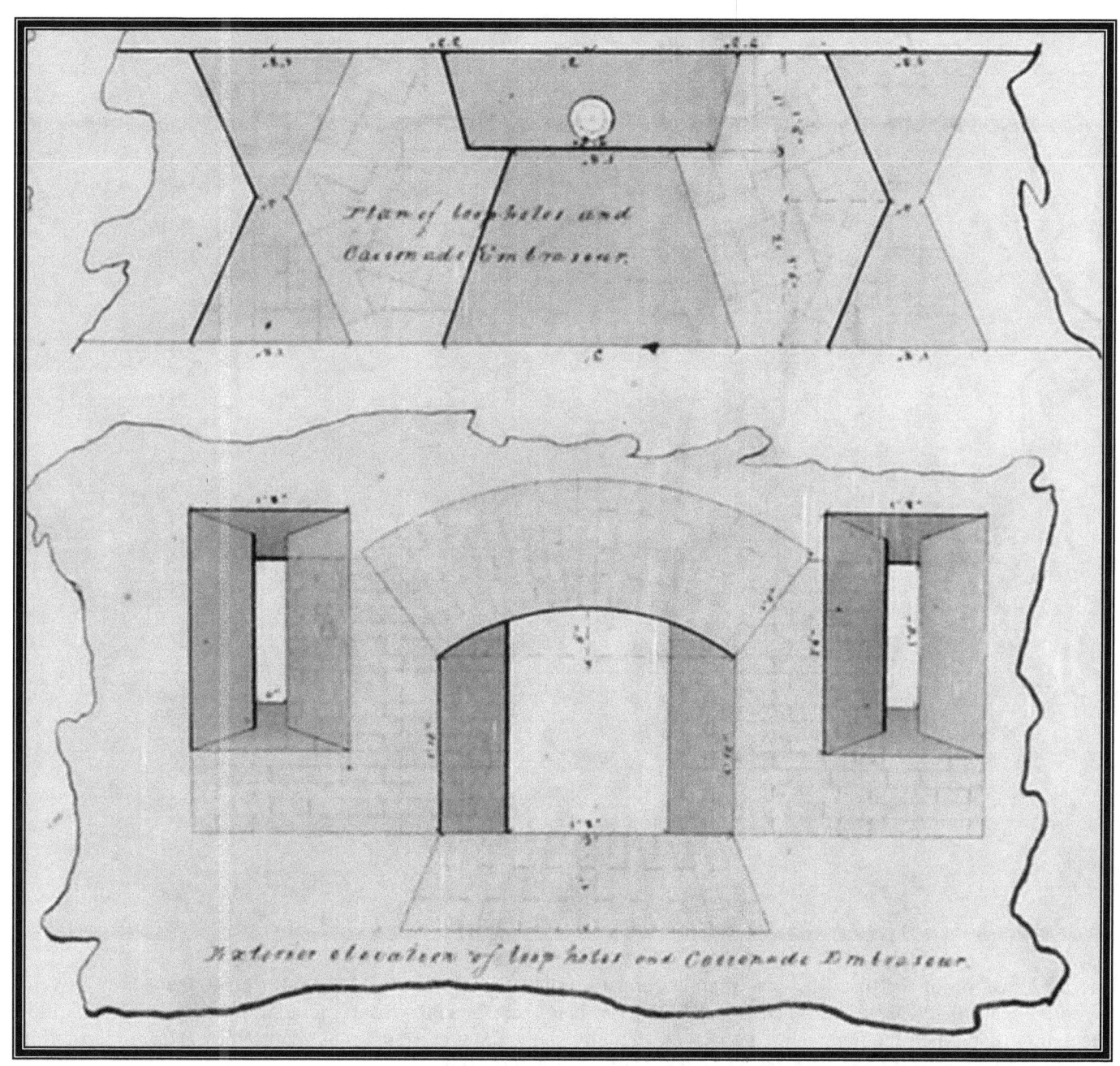

Upper: Plan of the casemate embrasure and loopholes. Lower: Exterior elevation of the plan for one of Fort Caswell's casemate embrasures, flanked by two musket loopholes. (National Archives and Records Administration, Cartographic Division)

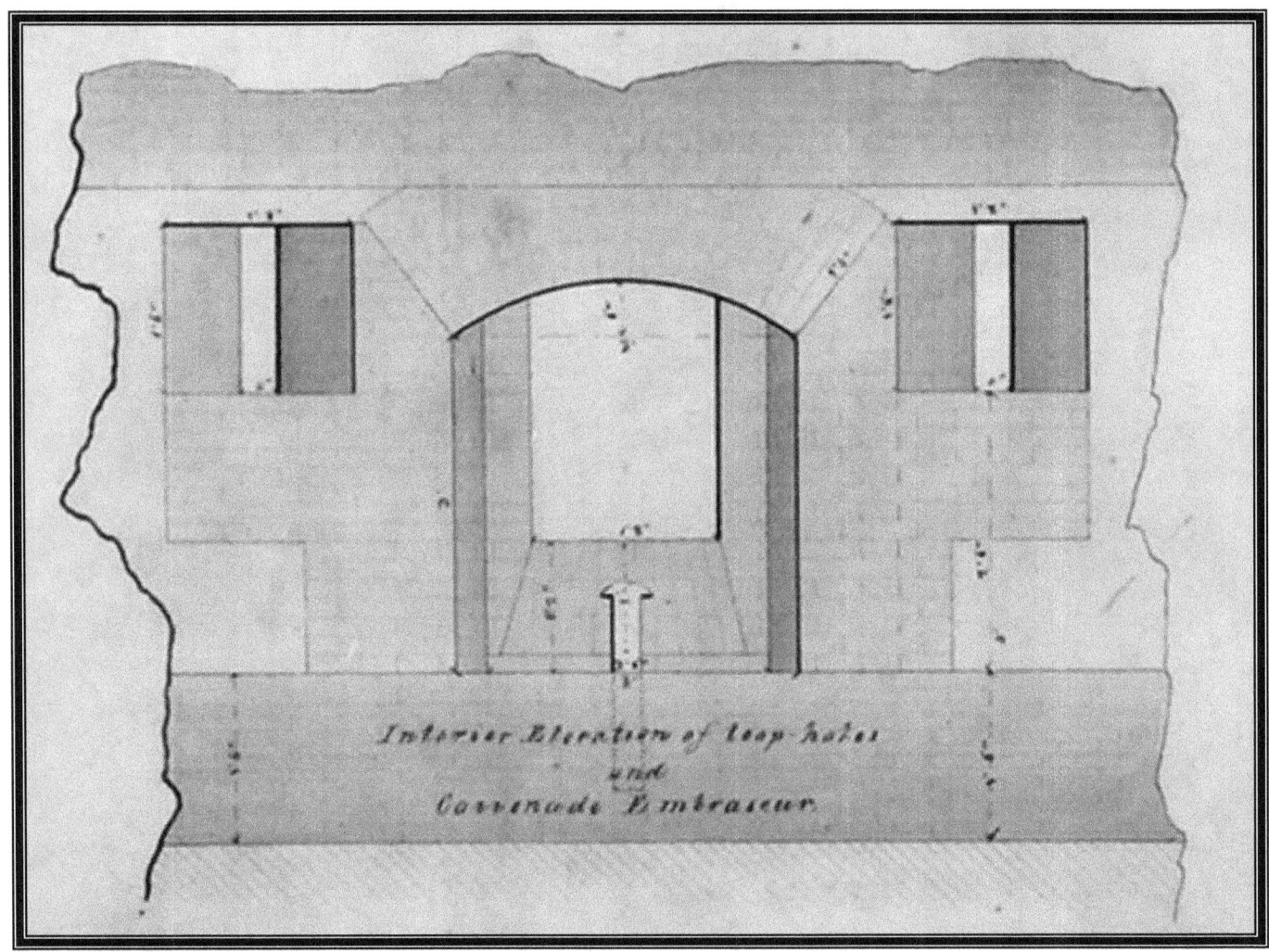

Interior elevation of the plan for a casemate embrasure flanked by loopholes. It is noteworthy that Fort Caswell's caponiere casemates were designed specifically for Navy carronades, front pintle mount. It is all the more interesting that, when the time came, there were actually some Navy carronades available for mounting in the fort. (National Archives and Records Administration, Cartographic Division)

Typical outwork casemate with traverse circle for a flank howitzer. This layout is highly similar to the casemates in the caponieres at Fort Caswell, complete with musket loopholes on the right and ventilation ports above. Fort Caswell, however, employed 32-pounder carronades in its caponieres. (Library of Congress, Prints and Photographs Division)

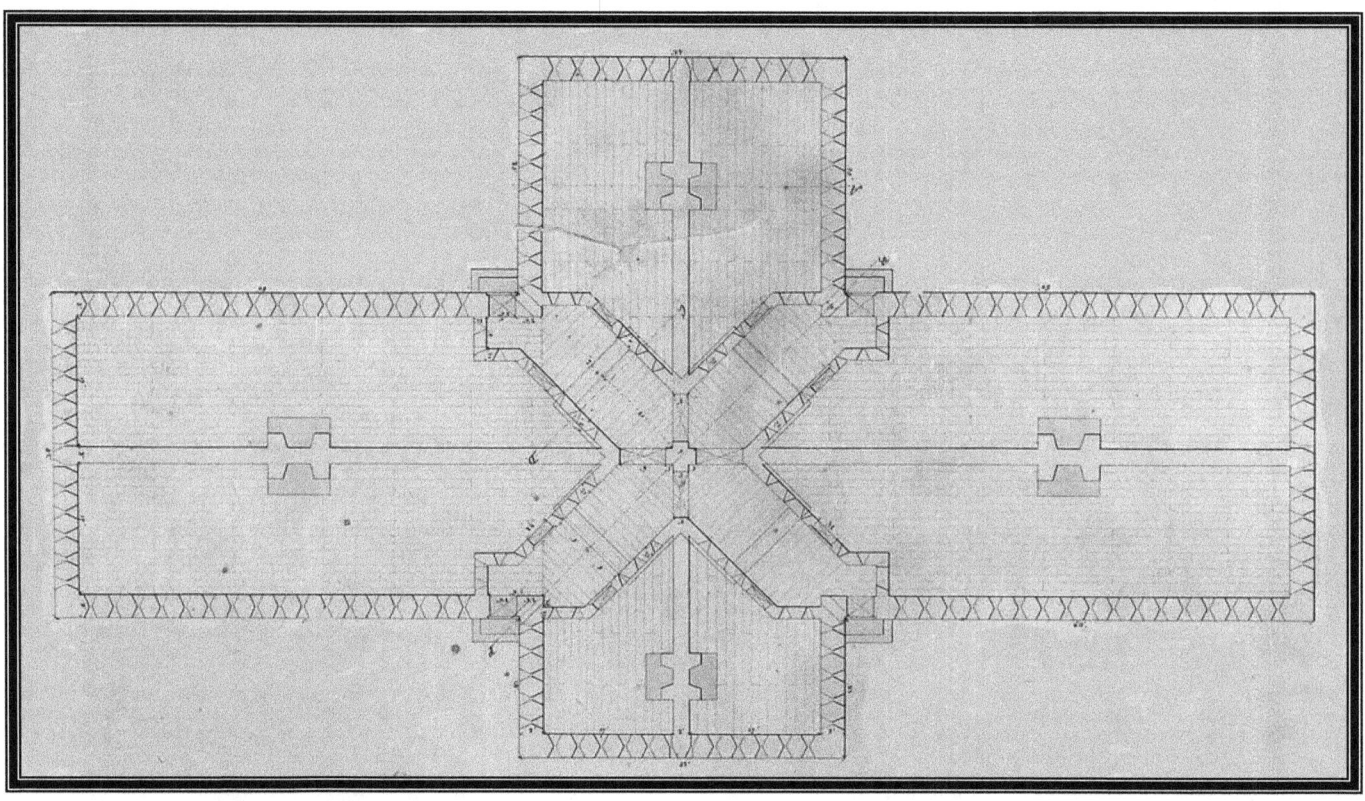

Plan of Fort Caswell's citadel - the last line of defense for an overpowered garrison. Home to the garrison, this fortified barrack was built with masonry walls three feet thick that were loopholed externally and internally. It was divided into eight self-contained dormitory rooms with a fireplace in each for heating and cooking, accessed by an X-shaped corridor in the center. The corridor was accessed by four iron doors, one at each point of the X, and could be isolated from the rooms, each of which had its own door. It is the author's opinion that the citadel was designed for occupancy by four companies, with the enlisted personnel housed in the large dormitories and the officers occupying the adjacent small ones. It's probable that command staff and company commanders occupied the smallest dormitory and line officers were housed in the slightly larger one. (NARA, Cartographic Division)

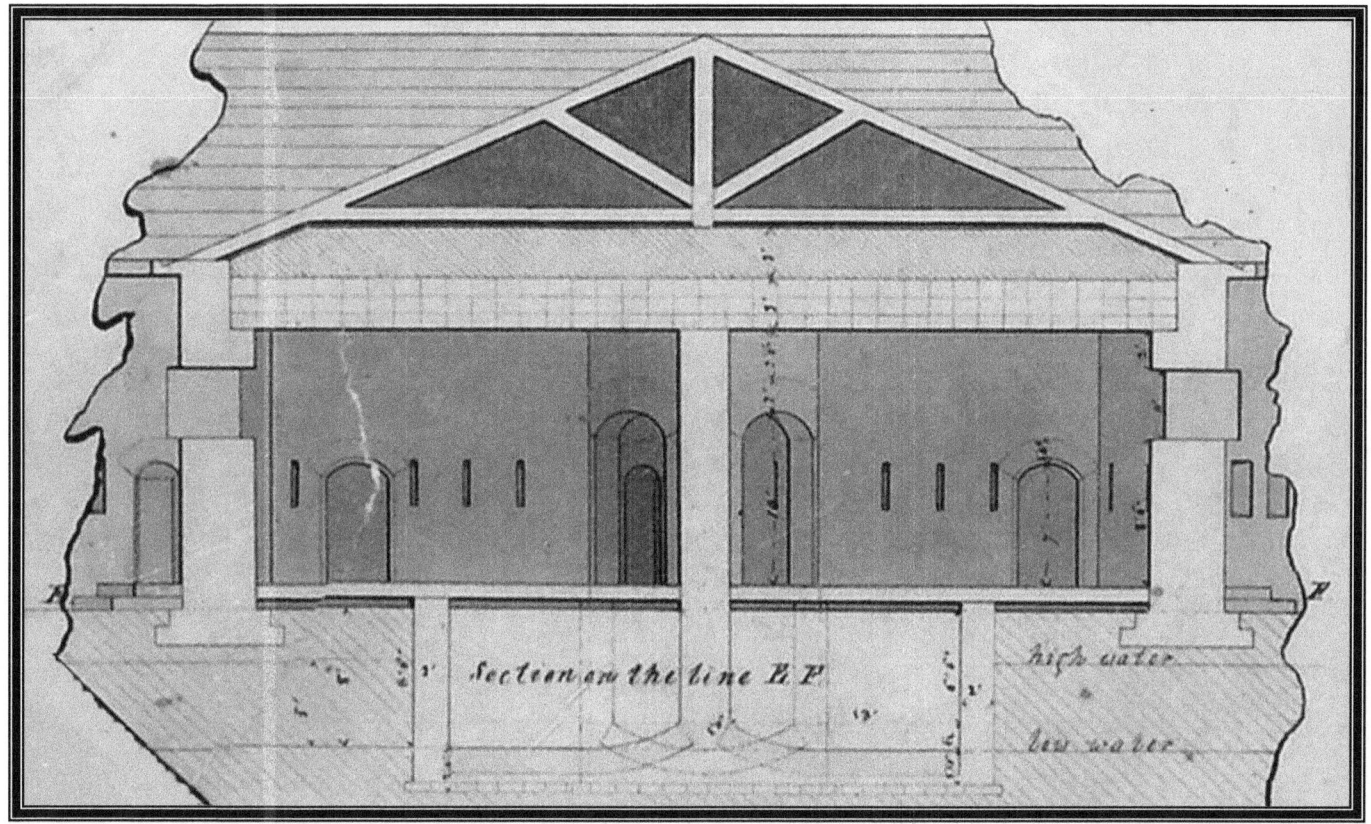

Section through the length of the corridor. The door at the far left is an outside portal and the other four are all dormitory doors. The doors appear to have been hinged inside the jamb and swung outward, so they could be pulled shut and barred from the inside. When closed, the doors rested upon the masonry jamb, the better to frustrate any attempt to batter them down from the outside. Once inside the outer doors, attackers were at the mercy of musketry from interior loopholes that not only delivered a crossfire, but enfilade fire as well. What appears here to be a dividing wall in the center of this section is actually a column of masonry that is seen as a cross in the center of the plan. Termed a pilaster, this column provides a bearing surface to support and tie together the arched lintels of the four open portals located there, in addition to supporting the beams for the roof. High water and low water levels are those of high and low tide, respectively. Caswell's footings were all perilously close to becoming immersed in water at high tide, an event that undoubtedly occurred from time to time, especially during stormy weather. (National Archives and Records Administration, Cartographic Division)

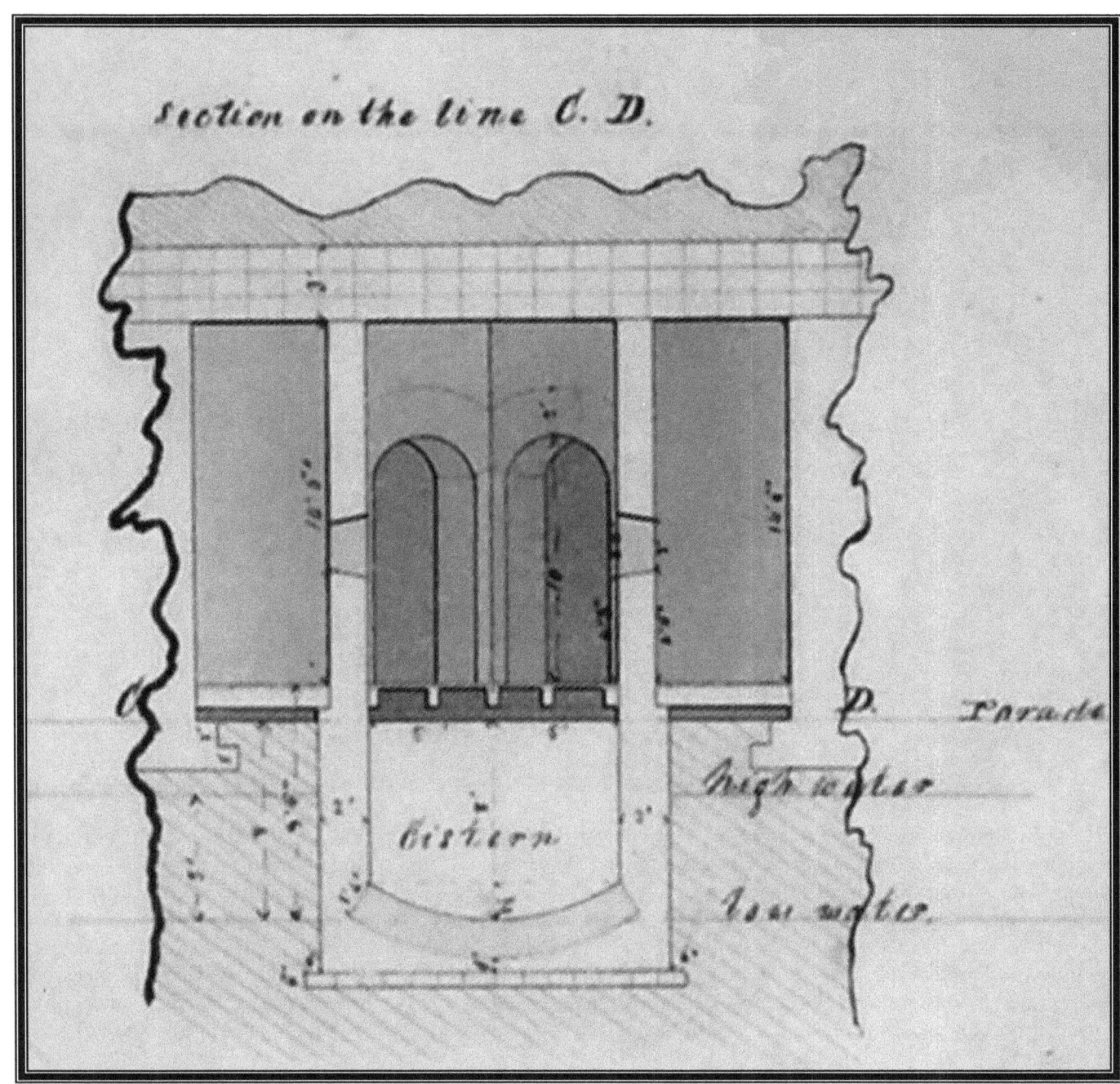

Section through the width of the corridor. The pilaster lies between the two arched open portals seen in this cross section. Each of the four branches of the X-shaped corridor had a cistern beneath its floor that served two dormitories. Rainwater from the roof was collected in scuppers and transported to the cisterns in downspouts. The water thus collected was hand pumped into the dormitories and used for cooking and drinking. (National Archives and Records Administration, Cartographic Division)

Fort Caswell | 45

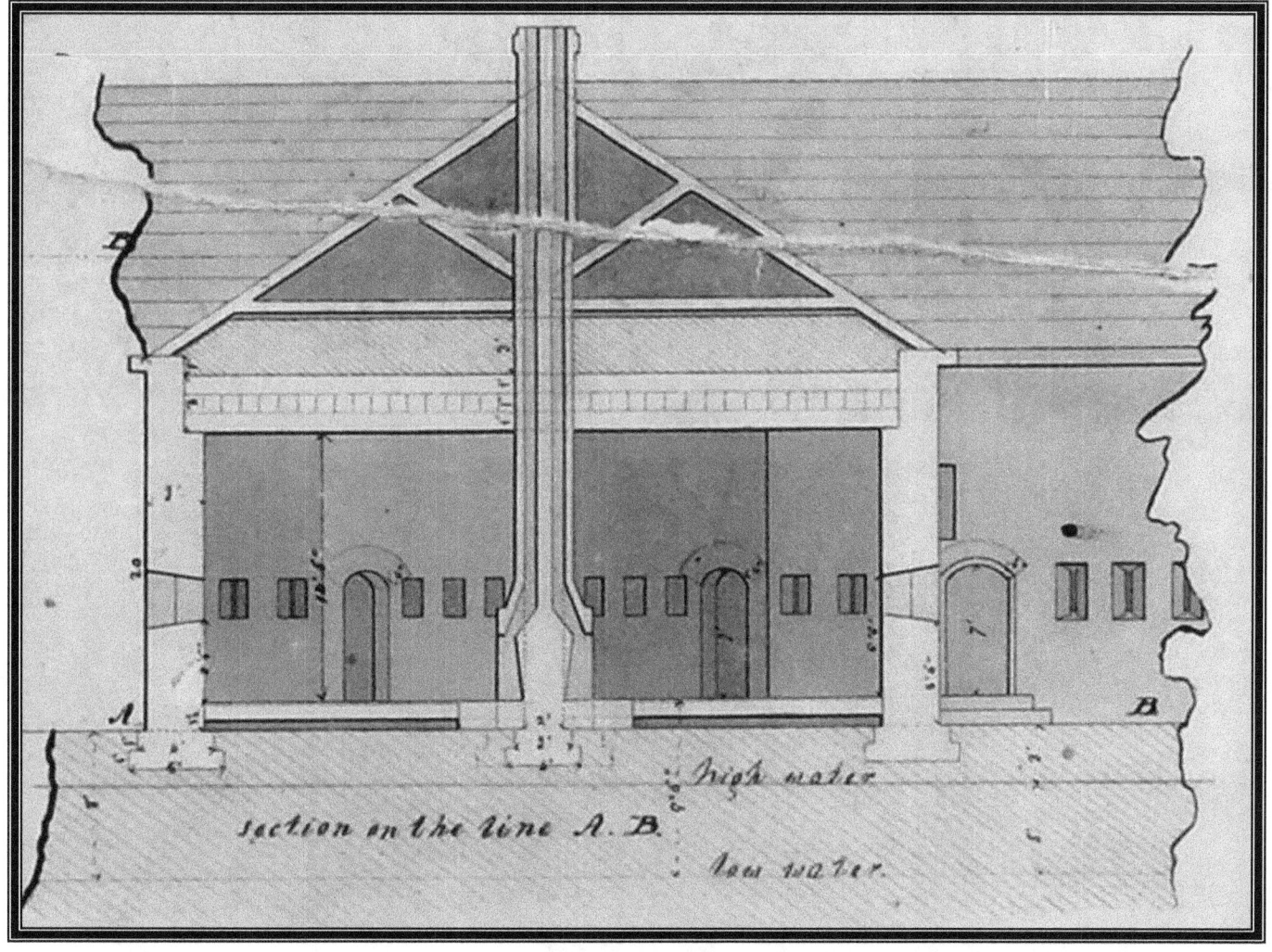

Section through two dormitories showing back to back fireplaces set into a masonry wall dividing the two rooms. Every dormitory was separated from every other dormitory by a masonry wall through which there were no portals. An outside door is seen at far right. (National Archives and Records Administration, Cartographic Division)

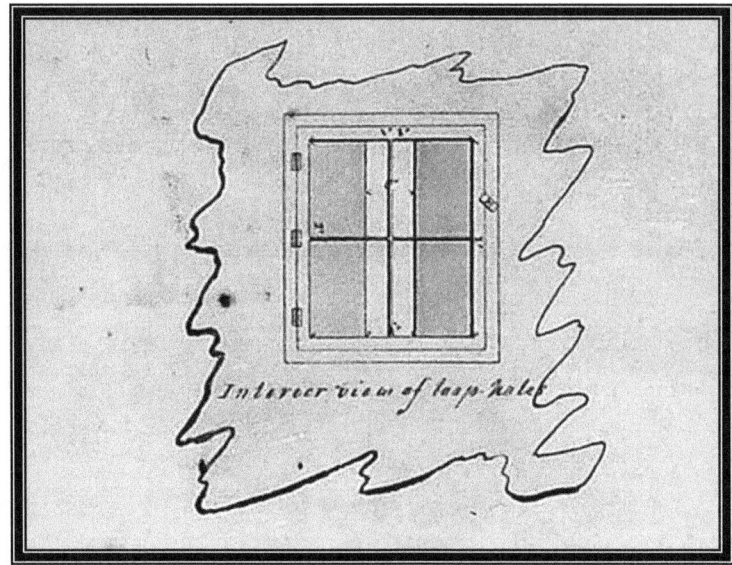

Interior detail of loopholes in Fort Caswell's citadel. The loophole is fitted with a hinged door that could be latched to deny access in the event of a surprise attack using incendiaries or hand grenades. (National Archives and Records Administration, Cartographic Division)

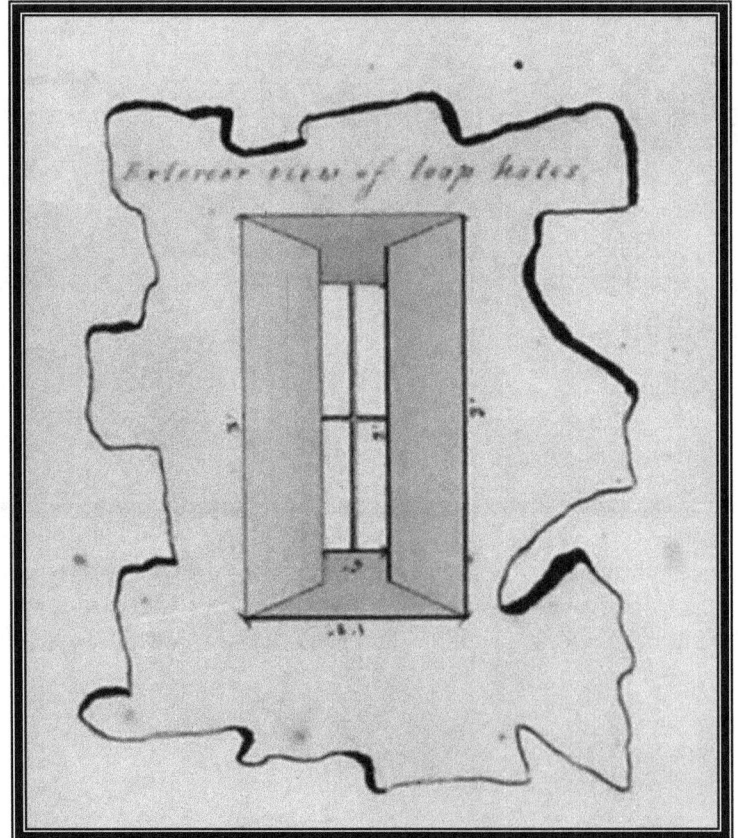

Exterior detail of loopholes in Fort Caswell's citadel. The crossed bars on the hinged door effectively decreased the opening size of the loophole in order to discourage the use of hand grenades. (National Archives and Records Administration, Cartographic Division)

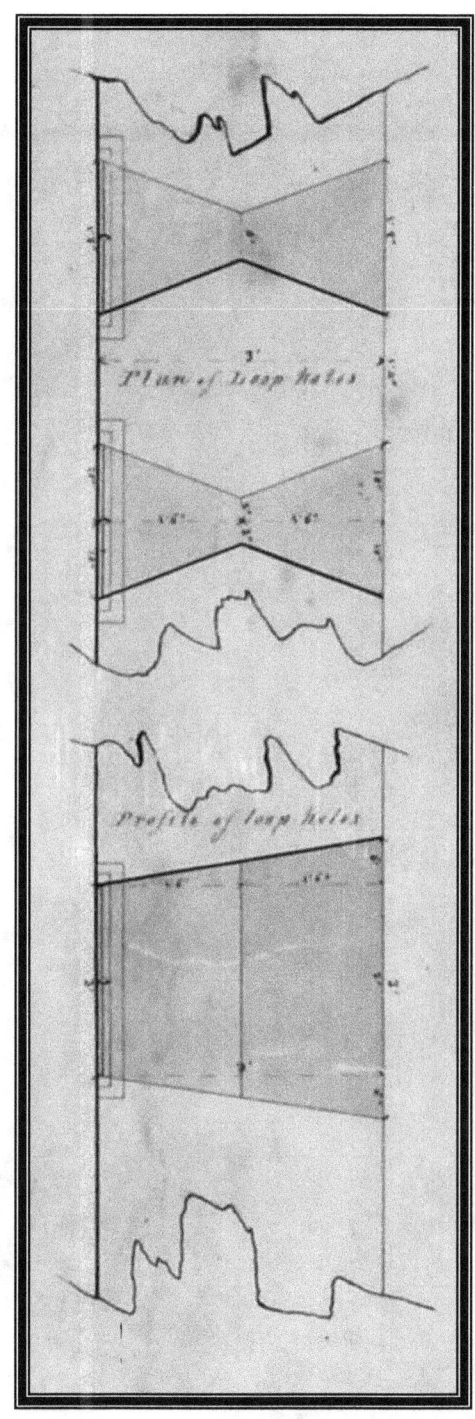

Plan of citadel loopholes - horizontal fields of fire.

Profile of citadel loopholes - vertical fields of fire.

(National Archives and Records Administration, Cartographic Division)

Confederate bronze 6-pounder field guns. (Library of Congress, Prints and Photographs Division)

Three

"Fort Caswell was badly served by old time siege pieces"
1st Lieutenant James H. Myrover

"The armament of Fort Caswell consists of the twenty 24 pounder guns above alluded to only two of which have been supplied with carriages, and one of those is disabled." Penned by a citizen's sub-committee of the Wilmington Committee of Safety on April 17, 1861, the statement painted a disheartening picture of the defensive capability of the fort seized by Militia forces only the day before. Common wisdom would suggest that all twenty were Pattern 1819 Siege and Garrison Guns, made in great quantity between 1825 and 1840, but evidence suggests that may have been only partially true. [1]

A Confederate officer once remarked, "Fort Caswell was badly served with old time siege pieces." Discovery of exactly which pattern or patterns lay in Caswell at the beginning of the war may rest with a surviving photograph taken after the fall of Fort Fisher in January of 1865. It was determined to be a 24-pounder by Federal engineers and appears as such on a map of the fort and its armament drafted by them soon after the surrender. [2]

The gun in the following image is clearly not the expected Pattern 1819 24-pounder, but is it even American? It has a few characteristics that provide clues to its genealogy: first, it has a short first *reinforce*; secondly, there are no *rimbases* to support the *trunnions* and center the gun between the *cheeks* of the carriage; third, the trunnions are centered on the axis of the *bore*; next, it was cast with an unbroken [smooth] *base of breech*; and last, the gun has no *breeching ring*, sometimes referred to as a ringknob.

24-pounder of presumed Pattern 1861 in the fourth battery from the left flank of the Fort Fisher land face. (Library of Congress, Prints and Photographs Division)

Perhaps the authors of the preeminent work on cannon of the nineteenth century encapsulated the state of manufacturing during the early part of the century, by stating, "Centered trunnions, without rimbases or breeching rings, may indicate American manufacture roughly between 1800 and 1816." Those features, together with the unbroken base of breech during this early period, fairly scream "Made in America." [3]

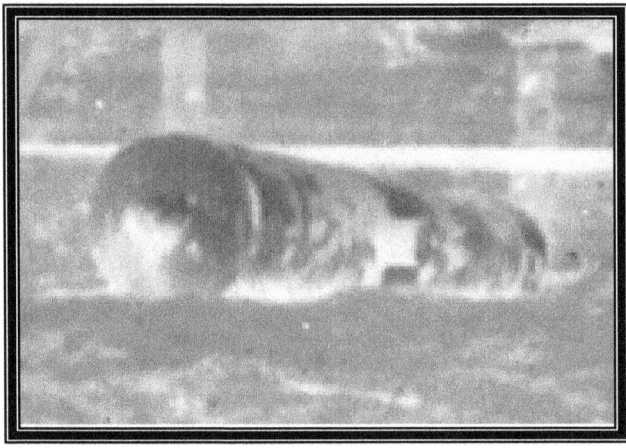

This negative view of the Fort Fisher 24-pounder confirms the presence of the short first reinforce enclosed by two raised rings and the lack of rimbases. Importantly, this gun features a round knob and rounded base of breech.

Its country of manufacture not in doubt, the pattern seems to be that of a transitional piece, blending the short first reinforce and nonexistent rimbases of Revolutionary War cannon with the unbroken breech base and centered trunnions of Pattern 1819 pieces.

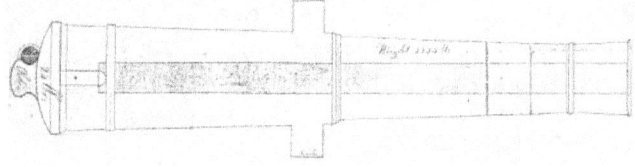

(Record Group 45, National Archives)

The preceding plan is that of a "long" 24-pounder manufactured for the U.S. Navy by Samuel Hughes of the Cecil Iron Works in Havre de Grace, Maryland, beginning in 1807. It is identified as such by its ringknob, a British Navy feature of many years' standing. The guns were specified to be about nine feet nine inches long and weighed about 50 hundredweight (cwt.), but the finished product actually ranged in length from 9' 7.3" to 9' 8.5" and weighed between 48 and 50 cwt. Guns of this pattern were cast both with and without the usual ringknob for use by Navy and Army alike. All were manufactured with off-centered trunnions, unlike those of the pictured gun. [4]

Army Regulations of 1816 standardized the 24-pounder for both siege and seacoast artillery pieces. The 1819 System of Land Artillery that followed solidified their standing as the largest big gun for land and coastal defenses of the United States, but plans for their manufacture weren't presented to the Secretary of War until 1820. John Clarke's Virginia-based Bellona Foundry delivered sixty 24-pounders of what is today an unknown pattern on August 28, 1817, fifty-five more on June 27, 1820, and another nine on 5 September 1821. Delayed approval of the 1819 System all but precludes Clarke's production from being cast in the 1819 pattern and suggests that his facility turned out the lion's share, if not all, of the 165 24-pounders procured by the United States Army from 1817 through 1821. Unknown until now, this production run is herein referred to as the Pattern 1816. [5]

If all twenty 24-pounders in the Cape Fear emanated from Fort Caswell, it's highly likely that as many as half of them were handed down from the sister fortification in Smithville. In July of 1811, Fort Johnston took delivery of eight seriously overdue 24-pounder guns of unknown pattern, with a like number there on December 31, 1818. By 1822, twenty more 24-pounders were in the fort, all of them probably new issues from Bellona, but only fourteen were counted there the following year. Then, in 1824, five of Johnston's 24-pounders and eight of its garrison carriages were condemned as unserviceable and eligible for sale at public auction, possibly from among the original eight sent there in 1811. By 1834, Fort Johnston inventoried eighteen 24-pounders, some of which may have come from the new Pattern 1819 production. [6]

The year 1840 saw Fort Caswell still under construction, with only an imaginative armament projected for it, while Fort Johnston held just ten ancient 24-pounders. Only too predictably, the lofty projection for arming Fort Caswell never came to pass, for on December 8, 1851, North Carolina Forts Macon and Caswell contained thirty-seven 24-pounder guns, seventeen in the former and twenty in the latter, and nothing else. Fort Johnston, on the other hand, was not even on the list of forts containing heavy cannon on that date.[7]

In 1861, the United States War Department inventoried all cannon situated in its forts and arsenals, arriving at the same total of thirty-seven *siege and garrison guns* in the entire State of North Carolina. There is little doubt that they were the same guns inventoried a decade earlier. There seems to be no question the Fort Fisher 24-pounder came from Bellona Foundry's 1817-1821 production, due to the dissimilarity of its pattern to that of the earlier Samuel Hughes production. Sometime between 1825 and 1834, however, it is a virtual certainty that Pattern 1819 guns were added to Caswell's armament.[8]

U. S. Pattern 1819 24-pounder Siege and Garrison Gun. Contemporary image showing the front pintle chassis and barbette carriage in profile. (Courtesy National Park Service, Fort Washington, MD, Photography by Park Ranger Barbara Wadding)

Regulations of the Army of the Confederate States for 1862, as well as Regulations for the Army of the United States for 1857, asserted pattern 24-pounders to be serviceable arms and referred to them as "24-pdr., iron cannon, old pattern, round breech." In order to distinguish the old pattern cannon from the Pattern 1819 24-pounders, the latter guns were listed separately in both sets of regulations as "24-pdr., iron cannon, U.S. Pattern 1819." On the other hand, the Regulations for the Army of the United States for 1861 deemed iron cannon of the class "24-pdr., old pattern, 5376 lbs." to be unserviceable. The weight of this pattern, incidentally, amounts to 48 hundredweight. It would appear that, in just a four-year period, old pattern guns serving in the Union Army were destined for the scrap heap, but that was not at all the case in the Army of the Confederate States.[9]

Weighing in at around 5,800 pounds, 24-pounder Siege & Garrison Guns fired a *solid shot* of 5.68" in diameter, weighing about 24.3 pounds. Using a six pound powder charge and five degrees of muzzle elevation, the maximum range was 1,901 yards.[10]

Shortly after the fall of Fort Sumter on April 13, 1861, some Wilmingtonians urged Governor Ellis to petition South Carolina Governor Francis W. Pickens for cannon to be mounted at Fort Caswell's parapets. "Can get guns immediately and anything else temporarily from Gov Pickins [*sic*] on request of authority," wrote Thomas D. Meares and James Fulton on 16 April. Governor Ellis immediately exercised his authority by dispatching his friend and Wilmington resident Duncan K. McRae to Charleston.[11]

The envoy's meeting with Governor Pickens was successful. "The Gov. will furnish to us eleven guns all mounted," he wired Ellis on the 17th. The following day, Pickens confirmed his understanding of the arrangement by wire. "Mr. McRae has received from me today eleven (11) cannon of large caliber. Five (5) large calumbiad [*sic*] and shot."[12]

The Columbiads, however, were not ready to ship on the 18th. Reporting to Governor Ellis from Charleston, McRae said, "Officers advise you to detach twelve (12) men of an artillery company to proceed here to be drilled in the management of columbiads. They can be familiarized to the work by the time the guns are ready." The preparedness of the Columbiads notwithstanding, McRae was ready to leave Charleston immediately with at least a portion of the ordnance. "I leave tonight with four (4) guns and supply ammunition." Two days later, the Wilmington ferriage partnership of James Orrell and Charles W. Hawes transported McRae and the ordnance supplies across the Cape Fear River from the Wilmington and Manchester Rail Road Depot to the Wilmington & Weldon Rail Road Depot for transshipment to Fort Macon.[13]

At 6:00 P.M. on April 17, North Carolina Convention delegate John D. Whitford arrived in Richmond to expedite fulfillment of a contract for cannon and ordnance supplies, entered into between the State of North Carolina and the Tredegar Iron Works on February 2, 1861. The day before Whitford's arrival, workmen from Joseph Reid Anderson's foundry loaded a fully equipped battery of four bronze 6-pounder field guns onto railroad cars bound for Goldsborough, in partial fulfillment of the contract with the Old North State.[14]

On the morning of the 18th, Whitford was able to buy two 6-pounder rifled guns from Anderson, one of bronze and one of iron, in addition to a supply of ammunition. Later in the day, Tredegar laborers dutifully loaded more railroad cars with the North Carolinian's purchases, less the iron rifled 6-pounder gun that wasn't quite complete enough to be mounted on its carriage.[15]

Of the twelve guns remaining in the contract, two 10-inch and two 8-inch Columbiads were to be divided between Forts Caswell and Macon. Frustrated in his efforts to obtain any 8-inch Columbiads from Richmond's Tredegar foundry, Whitford met with Virginia's Governor John Letcher on April 18 and obtained his permission to purchase four from Tredegar's competitor, Dr. Junius L. Archer's Bellona Foundry. The guns were part of a batch of forty-six pieces of heavy artillery lately manufactured to complete a U.S. contract dating from 1857, and then detained by the State of Virginia just prior to her secession from the Union. An average shipping weight of 9,245 pounds each confirms they were indeed U.S. Pattern 1857 New Columbiads.[16]

On April 19, Whitford anticipated receipt of a schedule for the imminent departure of the State's ordnance and ammunition, and wired Governor Ellis to request orders for placing them where they were needed most. "Will inform you and await orders for a division." Insofar as Whitford knew, the battery and the rifled gun were to ship in the company of a delegation from Wilmington and one N.S. Carpenter, a volunteer familiar with the rail system. On the 21st, Mr. Carpenter wired Ellis from Petersburg, asking that "an armed guard be placed at Weldon and Gaston Bridges," a certain indication the prized cargo was well on its way, but the Gaston Bridge was on the Raleigh and Gaston Railroad line. Had there been a change of plan? It seems so. On the same day, Ellis wired Adjutant General John F. Hoke. "Countermand the order sending Artillery Cannon to Wilmington. I have concluded to keep them here." Despite good intentions, it would appear that the delegation from the Cape Fear went home empty-handed.[17]

On April 27, four U.S. Pattern 1857 8-inch Columbiads and two 10-inch Columbiads of the same pattern, as well as two 12-pounder guns from the Tredegar Foundry were shipped to Goldsboro, but the six big cannon went without their carriages. Whether it was with Letcher's permission or without it, the 10-inch guns were acquired nonetheless, and the plan still called for the Columbiads to be divided equally between Forts Caswell and Macon. Available evidence, however, suggests that all the Bellona Foundry U.S. Pattern 1857 New Columbiads intended for Caswell were not immediately sent there.[18]

So what artillery patterns were shipped to the Cape Fear defenses from Charleston? Without equivocation, the 8-inch Seacoast Howitzers sent to the Cape Fear were of the U.S. Pattern 1839 or 1840 profile, of which Fort Sumter had four on April 14, 1861. An image taken in Fort Sumter immediately following its capitulation shows six cannon on the north face of the barbette tier. A surviving schematic of Fort Sumter's armament prepared on March 30 lists the calibers of all six, two of which are identified as "8" H," for 8-inch howitzer. A comparison of two cannon in the image to the schematic reveals their profiles to be identical to that of a Pattern 1839 or 1840 Seacoast Howitzer. Of greatest importance, the two do not nearly fit the profile of the so-called Bomford Pattern 1842, which was the only other Seacoast Howitzer pattern then extant.[19]

U. S. Pattern 1839 8-inch Seacoast Howitzer. (Courtesy of Jerry Dougherty)

From a barbette carriage and firing *spherical shell* only, these antiquated pieces of heavy artillery could send a 45 pound projectile down range a distance of 1,800 yards using eight pounds of powder and 5° of muzzle elevation.[20]

U. S. Pattern 1844 8-inch Columbiad. (Courtesy of Ben Jacobson under GNU Free Documentation License, Version 1.2)

There is also no doubt that the Columbiads were U. S. Pattern 1844's. The United States Army garrison of Fort Sumter had situated five of them on the parade "to serve as mortars," four of which were 8-inch caliber and the last a 10-inch piece. Military authorities at Sumter were clear as to just which guns Governor Pickens should send on to North Carolina. "We can without detriment let them have three 8-in. columbiad [*sic*] guns and carriages complete, the guns now lying on the parade."[21]

The Pattern 1844, quite unlike the Seacoast Howitzer, was said to be capable of sending a 65 pound solid shot down range 3,583 yards, using 10 pounds of powder and a muzzle elevation of 15 degrees. Its range using a 50 pound shell and the same charge and elevation, was theoretically 3,556 yards.[22]

U.S. Pattern 1857 New Columbiad. The gun in this image is of the pattern shipped to North Carolina from the Bellona Foundry via the Tredegar Foundry. Although two of the original four 8-inch Columbiads were intended for Fort Caswell, surviving records do not indicate that such a division ever occurred. In fact, the only evidence that Caswell received any guns of this pattern is a photograph of one in Fort Fisher near the end of the war. (Library of Congress, Prints and Photographs Division)

Early in the war, all of the Cape Fear heavy cannon were smoothbores that fired *spherical projectiles* in addition to grapeshot and *canister*. According to the U.S. Army, "The caliber of balls [shot] is expressed by the round number of pounds contained in them." Based on the weight of their solid shot, then, smoothbore cannon of the period that fired spherical projectiles came to be known as 128, 68[64], 42, 32, 24, 18, 12 [field and siege], and 6-pounders [field only]. The 128-pounder fired a 10-inch shot and the 64-pounder fired an 8-inch shot. The Seacoast and Siege Howitzers and all Mortars were precluded from firing solid shot.[23]

54 | **Guns of the Cape Fear**

This image, taken the day after Sumter's fall, clearly depicts the Pattern 1844 Columbiads on the fort's parade. (*Interior view of Fort Sumter on the 14th April 1861, after its evacuation by Major Robert Anderson, 1st Artillery. U.S.A. Commanding: 1857-1942*. Still Picture Records Section, Special Media Archives Services Division (NWCS-S), National Archives and Records Administration)

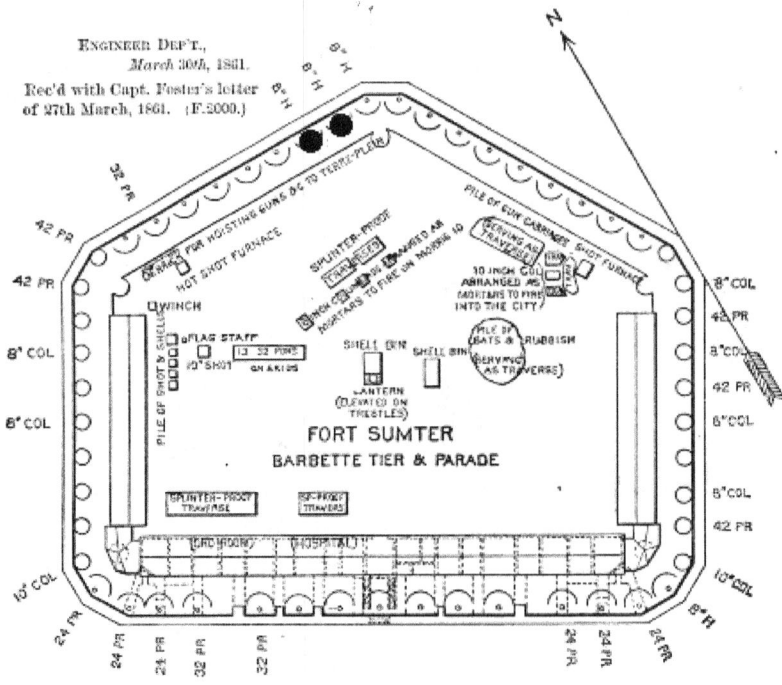

Schematic of the armament of Fort Sumter prior to the bombardment on April 12 – 13, 1861. The two cannon shown as black circles and identified as '8" H' [8-inch Howitzer] may be seen at the right in the image on the preceding page. (Foster to Totten, March 28, 1861, *OR* Series 1, Volume 1, P. 225)

Spherical *shell* was the oldest form of hollow explosive projectile. Also referred to as common shell, this thick-walled projectile was filled with black powder. Very early in the war, shells were armed by driving a tapered wood *fuze plug* into the top of the projectile with a mallet, after which a tapered paper *time fuze* was seated in the plug. The time fuze was ignited at the time of firing as the flame from the exploding powder charge engulfed the projectile.

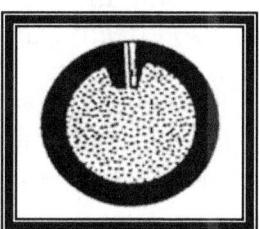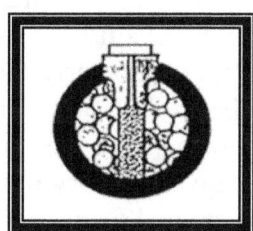

Left: Cross section of a spherical shell. Right: Cross section of a spherical case shot. The fuze depicted here is of a later type, but the image is representative of the contents of case shot, which remained constant no matter what type of fuze was used. (United States Army Center of Military History)

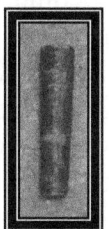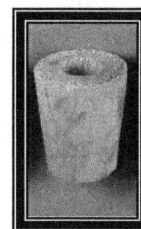

Left: C.S. 8-second paper time fuze. (Author's Collection) Right: Wood fuze plug. (Courtesy of Harry Ridgeway, The Relicman) The fuze plug was driven into the fuze hole of spherical shell or case shot in advance of taking the field. Once there and engaged, the paper time fuze was cut to length for estimated burn time and pressed into the fuze plug with the gunner's thumb before loading the projectile into the tube.

When the fuze burned down to the bursting charge, the resulting explosion shattered the projectile and its fragments rained down onto the target. Its thick wall also allowed the shell to penetrate buildings or fortifications without fracturing, thereby damaging the works from within and reaching otherwise concealed enemy troops. Of all the artillery in the service of the U.S. Army, only the 6-pounder field gun was excepted from firing shell projectiles.[24]

Spherical *case shot* is an anti-personnel projectile that was also called shrapnel in honor of its inventor, British General Henry Shrapnel. Case shot was a thin-walled hollow projectile filled with iron or lead balls and sometimes bullets set in a matrix of sulfur or tar, with a small bursting charge at its center. This type of projectile was armed and detonated in the same manner as a shell, but the larger number of pieces of metal introduced onto the target had a more devastating effect on enemy troops. Case shot was not acceptable for use in any 10-inch cannon or in Mortars.[25]

"Canister shot [*sic*] is a tin cylinder with iron heads, filled with balls packed in with sawdust," was a teaching principle set forth at the U. S. Military Academy. Effective at ranges from 300 to 600 yards, with the most effective range at 400 yards, canister provided the single most demoralizing effect on infantry of any artillery round of the Civil War. The little solid shot ranged in size from 1.14 inches for a 6-pounder gun to 1.84 inches for cannon with an eight inch bore. The U.S. Army's definition of grapeshot clearly differentiates it from canister. "A stand of grape consists of nine shot of a size appropriate to the caliber used, which are held together by two rings, and a plate at each end of the stand connected by a rod or bolt." The solid shot contained in a stand of grape ranged in size from 2.02 inches in a 12-pounder to 3.54 inches for an 8-inch cannon.[26]

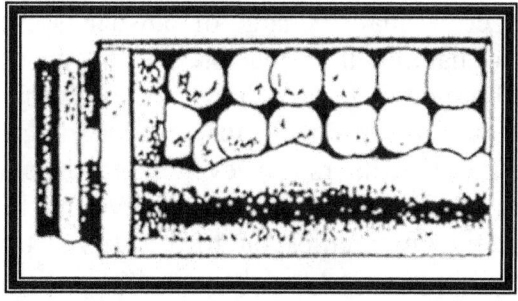

Cross section of the interior of a canister round containing metal shot and sawdust packing media. (United States Army Center of Military History)

Instruction at the U. S. Military Academy before the Civil War was unambiguous when it came to artillery practice. "Ordnance for the land service is divided into three classes, according to form and the kind of projectile used with each, viz.: *Guns, Howitzers* (including *Columbiads*), and *Mortars*." According to Academy training, "A howitzer is a gun with a chamber in it." Columbiads were included in the howitzer class due to the preponderance of the chambered U.S. Pattern 1844, which badly outnumbered the unchambered Pattern 1857 "New Columbiad" gun by a ratio of three to one. [27]

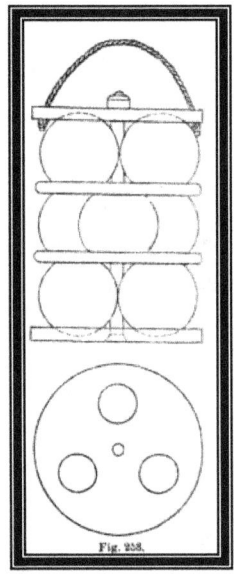

Stand of Grapeshot. (*The Artillerist's Manual*, page 352)

Howitzers were most valued for the delivery of shell projectiles, but shells "are liable to break if too much powder is fired behind them." In any howitzer, a smaller charge of powder is used to fill its chamber than that used in a gun of the same bore diameter, resulting in a high projectile trajectory, one rationale for reduced range and accuracy. Howitzers, however, more than made up for their shortcomings by delivering highly destructive projectiles on fortifications, troops, and buildings. Early in the war, the U. S. Army recognized ten types of chambered cannon: U. S. Pattern 1844 10 and 8-inch Columbiad; 8-inch Siege Howitzer; 12-pounder Mountain Howitzer; 10 and 8-inch Seacoast Howitzer; 32, 24, and 12- pounder Field Howitzers; and a short 24-pounder Howitzer for siege and garrison duty. [28]

If a howitzer is a gun with a chamber in it, then logic demands that a gun have no chamber. Accordingly, such artillery pieces maintain the same bore diameter from muzzle to breech and use a large charge to achieve a relatively flat trajectory for directly striking distant hard targets with solid shot. In a seacoast defense role, such targets included ships at sea or, in the event of land attack, enemy artillery. Using the principle of *ricochet*, solid shot was also effective against infantry, particularly those in groups or marching in column, but only when the ground was solid enough to resist the weight of the ball. Guns in the Army inventory immediately before the Civil War were: 42 and 32-pounder guns for use in seacoast defenses; 12, 18, and 24-pounder guns for siege and garrison duty; and bronze field pieces of 6-pounder and 12-pounder caliber. [29]

Mortars have very short barrels and equally short chambers and are designed to fire spherical shell only. They lob the explosive projectiles in a very high trajectory over and behind fortified ramparts "to crush the vaults and shelters of the enemy, and set fire to them." The U. S. Army maintained seven types of mortars in its service before the Civil War: 10 and 13-inch Seacoast; 8 and 10-inch Siege and Garrison; 16-inch Stone; 24-pounder Coehorn for trench warfare; and an Eprouvette for testing powder. [30]

While the U. S. Pattern 1844 Columbiad was nothing more than a heavy seacoast howitzer, the U. S. Pattern 1857 New Columbiad Gun had no chamber and was, as its name implied, a gun. The 8 and 10-inch calibers of the latter pattern came to be known as 64-pounders and 128-pounders respectively, reflective of the weights of their solid projectiles. The Confederacy never produced a Seacoast Howitzer or a chambered Columbiad, but the Tredegar Iron Works did produce its own version of the New Columbiad Gun in very limited quantity. [31]

"The shot used with heavy guns is generally without a *sabot*, but the shells are strapped to sabots made of thick plank, with strips of tin." Simply put and easy to understand, this was the guiding principle of heavy artillery before the Civil War began. But what about case shot? Omitted from specific mention in both the 1850 *Ordnance Manual for the Use of the Officers of the United States Army* and *The Artillerist's Manual* of 1860, strapping of case shot was finally given specific treatment in the 1862 version of the former publication. "The shells and spherical case shot (except for the 8-inch siege-howitzer) and the 8-inch siege and seacoast howitzer canisters are attached to sabots; the other projectiles are not strapped." It's now clear that Gibbon intended for the word *shell* to be inclusive of both case shot and shell, and that both types were to be strapped to sabots. [32]

The method for strapping shell and case shot to sabots for use in the big guns was relatively simple. First, the projectile was cradled into the sabot, and then two tin straps were crossed over the top of it. A slit was cut in one strap to allow passing the other through it before nailing the straps to the sabot, thereby locking the straps in position. Care was exercised to position the fuze hole in the angle of the straps, at a 45 degree angle to the vertical axis of the sabot before the straps were affixed to the sabot. [33]

A 32-pounder shell on its sabot, strapped according to the textbook. (Library of Congress, Prints and Photographs Division)

C.S. Spherical Shell. Here, the straps were attached to a collar of tin encircling the fuze hole positioned on the sabot opposite the powder charge. The paper time fuze was cut for burn time and inserted into the wood fuze plug just before loading the projectile into the tube. (Library of Congress, Prints and Photographs Division)

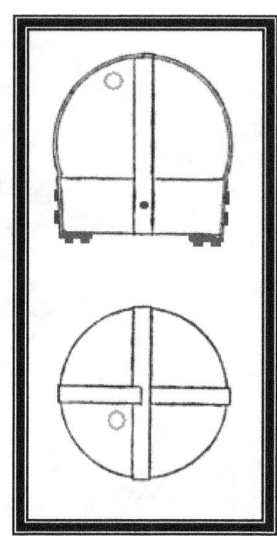

The method taught at the United States Military Academy for strapping a heavy artillery shell or case shot to its sabot. Seacoast Howitzer and Pattern 1844 Columbiad sabots were conical. (Adapted from *The Artillerist's Manual*, pp. 342, 350)

The only artillery pieces exempted from the requirement for saboted shells were 8-inch Siege Howitzers and all Mortars, which, by virtue of their short barrels, could all be hand-loaded and still maintain the fuze hole opposite the firing charge. The bottom of Siege Howitzer canister and grapeshot sabots were hemispherical to match the shape of half of a solid shot, a trait shared with no other cannon in the U.S. Army's service. In addition, conical sabots were to be attached to canister and grapeshot rounds intended for use in 8-inch Seacoast Howitzers and Columbiads, since "the cartridge should always occupy the whole length of the chamber." Sabots for both types of cannon were identical. Canister was not prescribed for the 10-inch Columbiads or Seacoast Howitzers for reasons unknown, other than the latter pieces had fallen into disfavor. [34]

When employing case shot or canister it was necessary to reduce the powder charge to avoid destroying the projectile upon firing. Keeping in mind that the cartridge must completely fill the chamber, the only way to reduce the charge was to put something else in its place. To do that, "a *cartridge-block* is placed in the bag, over the powder. The length of this block for any charge is easily deduced from the length occupied by 1 lb. of powder." The same cartridge block was used for both the Pattern 1844 Columbiad and the Seacoast Howitzer. [35]

Ammunition preparation and firing practice for field artillery was entirely different than for heavy artillery. Solid shot for use in field guns, for example, was always strapped to a sabot, which was never the case with the big guns. Additionally, the cartridge was tied to the sabot, thus creating a round of *fixed ammunition* for field artillery, whereas the cartridge was always loaded separately from the projectile with heavy artillery. Fixed ammunition was also applicable to case shot, shell, and canister when used in the little guns, but not so with the heavy howitzers. Here, solid shot, canister, case shot and shell were all saboted, but never fixed. Instead, the cartridge bag was tied to a cartridge block, creating a howitzer *cartridge*, which was loaded into the tube prior to the saboted projectile. [36]

Foreground: U. S. Pattern 1819 24-pounder Siege and Garrison Gun in a Confederate battery at the Warrington Navy Yard in Florida. Note the various patterns and calibers of artillery in this image (National Archives)

U.S. Pattern 1839 or 1840 8-inch Seacoast Howitzer. Even though the cannon in this photograph is identified in the Library of Congress as a 24-pounder siege gun, close examination reveals that it is not. Note the 8-inch saboted canister and stand of grape on their conical sabots. (Library of Congress, Prints and Photographs Division)

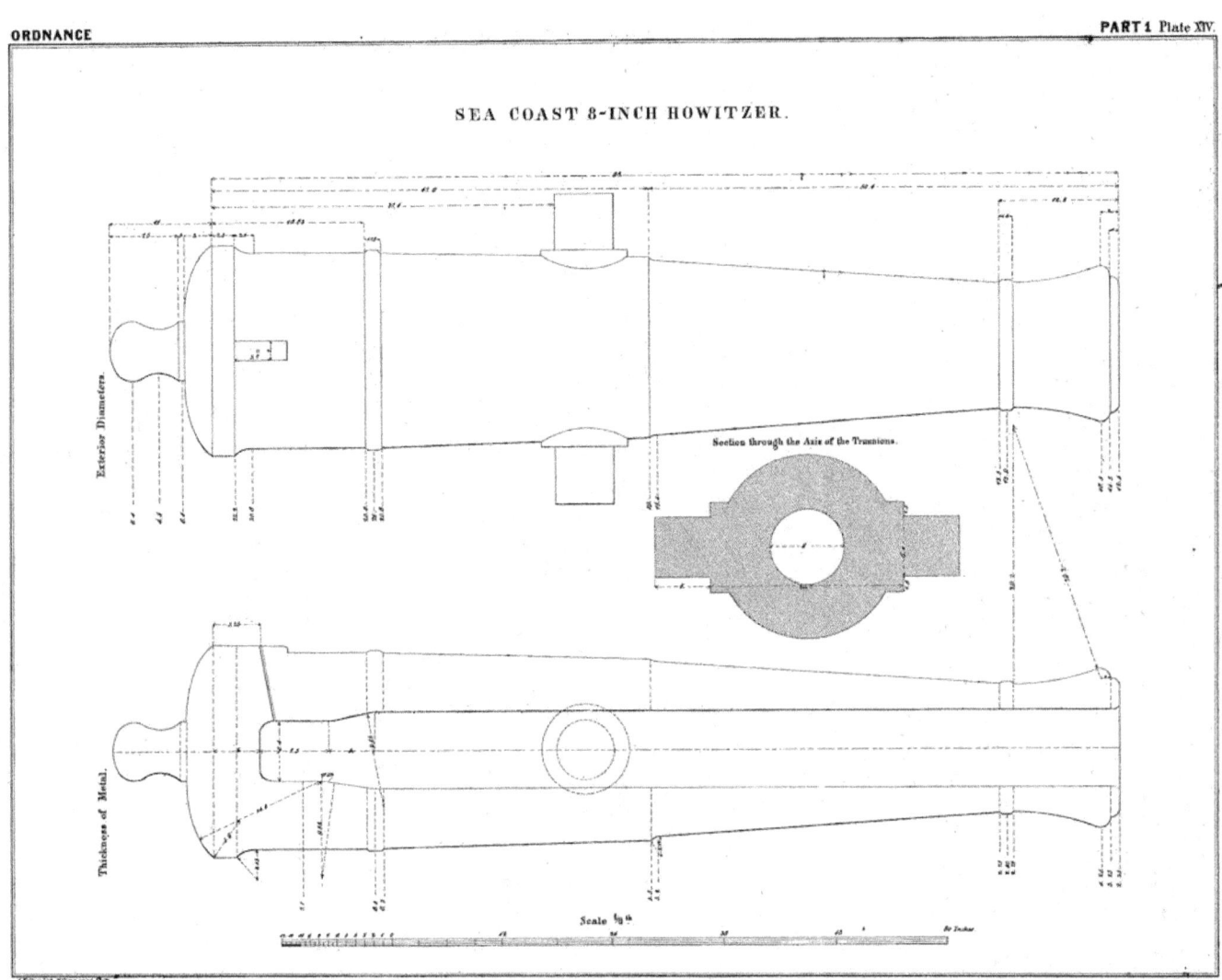

Plan and cross-section of the U. S. Pattern 1839/1840 8-inch Seacoast Howitzer. The cross-section clearly shows the chamber at the breech. There is a taper from the end of the bore to the beginning of the chamber, into which the conical sabot fits to ensure that the cartridge fills the chamber completely. (Courtesy Harpers Ferry Center, U. S. National Park Service)

Siege Pieces | 61

U.S. Pattern 1844 8-inch Columbiad. (Courtesy of WorldIslandInfo.com under Creative Commons License, Attribution 2.0 Generic, <http://creativecommons.org/licenses/by/2.0/deed.en>)

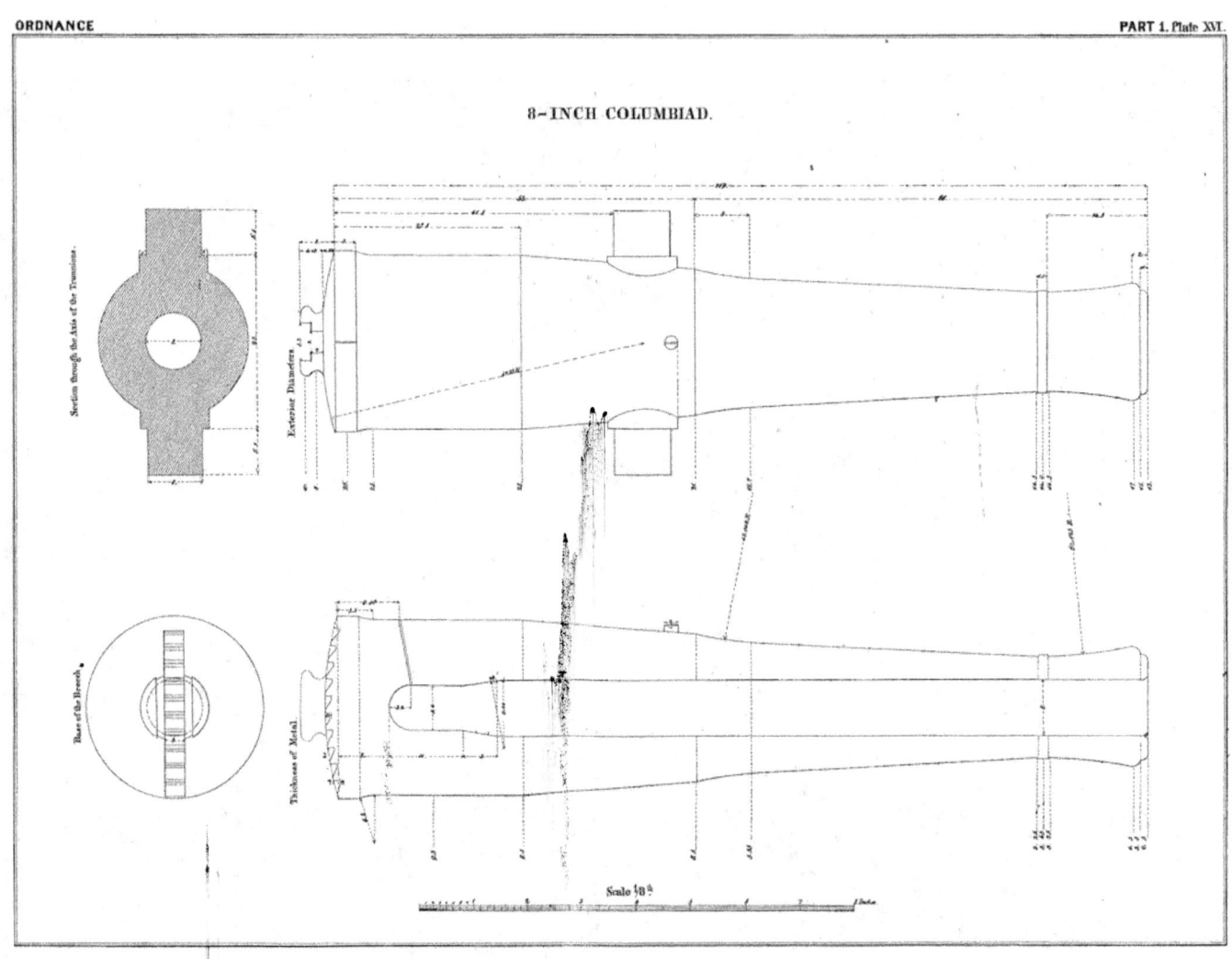

Plan and Profiles of the U. S. Pattern 1844 8-inch Columbiad. Based on the distinctive muzzle swell alone, this is the pattern sent to Fort Caswell after the fall of Fort Sumter in April, 1861. The cross-section clearly shows the chamber at the breech, effectively rendering this cannon nothing more than a seacoast howitzer. In fact, the sabot for this piece is identical to that of the Seacoast Howitzer. (Courtesy Harpers Ferry Center, U. S. National Park Service)

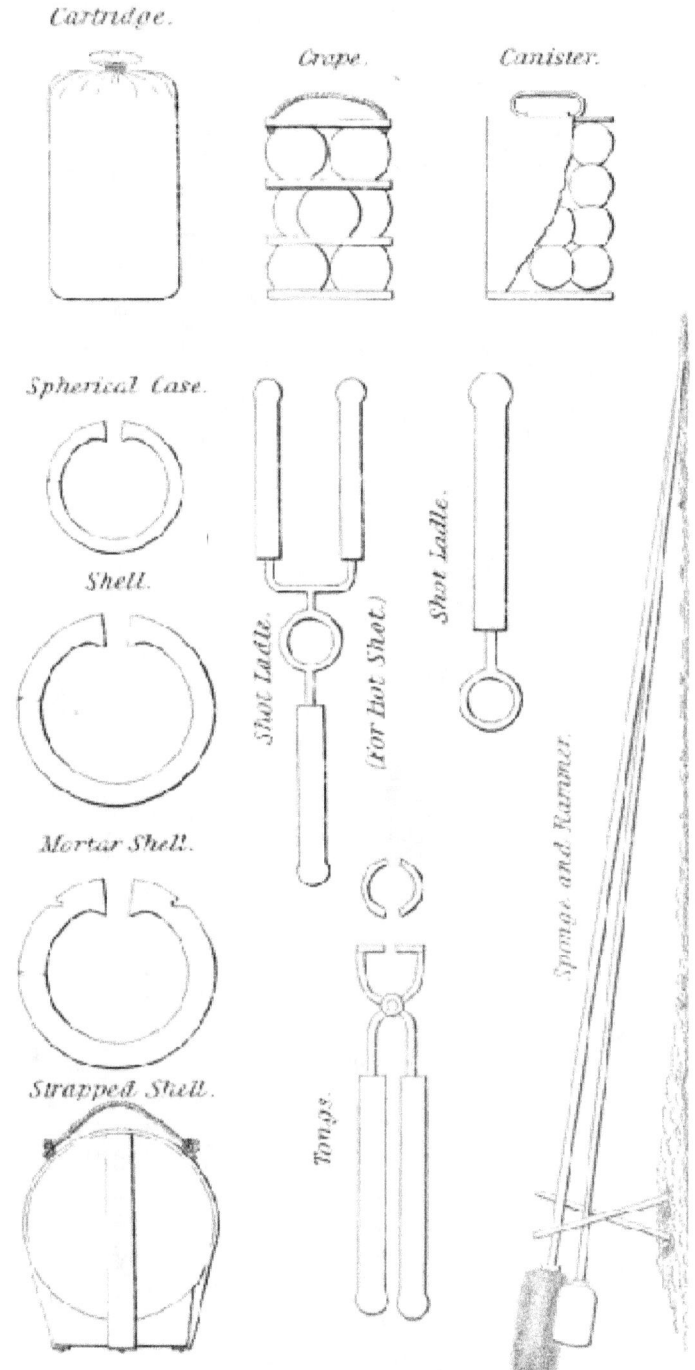

Heavy artillery ammunition and implements. The big guns used a bag filled with powder called a cartridge, unless the firing was to take place with reduced powder charges, in which case a cartridge block was inserted into the bag on top of the powder, in order to take the place of one pound of powder. Reduced powder charges were used when firing thin-walled case shot projectiles. All case shot and shell projectiles were saboted, as were canister and grape shot for the 8-inch Seacoast Howitzer and Pattern 1844 Columbiad. Everything else was deployed without a sabot. Tongs were used to engage lifting ears cast into mortar shells to keep the fuze directly opposite the charge. (*Instruction for Heavy Artillery*; Prepared by a Board of Officers for the Use of the Army of the United States, Charleston: Evans & Cogswell, 1861 [hereinafter cited as Confederate *Instruction for Heavy Artillery*], Plate 6)

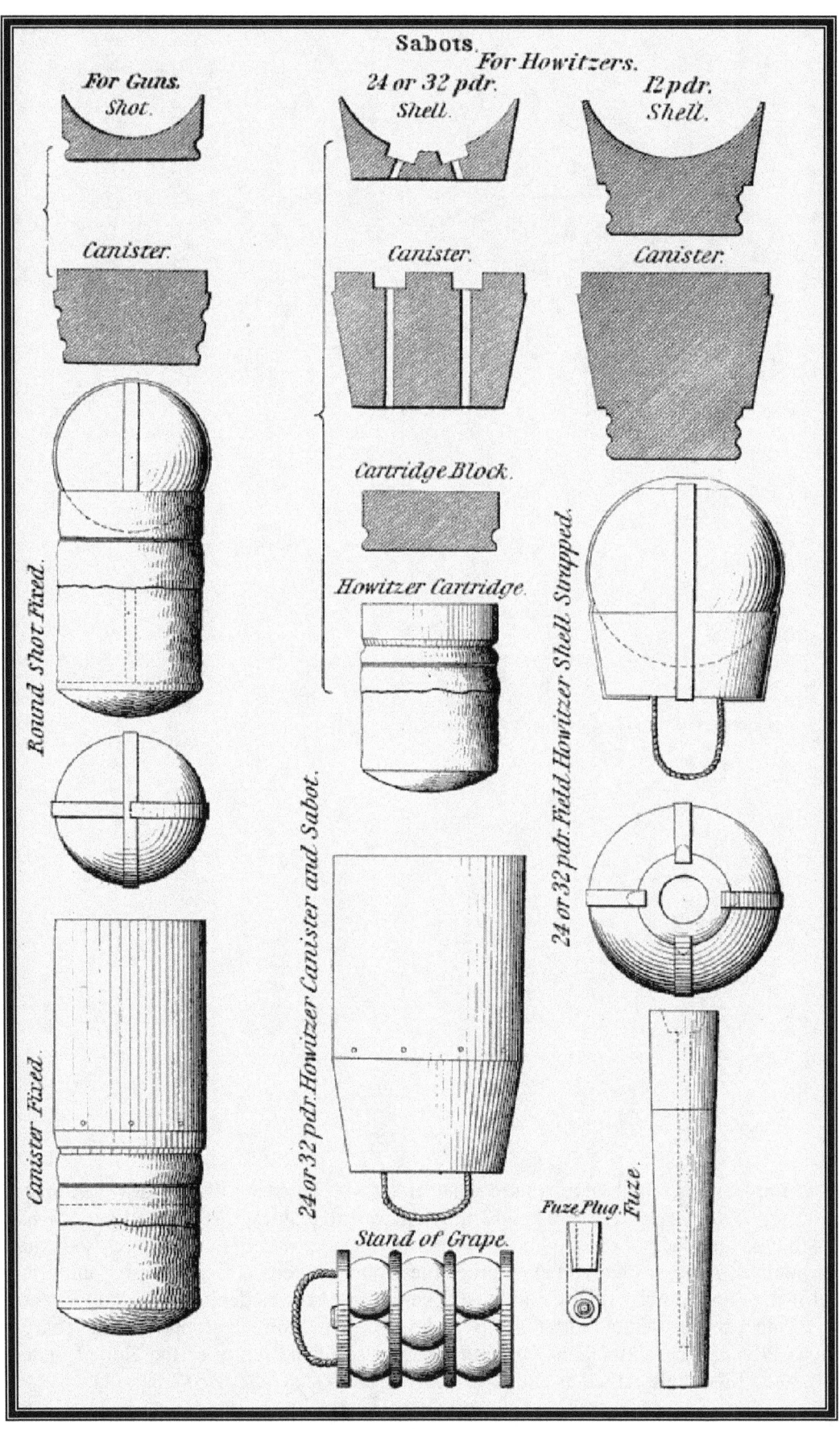

Field Artillery sabots, fuzes, and projectiles. Guns and 12-pounder howitzers used "fixed" ammunition, which was essentially a spherical projectile, shell, case shot, or canister strapped to a sabot with a cartridge bag tied to it. Large-caliber howitzers also fired shell and canister affixed to a sabot, but the powder charge was not tied to the assembly. Solid shot, however, employed a cartridge block of wood, to which the cartridge bag was tied, but the ball was loaded separately. (U.S. Ordnance Manual, 1850, Plate 16)

Four

"Major Whiting informs me that he is appointed inspector Gen'l.."
Adjutant General John F. Hoke, North Carolina State Troops

Major W. H. C. Whiting of the Confederate Corps of Engineers was appointed by North Carolina Governor John W. Ellis to the post of Inspector General of North Carolina's defenses on April 21, 1861, and was plugging away at his desk in Wilmington the next day. Just ten days earlier, he was second in command on Morris Island during South Carolina's bombardment of Fort Sumter in Charleston Harbor, to him mere "child's play" compared to the reality he now faced. Hand-picked by President Davis, Whiting had been charged with the daunting task of building a defensive system around a nucleus of fewer than two hundred raw volunteers with just twenty unmounted heavy artillery pieces in one fort and eight small caliber smoothbore field guns in another. Choosing his words carefully, he said, "Here they are willing enough, but the military has yet to grow." [1]

♦ ♦ ♦ ♦ ♦

William Henry Chase Whiting was born at Biloxi, Mississippi on March 22, 1824 to Mary A. and Levi Whiting. His father was a native of the Commonwealth of Massachusetts and career army officer who had ascended to the rank of Lieutenant Colonel of the 1st Artillery by the time of his death. A truly gifted scholar, young Whiting entered English High School in Boston at age 12, and graduated as the valedictorian of his class just two years later. Subsequently, he enrolled in Georgetown College, also known as Georgetown University, in Washington, D. C., and graduated second in his class two years later at the age of sixteen. Whiting was appointed to the United States Military Academy in 1841 and graduated at the top of his class in 1845. He earned the top score in every class he attended in his four years at West Point, thereby attaining the highest grade point average hitherto recorded at that venerable institution. [2]

Commissioned as a Second Lieutenant in the Corps of Engineers on July 1, 1845, Whiting was first posted to Pensacola, Florida as an assistant engineer until 1848, when he was assigned duties in Texas. His efforts there led to the location of the principal wagon route between San Antonio and El Paso, in addition to surveying a number of frontier military forts in the State. Whiting was promoted to 1st Lieutenant on March 16, 1853, by which time the well-traveled engineer had been singled out for service in no fewer than three States. In 1856, he was transferred to the

Cape Fear region of North Carolina, where he met and married Kate Walker, the daughter of Major John Walker of Wilmington, in April of 1857. He was promoted to Captain on December 13, 1858. [3]

The last transfer in Chase Whiting's U.S. military career was to Fort Pulaski, Georgia and Fort Clinch in Florida, both of which became subject to his oversight. On January 7, 1861, he reported the seizure of Fort Pulaski just four days earlier by Georgia State Troops acting under orders from Governor Joseph E. Brown. Then, on January 28, the Oglethorpe Barracks were seized by the same State Troops, heightening the pressures within Whiting's sphere of influence. Those events undoubtedly created a conflict for the Captain, torn between loyalty to his native country and the emotional bonds he had formed with friends and family in the new country he called home. [4]

Major William Henry Chase Whiting, ACSA.
(South Carolina Historical Society)

Opting to cast his fate with that of his adopted country, Captain William Henry Chase Whiting resigned from the United States Army on the 20th of February 1861, and accepted appointment as a Major in the Corps of Engineers of the Army of the Confederate States of America (ACSA) on 16 March. On February 23, his appointment not yet approved by the Confederate Congress, he was ordered to Charleston by President Jefferson Davis with orders to inspect and then to prepare the scattered works in the region "for active operations," both defensive and offensive. This done by 6 March, the Major was immediately dispatched to Savannah to inspect and improve the defenses of that city. With the deteriorating situation at Fort Sumter, however, Whiting was ordered back to Charleston, reporting for duty there on 18 March. [5]

On 11 April 1861, Brigadier General Pierre Gustave Toutant Beauregard assigned to Major Whiting the staff position of Acting Assistant Adjutant and Inspector General of the forces on Morris Island, reporting to Brigadier General James Simons of the South Carolina Volunteers. The next day, South Carolina forces opened fire on the U. S. garrison in Fort Sumter, forcing its capitulation on April 13, thereby marking the beginning of the American Civil War. Major Whiting's performance on those two days in April of 1861 would earn for him high marks with General Beauregard, and the two men would cooperate amicably many more times during the course of the war. [6]

To Inspector General Whiting, the situation he faced in Wilmington seemed to be nothing less than "a babel of confusion." Confiding in General Beauregard, he admitted, "I try to be as cool and patient as you are, but it is awful hard work." There was a very good reason for his frustration. "The worst is I have nothing to work with." [7]

A man possessive of innate intelligence and organizational skills, Whiting first sought to assemble a staff capable of following orders and establishing a military presence in the region. Captain Frederick L. Childs, ACSA, came with him from Charleston and was stationed at Fort

Caswell as Chief of Artillery and Ordnance. Samuel A'Court Ashe was commissioned as a 2nd Lieutenant by the State of North Carolina and was assigned to duty as an assistant to Captain Childs. Captain John C. Winder was personally commissioned by Governor Ellis and reported to the Inspector General for duty as Chief Engineer. With this small nucleus of staff officers in place, Whiting turned to the business of preparing to defend Wilmington with the limited resources then available to him. [8]

Colonel Theophilus Hunter Holmes, ACSA, commanding North Carolina Defenses. (Wikipedia)

U.S. Army Major Theophilus Hunter Holmes was commissioned Colonel in the Confederate States Army on March 16, 1861, but, for reasons unknown, he didn't resign his U.S. commission until April 22, at which time he was ordered to report to Governor Ellis for duty. On the 26th, he was given command of the coast defenses of the State of North Carolina with headquarters in Wilmington. Advanced to the rank of Brigadier General of North Carolina Volunteers by the Governor, Holmes held sway over the widely scattered defenses within a large geographical area, but he couldn't be everywhere at once. [9]

Inspector General Whiting was given great latitude in advancing the defenses of the Cape Fear, a delegation of authority that permitted Holmes to relocate his headquarters. "Feeling thus comparatively secure, and having full confidence in Gen. Whiting, as my successor in command at Wilmington, I shall proceed this morning to Newbern," Holmes reassured the Governor. [10]

The top priority for Whiting and his Chief of Artillery was the mounting of guns. With no carriages to be found in North Carolina and apprehensive of the unfinished state of the *barbette tier* at Caswell, he was determined to take matters into his own hands. "I want Gomez to send me drawings of the columbiad platform and carriage, and of the 32 and 24 pounder carriage *barbette*," Whiting requested of General Beauregard, his former commanding officer and mentor in Charleston. Acknowledging that there were sufficient 8-inch shells for the columbiads and seacoast howitzers, there weren't nearly enough fuzes, a shortfall he wasn't hesitant to request his superior to supply. [11]

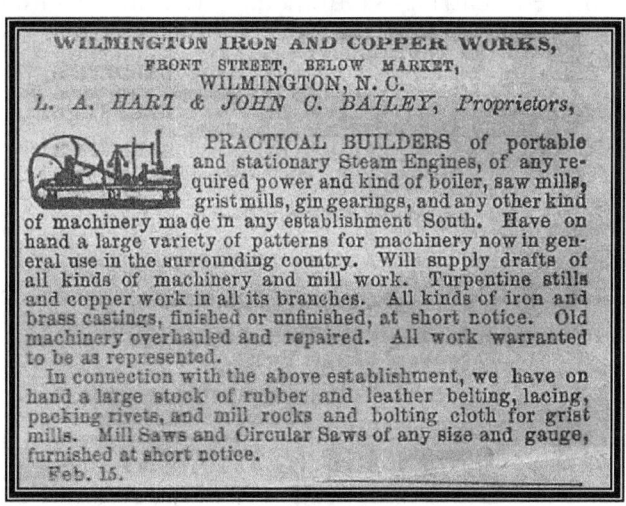

Advertisement by Hart & Bailey.
(*The Daily Journal*, May 31, 1861)

As pressing as the need for mounted guns was, though, it quickly became apparent that the needs of the men came first. In fact, Inspector

General Whiting issued an order that dealt with that very issue. "Hart & Bailey to repair the pumps & furnish the pipe for Caswell," he directed, addressing the problems with the fort's water supply. Thus began a relationship between civilian enterprise and military authority that would provide the necessities for defense of the Cape Fear. [12]

Levi A. Hart and John C. Bailey, principals of the Wilmington Iron and Copper Works, were the first of several qualified entrepreneurs to whom Inspector General Whiting turned for the implements of war. Barely minimal at first, their service to the Cape Fear began with the long overdue repair of Caswell's pumps, but it soon became clear that the Wilmington ironworker was destined for a much larger role in shaping the defenses. As early as April 26, labor to date on carriages and chassis for the 24-pounder guns was invoiced to Captain Childs, who noted substantial progress toward completion of ten chassis, "The work charged for being the iron work on ten *pintle* crosses." [13]

Not one to pass up an opportunity to advance his defensive scheme, Inspector General Whiting requested "twenty 32-pounder *carronade* guns with deck carriages" from the State of Virginia on April 29, to be used for flank defense of the ditches in the coast's two masonry forts. "Eight would serve Fort Macon and the same number Fort Caswell," he ventured. On May 6, 1861 the Seaboard and Roanoke Railroad consigned twenty Carronades from Portsmouth to Weldon, for the benefit of the Commonwealth of North Carolina. Noticing Whiting's success, Governor Ellis himself applied to Governor Letcher for additional heavy cannon. The Advisory Council to the State of Virginia, also known as The Council of Three, didn't disappoint. "Advised unanimously that the Governor supply the Governor of North Carolina with fifty pieces of heavy ordnance – 32-pounders, with shot and shell to correspond." [14]

But how did the Commonwealth acquire so many Navy cannon? On the night of April 20, 1861, the commandant of the U.S. Gosport Navy Yard in Norfolk ordered the destruction of every building, ship, and piece of ordnance property in response to the threat of seizure by Virginia Militia commanded by Major General William Booth Taliaferro. The militia forces entered the yard the following morning and were astonished to find that 1,198 pieces of heavy artillery had survived the botched demolition attempt and conflagration that followed, including the twenty Carronades requisitioned by Whiting. William H. Peters, a Navy Agent employed by the State found the guns in various states of repair. "Many heavy cannon were spiked and for the time rendered useless, some had their trunnions broken off." Cannon powder, shot, shell and other stores were taken as well, and together with the bonanza of ordnance, the Confederacy had the basis with which to defend its borders. [15]

May proved to be a pivotal month for Hart & Bailey, one that would affirrm not only their production capability, but their diversity as well. They were more than equal to the tasks at hand. From wood tompions for protecting cannon bores to priming wires for puncturing cartridge bags, and from ordnance gauges to gunner's levels, the ironworking firm produced everything needed with which to man the big guns. [16]

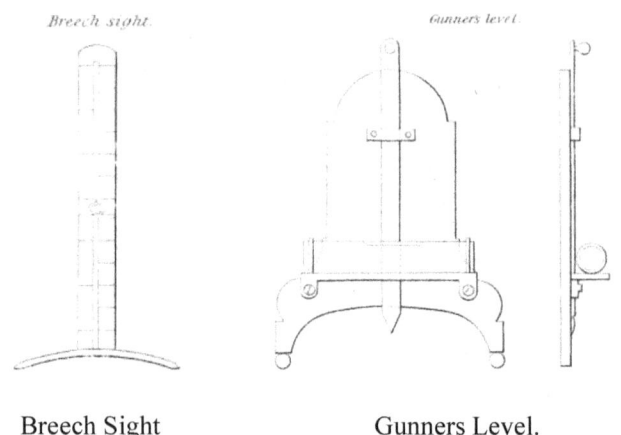

Breech Sight   Gunners Level.

Artillery implements presumed to be of the types made by Hart & Bailey for the guns at Fort Caswell. (Confederate *Instruction for Heavy Artillery*, 1861, Plate 5)

Hart & Bailey manufactured enough sabots, sets of straps, and tacks to assemble 400 units of spherical shell for the 24-pounders and enough of the same materials to assemble 600 units of spherical shell for the 8-inch Columbiads. After molding 80,500 shot for canister, the company produced the components and then assembled 150 canister rounds for the 24-pounders. They also manufactured 300 *columbiad blocks* just for the Pattern 1844 Columbiads.[17]

The missing traverse circles at Caswell's right flank, gorge, and covered way were of concern. Due to a shift in the river's main channel over the years, the principal points of defense had changed from the north angle to the very points where cannon couldn't be mounted. It may well have been fortuitous that no circles had been installed at those points while the fort was under construction, since it would have been necessary to remove them anyway. The traverse circle for a Columbiad was exactly that – a 360° circle, as opposed to the 180° circle common to the use of old pattern siege guns mounted on front pintle barbette chassis.[18]

The resourceful partnership of Hart & Bailey managed to manufacture five *wood circles* for Columbiads, three Columbiad carriage/chassis assemblies, and fifteen *pivots* in the month of May, in addition to beginning work on four Columbiad platforms. It seems reasonable to assume that the pivots were intended for ten 24-pounders, three 8-inch Columbiads and two 8-inch Seacoast Howitzers. The wood circles were manufactured for all five 8-inch cannon.[19]

Notwithstanding the diversity demonstrated by Messrs. Hart & Bailey, the enormity of the workload demanded the participation of more skilled manufacturers. Thomas E. Roberts was one of them. His enterprise, the Clarendon Iron Works, was recruited by General Holmes and Inspector General Whiting sometime in early May to build carriages and cast round shot projectiles for the batteries and forts of the Cape Fear defenses. Roberts' manufactory responded quickly, delivering the first installment of the carriages as early as 17 May. Three days later, the transport partnership of Orrell & Hawes ferried thirteen Carronades from the Wilmington & Weldon Rail Road Depot downriver to the Clarendon Iron Works, where carriages were to be made for them before their deployment at Fort Caswell. It wasn't until June 29, however, that he delivered the balance of his original contract to the State of North Carolina, making in all twelve 32-pounder and fourteen 24-pounder *barbette carriages.*[20]

With the ladies of Wilmington stitching up cartridge bags and Captain Childs instructing Fort Caswell's garrison in the fundamentals of artillery drill, Colonel Cantwell was rapidly approaching the capability for mounting a defense, limited though it might have been.[21]

Great progress at Fort Caswell, however, would not be enough. The original concept for the most significant initiative to be undertaken by the defenders of the Cape Fear can be traced far back in time to Lieutenant Joseph Gardner Swift's superintendence of the construction of Fort Johnston in 1804. In his report to the War Department in July of that year, Swift stressed the importance of erecting "an enclosed battery at Federal Point, at New Inlet," a project that remained a high priority for over four decades, but, for reasons undiscoverable, never received the necessary appropriation from Congress.[22]

After the sub-committee of the Wilmington Committee of Safety completed its inspection of "the works and points of defence at the mouths of the Cape Fear River" on April 16, 1861, their first recommendation was a little less to the point, but echoed Swift's sentiments nonetheless. "New Inlet should be protected by *two batteries* of seige [*sic*] guns covered by epaulments [*sic*] of sand bags – The first one, of six to ten guns, should be placed on Federal Point." On the day of the inspection, Colonel Cantwell was directed to "make a sand battery" on the peninsula, but the directive wasn't obeyed right away, probably due to a lack of engineering expertise.[23]

The project remained on hold until Inspector General Whiting assumed command of the Cape Fear Defenses, whereupon there was no time lost in selecting Charles Pattison Bolles to erect the battery on Federal Point. Bolles was a gifted engineer who had been working for the Federal Government on the United States Coast Survey of the Cape Fear since 1851. At the time of his assignment, Bolles was a Captain in the service of the State of North Carolina and, perhaps not altogether surprisingly, Inspector General Chase Whiting's brother-in-law. [24]

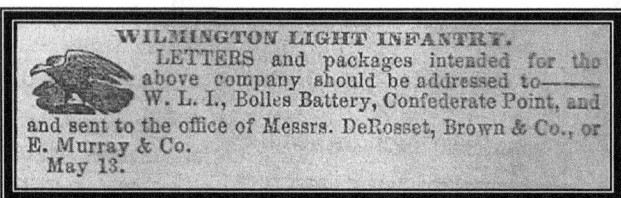

Earliest noted use of the terms Bolles Battery and Confederate Point. The date this military notice was first placed establishes a timeline for the relocation of the Wilmington Light Infantry from Fort Caswell to the peninsula. (*The Daily Journal*, May 31, 1861)

Near the end of April, Captain Bolles began the work that would bear his name throughout the war. Bolles Battery, as it came to be known, was located a little over a mile north of New Inlet, on the peninsula whose name would soon be changed from Federal Point to Confederate Point. The battery began as a very basic two-gun barbette affair made of sand surmounted by marsh turf, but quickly evolved into two adjacent batteries mounting three siege guns. [25]

It was first garrisoned by Captain William Lord DeRosset's Wilmington Light Infantry, detached from Colonel Cantwell's garrison at Fort Caswell sometime around the 7th of May. Captain DeRosset and his company of sixty volunteers were to continue the important work of establishing the first battery on the peninsula. When Captain DeRosset was commissioned as a Major in Field and Staff of the 3rd Regiment North Carolina State Troops on May 16, 1861, his tour of duty in the Cape Fear defenses was at an end. Command of the company passed to Wilmington merchant Henry Savage, then a 3rd Lieutenant, charged with overseeing completion of infantry breastworks and mounting the heavy artillery at Bolles' Battery. [26]

"There should be erected on the beach of Oak Island near the two beacon lights a battery of long range guns say from four to six," reported the now familiar subcommittee of Wilmington's Committee of Safety after their inspection of the works on the lower Cape Fear. Their suggestion wouldn't be ignored. A week or so after Captain DeRosset's promotion and transfer, Captain Bolles was sent to Oak Island to commence a sand battery some 800 yards below Fort Caswell. This advanced work was known as the Radcliffe Battery by Captain Nelson Slough and his "Cabarrus Guards," who were detailed to assist Bolles in the construction effort and to serve the 24-pounders sent there from Caswell. [27]

By May 11, the state of Whiting's defensive capability was much improved.

> We now have one 8-inch columbiad, mounted, two 8-inch sea-coast howitzers, and nine 24-pounders. In a few days two more columbiads, six 24-pounders, and some flank-defense 32-pounder Carronades will be in position. An advanced battery has been erected some 800 yards from the fort, bearing directly on the bar, for three 24-pounders. The guns, however, are not in position yet, from the want of carriages. Infantry breast-works for the supporting troops are under construction. At Federal Point, near New Inlet, two batteries have been erected, but not mounted for the reason above stated, and infantry breast-works for the guard. [28]

In the month following the seizure of the Cape Fear River forts, Inspector General Whiting experienced an outpouring of patriotic sentiment that swelled the ranks of volunteer companies throughout the region. From just four militia companies with an aggregate strength of 120 men at Forts Johnston and Caswell, the volunteer companies had mushroomed to eighteen, totaling over 1,050 recruits at five different locations. [29]

Post of Fort Caswell
Colonel John Lucas Paul Cantwell

- ❖ Cape Fear Light Artillery, Captain John J. Hedrick
- ❖ Rifle Rangers, Captain Edward Dudley Hall
- ❖ Fair Bluff Volunteers, Captain Burrell Smith

- Columbus Guards, No. 3,
  Captain Forney George
- Columbus Guards, No. 2,
  Captain William H. Toon
- Iredell Blues, [30]
  Captain Absalom K. Simonton
- Wilmington Rifle Guards,
  Captain Oliver Pendleton Meares
- German Volunteers,
  Captain Christian Cornehlsen

Radcliff Battery on Oak Island
- Cabarrus Guards,
  Captain Nelson Slough

Bolles Battery on Confederate Point
- Wilmington Light Infantry,
  3rd Lieutenant Henry Savage

Post of Fort Johnston
Captain Joseph P. Jones [31]
- Cabarrus Black Boys Riflemen, [32]
  Captain James B. Atwell
- Rowan Rifle Guards, [33]
  Captain Francis M. Y. McNeely
- Sampson Rangers,
  Captain Franklin J. Faison
- Columbus Guards, No. 4,
  Captain John Bunn Stanly
- Confederate Greys, [34]
  Captain Claudius B. Denson

Reserves at Wilmington
Inspector General W.H.C. Whiting
- Cape Fear Rifles,
  Captain M. M. Hankins
- Bladen Guards, [35]
  Captain George Tait
- Bladen Infantry, [36]
  Captain Robert Tait

The Inspector General felt a genuine sense of pride in the volunteers. "I am happy to report the creditable progress of the troops in drill and organization, especially their unflagging zeal, obedience, and great willingness." This was no small praise from a man whose entire life was connected to the military and who, as a child, began a thorough education in its ways. [37]

As delighted as he was with his troops, he was equally as unhappy with the command situation at the cornerstone of the Cape Fear defenses, Fort Caswell. "It is absolutely essential that the command of this work be placed in the hands of some regular officer familiar with routine of garrisons." Then he made his point. "The colonel commanding is energetic and does as well as he knows how, but he does not know how." Doubtful of finding a replacement for Colonel Cantwell, Whiting offered great praise for his Chief of Artillery and Ordnance, all the while eliminating him as a candidate. "Captain Childs, chief of artillery, has drilled the men well for artillery and is indefatigable in his duty as ordnance officer at the fort, but he is not in command, and cannot well be placed there now."[38]

The command situation at Caswell worried General Holmes too. "I should feel entirely free from apprehension if the Commander of Fort Caswell had more experience." He even had a replacement in mind. "I applied two days ago for Col. Winder to be sent there." Practical to the last, though, Holmes had to concede the inevitable. "If Col. Winder cannot be had for the service, I know of no other man available to replace him," referring, of course, to Colonel Cantwell. While it came to pass that John H. Winder was indeed offered command at Fort Caswell, he wasn't happy about it. "I was offered the commission of colonel of the 1st Infantry, coupled with an inferior command not at all connected with the appointment." He summed up his opinion of the Governor's offer of appointment when he wrote, "self respect forbids my acceptance." Those few words ended the search for Cantwell's replacement, at least for the time being. [39]

On May 15, 1861, Inspector General Whiting was called to serve his adopted country on the fields of Northern Virginia, but not before he had well begun the crucial work of improving the Cape Fear's defensive capabilities. While the seedlings of defense planted by Whiting were modest by most standards, his actions were all the more remarkable in that he had done as much with as little in less than a month's time.[40]

Wilmington needed a new leader. Brigadier General Holmes was still in command of the coast defenses for the State of North Carolina, but the job was simply too much for one general, no matter how large his staff. Walter Gwynn's resignation from command of the Virginia forces at Gosport on May 25 presented the opportunity Governor Ellis needed. Orders were issued on May 27 dividing the coastal defenses into two departments, naming Brigadier General Holmes to assume command of the Southern Department and directing Brigadier General Gwynn to do likewise in the Northern Department. All should have been well at this point, but the Confederate high command had something else in mind. It seems that Theophilus Hunter Holmes was destined for promotion to Brigadier General of the Provisional Army of the Confederate States (PACS), commanding the distant Department of Fredericksburg in Virginia.[41]

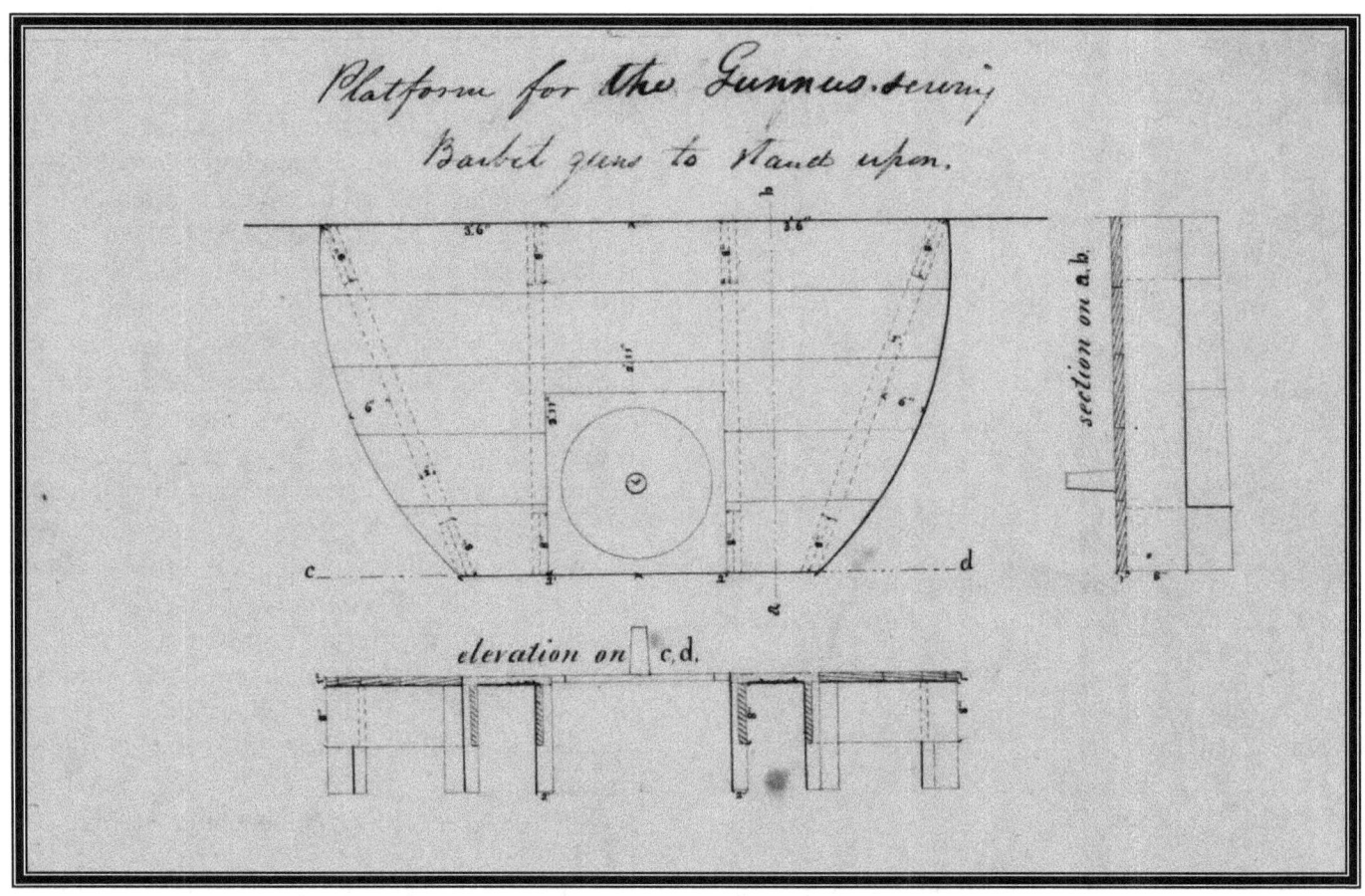

Plan of front pintle barbette platform for the anchorage guns on Fort Caswell's barbette tier. (National Archives and Records Administration, Cartographic Division)

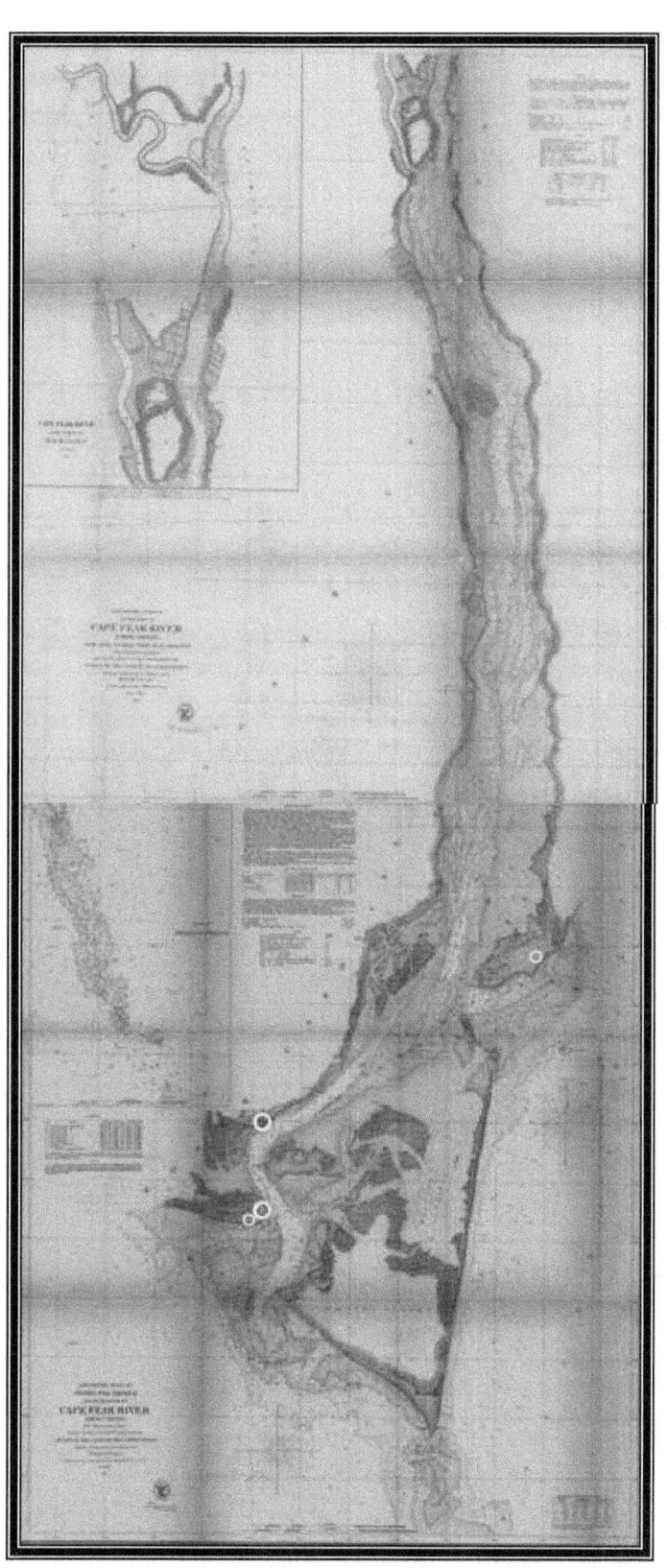

The approximate position of Bolles' Battery on Confederate Point and its proximity to Forts Caswell and Johnston. The sand battery known briefly as "Radcliffe Battery" appears about 800 yards below Fort Caswell on Oak Island. The largest circled positions are Forts Caswell and Johnston. The smallest circles represent the sand batteries. (National Oceanic and Atmospheric Administration)

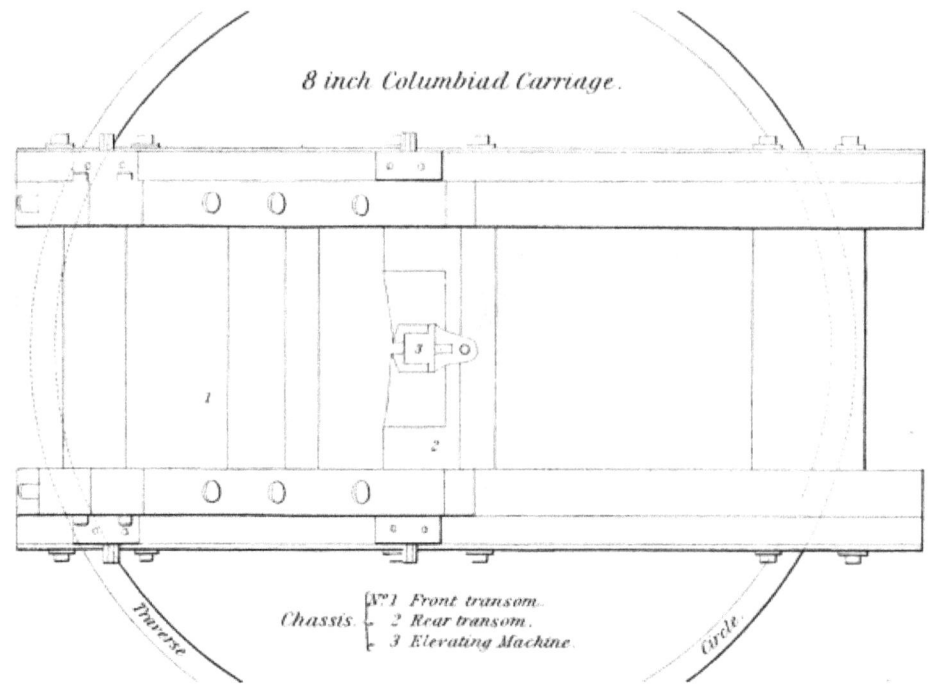

Plan of traverse circle and chassis for an 8-inch Columbiad. The circle is either made of iron or heavy wood planks with a void in the center. That void is then filled in by a platform, upon which the gunners stood to work the piece. (Confederate *Instruction for Heavy Artillery*, 1862, Plate 19)

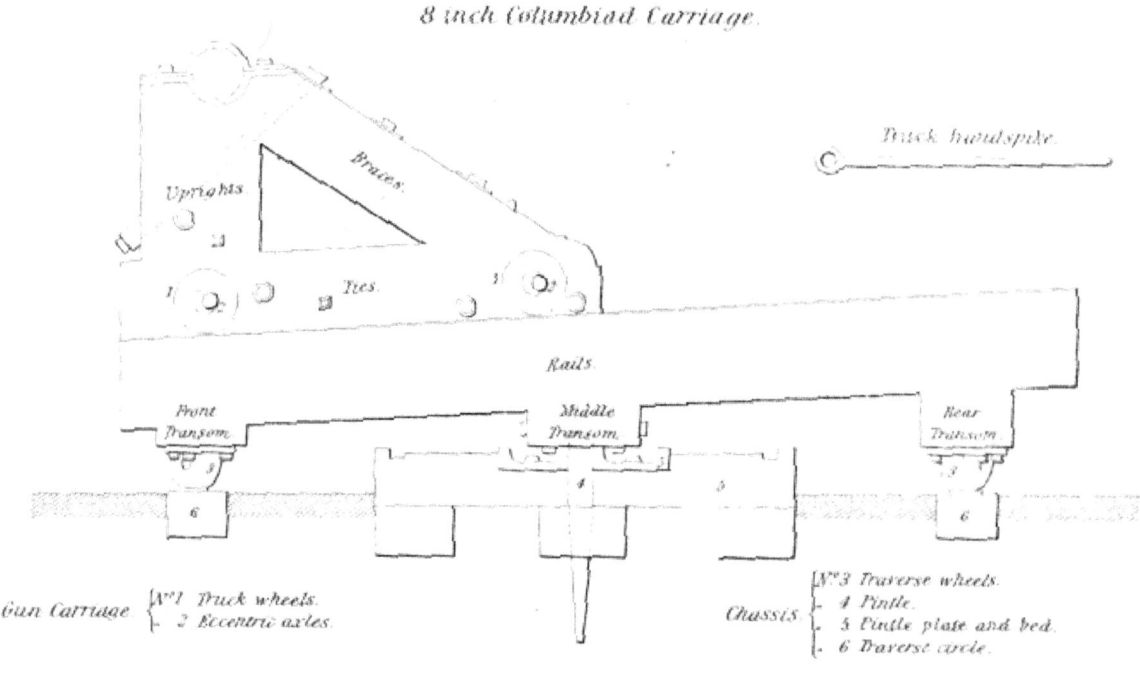

Profile of Columbiad carriage on its chassis. The pintle inserts into the center transom, allowing for a 360° traverse. Hart & Bailey built three sets of this assembly for Fort Caswell in May, 1861. (Confederate *Instruction for Heavy Artillery*, 1861, Plate 18)

Inspector General Whiting | 75

Wood traverse circle with a Columbiad chassis mounted on it. The method of construction here is by the book, but the circle is elevated, making service of the piece difficult. A platform built to the height of the circle or burying the circle in the earth alleviated this problem. (Library of Congress, Prints and Photographs Division)

Wood Columbiad traverse circle and platform to provide a level working surface for the gunners. While their work may not have followed this exact pattern, Hart & Bailey built five traverse circle/platform assemblies for Fort Caswell in May, 1861. (Library of Congress, Prints and Photographs Division)

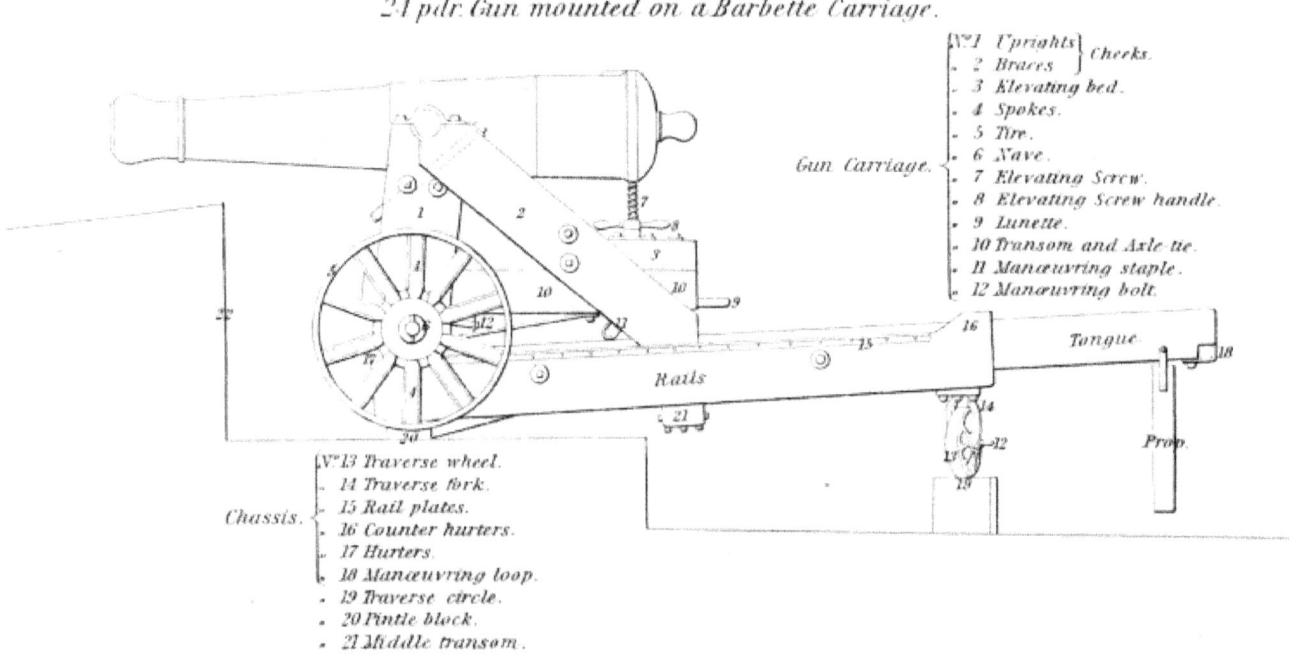

Pattern 1840/1845 24-pounder gun on a barbette carriage, front pintle. Hart & Bailey manufactured ten of this type of carriage for Fort Caswell in May, 1861. (Confederate *Instruction for Heavy Artillery*, 1861, Plate 11)

Five

"My excellent friend General Gatlin..."
Brigadier General Theophilus Hunter Holmes

North Carolina Governor John W. Ellis had a problem. Knowing full well that command of the Southern Department of the State's coast defenses couldn't be entrusted to a Colonel of militia at such a critical time, he needed someone with the experience to continue the task Whiting and Holmes had so well begun. Purely as a stopgap measure, the Governor ordered Colonel Charles Courtenay Tew to relieve Brigadier General Holmes of command of the Southern Department on 1 June. At the same time, Major William Lord DeRosset of the 3rd Regiment North Carolina State Troops replaced Tew in command at Fort Macon. This structure lasted only until June 18, when Ellis and the North Carolina Military Board appointed Colonel Richard C. Gatlin, ACSA to the state rank of Brigadier General and ordered him to assume command of the Southern Department of the North Carolina coast defenses. [1]

◆ ◆ ◆ ◆ ◆

Richard Caswell Gatlin was born on January 18, 1809 at Kinston, in Lenoir County, North Carolina to John Slade Gatlin and Susannah Caswell Gatlin. His mother was the daughter of Richard Caswell, the Old North State's first Governor. [2]

Captain Richard Caswell Gatlin, U.S.A.
(Generals of the Civil War)

Gatlin entered the U. S. Military Academy at West Point, N.Y. on July 1, 1828 and graduated

35th in his class on July 1, 1832, at which time he received an interim appointment to Brevet 2nd Lieutenant in the U.S. 7th Infantry. He served in some capacity in the Black Hawk Expedition of 1832, "but not at the seat of war." Subsequent to to cessation of hostilities there, the 7th Regiment was sent to Fort Gibson, Indian Territory until 1834, thence to the State of Louisiana, where Gatlin was promoted to 2nd Lieutenant of the 7th Infantry on July 31, 1834. [3]

The whirlwind of transfers continued with a return to Fort Gibson, then back to Louisiana, and then on to Camp Nacogdoches, Texas, where Gatlin was promoted to 1st Lieutenant of the 7th Infantry on August 31, 1836. After recruiting duty from 1837 to late 1838, the Lieutenant was returned with his regiment to Fort Gibson, where he was elevated to Adjutant of the 7th Infantry on December 13, 1838. [4]

Gatlin and the 7th Infantry left Fort Gibson for duty in the Florida War, better known as the Seminole War, from 1839 to 1842, after which time the regiment was ordered to New Orleans Barracks, Louisiana; Pass Christian, Mississippi; back to New Orleans; Pass Christian again; then the Military Occupation of Texas in 1845. It was while posted there that Gatlin was promoted to Captain on September 30, thus relieving him from Adjutancy with the 7th Regiment.

From the opening of the War with Mexico until 1846, Captain Richard C. Gatlin was there, participating in the successful defense of Fort Brown during the terrific bombardment from May 3 through 9, 1846, and then in the storming of the enemy works at the Battle of Monterey on September 23, when he was wounded and awarded a promotion to Brevet Major for gallant and meritorious conduct. He was then ordered on recruiting duty to recuperate from his wounds for the balance of the year and into 1848. During that service, he was offered an appointment to Colonel of North Carolina Volunteers, which he summarily declined, choosing instead to return to Mexico in 1848.

The war with Mexico ended soon after his return, however, and another dizzying array of transfers dominated the next 13 years of Gatlin's service in the U. S. Army, fourteen in all:

Jefferson Barracks, Missouri
Baton Rouge, Louisiana
Florida for "hostilities against the Seminole Indians"
Jefferson Barracks, Missouri
Fort Leavenworth, Missouri Territory
Jefferson Barracks, Missouri
Fort Gibson, Indian Territory
Upper Arkansas River
Fort Gibson, Indian Territory
Fort Smith, Indian Territory
Fort Laramie, Missouri Territory
Utah Expedition
March to New Mexico
Fort Craig, New Mexico Territory

The assignment to Fort Craig was coupled with a promotion to Major of the Fifth U. S. Infantry on February 26, 1861. [5]

While on a visit to Fort Smith, Major Gatlin was taken prisoner by Arkansas militia forces on April 23, 1861. He was subsequently paroled, based upon his agreement not to take up arms against the State or the Southern Confederacy, "unless exchanged." Since the United States government then held no prisoners with which to transact an exchange for the Major, he was effectively relieved from active duty and free to return to his home. Perhaps by design, Gatlin resigned from the U. S. Army on May 20, 1861, the very day that the State of North Carolina seceded from the Union. [6]

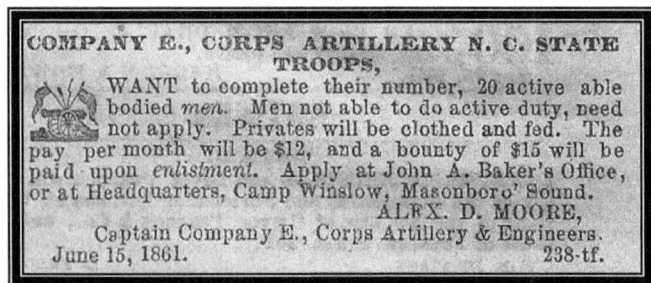

Locally designated as the Wilmington Light Artillery, Moore's Battery began its organization very near the date of this recruiting ad. (*The Daily Journal*, July 2, 1861)

The venerable subcommittee of Wilmington's Committee of Safety was just as unambiguous in its recommendation for Zeek's Island as it was in its vision for New Inlet and Oak Island. "There should also be a battery of four guns on Zeke's [sic] Island." On 12 June, Captain John Jackson Hedrick's Cape Fear Light Artillery battery transferred from Fort Caswell to Winder Battery, named for Captain of Engineers John C. Winder. Inasmuch as the company's muster into State service didn't occur until 17 June, the date of transfer may have been coincidental to the arrival of the battery's guns. [7]

Captain Samuel R. Bunting's "Wilmington Horse Artillery" was close on the heels of the Cape Fear Light Artillery when it became the second light artillery battery from the Cape Fear region to organize. Mustered into State service for twelve months on June 18, the company soon after went into camp near Camp Davis on Masonborough Sound, where it "served at first as coast guard." [8]

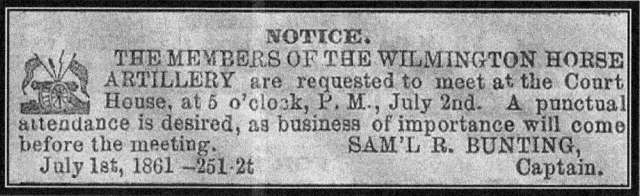

(*The Daily Journal*, July 2, 1861)

In mid-June, all ten companies of the 10th Regiment North Carolina Volunteers, then in service at Forts Johnston and Caswell and at Radcliffe Battery on Oak Island, assembled for the purpose of finalizing their organization and electing officers. At last shedding their local designations, the below listed companies were mustered into State service on June 18, 1861:

- Company A, Captain Nelson Slough
- Company B, Captain James B. Atwell
- Company C, Captain Burrell Smith
- Company D, Captain John B. Stanly
- Company E, Captain Claudius B. Denson
- Company F, Captain Owen L. Chesnutt
- Company G, Captain John S. Brooks
- Company H, Captain Uzz Cox
- Company I, Captain James A. Faison
- Company K, Captain William H. Toon

Alfred Iverson was elected Colonel of the 10th and Franklin Julien Faison became its Lieutenant Colonel. Faison's election, however, created the necessity for another election to replace him in the Sampson Rangers. [9]

Captains William Stewart Devane and James C. Holmes each had their supporters among the men of Sampson County, but neither faction wished to serve with the other, nor did either of them want to serve with the 10th Regiment. In an attempt to appease both sides, Governor Ellis directed the Rangers to form two companies and to dispatch recruiting officers to bring both to full strength prior to mustering into State service. Holmes' Company apparently retained the local designation Sampson Rangers and went on to an infantry assignment. Officially mustered into State service as Captain William S. Devane's Independent Company (Confederates), North Carolina Troops, the company remained on duty at Fort Johnston while awaiting its organization with a regimental unit. [10]

Soon after mustering into the service of the State of North Carolina on March 14, Captain Patrick M. Edmondston's Company of North Carolina Volunteers, known as the Scotland Neck Mounted Riflemen, went into camp at Camp Winslow. Newspaper accounts proudly supplied details of the first cavalry company to serve in the Cape Fear defenses:

> This splendid company of Dragoons, commanded by CAPT. P.M. EDMONDSON [sic] was mustered into the service of the State by MAJ. W. J. CLARKE at Clarksville, Halifax County on the 14th inst., and left for Wilmington on the following Monday. The company numbers about 70 fine young men, superbly mounted. They are armed with sabres, pistols and double-barrel shotguns. [11]

After his formal assumption of command of the Southern Department's defenses, General Gatlin's first order of business was to protect the vulnerable works on Confederate Point from land attack by establishing a camp for a regiment of infantry about five miles north of Bolles' Battery. Camp Wyatt, as it came to be known, was the brainchild of Major Whiting, but its value to the defense of the region was soon recognized and its development attended to by General Gatlin.[12]

The first official ordnance inventory for the Wilmington area appears under a June 30, 1861 date and was published by the Confederate Ordnance Department:

Fort Caswell:
   3 – 8-inch Columbiads
   3 – 8- inch Seacoast Howitzers
   9 – 32-pounder Iron Guns
   2 – 8-inch Navy Guns
   3 – 6-pounder Field Guns
   13 – 24-pounder Iron Guns
Fort Johnston:
   2 – 24-pounder Iron Guns
   5 – 6-pounder Field Guns
New Inlet:
   3 – 24-pounder Iron Guns
   1 – 6-pounder Field Gun
Oak Island Battery:
   2 – 24-pounder Iron Guns
Zeek's Island (Winder Battery):
   2 – 32-pounder Iron Guns
   1 – 8-inch Seacoast Howitzer
Wilmington:
   13 – 32-pounder Carronades [13]

Surprisingly, the supply of 24-pounder guns remained constant at twenty, but that's the only class of ordnance that did. It appears that Fort Sumter had cleared its barbette tier of another pair of 8-inch Seacoast Howitzers and sent them to the Cape Fear. The Carronades housed in Wilmington mysteriously numbered more than originally projected for Fort Caswell, seemingly by mistake. The Wilmington & Weldon Rail Road Co. billed for shipping two cars to New Berne and one to Wilmington but the opposite happened, leaving Fort Macon out of the mix altogether. Additionally, two Navy 8-inch *shell guns* and eleven Navy 32-pounders came to the Cape Fear defenses in May, part of a 24-gun shipment of Navy guns transported to Weldon aboard cars of the Seaboard & Roanoke Rail Road Company. That shipment represented the balance of the original fifty cannon promised to the State of North Carolina by Governor Letcher of Virginia, exclusive of the Carronades, the requisition for which was approved later, but arrived sooner than the original allotment.[14]

The vast majority of Gosport 32-pounders were shipped without carriages, since only 138 could be saved from the flames, but 60 Navy *four-truck* carriages for the 79 8-inch shell guns were salvaged. Early in July, Levi Hart and John Bailey delivered nine barbette carriages, chassis, and traverse circles to Fort Caswell for its 32-pounder guns, suggesting that the two 32-pounders on Zeek's Island were mounted on Navy carriages, as were both 8-inch shell guns at Caswell.[15]

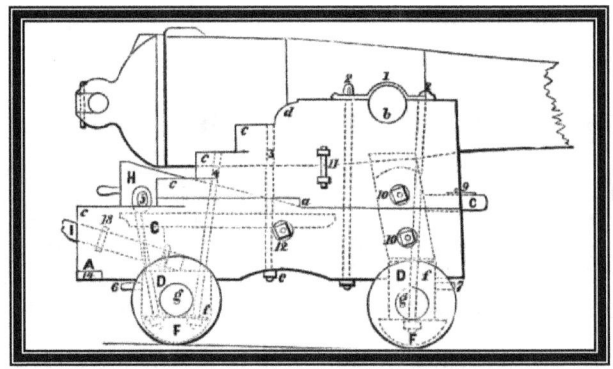

Profile of a U. S. Navy four-truck carriage. (Simpson, *A Treatise on Ordnance and Naval Gunnery*)

The U.S. Navy managed to introduce so many patterns and types of cannon in the first half of the 19th century that understanding the system completely is challenging. As luck would have it, the only patterns of importance to the defenses of the Cape Fear were those that were cast many years before the Civil War and were appropriated by Virginia troops when the Gosport Navy Yard was seized. Those were the guns that were later dispersed among the Confederate States and formed the basis for defending their vital harbors and forts.

The Navy's confusing system can be traced to 1816, when Congress granted an appropriation for the gradual growth of the U.S. Navy. More than 600 cannon were cast between 1817 and 1827. "Gradual Increase" guns came in just four patterns: a 60 hundredweight (cwt.) 32-pounder, a 42-pounder of 70 cwt., a 32-pounder carronade weighing 17 cwt., and a 42-pounder carronade of 27 cwt. Gradual increase cannon featured a ringknob at the base of the breech. Carronades were chambered, but the heavier cannon were guns in the truest sense, and consummately reliable, at the very worst. [16]

Each hundredweight was understood to be 112 pounds, therefore 60 cwt. guns should have weighed about 6,720 pounds, on average. Unfortunately, reporting of the weight in cwt. at the time of the Civil War was completely dependent upon the individual preparing the report. Weights were often expressed as one cwt. higher or lower than those now recognized as the true classification intended by the Navy.

The introduction of future patterns of naval ordnance resulted in the guns manufactured during the Navy's period of gradual increase becoming known as old style guns, old pattern guns, or just old guns. For reasons unknown, the demise of the old pattern guns began a period of experimentation with the Navy's ordnance that resulted in a bewildering assortment of patterns, sizes, and profiles. [17]

Beginning in 1844, the U.S. Navy recognized three classes of 32-pounder chambered cannon, the first two of which weighed 27 and 32 cwt. The latter weight is universally referred to as 33 cwt. in Civil War records, and that designation is therefore adopted for use herein. As it turned out, however, the Navy really didn't want those early guns to have chambers, so new production omitted them and most, if not all, existing cannon had their chambers reamed out and were reissued as guns. The third class included forty "light" 32-pounders that were cast specifically for *USS Cyane* and the recently commissioned *USS Levant* in 1837, as well as twenty-four cast with the same weight but of a variant pattern for *USS Saratoga* in 1842. Both of those patterns were referred to in the inventory of captured ordnance at Gosport as 40 cwt. "Shubrick Guns," but whether they were so named in honor of Lieutenant, later Admiral, William Branford Shubrick, or Commander Irving Shubrich is conjectural. The former officer served aboard *USS Constitution* during its capture of *HMS Cyane* and *HMS Levant* from the British in February, 1815 and the latter officer commanded *USS Saratoga* in 1845 and 1846. It should be noted that none of these 32-pounders exceeded 84 inches in length, causing them to be referred to more often than not as *short guns*. [18]

From one foot to almost 2.5 feet longer than their predecessors, the *long guns* came next in the parade of Navy patterns. The Navy cannon of 42 cwt., 4th pattern was the forerunner of unchambered guns, with four heavier guns that followed. Of the four, two were referred to as unchambered guns, those being the 47 and 51 cwt. The last two long guns were classified as *round shot guns*, with the 57 cwt. herein called *The Long Gun* and the 62 cwt. gun herein termed *The Heavy Gun*. It should be noted that the 47 cwt. gun and the 62 cwt. gun were most often listed in official correspondence as 46 cwt. and 61 cwt., respectively, so they will henceforth be referred to as such. [19]

8-inch Navy Shot Guns of 106 cwt., not unlike Army 8-inch Columbiads, were styled unofficially as 64-pounders, but, just as often, they were referred to as 68-pounders. It comes as no surprise, then, that 8-inch Navy guns, shot or shell, came to be called 64 or 68-pounders by some Confederate Army personnel. [20]

By way of recapitulation, Navy personnel referred to unchambered cannon as such or as shot guns, and chambered pieces were termed shell guns. To Army personnel, unchambered cannon were guns, and chambered pieces were howitzers, apparently regardless of what names they may have been given by another branch of the service. Therefore, to a Confederate Army unit serving an 8-inch Navy shell gun, the piece was nothing more than a seacoast howitzer, logically speaking. Gradual Increase Navy guns were often referred to as either old or old style in ordnance vernacular of the time. According to Navy ordnance manuals, all of their 32-pounder guns could fire spherical shot, shell and case shot using variable powder charges, whereas 8-inch Navy shell guns were believed unreliable for firing shot due to the smaller powder charge employed in them. [21]

◆ ◆ ◆ ◆ ◆

Eighty guns were shipped to North Carolina from the Navy Yard at Gosport by June 10, 1861. Only twenty carronades and fifty 32-pounders were allocated to the Old North State by the Governor of the State of Virginia, so it appears that ten 8-inch shell guns were acquired without official sanction. The list of guns and their weights are as follows:

   2 – 32-pounders of 42 cwt.
   4 – 32-pounders of 27 cwt.
   4 – 24-pounders of 31 cwt.
   10 – 32-pounders of 46 cwt.
   10 – 32-pounders of 57 cwt.
   20 – 32-pounders of 61 cwt.
   10 – 8-inch guns of 63 cwt.
   20 – 32-pounder carronades 17 or 18 cwt. [22]

All too seldom does an opportunity arise to positively identify the weight of a Navy cannon used in the Cape Fear defenses. Two surviving images of the same gun taken in Fort Fisher present a unique opportunity to view a pattern of Navy cannon that didn't survive the war. Taken together, these images provide every feature of the U.S. Navy 32-pounder unchambered cannon of 42 cwt., fourth pattern, nominal length 96 inches. The first three patterns of this weight were chambered, but the chambers of most such pieces were reamed out later. From the second image, the pattern's muzzle swell, as well as its rounded breech base and gusseted breeching jaws are easily discerned. From the first image, the gun's length is easily calculated by using the known dimensions of the 32-pounder projectiles on the right as a ruler. [23]

It's the author's considered opinion that the 42 cwt. gun pictured in the following images is one of two that served in the Winder Battery on Zeek's Island. The logic flows like this: first, only two 42 cwt. Navy 32-pounders were ever shipped from Virginia to North Carolina; second, both were shipped prior to June 10, 1861, in time to be counted in the June 30 inventory; next, Fort Fisher had no 32-pounders on 30 June whereas the Winder Battery had two; and last, the guns were more likely to have come from Zeek's Island when operations there closed in 1863 than from Fort Caswell at a time when longer range cannon were the order of the day.

(Library of Congress, Prints and Photographs Division)

(Library of Congress, Prints and Photographs Division)

Presented next is yet another surviving image from the formidable Fort Fisher that provides positive identification of a gun that served in the Cape Fear defenses. It is without doubt a U.S. Navy 8-inch chambered shell gun of 63 cwt., nominal length 106 inches. It being a chambered cannon, this piece was relegated to the same mission as a Seacoast Howitzer – firing shell at infantry beyond 400 yards and canister or grape at a range of 400 yards and nearer. As a defense against naval vessels beyond a mile, such guns were utterly worthless.[24]

(Library of Congress, Prints and Photographs Division)

On July 1, 1861, all ten companies of the 8th Regiment, North Carolina Volunteers assembled at Camp Wyatt for the purpose of electing officers and mustering into Confederate Service. The following officers were elected to command of their respective companies:

- ❖ Co. A, Captain Christian Cornehlsen
- ❖ Co. B, Captain Robert Tait
- ❖ Co. C, Captain Forney George
- ❖ Co. D, Captain William Stokes Norment
- ❖ Co. E, Captain John R. Hawes
- ❖ Co. F, Captain Charles Malloy
- ❖ Co. G, Captain Henry Savage
- ❖ Co. H, Captain Edward Dudley Hall
- ❖ Co. I, Captain Robert D. Williams; replacing Oliver Pendleton Meares, elected Lieutenant Colonel.
- ❖ Co. K, Captain Thomas James Purdie; replacing George Tait, elected Major.

The officers of the Regiment elected James D. Radcliffe to serve as their Colonel, following the custom of U. S. volunteer military organizations of the middle 1800's. It seems Colonel Radcliffe was held in high regard by the private soldiers. "Our Colonel is not at all a tight man I don't think," ventured Private William H. Best of Company H. Of his surroundings, Best said, "I find Camp Wyatt to be a fine place." But, he went on to conclude, "The musketoes [sic] are worse here than I ever saw them."[25]

The urgent demand for light artillery batteries in Virginia compelled the Governor to order the Wilmington Light Artillery to Camp Boylan near Raleigh for equipment and instruction. By then known only as Moore's Battery, the company was at the camp of instruction when Governor John Willis Ellis suddenly passed away on 7 July 1861, while vacationing in Virginia. The battery had the distinct honor of serving on the detail to return the Governor's body to Raleigh. Henry Toole Clarke, Speaker of the North Carolina Senate and first in the State's line of succession, rose to the Governor's office.[26]

Brigadier General Richard Caswell Gatlin found himself in command of the Cape Fear defenses with even less to work with than his predecessor had complained of. Unbeknownst to him, it would get worse. Just prior to Gatlin's ascendancy to command in Wilmington, 2nd Lieutenant Ashe received travel orders from Fort Caswell to the arsenal at Harpers Ferry, Virginia to remove its rifle-making machinery to the North Carolina arsenal at Fayetteville. Some ten days later, Ashe returned to duty at Caswell, but mere days afterward he fell desperately ill and went home to Wilmington to convalesce. His superior, Captain Frederick L. Childs, received orders to assume command of the Charleston Arsenal on 11 July, leaving General Gatlin with no experienced ordnance officers in all of the Cape Fear defenses. Then, in mid-July, Colonel James A. J. Bradford of the North Carolina Corps of Artillery, Ordnance and Engineers ordered Captain John C. Winder from the Cape Fear to recruiting duty. Captain Winder was at that time the Cape Fear's Chief Engineer, and the only engineer officer remaining in the region. It might have been a bad time for Gatlin to be shorthanded.[27]

At 9:45 A.M. on July 12, 1861, Flag Officer G. J. Pendergrast, USN, anchored *USS Roanoke* inside the mouth of the Cape Fear River. The commander of the West India Squadron dutifully memorialized what he saw. "Found the rebel flag flying on Fort Caswell and in the town of Smithville," he recorded in his ship's log. Aided by a telescope, the Flag Officer "could count fourteen guns (barbette) on Fort Caswell and several fieldpieces [*sic*]." An inquiring mind can only wonder exactly what ordnance Pendergrast was looking at. [28]

The key to the deployment of Caswell's guns rests with the presence or absence of traverse circles. Recalling that traverse circles had never been placed at the right flank or gorge of Fort Caswell but had been installed at the remaining three faces, the output of Hart & Bailey is specific enough to pinpoint the locations of the heaviest guns to be mounted.

Five circles for Columbiads were delivered in May and nine 32-pounder carriages and circles were completed in early July, implying that they were intended for placement where there were no traverse circles, namely at the right flank and gorge of the fort. Conversely, no traverse circles were manufactured for the 24-pounder guns, a certain indication that at least the first guns of that caliber were to be mounted somewhere at the remaining three faces of the fort, most likely the two faces of the northern salient angle. [29]

From his vantage point, Pendergrast could see the right face of the northern angle, the gorge, and the right flank of Caswell's barbette tier, so virtually everything that had been mounted to date was visible to him. It is highly unlikely that the 32-pounders had been mounted yet, since the carriages had been delivered just four days before the U. S. Navy's visit. So, the probability exists that the Flag Officer was looking at two 8-inch Seacoast Howitzers on Caswell's right flank for short range work on ships attempting to pass the fort and ascend the river; three 8-inch Columbiads divided between the gorge and the right flank for long range engagements on the western bar and main ship channels; and nine 24-pounder Siege Guns at the northern salient angle to protect the anchorage in the river. [30]

Perhaps emboldened by Pendergrast's report, *USS Daylight* chased steamer *Laura* into the Cape Fear River on July 17, in full view of Fort Caswell. Colonel Cantwell then took an unusual course of action. "I went out with two or three companies of the garrison some ½ mile or thereabouts to her protection. The *Daylight* fired a shot or two at the troops," recalled the Colonel. The threat of being under the guns of Caswell moved the Federal vessel's commander to put out to sea and Colonel Cantwell noted a happy conclusion to the incident. "The schooner got in safely." To demonstrate his gratitude for the assistance, *Laura's* captain presented a First National Confederate flag to Colonel Cantwell. "I used it as a garrison flag at Fort Caswell," he proudly recounted. [31]

In the middle of July, Raleigh reminded the general of the availability of the heavy artillery left in Weldon the previous May. Gatlin was quick to reply. "I shall be glad to receive the eleven 32-pounders, but the order to discontinue expenditures on account of the State will prevent their immediate use," he gently reminded the Governor's Military Secretary. Then he abruptly delivered the bad news. "The batteries for which they were required have not been erected." As a consequence of his candor, Gatlin would obtain fewer of those cannon for his command. [32]

While it was true that the Zeek's Island battery, the Oak Island water battery, and Bolles' Battery on Confederate Point had been erected and their guns mounted, other batteries advised by Inspector General Whiting hadn't yet been started. Specifically, Whiting had envisioned batteries at Price's Creek, Reeves' Point, and the site of Old Brunswick. Work on another battery near Confederate Point lighthouse had begun, but work was suspended prior to its completion. According to General Gatlin, "The defensive works there in progress were continued to completion, but no others were undertaken in as much [*sic*] as the Governor, directed, early in July, that all expenditures on account of

Engineering and Ordnance should cease." [33]

Feeling that the nine companies of the 8th Regiment at Camp Wyatt rendered Confederate Point secure enough from an attack by land, General Gatlin thought more was necessary to protect the peninsula from harassment by the U.S. fleet. "By erecting a battery near Camp Wyatt and another some two miles and a half nearer Confederate Point, the vessels of the enemy would be compelled to keep at least two miles from shore," he wrote, thus voicing his convictions to Warren Winslow. Conveying the urgency of the situation, he concluded, "These two batteries ought to be erected at once." The General made his needs for additional batteries known to anyone in a position to help, including the Wilmington Committee of Safety. [34]

General Gatlin's communications with the Committee and the influential Warren Winslow may have prompted a proposal to President Davis on 22 July, seeking to end the stalemate. On behalf of the State of North Carolina, Winslow suggested that the State advance the necessary funds to restart the construction of batteries all along the state's coastline, in exchange for $50,000.00 in Confederate bonds and the promise to supply the necessary engineer officers. [35]

The approval process churned slowly into the month of August with no appreciable movement toward acceptance of the Governor's offer. Moreover, there was no significant progress in furthering the defenses of the Cape Fear except for the muster of Second Lieutenant John W. Galloway's Detachment of North Carolina Volunteers, also known as Coast Guard, into State and then Confederate service on 20 August at Fort Johnston. This detachment of seafaring men was encamped on the beach about three miles from Fort Caswell, serving on picket duty for that section of the coast. The camp's initial location is thought to be at Piney Point, not far from property owned by Galloway. A renowned pilot in his own right, the Lieutenant and many of the detachment's men of the sea also served as guides for blockade runners. [36]

The important post of commander of the North Carolina Coast Defenses had been vacant since June, when Brigadier General Theophilus Hunter Holmes was assigned to command the Department of Fredericksburg in Virginia. In a telegram dated 19 August 1861, Richard Caswell Gatlin was notified of his appointment to the rank of Brigadier General in the Provisional Army and simultaneously given command of "the North Carolina forces on the coast of that State." [37]

August 19, 1861 was an eventful day for the State of North Carolina. It marked the transfer of all things military to the Confederate States of America, including the necessary funding to erect the two advanced works proposed for Confederate Point by General Gatlin. Outwardly confused as to just what the nationalization of North Carolina's defenses held in store for him, General Gatlin presumed he was to assume command of the state's coast defenses, thereby replacing General Holmes, but that was not at all what Confederate authorities had in mind. By August 26, however, he seemed to have a clearer understanding of his new responsibilities. On that day, he informed his new employers in Richmond from headquarters, Department of North Carolina that Colonel Sewall L. Fremont, 1st Artillery Regiment North Carolina State Militia had reported to him pursuant to orders from Governor Clark. [38]

Sewall L. Fish graduated with the class of 1841 at West Point, ranked 17th. A little later, he informally changed his surname to Fremont, by which alias he was ever after known. With wide experience as both an engineer and an artillery officer, Gatlin sought to have Fremont mustered into the Provisional Army and put to work on the defenses so long neglected in the Cape Fear and elsewhere on the coast. Then on leave from the Wilmington & Weldon Railroad where he served as its superintendent, Colonel Fremont didn't receive the requested appointment, despite a passionate appeal from the town of Wilmington. General Gatlin determined that the long-dormant Cape Fear defenses were to be Fremont's top priority, where the Colonel would be assisted by an engineer who was no stranger to the region, the returning Captain John C. Winder. Both of Confederate Point's advanced works north of Fort Fisher would come under the latter officer's capable supervision. [39]

The transfer of control over the batteries and forts in North Carolina to the Confederate States left Fort Caswell without a leader, for which there was a reasonable explanation. A Militia officer could not command a Confederate Army post without first being duly commissioned in that army. Appointment of Franklin J. Faison of the Tenth Regiment North Carolina Volunteers to Lieutenant Colonel in the Provisional Army on 20 August solved that problem, however. With Colonel Alfred Iverson commanding the bulk of the Tenth Regiment at Fort Johnston, Faison became the next-highest ranking officer on that side of the river and the logical choice to command Fort Caswell. Not one to shrink from duty, the displaced Colonel Cantwell requested authorization from the State Adjutant General to accompany Colonel Reuben Campbell's Seventh Regiment North Carolina Troops to Hatteras Inlet as a volunteer combatant. His request was granted just the day before the U. S. Navy bombardment of the forts there began, saving him from the fate that befell so many. [40]

Following an unprecedentedly furious naval bombardment, Forts Hatteras and Clark fell to a combined U. S. Army/Navy assault force on 29 August 1861, with the resultant loss of twenty-five pieces of heavy artillery. Excepting one unmounted 10-inch Columbiad, all of the captured guns had recently been issued by the Gosport Navy Yard in Norfolk. Unfortunately, the loss of the Hatteras forts precipitated the unwarranted abandonment of all the fortifications at Beacon Island and the town of Portsmouth, along with another 22 pieces of heavy artillery. [41]

The fall of the forts at Hatteras Inlet must have brought on some feeling of vulnerability throughout the North Carolina coastal defenses. Fort Macon, at least, received the seven 32-pounder Carronades it had been promised, but not from the expected source. On 31 August, seven Carronade carriages and six 32-pounder gun carriages assembled by the Clarendon Iron Works were shipped via the Wilmington and Weldon Rail Road Company, destination Fort Macon. This shipment carried only carriages, no guns, suggesting that the guns were already there. Had Wilmington sent seven of its thirteen Carronades to Fort Macon as planned, or had the guns sent to New Berne in May been forwarded to Bogue Sound? It must have been the latter case, since all thirteen Carronades sent to the Clarendon Iron Works to have their carriages built were still there, destined for distribution to Fort Caswell for flank defense of its ditch and to Fort Fisher for use in its land face defenses. [42]

Referring not too subtly to the catastrophe at Hatteras, North Carolina's native son, Brigadier General Theophilus Hunter Holmes, implored Jefferson Davis to replace General Gatlin, citing deep anxiety for the safety of his home. "The energy, science, and industry of General Whiting point to him as the proper commander to guard against further injury in that quarter," said Holmes, pointedly. It doesn't matter how well-intentioned, Holmes' entreaty could have had no other effect than to unfairly cast doubt on the abilities of the man who had been in command of the Department of North Carolina for less than two weeks. [43]

General Gatlin | 87

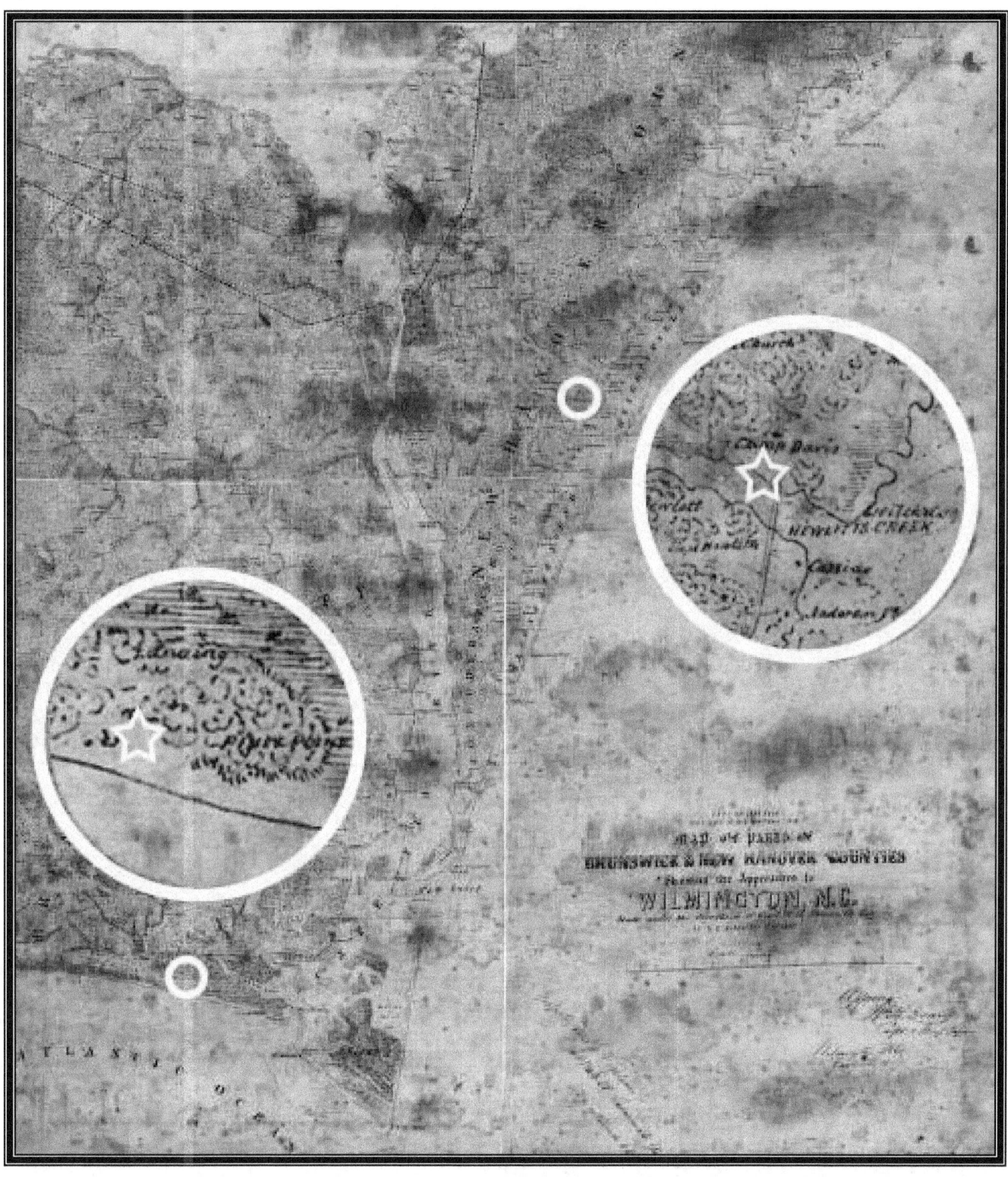

The sites of Camp Davis at Masonboro' Inlet and Lieutenant Galloway's camp near Piney Point. *Map of parts of Brunswick and New Hanover Counties showing the approaches to Wilmington, N.C.*, in the Jeremy Francis Gilmer Papers, Collection #276, Southern Historical Collection of the Wilson Library, University of North Carolina at Chapel Hill, hereinafter cited as Gilmer Papers, SHC, UNC-CH)

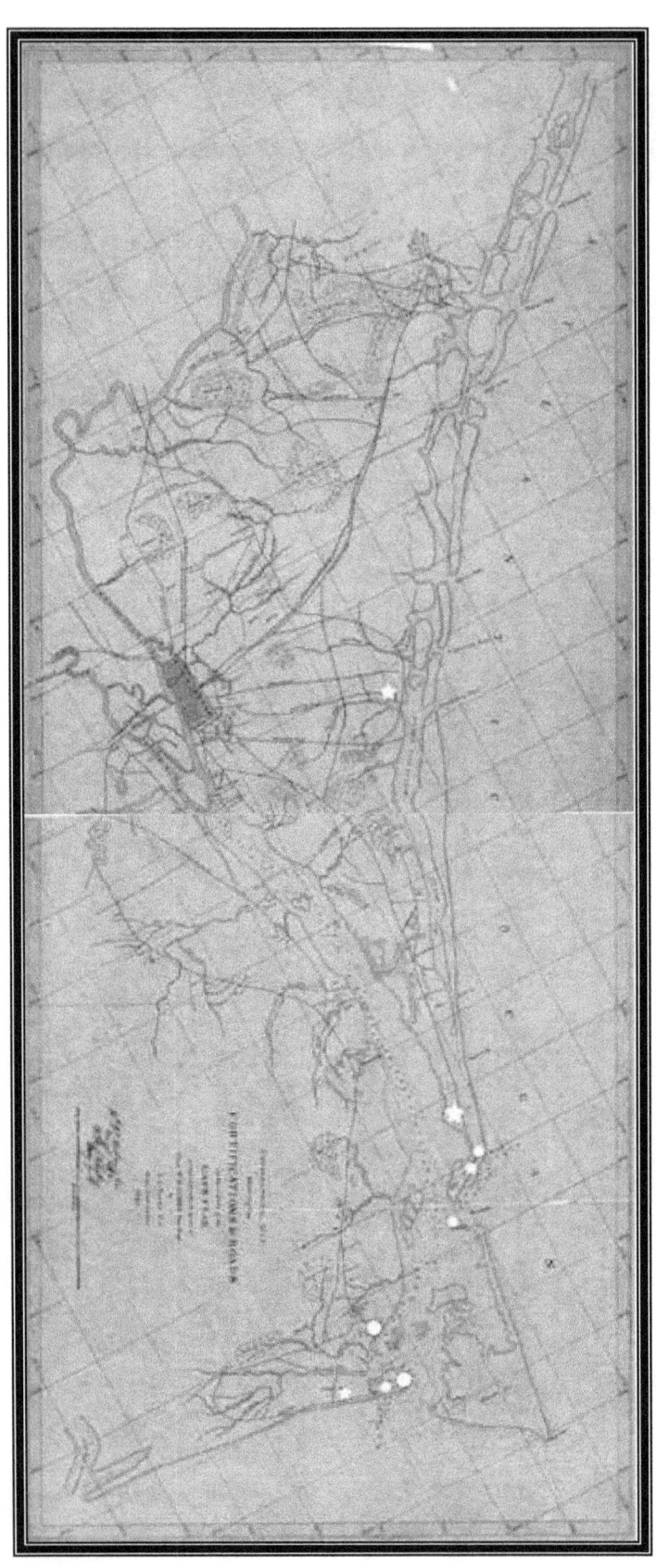

Cape Fear defenses as they were in August, 1861. On the left bank of the river, beginning near its mouth: Lieutenant Galloway's Detachment of Coast Guards camp, Radcliffe Battery, Fort Caswell, and Fort Johnston. On the right side of the river, beginning on the south side of New Inlet: Winder Battery on Zeek's Island, Bolles Battery, the incomplete "Lighthouse Battery," Camp Wyatt, represented by the large white star, and ending with the site of Camp Davis at Masonborough Inlet, which is also the approximate location of the unidentified Camp Winslow. *Topographic Map Showing the Fortifications and Roads in the Vicinity of the Cape Fear*, Gilmer Papers, SHC, UNC-CH)

U.S. Navy 32-pounder carronade of 17 or 18 hundredweight, mounted on a modified siege carriage and limber at Morris Island, Charleston defenses. This method of mounting carronades was routinely used in land and harbor defenses throughout the Confederacy. (Library of Congress, Prints and Photographs Division)

U.S. Navy 32-pounder chambered cannon of 27 hundredweight, length 72 inches. Only four guns of this pattern were issued from the Gosport Navy Yard to the State of North Carolina in June of 1861, so the likelihood of its presence in the Cape Fear defenses is remote. (Library of Congress, Prints and Photographs Division)

U. S. Navy heavy (round shot) gun of 61 hundredweight, length 112 inches, mounted on a front pintle barbette carriage. Twenty guns of this pattern were sent to North Carolina prior to June 10, 1861, hence there is a possibility that guns just like it were serving in the Cape Fear on 30 June. Ultimately, 107 pieces of this pattern were shipped to North Carolina for safekeeping by June 30. Even though 234 of these cannon were manufactured, only one survives to the present day. (Library of Congress, Prints and Photographs Division)

U. S. Navy 32-pounder (round shot) gun of 57 hundredweight, length 112 inches, mounted on a Navy four-truck carriage. Also known as the long gun, this unchambered cannon was the most common pattern of all the 32-pounders captured by the Confederacy at Gosport. It was, in fact, the most prevalent pattern of all iron Navy cannon of the era, but only sixteen of them were shipped to North Carolina prior to June 30, 1861. (Library of Congress, Prints and Photographs Division)

U. S. Navy 8-inch chambered shell gun of 63 hundredweight, 2nd Pattern, length 106 inches. Sixteen guns of this weight were shipped to North Carolina in May and June, 1861. This piece was the Navy equivalent of an Army Seacoast Howitzer, and was often referred to as such by Confederate Army personnel. The presence of this very pattern in the defenses of the Cape Fear is thoroughly documented, and some of them served there from early in the war until its end. (Photography courtesy of Eric Ramey)

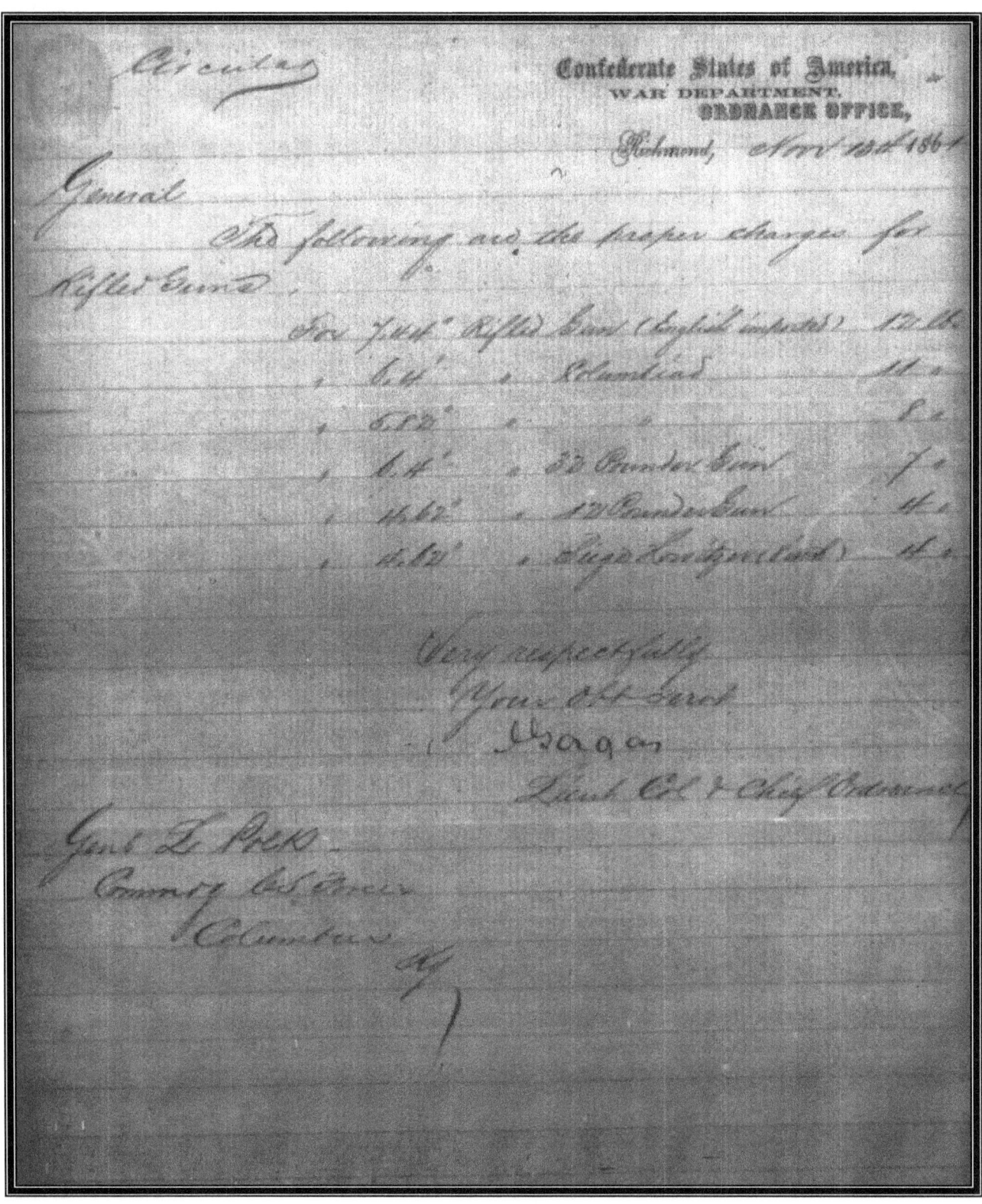

1861 Circular issued by Confederate Chief of Ordnance Lieutenant Colonel Josiah Gorgas specifying the propellant charges to be used in rifled guns of the Confederate Army. Some of these early charges would prove to be excessive. (NARA)

Six

"General J. R. Anderson . . . appears to inspire our people with much confidence."

William S. Ashe

On September 3, 1861 Virginian Joseph Reid Anderson was appointed to the rank of Brigadier General (PACS) and ordered to report to General Gatlin in Goldsborough "for duty connected with the defenses of the coast of that State," not quite the local command autonomy most residents of the Cape Fear wanted. [1]

Brigadier General Joseph Reid Anderson, PACS. (Library of Congress, Prints and Photographs Division)

Joseph Reid Anderson enrolled in the U.S. Military Academy on July 1, 1832 and graduated fourth in his class exactly four years later, whereupon he was promoted to 2nd Lieutenant of the Third Artillery Regiment. On 1 November 1836, Anderson transferred to the Army Corps of Engineers with a rank of Brevet 2nd Lieutenant, but that transfer was reversed by order of December 31, 1836 and his original appointment to the 3rd Artillery reinstated. Then, on July 1, 1837, he relinquished his appointment in the 3rd Artillery for an appointment to Brevet 2nd Lieutenant in the Corps of Engineers. While the paperwork was being shuffled in Washington, the young officer was busy building Fort Pulaski, the foreboding masonry fortress guarding the river approach to Savannah, Georgia. Anderson resigned on September 30, 1837 to become the Assistant Engineer for the City of Richmond, followed in 1838 by a three-year stint as Chief Engineer of the Valley Turnpike Company in Virginia. In 1841, Joseph Anderson was named Superintendent and a full partner in the Tredegar Iron Works. He also served as a member of the

House of Delegates of the State of Virginia from 1852 to 1855. [2]

♦ ♦ ♦ ♦ ♦

General Anderson reported to General Gatlin's headquarters on 7 September 1861 with orders "to take charge of the Coast Defenses of North Carolina," as directed by the Confederate high command. But there was a problem. "It was soon perceived that it would be impossible for Gen'l [sic] Anderson to give proper attention to the entire coast," Gatlin observed. Governor Clark was in complete accord. That same day, he presented Gatlin's sentiments to the Secretary of War and took the opportunity to recommend that Brigadier General D. H. Hill be assigned specifically to the Cape Fear. [3]

At Fort Caswell, Captain John A. Brown was ordered to duty on September 12, replacing Captain Frederick L. Childs as Chief of Artillery and Ordnance. A resident of Maryland, Brown was a West Point graduate and an officer in the old U. S. Army since July 1, 1846. As it turned out, the very capable Lieutenant Samuel A. Ashe returned to Caswell in September to resume his former duties, but this time it was as Captain Brown's assistant. [4]

In late September, residents of Wilmington again lobbied Jefferson Davis for the assignment of a general officer duty-specific to the Cape Fear. Pointing out the enormity of the North Carolina coastline and the inability of General Gatlin to oversee the entirety, W. S. Ashe wrote to the President to recommend officers deemed suitable to assist the general. It wasn't long after Mr. Ashe's communiqué that Lieutenant Colonel Faison was felled by illness, rendering him unfit to command the important post of Fort Caswell. Coincidentally or not, the situation at Caswell seems to have set in motion a series of events that would finally lead to autonomy of command at Wilmington. [5]

While on an inspection tour of the various coastal defenses under his command on the 21st of September, General Anderson checked in at General Gatlin's headquarters in Goldsborough. For reasons suspected yet unsubstantiated, Gatlin directed Anderson "to return to Wilmington and remain in command of the defenses of Cape Fear until some responsible officer could be assigned to that duty." The general's order effectively established a separate and distinct district within the Department of North Carolina. Eight days later, Brigadier General Daniel Harvey Hill was ordered to report to General Gatlin for duty in the military subdivision formerly known as the Northern Department of the North Carolina Coast Defenses, lately redesignated the District of the Pamlico. [6] Meanwhile, Colonel Fremont wasn't standing idly by to see what was going to happen next. Fresh from his selection as Chief Engineer of the coastal defenses of North Carolina and armed with the knowledge that he had the support of the people of Wilmington, Fremont began the task of breathing new life into the sidelined lighthouse battery on Confederate Point. In concert with Captain John Winder of the Engineers, he prosecuted completion of that work with vigor, almost to the exclusion of the other coastal defenses. [7]

The work progressed somewhat slowly and by September 21 it became necessary to move Companies F and I of the 8th Volunteers from Camp Wyatt, not only as an infantry support for the work parties, but to supply additional labor as well. As it was with so many coastal sand batteries and forts, the majority of its guns would initially be mounted on Navy carriages, except for some few 24-pounders mounted on barbette carriages, built by Wilmington Iron and Copper Works. On September 24, 1861, the battery was referred to for the very first time in official correspondence as Fort Fisher. It was christened by Colonel Fremont in honor of Colonel Charles Frederick Fisher of the 6th North Carolina, killed in action at the First Battle of Manassas. [8]

As a member of the subcommittee selected by the Wilmington Committee of Safety to inspect the various points of defense in the Cape Fear in April, Colonel Fremont had a vision of what needed to be done, and he determined to better protect the men and guns on Confederate Point with a larger, more modern battery. As it was designed, the new battery would be a four-gun casemated affair, utilizing heavy timbers for its framework, all of which was to be covered with sand surmounted by marsh turf. Palmetto logs from Smith's Island provided the framework for the embrasures. In spite of Colonel Fremont's belief that the batteries at the mouth of the river would be complete by the end of the month, there was much more still to be done. [9]

The Department of North Carolina's return for the month of September, 1861 included the first known reference to the "District of Cape Fear," Brigadier General J. R. Anderson commanding. Without reproducing that return it its entirety, the various duty stations with their complement of officers and men are presented as an abstract below. Only the troops present for duty are indicated.

Fort Caswell: 13 Officers, 371 Men
Fort Johnston: 31 Officers, 412 Men
Camp Wyatt: 36 Officers, 609 Men
Confederate Point: 4 Officers, 82 Men
Camp Davis: 36 Officers, 965 Men
Wilmington, etc.: 78 Officers, 1,668 Men
Camp Winslow: 4 Officers, 68 Men
Camp Hopkins: 4 Officers, 96 Men [10]

As might be expected, the return doesn't contain sufficient detail to do justice to the troops that served in the Cape Fear defenses, particularly when sufficient information to right the record is available. Following is a detailed rendition of the September 30, 1861 District of Cape Fear return:

September, 1861
Brigadier General Joseph Reid Anderson,
commanding District of Cape Fear

Fort Johnston: Colonel Alfred Iverson,
   10th Regiment, N.C. Volunteers: [11]
      Co. A, Captain Nelson Slough
      Co. C, Captain Burrell Smith
      Co. G, Captain John S. Brooks
      Co. H, Captain Uzz William Cox
      Co. I, Captain James A. Faison
      Co. K, Capt. Thomas Fentress Toon
   Capt. Wm. S. Devane's Co. (Confederates) NC Vols. [12]

Fort Caswell: Captain John A. Brown
   10th Regiment, N.C. Volunteers: [13]
      Co. B, Captain James B. Atwell
      Co. D, Captain John Bunn Stanly
      Co. F, Captain Owen L. Chesnutt
Oak Island (Radcliffe Battery):
      Co. E, 10th Reg't., Captain Claudius B. Denson [14]
Fort Fisher: [15]
      Co. F, Captain Charles Malloy
      Co. I, Captain Robert D. Williams
Zeek's Island (Winder Battery):
      Cape Fear Light Artillery, Captain John J. Hedrick [16]
      Co. K, 8th Reg't, Captain Thomas James Purdie [17]
Camp Wyatt: Colonel James D. Radcliffe
   8th Regiment, N.C. Volunteers [18]
      Co. A, Captain Christian Cornehlsen
      Co. B, Captain Robert Tait
      Co. C, Captain Forney George
      Co. D, Captain William Stokes Norment
      Co. E, Captain John Robert Hawes
      Co. H, Captain Edward Dudley Hall
Confederate Point (Bolles Battery):
      Co. G, 8th Reg't., Captain Henry Savage [19]
Camp Hopkins:
      Moore's Battery, Captain Alexander D. Moore [20]
Camp Davis and vicinity:
      Bunting's Battery, Captain Samuel R. Bunting. [21]
      15th Regiment, N. C. Volunteers [22]
Camp Winslow:
   2nd Lt. Atherton B. Hill's Company of N.C. Volunteers, known as Scotland Neck Mounted Rifles [23]
Wilmington and vicinity:
      28th Reg't N. C. Volunteers, Col. James H. Lane [24]
      30th Reg't N. C. Volunteers, Col. Francis M. Parker [25]
Beach West of Fort Caswell:
      Coast Guard Detachment, 2nd Lt. J. W. Galloway [26]

By way of clarification, it should be noted that there were omissions from the September return. Radcliffe Battery wasn't listed on the return as a separate duty station, neither was the Winder Battery on Zeek's Island, nor was Camp Walker near Smithville. Fort Fisher was not referred to as such, even though it had been so named by Colonel Fremont in September. The continued occupation of the unnamed camp on the beach below Fort Caswell by Lieutenant J.W. Galloway's Coast Guard detachment also went unnoticed. It is doubtless the case that all of these units were carried on regimental returns elsewhere, such as Fort Caswell, Fort Johnston, Camp Wyatt or even the Wilmington garrison.

In spite of the much-needed influx of new

troops into the Cape Fear, one aspect of the rush to muster stands out: infantry arms. Of the three infantry regiments that reported for duty that September, only one was armed. Of the others, one was only partially armed and the last had no arms at all. In fact, Colonel James Henry Lane's troops would not be armed until the old flintlock muskets in the State's arsenals could be altered to the more modern percussion system. Of his regiment's service in the defenses of the Cape Fear Colonel Lane said, "During its stay in that kind and hospitable town it performed post duty and guarded various bridges on the Wilmington & Weldon Railroad." Once armed and properly drilled, the 970 men of the regiment in marching formation presented a stirring sight. "The 28th moves down Second Street, with steady tramp, the long line of their bayonets gleaming in the sun, and the firm bearing of the men indicative of determination and giving promise of gallant service when called upon," the *Wilmington Journal* proudly reported.[27]

Captain Moore's artillery company reported to General Anderson with no field pieces, having been unable to appropriate any in Raleigh. In anticipation of the Captain's arrival, however, Anderson managed to stockpile two 12-pounder howitzers and six of the lighter 6-pounder guns. In fact, the Tredegar Iron Works completed Captain Moore's September 11 requisition for four 6-pounder caissons near the end of the month, and shipped them to Wilmington along with 12-pounder howitzer and 6-pounder gun ammunition in a ratio of one each of the former to every two of the latter. This combination of ammunition and caissons positively establishes Moore's initial armament at two 12-pounder howitzers and four 6-pounder guns. Needless to say, his guns were the lightest of artillery pieces, useful primarily as infantry support at close range. Against rifled pieces in distant counter-battery fire, there would be no contest. Firing a spherical shell projectile with a muzzle elevation of 5°, the howitzers could achieve a range of only 1,072 yards using a one pound powder charge. With a powder charge of .75 pounds and a muzzle elevation of 3.75°, their range was reduced by an insignificant 22 yards when firing spherical case shot.[28]

Confederate bronze 12-pounder howitzer that served in 1st Lieutenant John Meredith Jones' section of Captain William Badham's Company B, 3rd Battalion North Carolina Light Artillery. (Courtesy of Lieutenant Jones' grandson, Commander Burton Hathaway Jones, United States Navy, retired)

The need for rifled cannon became evident at an early stage in the development of the Cape Fear defenses, especially so after Hatteras Inlet's fall in August of 1861. Smoothbores weren't able to achieve the range of rifles in any case, and Confederate coastal defenses needed to keep Federal Navy vessels a respectable distance from their shores. Problematically, many old patterns were unsuitable for rifling and blacksmith shops weren't equipped to do the work anyway.

One prerequisite for rifling was that the piece be unchambered to accept the larger powder charge required to discharge the projectile from the cannon at its maximum initial velocity. Next in importance was the presence of sufficient metal mass at the gun's breech, so that it could withstand the increased pressures generated in a rifled gun. Finally, and of greatest importance, specialized machinery was required to rifle a gun, essentials normally found only in arsenals and ironworking manufactories.

Early in the Civil War south, metalworking facilities were few and far between. There were no sophisticated means in Wilmington at this point in the war, so the only options for securing rifled guns were: get them from somewhere else; send existing smoothbore guns to the nearest manufactory to be rifled; or buy the machinery and do the work locally.

Conversion of Confederate smoothbores was first commenced under government supervision at the Gosport Navy Yard, where the important work of repairing, rifling, and banding captured 32-pounders was initiated. One such gun of 57 cwt. aboard CSS *Harmony* was tested under combat conditions against USS *Savannah* on August 31, 1861. News of the gun's success in the engagement spread quickly throughout the Confederacy and demand for the long range gun escalated. To the extent possible, and then only under intense political pressure, Gosport shipped some of the altered guns to coastal fortifications, but never to the exclusion of outfitting naval vessels. "Went up to Norfolk . . . we cannot get any of the guns that are being rifled," lamented Lieutenant Colonel John Thomas Lewis Preston, commander of the defenses on Craney Island, Virginia. Twenty-three rifles from Gosport were shipped to various points in the Confederacy between August 31 and October 2, six of them to North Carolina. By October 4, the forges at the Navy Yard were turning out enough bands to enable the output of just one rifled and banded gun per day.[29]

While the rifling of guns was comparatively uncomplicated, banding them was not. First, the last two feet or so of the breech had to be turned on a lathe to reduce the gun's contoured surface to a cylindrical shape. Transporting a large lathe to a remote location was not logistically possible and that type of equipment was simply not available in villages of the largely agrarian South. Next, four six-inch wide forged rings of one inch thickness were heat-shrunk onto the breech of the cannon, requiring facilities for the production of high heat. Taken together, those two steps were beyond the capabilities of small-town artisans and their machinery, so the guns rifled in the Cape Fear by the brothers Eason were without doubt deployed unbanded and they certainly must have remained that way for the remainder of the war.

The "Gosport Rifle," as it shall henceforth be termed, bore a distinct method of manufacture that would distinguish it from others altered throughout the Confederacy. One insightful U.S. Army Ordnance officer offered a nearly perfect description of the pattern.

> It has seven grooves, the bottom of the groove being cylindrical in form, intersecting at one edge with the surface of the bore. At the other edge the groove is eleven-hundredths of an inch deep. It has thus but one shoulder, which is at the right edge of the groove, as the twist is to the left. The grooves and bands [*sic*] are of equal width, and have a uniform twist of one turn in 32 feet. The gun is manufactured from a 32-pounder navy gun of 61 cwt. A portion at the breech was turned down to a perfect cylinder, and then wrought-iron cylinders shrunk around the breech, similarly to the Parrott gun. The cylinder, when complete, is 24 ½ inches long and 1 ½ inches thick.[30]

Confederate banding using four 6-inch wide iron rings of 1½ inch thickness that have been heat shrunk onto the lathe-turned breech of a Navy smoothbore. (Library of Congress, Prints and Photographs Division)

Thus did the Ordnance specialist accurately describe the banding and so-called "hook-slant" rifling features of the Gosport Rifle. Lieutenant John Mercer Brooke, CSN, coined the term "ratchet rifling" to describe the pattern that came before his assignment to ordnance duties. Even though he does not appear to be responsible for its design and evolution, Brooke's selection of the pattern for use in the rifles of his invention led to the sobriquet "Brooke Rifling," as it is still known today. Scholars have variously identified the pattern as a variant of "sawtooth," Scott's, or even Blakely rifling, and well it may be, but the final determination of just which attribution is proper is highly technical and must be left for the true experts to sort out.[31]

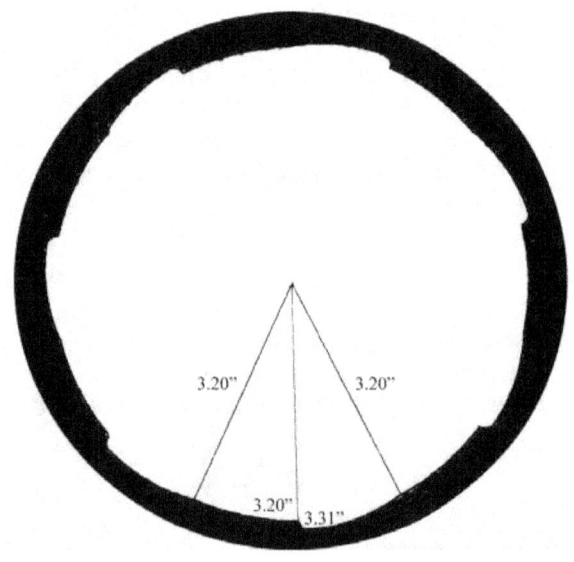

Hook-slant rifling with seven lands and grooves in a 6.4" bore, the same as that of a smoothbore 32-pounder. A hybrid form of rifling that combines the single-shouldered groove of the Blakely pattern and the equidistant lands and grooves of the Scott's pattern. (Adapted from Brooke, Plate VIII, Record Group 74, National Archives)

Hook-slant rifling in a Gosport Rifle. (Courtesy of Fort Branch, North Carolina, photography by Don Torrance)

The practice of supplying rifled guns to other than warships was curtailed completely by the Confederate Navy Department in October, 1861, after which the only option left for obtaining newly-manufactured rifles was to submit a requisition to the harried Confederate Ordnance Department and then wait an indeterminate length of time for their delivery.[32]

As for rifling existing smoothbores, the choices were limited: either develop resources locally or send the guns elsewhere, the latter of which proved to be unworkable. Dismounting guns and transporting them to either Richmond or Charleston involved great delays and ran the risk of having too few guns in the defenses in the event of attack. The do-it-yourself approach seemed the sensible thing to do.

In the beginning, the only guns available to the Confederacy for rifling were those that had been captured in southern arsenals and forts at the onset of war. Falling into that category were Pattern 1840 and 1845 24-pounder Siege and Garrison Guns, as well as 32-pounder and 42-pounder Seacoast Guns. With significant iron mass at the breech, all were thought to be the most acceptable candidates for alteration. The Cape Fear, however, was not fortunate enough to have acquired those patterns when Forts Caswell and Johnston were seized. Wilmington's ancient U.S. Pattern 1816 and decidedly fragile Pattern 1819 24-pounder Siege and Garrison Guns would have been, in normal times, rejected as good candidates for rifling. As the Navy guns from Gosport became available, they obviously met the criteria for conversion, but lack of local resources was still a problem, one that would be solved in an unexpected manner.

The foundry of James M. Eason and Brother in Charleston successfully built machinery and began rifling a 24-pounder gun shortly after the fall of Fort Sumter in April of 1861. Testing of the first Eason rifled 24-pounder in July was an unqualified success. "It has been demonstrated that the Eason gun will throw solid shot or shell, with accuracy, further than any other cannon now in our possession," crowed the *Charleston*

Mercury. By September, the Eason Brothers had more than twenty guns awaiting rifling at their manufactory in Charleston. Perhaps it was the crush of heavy artillery pieces overcrowding his foundry floor that influenced James Eason to develop portable machinery for cutting grooves in a cannon onsite, without the need to remove it from the carriage.[33]

While the precise pattern of rifling employed by the Eason firm is unknown, the lands and grooves were undoubtedly not hook-slant, but rectangular, as was the rifling done by Skates and Company's Mobile, Alabama, foundry and others throughout the deep South. The only documented Cape Fear battlefield recovery of a fired projectile made specifically for a rifled 32-pounder exhibits rectangular 11-groove rifling on its sabot. It must be noted, however, that other Confederate projectiles for the rifled 32-pounder have been recovered from Eason's Charleston area of manufacture with rectangular 8, 10, and 13-groove rifling. Rifled 24-pounder projectiles survived the war with 5, 9, and 18-groove rifling, but no battlefield recoveries from the Cape Fear have been documented to determine which, if any, of those patterns might be attributable to Eason's portable machinery.[34]

When Governor Clark learned of the Eason portable rifling apparatus in September, he immediately inquired into its availability. "The Wilmington guns will be rifled as many as are needed," the Governor vowed. This undertaking would require an army ordnance officer to act as a liaison in the effort, one that was familiar with not only the Cape Fear defenses in general, but with Fort Caswell in particular.[35]

C. B. Denson of the Confederate Engineers remembered just who that man was. "Lieutenant Ashe equipped the batteries and superintended the rifling of old smooth-bore guns with machinery designed by Messrs. Easons, [*sic*] of Charleston." It seems his return to duty from a recent illness couldn't have come at a better time. The Easons were finished in Wilmington and gone from there by September 26, a poorly timed surprise for Governor Clark. "I received no report that you had concluded your work at Wilmington, till I heard it was carried back to Charleston," he wrote of the rifling apparatus. Then the Governor made it clear just what his expectation was. "I now desire you will carry it forthwith to New Bern for such work as shall be indicated there." To hear General Anderson tell it, though, the Cape Fear hadn't received any of the Gosport Rifles, and indeed had no rifled guns whatsoever. "I have no guns of sufficient range on these works," he complained, just a few days after the Eason Brothers left Wilmington.[36]

Based on an estimated time of one day to rifle one cannon, the Easons could have turned out an absolute maximum of 15 guns had they begun the same day Governor Clark wrote his letter of inquiry into their services. Available evidence, however, suggests that they initially rifled ten guns: five 24-pounder siege guns and five 32-pounder Navy guns, all of them unbanded.[37]

The Cape Fear's first production rifle was consigned to the Richmond & Petersburg Rail Road Co. on the third of October, 1861. The Tredegar Foundry was then producing rifled 8-inch and 10-inch Columbiads on the Rodman pattern in respective calibers of 5.82 and 6.4-inches. Wilmington's gun was cast in the profile of an 8-inch Columbiad, and therefore of the smaller caliber, identical to a rifled 24-pounder. Three weeks later, on the 26th of October, the Wilmington depot delivered the big gun and its iron carriage to Fort Caswell, together with its related implements. Six long delayed 32-pounder carronades completed what was a very important ordnance shipment.[38]

Lieutenant Franklin Faison's protracted leave of absence from command at Fort Caswell prompted General Gatlin to recommend Captain John A. Brown for temporary promotion to Colonel and assumption of command at that post. On October 10, Brown was promoted to the temporary rank of Colonel in the Provisional Army and assumed his new duties.[39]

Brown and the other commanders in the Cape Fear defenses presided over the muster of the below-listed independent companies over the months to come. Cavalry, prized for its mobility, amounted to forty percent of the new recruits.

- Captain William C. Howard's Company of Cavalry, North Carolina Volunteers - Swansborough. [40]
- Captain A. F. Newkirk's Company of Cavalry - Camp Heath. [41]
- Confederate Guards Artillery, Captain John O. Grisham - Wilmington. [42]
- Captain John A. Richardson's Company (Bladen Artillery), North Carolina Volunteers Fort Fisher. [43]
- Captain Malcom McNair's Company (Scotch Greys Artillery), North Carolina Volunteers Wilmington. [44]
- Captain Henry Harding's Company of North Carolina Volunteers - Wilmington Camp of Instruction. [45]
- Captain James M. Stevenson's Company of Artillery, North Carolina Volunteers (King Artillery) - Fort Caswell. [46]
- Captain Thomas G. Walton's Company of North Carolina Volunteers (Davis Dragoons) Camp Anderson. [47]
- Captain Edward W. Ward's Company of Cavalry of North Carolina Volunteers - Swansborough. [48]

Captain John Grisham's "Confederate Guards Artillery" brought a hitherto unseen class of light artillery to the Cape Fear. "This gun was a 12 pounder brass gun, with swell muzzle *mouldings*, handles over the trunions [sic], with knob and band at the breach [sic] and when nicely polished was a thing of beauty, when lying quietly on its carriage," recalled Lieutenant Patrick C. Hoy. This description leaves no doubt that Captain Grisham's battery was armed with four Pattern 1841 Heavy Field Guns, weighing some 1,800 pounds each. "A heavy load for four horses," Hoy said, perhaps understating the case. With a muzzle elevation of 5° and using a 2½ pound powder charge, these heavy, small caliber guns could propel a 12-pound solid shot down range a distance of 1,663 yards. Charged with a pound and a half of powder and 2½ degrees of muzzle elevation, spherical case shot could achieve a maximum range of 1,250 yards. [49]

Captain Stevenson's company, among others, was in dire straits when it came to the barest of essentials. In anticipation of a hard winter, the ladies of the Lisbon Soldiers Aid Society came forward with some necessities for the company, as they had done in the cities of Portsmouth, Norfolk, and Goldsborough. Moved by the Society's generosity, the Captain addressed its president. "I do heartily thank you, and all the members of your society for the many valuable articles so necessary for the comfort and health of our men." In conclusion, he vowed, "Accept from me ladies, tho' a stranger, my warmest thanks and full assurance that my right arm shall always be raised in your defence [sic] and for my country." Captain Stevenson would prove to be a man of his word. [50]

Just as his troop strength began to approach the levels General Anderson deemed adequate to defend Wilmington, a Yankee fleet menaced the coast of South Carolina. On November 7, 1861, Colonel Clingman's 15th and Colonel Radcliffe's 8th Regiments of North Carolina Volunteers and Captain Moore's light artillery battery were all ordered to Charleston. The 15th Regiment from Camp Davis and Moore's Battery from Camp Hopkins, being nearest to Wilmington, were first to board the train. [51]

Radcliffe's 8th Regiment, on the other hand, was 20 miles downriver and, according to 1st Lt. William H. McLaurin, their movement didn't go nearly as planned. "On 7 November, orders were received to go to the aid of Port Royal, S.C., and in a few hours all of our equipage was on the banks of the Cape Fear, at Sugar Loaf Landing, awaiting transportation, where, by a miscarriage of orders, steamer after steamer passed us by, and we remained thirty-six hours." The men of the 8th likely wouldn't miss drilling on Fisher's big guns, but their contributions were many. They toiled on the Lighthouse Battery and the unfinished casemate battery, both of which were assimilated into Fort Fisher. They participated in the construction of Gatlin's vision, the advanced works of Battery Anderson and Battery Gatlin, the former about three miles from Fort Fisher and the latter about 5½ miles distant. All well and good, but the quest for glory beckoned. [52]

For many months, the numbering system of the North Carolina Volunteer Regiments had been in a confused state, the reasons for which are far too tedious to be detailed here. Suffice it to say that the situation was finally addressed on November 14, 1861, when the Confederate high command renumbered not a few North Carolina volunteer regiments by adding a factor of ten to their existing numerical designations. Both of the recently departed regiments were affected by the change, when Clingman's regiment became the 25th Regiment North Carolina Infantry (State Troops) and Radcliffe's command was changed to the 18th Regiment North Carolina Infantry (State Troops). Of the units remaining in the Cape Fear, the 28th and 30th Regiments were not affected, but Colonel Iverson's command was redesignated the 20th Regiment North Carolina Infantry (State Troops). [53]

Following the reassignment of two infantry regiments and an artillery battery, General Anderson reallocated his resources, which meant a change of duty station for more than a few companies, the designations and changes of station as listed below.

- Captain William S. Devane's Company (Confederates) North Carolina Volunteers - Fort Johnston to Fort Caswell. [54]
- Company B, 36th Regiment North Carolina Troops (Purdie's Battery) - Zeek's Island to Fort Fisher. [55]
- 30th Regiment North Carolina Troops - Camp Walker near Smithville to Camp Wyatt. [56]
- Captain William C. Howard's Company of Cavalry, North Carolina Volunteers - Swansborough to Camp Hopkins, thence to Fort Fisher. [57]
- Bunting's Battery - Camp Davis to Camp Anderson, thence back to Camp Davis. [58]
- Captain Atherton B. Hill's Company of Cavalry – Camp Winslow to Camp Grant. [59]
- Captain Malcom McNair's Company (Scotch Greys Artillery), North Carolina Volunteers Wilmington to Fort Caswell. [60]
- Confederate Guards Artillery - Wilmington to Fort Fisher. [61]
- Cape Fear Light Artillery - Zeek's Island to Fort Fisher. [62]

By early December, General Gatlin fretted over the security of the northern sounds of North Carolina. "In regard to the battery at Huggins' Island, I don't see exactly where the troops are to come from," he complained to General Anderson. Between the two of them, though, a plan must have taken shape, for on December 6, Gatlin made his wants known to the State of North Carolina. "I desire to receive into service three companies of artillery to serve at the heavy batteries on the Pamlico, Neuse, and White Oak Rivers." From the language in Gatlin's dispatch, it would seem the batteries had already been completed. [63]

Huggins Island, situated at the mouth of the White Oak River, was, in spite of its remote location, part of General Anderson's District of the Cape Fear. One of the three companies to be mustered into service was then organizing in Wilmington under the designation Captain Daniel Munn's Company of Artillery, North Carolina Volunteers, also known as the Bladen Stars. Captain Munn's Company was mustered into service on 1 January 1862 for "local defense and special service," under the auspices of the now familiar Local Defense Act. Soon after mustering in, Munn's Bladen Stars took its place in the most far-flung defensive position in Anderson's district, overlooking Bogue Inlet. [64]

Even though Lieutenant Colonel Franklin J. Faison had fully recovered from his illness and returned to duty on October 28, 1861, John A. Brown remained in command of Fort Caswell by virtue of his rank of Colonel, even though it was awarded temporarily. While the situation seems simple enough, there remained a problem of military protocol. Lt. Colonel Faison had never been relieved of command at Fort Caswell. This oversight persisted until December 17, when Special Orders No. 143 formally relieved him from duty at Caswell and returned him to his parent unit, the 20th Regiment North Carolina Infantry. Colonel John Brown formally assumed command on January 1, 1862. [65]

On January 24, Fort Johnston's Cadet of Engineers Thomas Rowland found himself in Wilmington. "I was ordered there by General

Anderson who wished me to take command of a detachment of heavy artillery at some battery on the Cape Fear River." That detachment may well have been the first eighteen or so early Hatteras parolees belonging to Captain Thomas Sparrow's Company K, 10th Regiment North Carolina State Troops (Washington Grays). The men went into camp near Fort French, the first in a series of proposed water batteries a few miles below Wilmington on the east bank of the Cape Fear River. [66]

Not yet 21 years of age, Rowland was nearing completion of some new water batteries at Fort Johnston, lacking just one important detail. "I have a few hands with an overseer turfing the batteries, but I cannot close up my affairs until Col. Freemont [sic] sends several guns to be mounted." As a river battery, Fort Johnston hadn't been viable for some time, serving instead as headquarters for the 20th Regiment North Carolina Infantry. [67]

Following is an extract from the return for the District of the Cape Fear for January, 1862:

> Wilmington: 43 officers, 677 men, no artillery
> Camp Grant: 4 officers, 69 men, no artillery
> Camp Davis: 4 officers, 64 men, 6 field pieces
> Camp Heath: 4 officers, 77 men, no artillery
> Camp Wyatt: 43 officers, 637 men, no artillery
> Fort Fisher: 15 officers, 232 men, 25 heavy guns; 4 field pieces
> Zeeke's Island: 2 officers, 73 men, 3 heavy guns
> Fort Johnston: 41 officers, 593 men, no artillery
> Fort Caswell: 14 officers, 217 men, 34 heavy guns; 1 field piece
> Camp Hopkins: 4 officers, 70 men, no artillery
> Swansborough: 3 officers, 64 men, no artillery
> Huggins' Island: 4 officers, 64 men [68]

As it was with the September, 1861 return, it's possible to link the units serving in the Cape Fear defenses with their respective duty stations.

January, 1862
Brigadier General Joseph Reid Anderson,
commanding District of the Cape Fear

Fort Johnston: Colonel Alfred Iverson [69]
   Nine Companies 20th Regiment N. C. Infantry
Fort Caswell: Colonel John A. Brown [70]
   (Heavy Artillery – 34 guns)
   One Company 20th Regiment N. C. Infantry
   Scotch Greys, Captain Malcom McNair
   King Artillery, Captain James Martin Stevenson
   Confederates, Capt. William S. Devane
Camp Wyatt: Colonel Frances Marion Parker [71]
   Nine Companies 30th Regiment N. C. Infantry
Fort Fisher: [72]
   (Heavy Artillery – 25 guns)
   One Company, 30th Regiment N. C. Infantry
   Cape Fear Light Artillery, Captain John J. Hedrick
   Bladen Artillery, Capt. John A. Richardson
   Confederate Guards Artillery, Capt. John O. Grisham
   (Light Artillery – Four 12-pounder guns)
Zeek's Island (Winder Battery): [73]
   (Heavy Artillery – 3 guns)
   Purdie's Battery, Captain Thomas J. Purdie
Camp Anderson:
   Captain Thomas G. Walton's Company of Cavalry
Wilmington:
   28th Regiment N. C. Volunteers, Col. James H. Lane
Camp Davis:
   Bunting's Battery, Captain Samuel R. Bunting [74]
   (Light Artillery – Six 6-pounder guns)
Swansborough:
   Captain Edward W. Wards Company of Cavalry
Huggins' Island:
   Bladen Stars, Captain Daniel Munn
Camp Grant:
   Capt. Atherton B. Hill's Company of Cavalry
Camp Heath:
   Captain Abram F. Newkirk's Company of Cavalry
Camp Hopkins:
   Captain William C. Howard's Company of Cavalry [75]
Beach West of Fort Caswell:
   Captain John Galloway's Company, Coast Guards [76]

On its face, the January return provides the basis for determining the nature of the artillery in the Cape Fear defenses as of the end of January 1862. There were 53 pieces of heavy artillery in the entirety of the defenses on 30 June 1861, compared to 62 big guns on the latest return, seemingly a net increase of just nine guns. One of those, it will be recalled, was an 8-inch Columbiad rifled to 5.82 inches and two were 8-inch Rodman Pattern 1861 C. S. Columbiads, recently arrived in the Cape Fear defenses. The latter smoothbore guns, bearing foundry numbers 1324 and 1329, were billed to the Confederate government on January 13, after first shipping from the Tredegar Iron Works to Wilmington via the Richmond and Petersburg Rail Road. Rounding out the known patterns and calibers were: thirteen 32-pounder Carronades; twenty 24-pounder siege guns, some rifled and some smoothbore; three U.S. Pattern 1844 8-inch Columbiads; one 8-inch Columbiad of unknown pattern; three Pattern 1839 or 1840 8-inch Seacoast Howitzers, and two 8-inch Navy Shell Guns. Only seventeen U.S. Navy 32-pounders could therefore have been present in all of the Cape Fear defenses, unquestionably of mixed weights. Of those seventeen, five were rifled, leaving thirteen in smoothbore configuration. [77]

A significant shuffling of resources at this point in the war muddies the water as to just which calibers and patterns were mounted where in the defenses. It is abundantly clear, however, that Wilmington and Fort Johnston reported no artillery on hand, indicating that Forts Caswell and Fisher had divided the thirteen 32-pounder Carronades and the ancient fort on the river had lost two 24-pounder siege guns, for which no replacements were forthcoming from Colonel Fremont. Moreover, some old Columbiads were in position at Fort Fisher in the fall of 1862, giving rise to the possibility that they came from Fort Caswell after some of its 32-pounders had been rifled in September, or that some had been obtained from a source outside the Cape Fear. Altogether too predictably, though, the Winder Battery on Zeek's Island still mounted three guns, almost certainly the same artillery serving there in June past. [78]

In early January, Lieutenant Daniel L. Braine, commanding the blockader *USS Monticello*, received valuable intelligence as to the armament on and about Confederate Point from two "contrabands," best described as escaped slaves, who fled the peninsula. He dutifully reported the situation to his superiors.

> At New Inlet in and about the fortifications (which consist of one battery of twelve guns, one earth casemate of six guns, one small battery of three guns, and one battery on Zeeke's Island of four guns) there are stationed about one regiment and a half (1,400 men) also four field pieces, horse artillery. All the guns in these batteries are short 32-pounders. [79]

Some of this intelligence confirms what is known to be the state of affairs with the works at New Inlet: the battery of twelve guns obviously referred to Fort Fisher; the earth casemate battery was a reference to the new work of Colonel Fremont; the small battery can certainly be ascribed to Bolles' Battery; and the existence of four field pieces of horse artillery were those of Captain Grisham's battery. Very little credibility attaches to the stated number of guns, either in total or by battery, nor can the number of troops be considered factual. The greatest piece of misinformation is the attribution of all the guns in the batteries as short 32-pounders. Certainly some of them were, particularly in the land face of Fort Fisher, where some Carronades were deployed. Given the known presence of siege guns, Columbiads, and seacoast howitzers, all of the guns could not have been short.

Vicinity of Scott's Hill and Camp Heath. Inset: The camp between Scott's Hill (triangle) and the more distant camp (star) is identified as an "Artillery Camp" on this 1864 map. The camp marked with the star is annotated on the map as an "Old Camp." It is the author's opinion that the latter camp is the site of the original Camp Heath where Newkirk's cavalry was stationed. (*Map of country between N. E. Cape Fear River and Topsail Sound*, Gilmer Papers, SHC, UNC-CH)

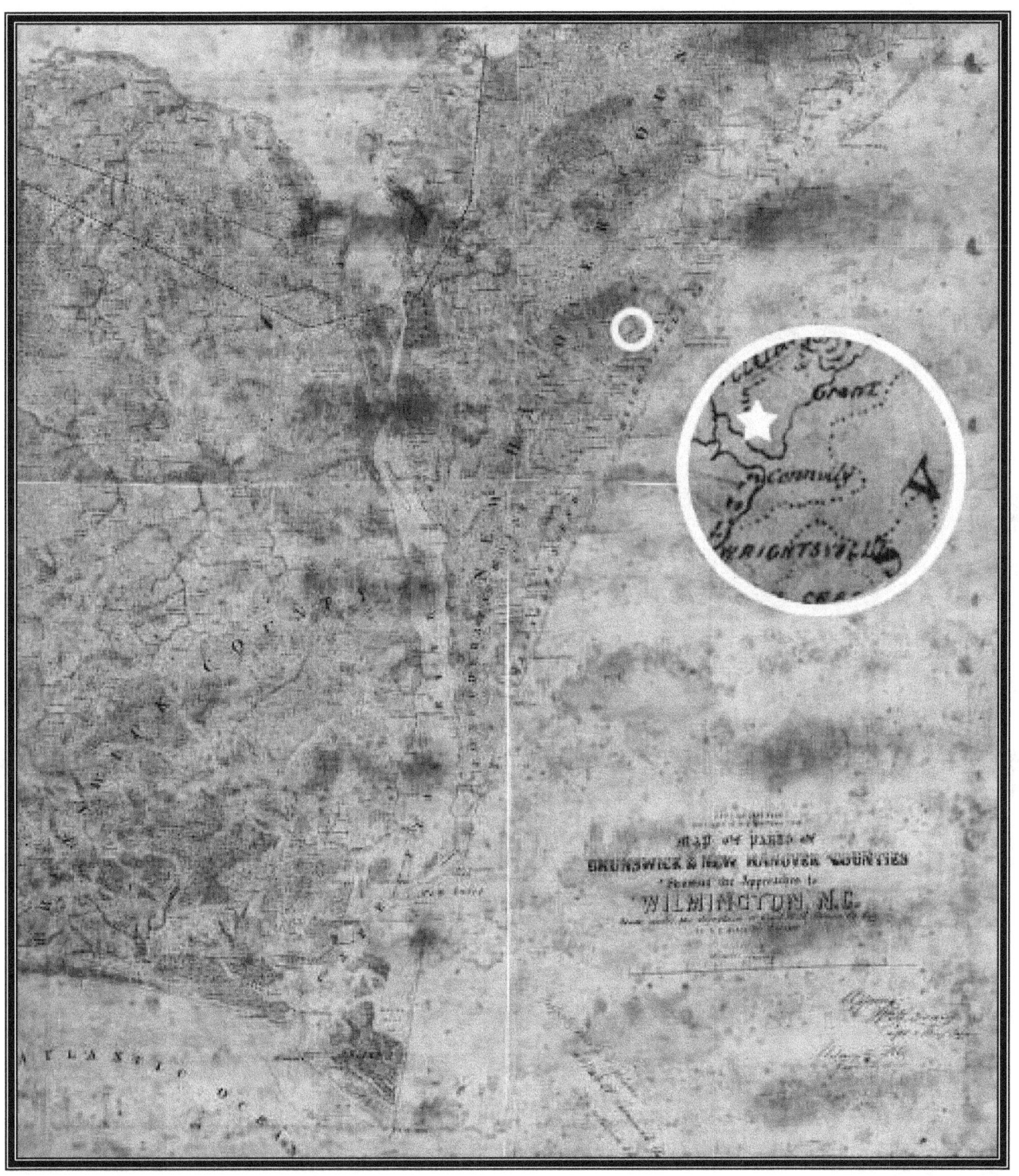

While it is only the author's opinion, the common practice of naming camps after the owners of land they were situated upon seems to favor this location as the site of Camp Grant. (*Map of parts of Brunswick and New Hanover Counties showing the approaches to Wilmington, N.C.*, Gilmer Papers, SHC, UNC-CH)

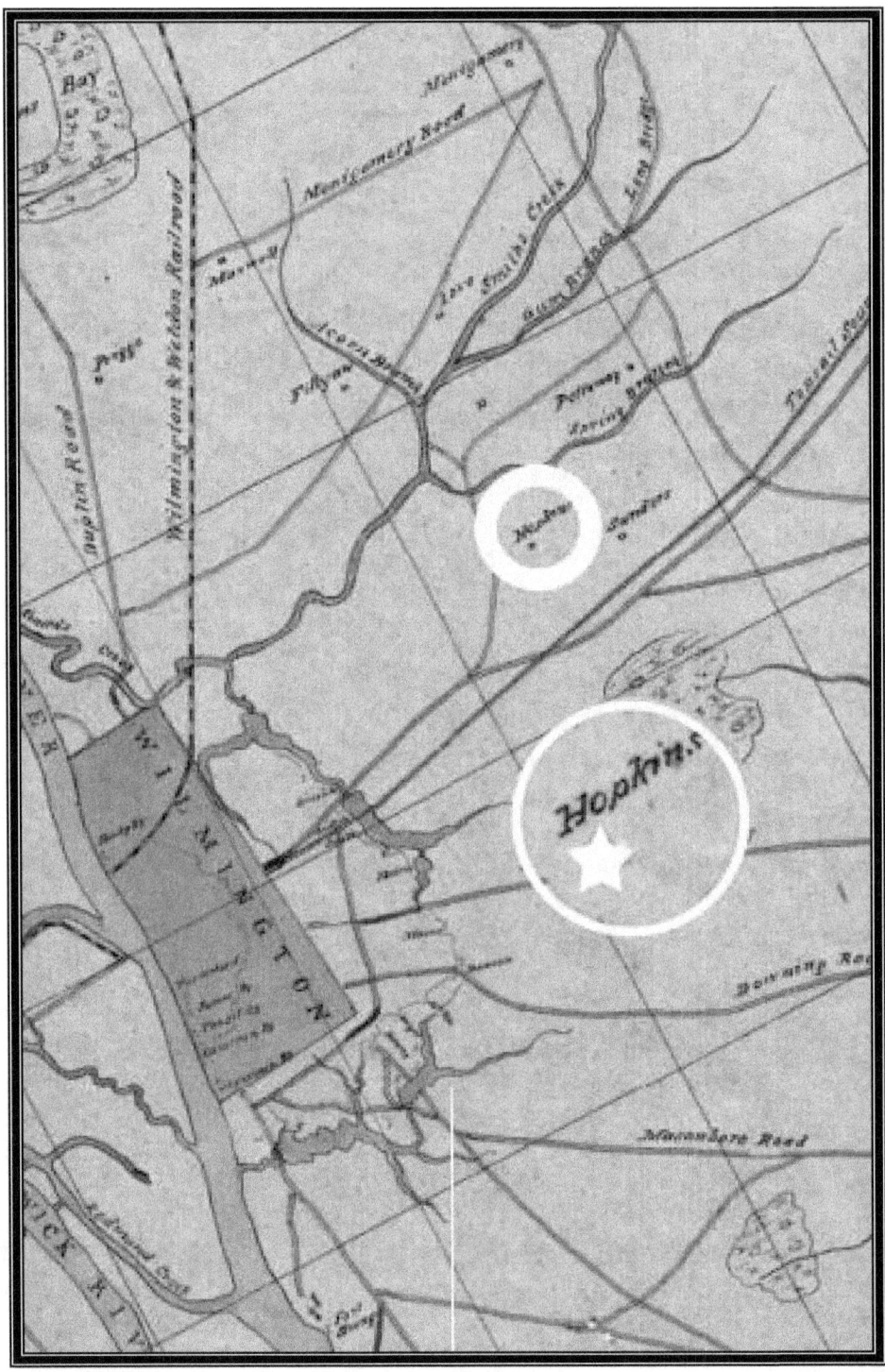

The probable site of Camp Hopkins near Wilmington. Although somewhat theoretical, the trend toward naming camps for the owner of the land upon which they were located points to this site as Camp Hopkins. (*Topographic Map Showing the Fortifications and Roads in the Vicinity of the Cape Fear*, Gilmer Papers, SHC, UNC-CH)

General Anderson | **107**

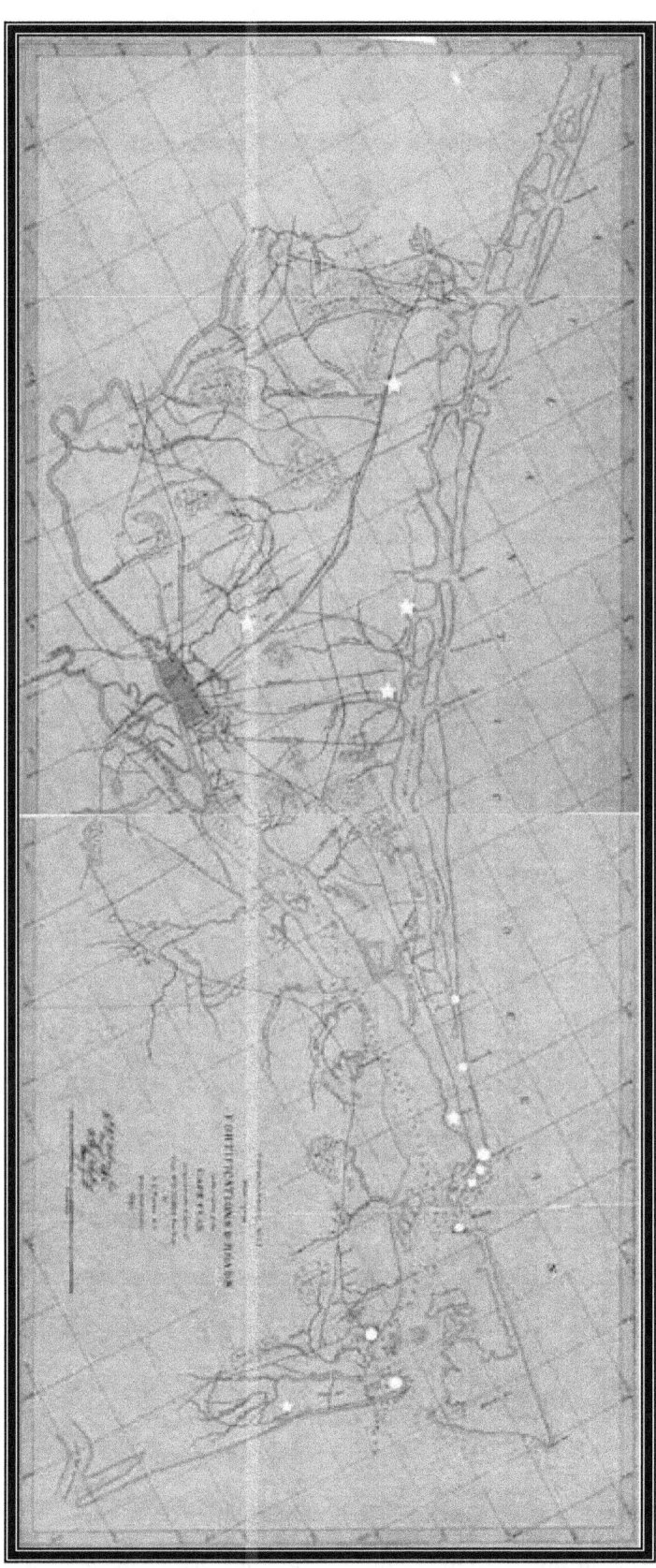

District of the Cape Fear defenses at year's end in 1861. The northernmost outpost of Camp Heath was occupied by Captain Abram Francis Newkirk's Company of Cavalry which patrolled the district's extensive coastline. It is the author's opinion that the property on the plank road nearest Wilmington that is shown on this map as being owned by "Hopkins" is the site of Camp Hopkins. With Bunting's Battery in Wilmington, Camp Davis was unoccupied, as was Camp Winslow, the exact location of which remains obscure, but it is known to have been "at Masonboro' Sound" and "near Camp Davis." Above Camp Davis, Captain Atherton B. Hill's "Scotland Neck Mounted Rifles established Camp Grant, thought to be located on land owned by one Mr. Grant on Wrightsville Sound. Far below that, on Confederate Point, Battery Gatlin and, below that, Battery Anderson were completed, their armament unknown. Camp Wyatt (large star) was garrisoned by the 30th Regiment North Carolina Infantry. The lighthouse battery and the casemate battery were all but combined into the ever-expanding Fort Fisher, below which was Bolles Battery. Winder Battery on Zeek's Island was, of course, the last line of defense for New Inlet. Gone was the Oak Island water battery on the east side of the river, replaced in manpower only by Lieutenant Galloway's detachment of "Coast Guards" about three miles from Caswell (small star). Fort Johnston was home to the 20th Regiment North Carolina Infantry and Fort Caswell was evolving into a truly autonomous command relying less and less on companies of that regiment to provide manpower for its garrison. (*Topographic Map Showing the Fortifications and Roads in the Vicinity of the Cape Fear*, Gilmer Papers, SHC, UNC-CH)

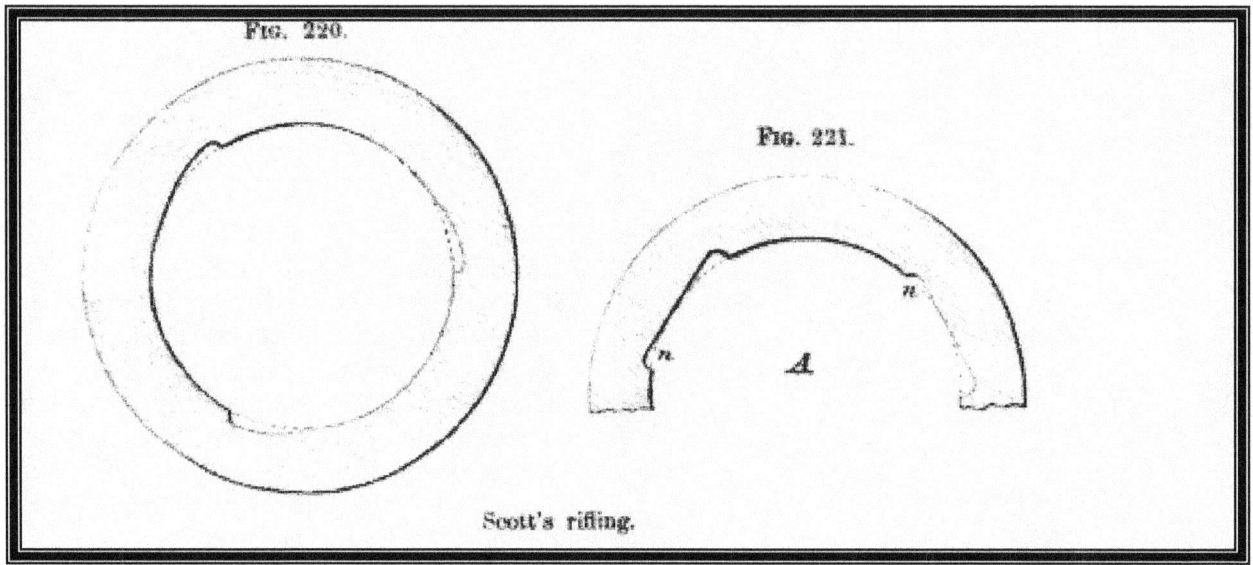

Left: At first glance, this Scott's hook-slant rifling seems to match the pattern of the Gosport Rifle.
Right: An enlargement of the Scott's rifling clearly shows grooves with <u>two</u> exaggerated shoulders.
The lands and grooves depicted here are equidistant.

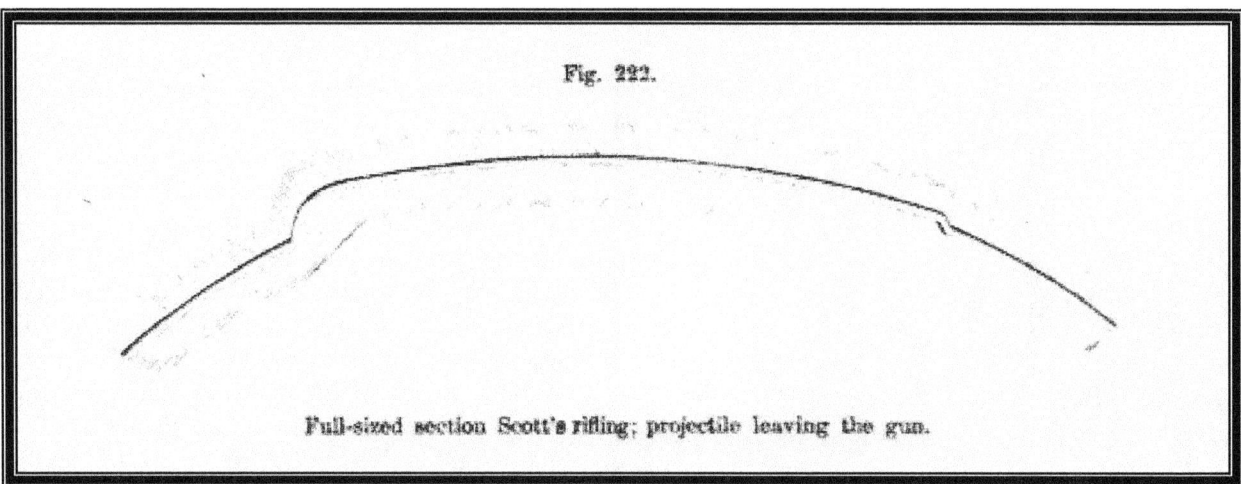

An enlarged cross section of Scott's rifling depicts the two shoulders of the groove
as they appear in the bore, less exaggerated than seen in the image at the upper right.

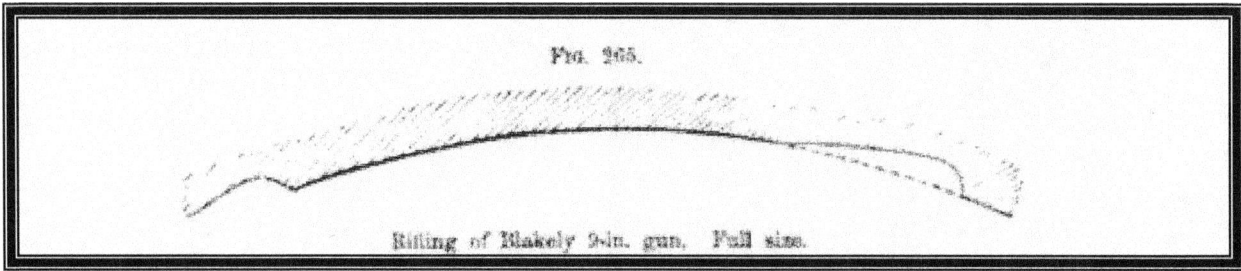

Blakely rifling, characterized by very large lands and small grooves having only one shoulder. All of the above
images are from Alexander L. Holley, *A Treatise on Ordnance and Armor*, New York: D. Van Nostrand, 1865.

8-inch C.S. Pattern 1861 Columbiads and carriages on center pintle Columbiad chassis. This is the pattern that the Tredegar Iron Works bored and rifled to 5.82 inches and shipped to Wilmington on October 4, 1861. In profile, there is no way to distinguish the rifled pattern from the smoothbore. Inset: Tredegar-made shells for the "hybrid" rifles carried pre-engraved sabots of lead or copper. 5.82 inch rifles had 6-groove rifling and 6.4-inch rifles had 5-groove rifling. (Library of Congress, Prints and Photographs Division)

U.S. unchambered Navy cannon of 57 hundredweight, banded and rifled.
(Library of Congress, Prints and Photographs Division)

Confederate bronze 12-pounder Howitzer. (Library of Congress, Prints and Photographs Division)

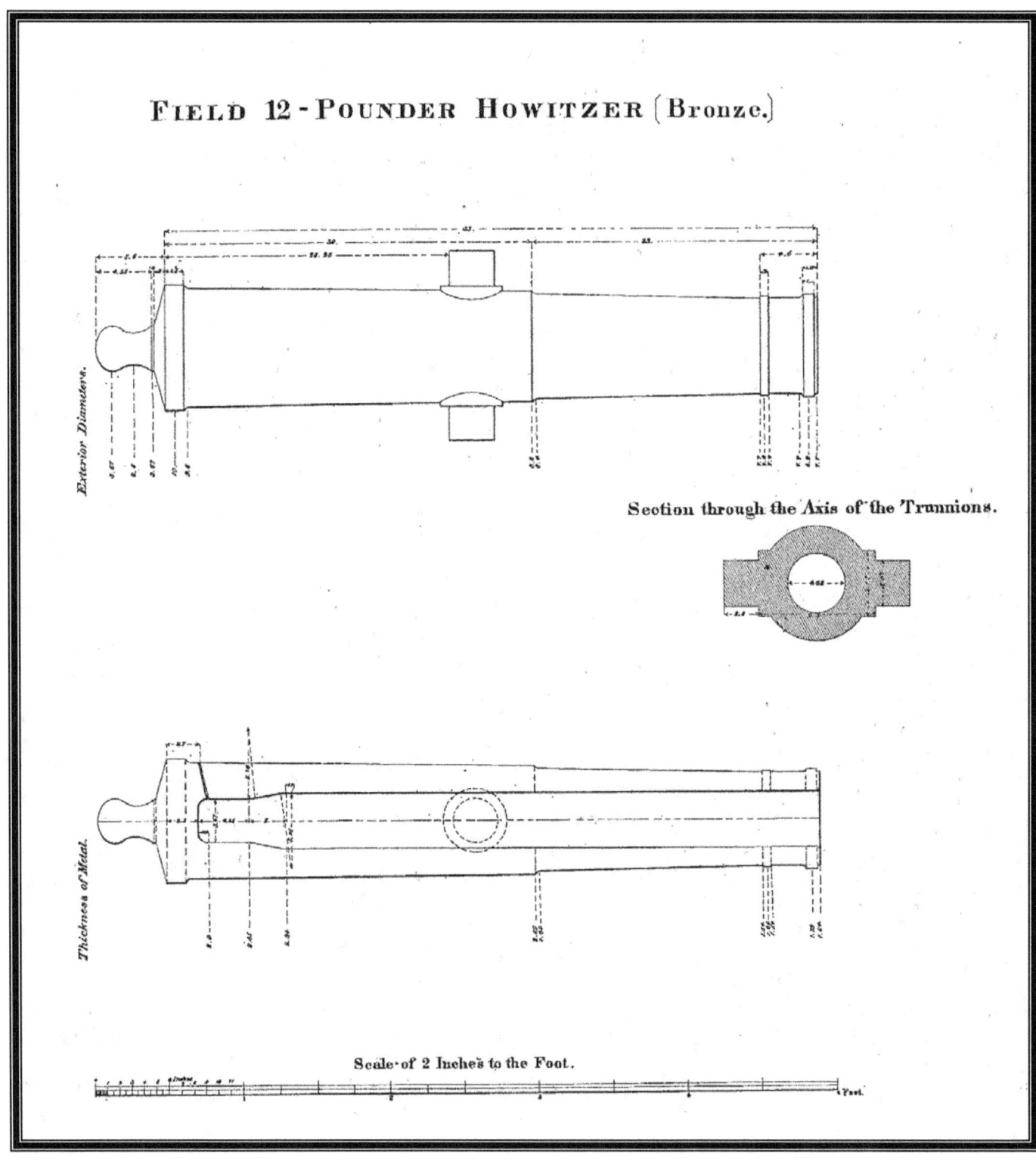

Plan and profile of Pattern 1841 bronze 12-pounder Howitzer. Again, the profiles of the patterns manufactured by Confederates and Federals alike were highly similar, if not identical. 12-pounder Howitzers weren't manufactured for the Confederacy by Tredegar after late 1862. (Courtesy Harpers Ferry Center, U. S. National Park Service)

U.S. or C.S. Pattern 1841 12-pounder Heavy Field Gun (bronze). This pattern was virtually obsolete when the war began, due primarily to its excessive weight. Other than bore size, the only difference between the profiles of this pattern and the Pattern 1841 6-pounder gun is the presence of mounting loops above the trunnions. Captain Grisham's "Confederate Guards Artillery" brought four of these heavyweights to the Cape Fear from Mississippi. (Library of Congress, Prints and Photographs Division)

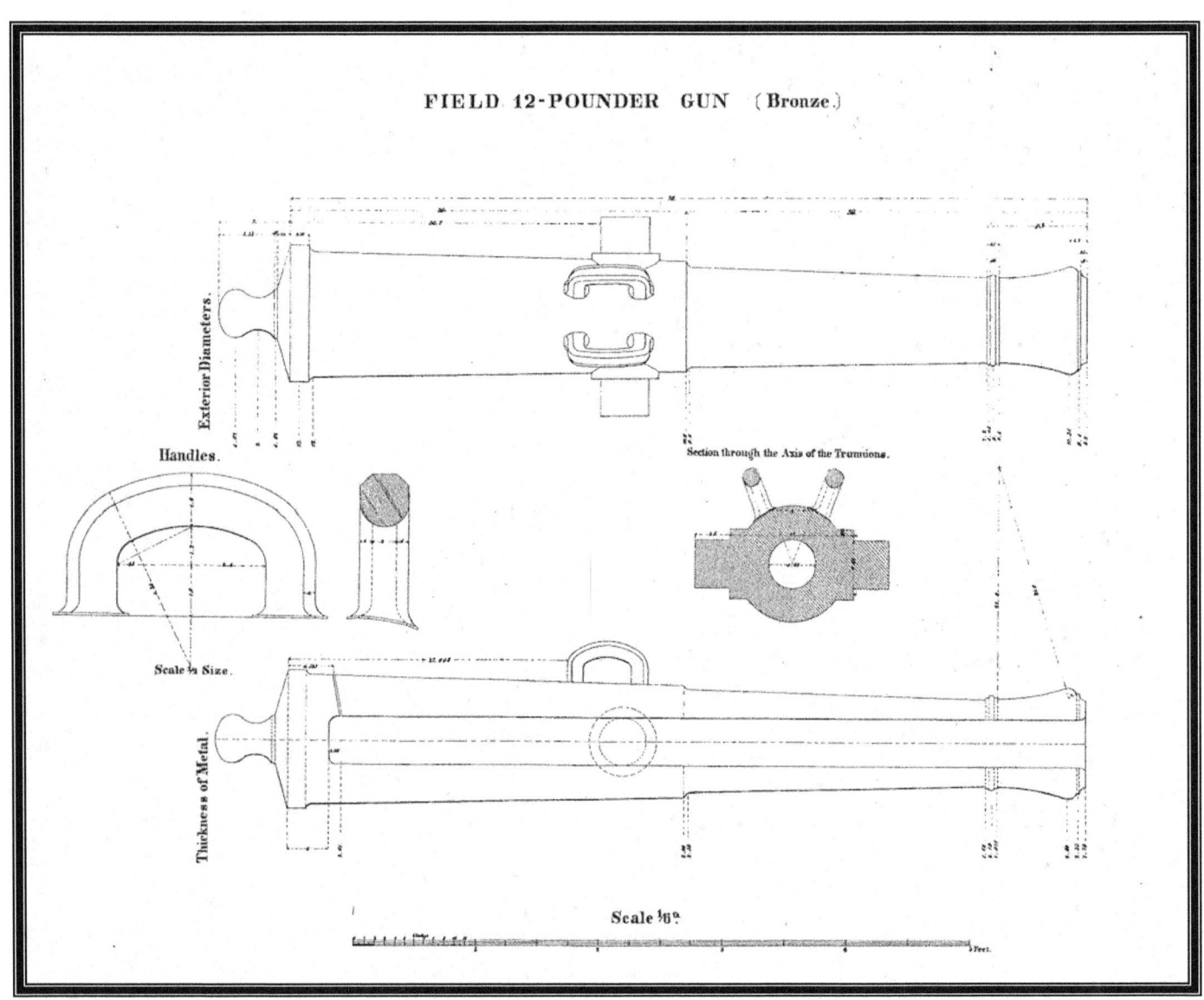

Plan and profiles of U.S. or C.S. Pattern 1841 12-pounder Heavy Field Gun (bronze).
(Courtesy Harpers Ferry Center, U. S. National Park Service)

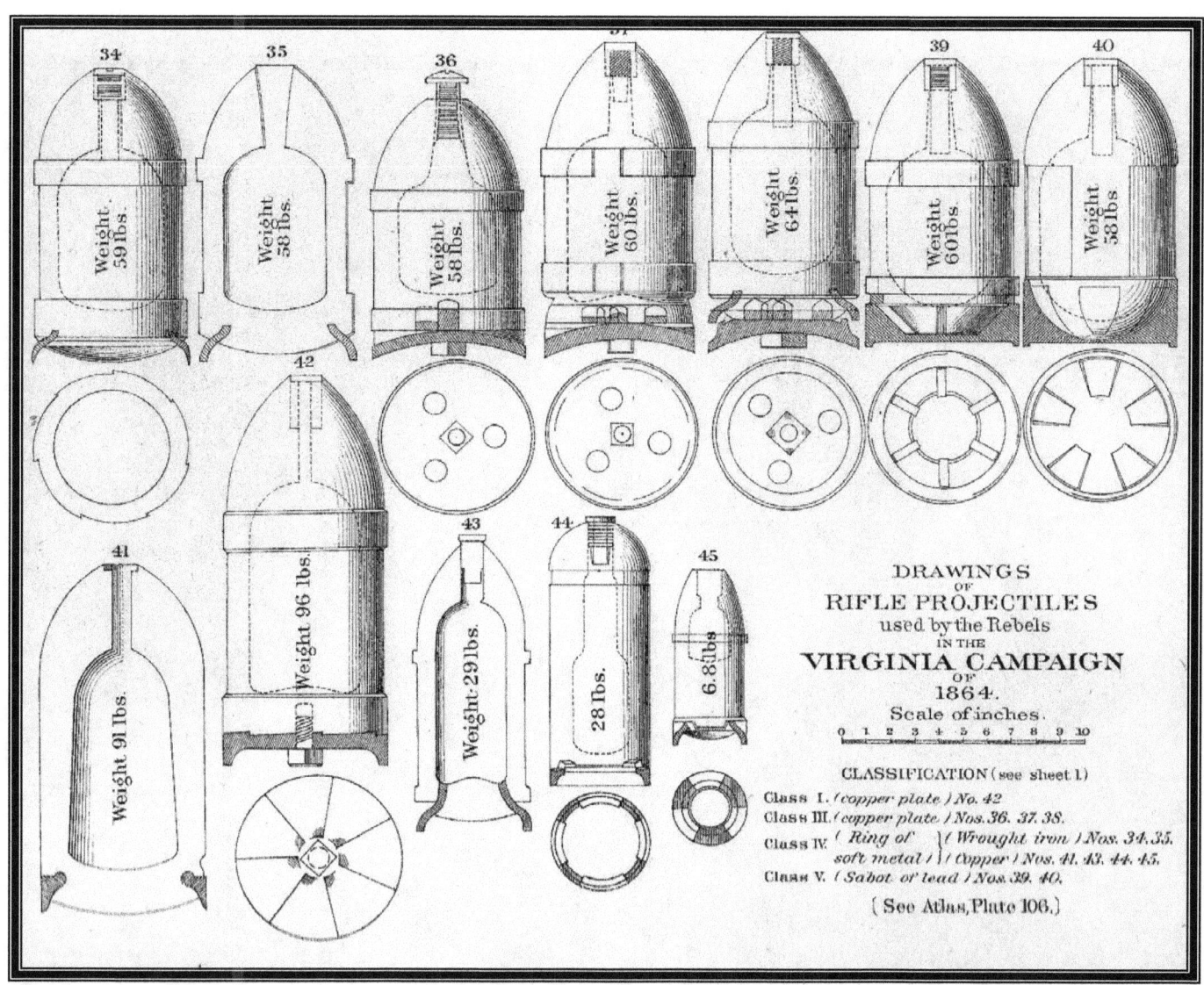

Examples of rifle shells and case shot employed by the Confederacy during the Civil War. Solid bolts are also found among the various types as well. The single most notable thing about Confederate projectiles is the rampant use of *bourrelets*, or raised rings around the body of the projectile. By using this technique, machinists had only to machine the bourrelets to size and not the entire projectile, thereby saving time and wear on cutting tools. The "classification" at the lower right identifies the various types and materials of the sabots found on Confederate projectiles. (United States War Department. *Atlas to Accompany the Official Records of the Union and Confederate Armies*. 1861-1865, Plate CVII, Washington: U.S. Government Printing Office, 1891-1895)

Joseph Reid Anderson's Tredegar Iron Works and Foundry, Richmond, Virginia.
(Library of Congress, Prints and Photographs Division)

Seven

"Fort Fisher was a small unfinished work..."
Brigadier General Samuel Gibbs French

Buoyed by their initial success at Hatteras Inlet in August, the bluecoat hordes once again determined to extend their reach into the Sounds of North Carolina. On February 8, Union forces overwhelmed and captured the garrison of 2,500 men on Roanoke Island, with the resultant loss of 34 pieces of heavy artillery and three of light artillery. Every one of the big guns had been furnished by the Gosport Navy Yard, including three 32-pounder rifles. It was a crushing blow that reverberated all the way to Richmond, where promises of assistance to the Governor had been uttered but only superficially honored, and too late, even then. [1]

In the month of February and into very early March, following the loss of Roanoke Island, the Cape Fear defenses garnered six companies and saw one returned to Wilmington from its remote outpost.

- ❖ Bladen Stars, Captain Daniel Munn - Huggins Island to Fort Fisher. [2]
- ❖ Brunswick Artillery, Captain John Douglas Taylor - Fort Caswell. [3]
- ❖ Blocker's Artillery, Captain Octavious H. Blocker - Fort Fisher. [4]
- ❖ Starr's Light Battery, Captain Joseph B. Starr Fort Fisher. [5]
- ❖ Captain Henry Harding's Company North Carolina Volunteers - Fort Fisher. [6]
- ❖ Captain John R. Lanier's (Infantry) Company North Carolina Volunteers - Pamlico River to Fort Fisher. [7]
- ❖ Company K, 10th Regiment North Carolina State Troops (1st Artillery), Captain Thomas Sparrow - Fort French [8]

February 9th found Cadet Engineer Thomas Rowland still awaiting orders. "A company of heavy artillery is being raised in Wilmington. As soon as it is completed it will be sent to Light House Battery about two miles below Wilmington, and I will be ordered there to command the battery." On 5 February 1862, the Convention of the State of North Carolina had authorized the Governor "to raise by voluntary enlistment not exceeding three Artillery Companies to serve at the batteries already erected or which may be hereafter erected on the Cape Fear River below or at and in the vicinity of the town of Wilmington . . ." Rowland's aspiration to command would be frustrated not long afterward. "I found that an order has just been issued, assigning me to new duties at Fort Johnson [sic]." [9]

In a pointed reference to the batteries on the Cape Fear River nearest Wilmington, Governor

Clark lamented the state of their preparedness in late February. "There are several batteries on the river below the town of Wilmington, with some guns, but are without garrison." Indeed, there were three batteries, one ready for a garrison and another not far behind. The third was in the final stages of planning. In fact, Fort French, located about 3 miles south of town, received its first garrison on February 28, 1861. Not as ready for garrison was the Light House Battery, sited approximately two miles south of the port city. Lazaretto Battery, about two months away from receiving its garrison, was about a half-mile south of Fort French. [10]

Not two months after assuming command of Fort Caswell, on February 26, 1862, Colonel John A. Brown was relieved of duty and ordered to Norfolk as a Captain of Artillery. Brown's successor was not named immediately, giving rise to speculation that his temporary promotion was never intended to become permanent. It may be, too, that the old fears of inexperience at Caswell were resurrected by the misfortune at Roanoke Island, or the transfer and demotion might have been for some unspoken egregious offense. Whatever the reason, the fort was in need of a new commander, an expectation that wasn't realized immediately. [11]

Two artillery companies mustered into the service of the Confederacy in the first half of March, enabling one very welcome transfer.

- 3 March: Captain Edward B. Dudley's Company North Carolina Volunteers Artillery Zeek's Island. [12]
- Company B, 36th Regiment North Carolina Troops (Purdie's Battery), Captain Thomas J. Purdie - Zeek's Island to Wilmington. [13]
- 12 March: Captain Nathan L. Williamson's Company of North Carolina Volunteers - Fort Caswell. [14]

In response to the unexpected appearance of Federal troops before the town of New Berne, four units were withdrawn from the Cape Fear to reinforce its threatened garrison.

- 28th Regiment North Carolina Infantry, Colonel James Henry Lane. [15]
- Bunting's Battery, Captain Samuel R. Bunting. [16]
- Confederate Guards Artillery, Captain John O. Grisham. [17]
- 1st Company B, 36th Regiment North Carolina Troops (2nd Artillery), Captain Thomas J. Purdie. [18]

The excision of three artillery batteries and an infantry regiment from the Cape Fear defenses precipitated a few urgent transfers to replenish the vacated duty stations.

- Captain Elisha A. Perkins' Company of Cavalry - Camp Anderson to Camp Wyatt. [19]
- Captain Howard's Company of Cavalry - Fort Fisher to Camp Wyatt. [20]
- Captain Edward W. Ward's Company of Cavalry - Swansborough to Montfort's Mill in Onslow County. [21]
- Captain Atherton B. Hill's Company of Cavalry - Camp Grant to Camp Saunders in Onslow County. [22]

Dispatched from South Carolina on March 16, Captain Alexander D. Moore's battery of light artillery and Colonel William E. Starke's 60th Virginia Infantry Regiment were detained in Wilmington by order of General Anderson, their services in the north no longer needed. Moore's Battery, another of the North Carolina units sent to the aid of South Carolina in November, went into camp at "Watson's Branch" soon after its arrival in Wilmington on March 19. [23]

The diminutive stream that was Watson's Branch fed Hewlitt's Creek, upon the banks of which Camp Davis was located. Any unnamed encampment didn't remain that way for very long, and the one on Watson's Branch was no exception. Known to have been in the vicinity of Masonborough Sound about seven miles from Wilmington and five miles from Camp French, it was likely the site of Camp Holmes. [24]

Even the 30th Regiment from Camp Wyatt and the 20th Regiment from Fort Johnston were moved to Wilmington on 14 March, but their advance was halted when news of New Berne's fall reached the city. Both regiments were then ordered into camp in the vicinity of the city. The 30th Infantry turned out to be the more mobile of the two, pitching their tents first at Camp Lamb, from which they removed to Camp French, and finally taking up residence at Camp Holmes on Masonborough Sound on 30 March. However temporarily, the 20th North Carolina stayed put in or about Wilmington, demonstrating just how providential it was to have a ranking Colonel as its commander. [25]

As for the Cape Fear Light Artillery, Captain John Jackson Hedrick, PACS, resigned from the company on 18 March to accept a promotion to Major, PACS, commanding the Post of Fort Fisher and Zeeks Island. Close on the heels of Hedrick's advancement, the officers of the company elected Lieutenant James D. Cumming as their new commander. From that day forward, the company was known only as Cumming's Battery and the local designation of the Cape Fear's namesake light artillery battery faded into history. It somehow seems fitting to retire the local designation of a company whose founder has moved on. [26]

The fall of New Berne marked the loss of a vital point on the Confederate map, in addition to the loss of twenty-seven Gosport 32-pounder smoothbores, six rifled cannon and one 8-inch Columbiad. Recriminations abounded and found only one target. Amid whispers of intemperance, Brigadier General Richard Caswell Gatlin became the scapegoat for every disastrous event occurring during his tour of duty as commander of the Department of North Carolina. Despite Gatlin's repeated pleas for men and materiel in the months prior to the attacks, the responses from Richmond were, every time, too little and too late. [27]

Loss of the northern sounds and 108 pieces of heavy artillery in only six and a half months, however, was just too much for the Confederate high command to bear alone, even had it been so inclined. Citing health reasons, General Gatlin was relieved of command of the Department of North Carolina on March 15. Brigadier General Joseph Reid Anderson was announced as his replacement in Goldsborough, leaving Colonel Alfred Iverson in command of the District of the Cape Fear. [28]

On the same day, Brigadier General Samuel Gibbs French was assigned by the Adjutant and Inspector General's Office (AIGO) in Richmond to command the District, but, strangely, General Anderson contravened the order. When French reported for duty on the 17th, Anderson gave him command of the District of the Pamlico, and, in spite of the breach of military protocol, General French formally assumed command the next day, thus extending Colonel Iverson's command duty in Wilmington. [29]

Three days prior to the fall of New Berne, George A. Cunningham was appointed to the rank of Colonel, PACS and ordered to report to General Gatlin for duty as the new commander of Fort Caswell. The relief of General Gatlin, however, changed everything. With the Cape Fear command situation still undecided, Colonel Cunningham's orders were countermanded until matters could be stabilized. [30]

In a reversal that almost certainly originated in Richmond, Brigadier General Samuel Gibbs French, in accordance with his original orders, assumed command of the District of the Cape Fear on the 22nd of March. At that point, the Adjutant and Inspector General's Office directed Colonel Cunningham to report to him for duty at Fort Caswell. Then, following orders received on the 23rd, Major General Theophilus Hunter Holmes relieved Anderson when he formally assumed command of the Department of North Carolina on 25 March. [31]

◆ ◆ ◆ ◆ ◆

Brigadier General Samuel G. French brought with him to the Cape Fear a wealth of military experience dating to the Mexican War, where he served with distinction. He was born on 22 November 1818 in Trenton, New Jersey and received his early education at the prestigious Burlington Academy. French was graduated from West Point on July 1, 1843, ranked 14th in a class of 39, and commissioned Brevet Second Lieutenant with the U. S. Third Artillery. He served on garrison duty on the frontier until the outbreak of war with Mexico, where he was in action at the battles of Palo Alto and Resaca de la Palma, earning him a commission as a Second Lieutenant on June 18, 1846.

Brigadier General Samuel Gibbs French, PACS.
(Wikimedia Commons)

French was brevetted First Lieutenant for gallant and meritorious conduct in the battles around Monterey, and received a promotion to Brevet Captain in February, 1847 for his actions at the Battle of Buena Vista, where he was seriously wounded. He was promoted to First Lieutenant in the Third Artillery in March, 1847, then to Captain in the Quartermaster Corps on January 12, 1848. On May 31, 1856, he resigned his commission in the U. S. Army and turned to planting near Vicksburg, Mississippi, at which avocation he was engaged when he once again heard the drums of war beat the long roll.

When the State of Mississippi seceded from the Union, Governor John J. McRae sent for Samuel G. French and appointed him Lieutenant Colonel and Chief of Ordnance in the Army of Mississippi on 12 February. In April of 1861, he was appointed Major, Corps of Artillery, ACSA, and six months later, President Jefferson Davis sent him a dispatch asking him to accept the position of brigadier general. On 23 October he was commissioned as such in the Provisional Army of the Confederate States of America, and from November 14, 1861 until he was sent to North Carolina, French was in command at Evansport, Virginia. [32]

◆ ◆ ◆ ◆ ◆

General French's assumption of command in Wilmington relieved Colonel Alfred Iverson and freed up his regiment for assignment elsewhere, which wasn't long in coming. The men of the 20th Regiment North Carolina Infantry packed their bags and departed the confines of the port city for the sand flea-infested Camp Wyatt soon after French's arrival. With French superceding Anderson in Wilmington, Major William Lamb lost his job as Assistant Quartermaster for the Cape Fear District. Expectedly, General French brought his staff with him, including his very capable Chief Quartermaster, Major John B. Morey. Obviously, there ensued a period of transition from Lamb to Morey, but the energetic young staff officer from Virginia wouldn't wait long for a new assignment. [33]

The defensive scheme for the Cape Fear River and the Town of Wilmington must have seemed daunting to the new commanding officer, at least in the beginning, but General French seemed to know what had to be done. "On arriving at Wilmington, the first duty was the immediate examination of the defenses at the mouth of the Cape Fear river." Accompanied by his staff and the knowledgeable Cadet Thomas Rowland, the

General's stop at Oak Island left him with a positive impression. "Fort Caswell was in fair condition for defense, and any vessels passing it would meet river obstructions while under short range of the guns." Across the river, however, the Brigadier found only a work in progress. "Fort Fisher was a small unfinished work, consisting of a casemate battery fronting the ocean, and a line of works, nearly at right angles with this, that ran back inland. This latter line constituted the land seaside defense, while the guns also commanded the channel and the entrance thereto." [34]

General French moved quickly to shore up one perceived weakness. On March 25, Cadet Rowland was housed at the nearby Orton Plantation, and not minding a bit of it. "The gentleman who owns the plantation gives us the use of his house, and servants to cook for us and wait upon us." Notwithstanding his elegant surroundings, the young Cadet had work to do. "I was ordered here to superintend the construction of a battery and a line of intrenchments [sic]." Located near Old Brunswick, Rowland used the ancient map site of Brunswick Point to describe the locus for the proposed fortifications, a label that would endure only until the work could be given a more historically relevant one. [35]

Reporting to Robert E. Lee on March 27, Major General Theophilus H. Holmes said, "I have ordered six companies who have been drilled at heavy artillery to report to General French in Wilmington." Those six were joined by several more that reached their duty stations in the last days of March and into April. [36]

- ❖ Co. I, 10th Regiment North Carolina State Troops, Captain John N. Whitford - "Old Brunswick Point Battery." [37]
- ❖ Herring Artillery, Captain William A. Herring Fort Johnston. [38]
- ❖ Gatlin Artillery, Captain James S. Lane - Fort Johnston. [39]
- ❖ Robinson Artillery, Captain Edward Mallett Fort Fisher. [40]
- ❖ McMillan Artillery, Captain William H. Tripp Fort Fisher. [41]
- ❖ Bridgers' Artillery, Captain William B. Rodman - Brunswick Point. [42]
- ❖ Captain Alexander McRae's Company Heavy Artillery - Brunswick Point. [43]
- ❖ Lenoir Braves, Captain William Sutton Wilmington. [44]
- ❖ Captain Charles C. Whitehurst's Company Fort Fisher. [45]
- ❖ 43rd Regiment North Carolina Infantry, Colonel Thomas S. Kenan - Wilmington. [46]
- ❖ 51st Regiment North Carolina Infantry, Colonel John L.P. Cantwell - Camp Morgan. [47]
- ❖ 1st Co. A, 2nd Regiment N. C. State Troops, Captain Calvin Barnes - Brunswick Point. [48]
- ❖ Co. B, 1st Regiment Maryland Infantry, Captain Charles C. Edelin - Brunswick Point. [49]

Despite the seemingly large influx of military units into the Cape Fear, two commands were ordered away. Just a little more than a month after its arrival, the 60th Virginia was ordered back to its home state for duty with the Army of Northern Virginia. Even though the regiment's stop in Wilmington had always been considered to be temporary, General Holmes wasn't going to give it up without a fight. Needless to say, the authorities in Richmond weren't the least moved by Holmes' reluctance. "I am directed by General Lee to acknowledge the receipt of your letter of the 18th instant, wherein you state that you cannot recommend the withdrawal of Colonel Starke's regiment from your department," wrote Walter H. Taylor on April 20. Robert E. Lee's Assistant Adjutant General continued, "He on yesterday telegraphed you to send this regiment." The frustration of the highest ranking general in the Confederate Army was evident in closing. "If the regiment has not started, the General desires you to send it immediately." [50]

Captain John N. Whitford's Company I, 10th Regiment North Carolina State Troops, stationed at the "Old Brunswick Point Battery" since March 29, received orders to report to Kinston for scouting duty on April 22. Leaving 23 of his men in the General Hospital at Wilmington, Captain Whitford and the remaining 76 men of his command took up the march immediately, reaching Kinston three days later. From there,

Whitford and 65 men were ordered to Swift Creek Bridge, Craven County, where they began their transformation from heavy artillery acting as infantry to partisan rangers. [51]

On April 18, Companies A, H, and D of the 30th Infantry were detached from the Regiment and ordered to Onslow County to join Captain Atherton B. Hill's Company of Cavalry already bivouacked at Camp Saunders. Two days later, Colonel Parker was ordered to march to Onslow with the balance of the regiment, there to reunite his regiment and join up with the cavalry. First detaching Company E for provost guard duty in Wilmington, six companies of the 30th departed Camp Holmes on 25 April, accompanied by Captain Abram F. Newkirk's Cavalry and one section of Moore's Battery, all of which arrived at Camp Saunders the night of 30 April. [52]

The first detailed gun-by-gun itemization of the armament of Fort Caswell in almost a year appears in a log book entry of *USS Monticello*:

> At 10 p.m. two deserters from the Confederate Army came off in a small rowboat. They state that Fort Caswell is garrisoned by 550 men, mounts 6 carronades to rake the moat, which has 5 feet of water in it. On the S.W. side of fort there are 6 rifle guns, 1 large 64-pounder, and 5 32-pounders; near there are 4 8-inch columbiads. The balance of the guns are 30, 32, and 24 pounders. [53]

This was a hurried entry, written sometime after 10:00 P.M. on the night of Lieutenant Daniel Braine's interrogation of Henry Garwood and George Henry of the King Artillery, but while the information was still fresh in the Navy officer's memory. That Fort Caswell mounted six carronades isn't a surprise, but the number was still half the cannon the fort's caponieres were designed for. The stated depth of the water in the moat is accurate, at least according to the plans presented in Chapter 2. The Lieutenant then appears to say there were twelve guns on the "S.W. side" in addition to four 8-inch Columbiads nearby, but the intimation that the balance of the guns consisted of "30, 32 and 24 pounders" is confusing, particularly when it comes to the ill-defined 30-pounders. As luck would have it, though, a clarification of the hastily prepared log entry is at hand. [54]

A few days after the interrogation, Lieutenant Braine penned a report that provides greater detail as to the numbers and calibers of the large guns in Fort Caswell but, at the same time, is in conflict with his own log entry on one very important point. First he said, "The fort mounts 36 guns in all." Braine went on to say, "The guns in barbette are 30 in number; 6 are rifle guns and look toward the entrance to the harbor, and with these are 4 8-inch columbiads looking in the same direction. The balance of the guns are light 32 and 24 pounders." With the six carronades reported in the log book, this description seems to be completely accurate, but another conflict is seen in the continuation of the Lieutenant's report, which states: "4 of them are carronades placed so as to rake the moat (which has 5 feet depth of water in it)." [55]

The Lieutenant had it right on his first try. It has been established that Caswell's capacity of two carronades for each of its six caponieres was in fact reduced to one for each as the log indicates. Four carronades would have left two scarp walls defenseless, an unacceptable scenario at best. This is, simply put, a case of erroneous transcription, either from the log entry to the report or from the report to the Official Records.

What can be learned from the results of Lieutenant Braine's interrogation? First, five 32-pounder rifled guns and one "large 64-pounder" rifled gun were pointing "toward the entrance to the harbor," an obvious reference to the Western Bar Channel and its land approaches to the fort. Fort Caswell's gorge was the only parapet on the barbette tier covering that entrance to the river. Four 8-inch Columbiads were mounted near the rifled guns, presumably at the southeast face to command the Old Inlet channel at Bald Head Point. This information matches up with what is known of the distribution and certain lack of traverse circles in the fort when it was seized in April of 1861. Not counting the six carronades, the remaining twenty guns consisted of a mixture of 24 and 32-pounders, categorized as "light," a nonspecific term that clarifies little. The rifled "64-pounder" was obviously the same rifled 8-inch Columbiad sent to General Anderson the previous October. Relying entirely upon the profile of a single surviving rifled 10-inch Confederate Columbiad, cast by Tredegar on 17 October 1861 and now located in Mobile, AL, it has long been accepted that the so-called "hybrid" 5.82-inch and 6.4-inch rifles bored from 8-inch and 10-inch Rodman Pattern 1861 Columbiad blocks were the earliest rifles made by Tredegar. The gun that came into Fort Caswell was invoiced as an "8-in Rifle gun," therefore of the smaller caliber and rifled with six rectangular grooves. [56]

"64-pounder confederate gun at Yorktown, Va., which burst in the effort to reach Federal siege [sic] guns. 1862." So reads the title of this ghostly image. The gun is a 10-inch Columbiad bored to 6.4 inches and rifled, two of which burst during the siege. Yorktown had no 8-inch rifled Columbiads. According to early thinking, rifling a 6.4-inch smoothbore allowed it to fire a bolt twice the 32-pound weight of its smoothbore counterpart. In that sense, the gun in this image is properly attributed. Note the obvious Rodman profile of both the U.S Pattern 1861 and Confederate Columbiads. (Library of Congress, Prints and Photographs Division)

The identification of the large rifled gun as a 64-pounder does not, however, coincide with what is known about the calibers of the time. In the early years of the Civil War, it was theorized that such a gun could fire a *bolt* that was double the weight of a smoothbore shot. Therefore, if a 6.4-inch shot weighed about 32 pounds, wisdom of the day advocated that the maximum weight of a rifle bolt should be 64 pounds. The image preceding and its caption demonstrate just such thinking, which, when applied to Fort Caswell's gun, means that its bolt should have weighed about forty-eight pounds based upon the 24-pound weight of a 5.82-inch shot. How then, did the deserters come to call the big gun a 64-pounder? The answer is almost too simple. [57]

Fort Caswell's parapet was graced with an additional 8-inch Columbiad over and above the June 1861 inventory of three. Calling to mind the presence an "old Columbia" at Fort Fisher in September, 1861, it seems likely that Caswell sent at least one U.S. Pattern 1844 Columbiad to Fisher, which was replaced by two Tredegar C.S. Pattern 1861 Columbiads on 13 January. An 8-inch smoothbore fired a 64-pound solid shot. If the big rifled gun was of the same profile as the new guns, as it almost certainly was, it's understandable how the deserters came to use the caliber of the smoothbore to describe the rifle. [58]

Caswell's five 32-pounder rifles were most certainly the work of the Eason Brothers, most likely the sum total of their rifling efforts on the 32-pounders of the Cape Fear. It is noteworthy that all three of the 8-inch Seacoast Howitzers present in June of 1861 were gone, as were both 8-inch Navy Shell Guns. Exactly where those guns went at this point in the war is strongly suspected, but the certainty is that they remained in the Cape Fear defenses.

Back on February 20, the Tredegar Foundry shipped two 8-inch Siege Howitzers and one 4.62-inch C. S. Siege Rifle to Colonel Fremont. Knowing that the siege rifle was not in Fort Caswell, it must be correctly surmised that it went to Fort Fisher. After all, Caswell already mounted a rifled Columbiad. As for the siege howitzers, surviving photographic evidence proves that at least one of the two served in the fort on Confederate Point. [59]

The 4.62-inch Siege Rifle was not just any old smoothbore 12-pounder manufactured and issued as such and then rifled later. This was one of a group of guns manufactured from 24-pounder iron siege gun blocks cast in molds left over from Tredegar's Pattern 1845 production. Since those rifles, as issued, weighed about 600 pounds less than a 24-pounder siege gun, it's obvious that it would have been necessary to alter the mold to produce a different design altogether. While the profile of the finished product was barely recognizable as that of a 24-pounder, its rounded breech and lack of reinforces gave it a profile more akin to a Dahlgren than to a siege gun. The Cape Fear gun was the fifth gun cast by Tredegar and was therefore most likely rifled with three rectangular grooves, the projectiles for which were pre-engraved by Tredegar in the style of those manufactured for the 5.82-inch rifled Columbiads. [60]

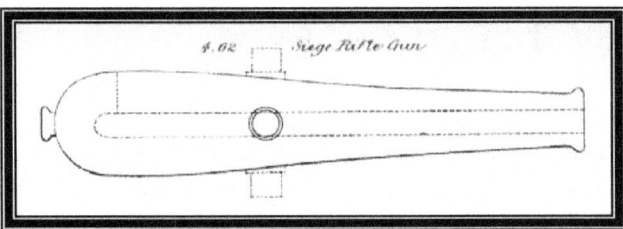

Confederate Siege Rifle 1st Pattern. This plan may be all that survives to show the profile of the first of its kind, a 4.62-inch rifle sculpted from a 24-pounder Siege Gun block. (*Confederate Ordnance Manual*, Plate 1)

4.62-inch Confederate Siege Rifles, at 114 inches long and weighing a little over 5,100 pounds, were capable of pushing a forty pound bolt to a maximum distance of about 2½ miles using a five pound powder charge and 15½° of muzzle elevation. Huge rifled Columbiads, on the other hand, could achieve a maximum range of about four miles using ten pounds of powder behind a 60-pound shell. [61]

Only two siege howitzers known to have been used by the Confederacy survive, but, being of the Pattern of 1840, they are not thought to be of Confederate manufacture. The preceding image of captured Confederate siege howitzers bears a profile more closely resembling that of a U.S. Pattern 1861 8-inch Siege Howitzer, but without the rounded breech and tapered muzzle. [62]

Notwithstanding its smallish length of about 60 inches and weight of around 2100 pounds, the 8-inch Confederate Siege Howitzer could propel a five second fuzed 45-pound shell a distance of 1,150 yards using a four pound propellant charge and 5° of elevation. At an extreme elevation of 12½°, the range increased to 2,280 yards. The ability to engage infantry at long range made the siege howitzer a formidable weapon indeed, but its awesome power was all the more devastating using grapeshot and canister at 400 yards. [63]

Confederate 8-inch Siege Howitzers on siege carriages. (Library of Congress, Prints and Photographs Division)

On April 11, the ferriage company of Orrell & Hawes lightered a "Big Cannon to Fort Fisher," presumably from a much larger vessel. If the assumption is that the contractor was accustomed to the weights of 32-pounders and such, then the likelihood is the gun was an 8-inch Columbiad from a source outside the Cape Fear, its weight being much greater than anything previously handled by them. On the same day, the firm lightered four additional guns to Fort Fisher, seemingly a net gain of five cannon to the sand fort. But was it a net gain or was it a case of upgrading assets and transferring the castoffs? Brunswick Point coincidentally received five guns and the partnership of Orrell & Hawes moved three others, for a total of eight at that maturing work. At this point, it's anyone's guess just which guns were involved, but chances are the transfer theory is valid. [64]

Following is a reasonably credible rendition of an otherwise nonexistent return for the District of the Cape Fear for April, 1862.

April, 1862
Brigadier General Samuel Gibbs French, commanding District of the Cape Fear

Fort Johnston:
    Gatlin Artillery, Captain James S. Lane
    Herring Artillery, Captain William A. Herring
Fort Caswell: Colonel George A. Cunningham
    Scotch Greys, 1st Lieutenant John S. McArthur
    King Artillery, Captain James Martin Stevenson
    Confederates, Captain William S. Devane
    Brunswick Artillery, Captain John Douglas Taylor
    Columbus Artillery, Captain Nathan L. Williamson
Fort Fisher: Major John J. Hedrick
    Bladen Artillery, Captain John A. Richardson
    Bladen Stars, Captain Daniel Munn
    Blocker's Artillery, Captain Octavious H. Blocker
    Starr's Light Battery, Captain Joseph B. Starr
    Captain Henry Harding's Company N. C. Volunteers
    Captain John R. Lanier's (Infantry) Co. N. C. Vols.
    Captain Charles C. Whitehurst's Company
    McMillan Artillery, Captain William H. Tripp
    Robinson Artillery, Captain Edward Mallett
Camp Wyatt:
    20th Regiment N. C. Infantry, Colonel Alfred Iverson
    Captain Elisha A. Perkins' Company of Cavalry
    Captain William C. Howard's Company of Cavalry
Zeek's Island (Winder Battery):
    Anderson Artillery, Captain Edward Dudley
Fort French:
    Washington Grays, Captain Thomas Sparrow

Light House Battery:
    River Guards, Captain Charles D. Ellis
Brunswick Point:
    Bridgers' Artillery, Captain William B. Rodman
    Captain Alexander McRae's Company Heavy Artillery
    1st Co. A, 2nd Reg't N. C. S. T., Capt. Calvin Barnes
    Co. B, 1st Reg't. Maryland Infantry, Capt. C.C. Edelin
Wilmington:
    43rd Reg't, N. C. Infantry, Colonel Thomas S. Kenan
    Lenoir Braves, Captain William Sutton
    Co. E, 30th Reg't. N. C. Infantry, Capt. J.C. McMillan
Camp Morgan:
    51st Regiment, North Carolina Infantry (8 companies), Colonel John Lucas Paul Cantwell
Camp Saunders, Onslow County:
    30th Reg't. N. C. Infantry, Colonel Frances M. Parker
    Captain Atherton B. Hill's Company of Cavalry
    Captain Abram F. Newkirk's Company of Cavalry
    Moore's Battery, Captain Alexander D. Moore
Montfort's Mill, Onslow County:
    Captain Edward W. Ward's Company of Cavalry
Camp Hedrick:
    Cumming's Battery, Captain James D. Cumming
Beach West of Fort Caswell:
    Captain John Galloway's Company, Coast Guards

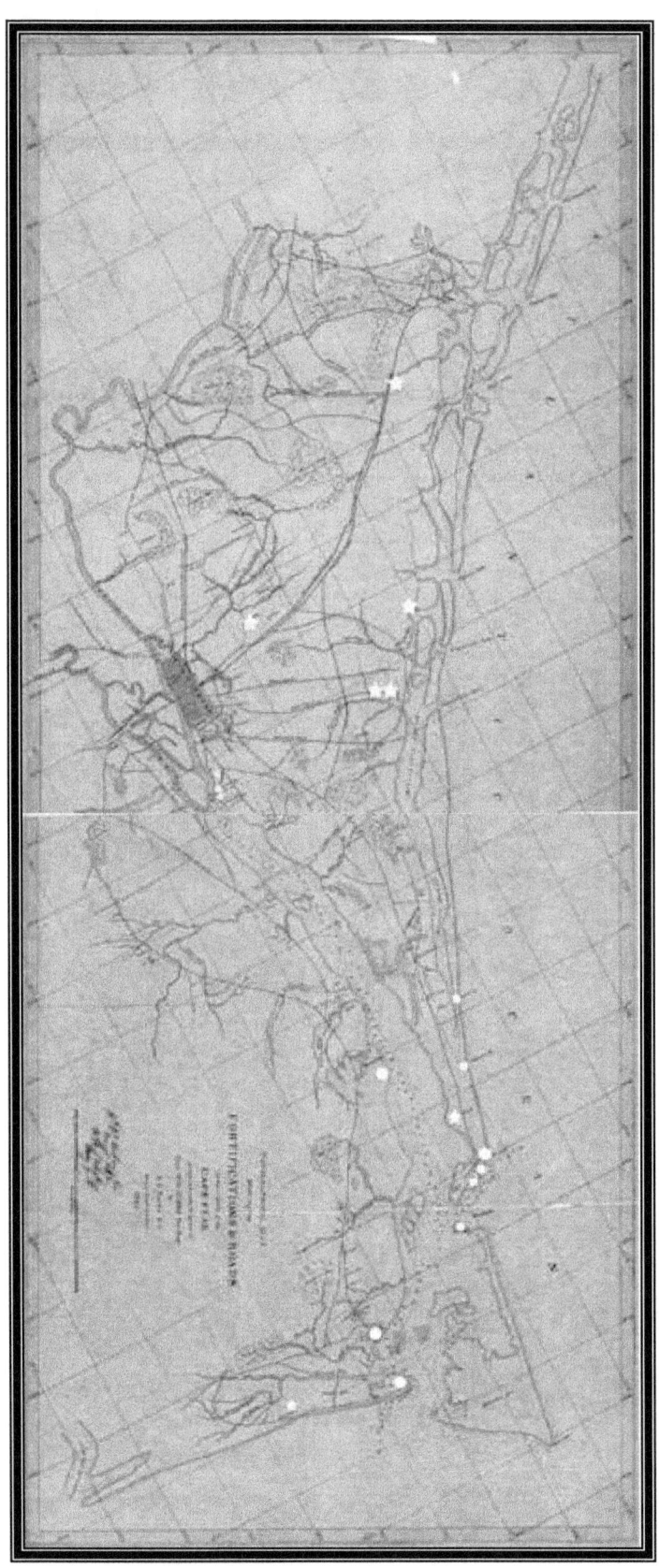

Left: Cape Fear defenses at the end of April, 1862. The three small emplacements below Wilmington are the Light House Battery, Fort French, and Lazaretto Battery. Further downriver on the west side is the site of Fort St. Philip, at this time not much more than a water battery and a line of entrenchments extending from water's edge to Orton Pond. Further down the river, near its mouth, stood Forts Johnston and Caswell, with the Coast Guard company to the west. On the right side of the river, beginning at the bottom of the map, is Winder Battery on Zeek's Island, followed by Battery Bolles and the casemate battery on the peninsula. Above that is the larger Fort Fisher, then the starred Camp Wyatt, followed by Batteries Anderson and Gatlin. Much further above are Camps Davis and Holmes, then Camp Grant, followed by the distant Camp Heath at Scott's Hill. The camp on the plank road to Wilmington is thought to be the site of Camp Hopkins. At this juncture, the expanding defenses are more reflective of fortifying the river first, and then providing an early warning system along the extension of the plank road and at Masonborough Inlet. While there were some entrenchments abutting the east side of the city at this time, they are believed to have been in transition from mere rifle pits to more substantial fortifications mounting cannon. (*Topographic Map Showing the Fortifications and Roads in the Vicinity of the Cape Fear*, Gilmer Papers, SHC, UNC-CH)

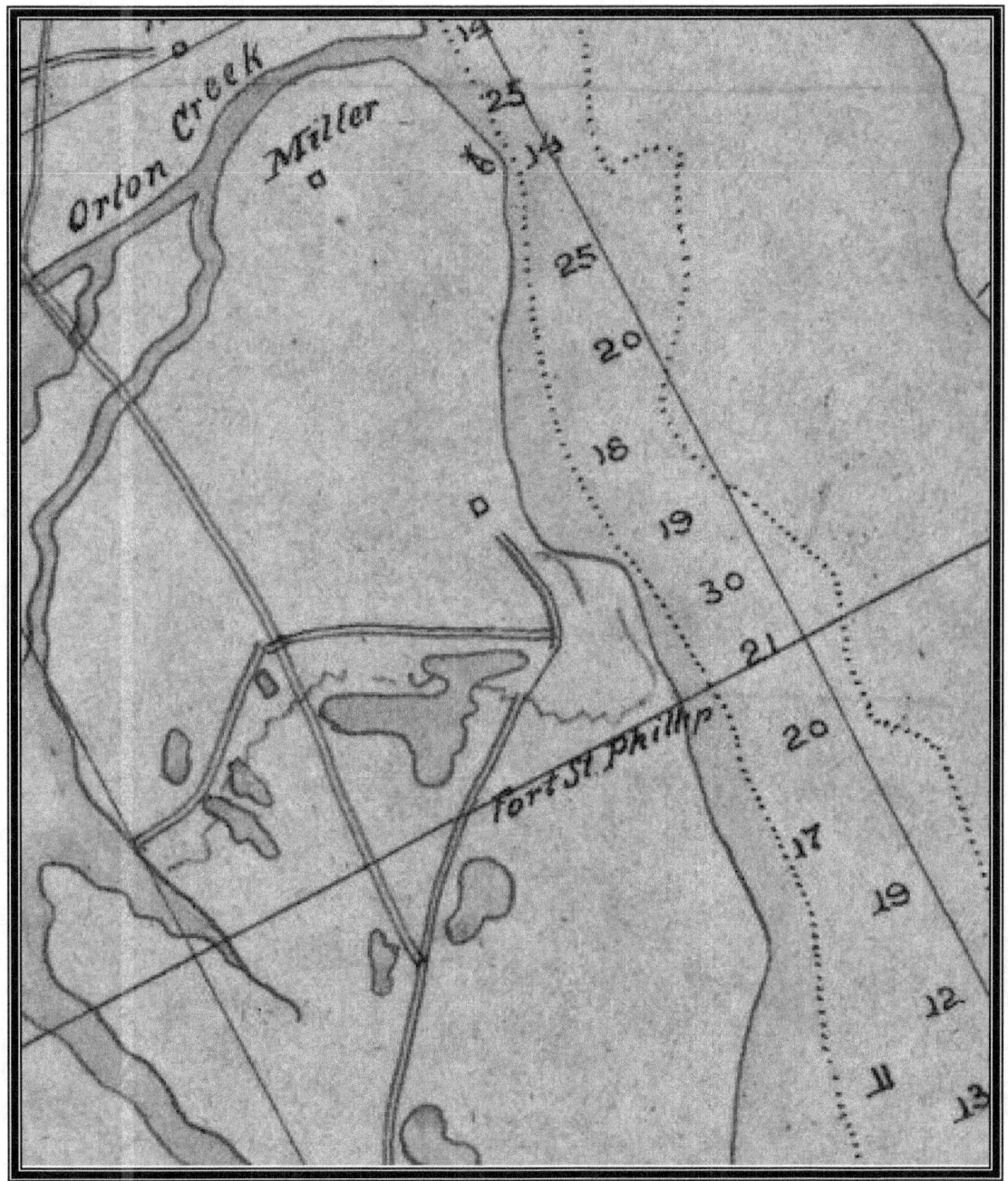

Enlargement of Fort St. Philip's site, with its battery parallel to the river and the line of entrenchments extending inland using several small ponds as obstructions. (*Topographic Map Showing the Fortifications and Roads in the Vicinity of the Cape Fear*, Gilmer Papers, SHC, UNC-CH)

128 | **Guns of the Cape Fear**

The supposed site of Camp Holmes on Watson's Branch and its proximity to Camp Davis. The author believes this camp to also be the site of old Camp Winslow. (*Map of the vicinity of Wilmington*, Gilmer Papers, SHC, UNC-CH)

Locations of the Light House Battery, shown here as Fort Strong; Fort French, shown here as Fort Lee; and Lazaretto Battery, shown here as midway between Fort Lee and Fort Campbell. The date of this map is not known, but chances are it is from 1864, after the names of all the batteries commanding the obstructions in the river had been changed. (*Map of the vicinity of Wilmington*, Gilmer Papers, SHC, UNC-CH)

The cannon in this image bears a strong resemblance to the plan of a 4.62-inch siege rifle bored from a 24-pounder siege gun block as shown in the Confederate Ordnance Manual of 1863. (Library of Congress, Prints and Photographs Division)

Eight

"I commenced the new Fort Fisher..."
Colonel William Lamb

The capitulation of Fort Macon on April 26, 1862 and the loss of 51 guns of heavy caliber struck a nerve with the Confederate command in Wilmington. Macon and Caswell were the only Third System masonry forts in North Carolina and early thinking regarded both to be the most secure of the State's coastal fortifications. The surrender itself was not as much the cause of their consternation as the manner in which it happened. Fort Macon was first invested by Federal troops who then successfully launched their siege operations among the many sand hills before the fort, thus shielding them from defensive artillery fire. [1]

Similarly, the sand hills below Fort Caswell were interposed between its heavily defended gorge and the very point from which a land attack was most likely to emanate. The sand hills offered an open invitation for the Federals to commence regular siege operations with enough shelter to ensure success. The lessons of Fort Macon were not lost on the Confederates in the Cape Fear, however. A little over two weeks after the loss of Fort Macon, Commander James F. Armstrong of the *U. S. S. State of Georgia* observed considerable activity on Oak Island. "The rebels at Fort Caswell are busy strengthening their fortification and leveling the sand hills to the westward of the fort." Private John B. McNeill of the Scotch Greys was one of those rebels. "I must go to work levelling [*sic*] sand hills in a few minutes, which is the worst work I ever did standing in the sunshine which is hot enough to roast an egg." [2]

Work on river fortifications continued apace elsewhere as well. Employing the services of twenty-two free blacks brokered by 44-year-old native of Massachusetts E. A. Keith, Cadet of Engineers Thomas Rowland accumulated 334½ man-days of labor on Brunswick Point by May 14. In fact, it wasn't much longer before he was able to report significant progress. "I have nearly finished the Line of Intrenchments [*sic*]; it is almost a mile in length, extending from the Battery on the river to a pond eight miles in length." Rowland also had a new name in mind for the fledgling fort. "On our line of defences is an old church one hundred and fifty years old. It was the church of the Parish of St. Phillip in the old colonial days, and has already witnessed the struggles of one revolution. We think of calling our battery Fort St. Phillip." [3]

Private Hugh McGoogan and the rest of the men of Company D, 51st North Carolina Infantry were "down 4 miles below Wilmington a building and [sic] iron battery." A casemated battery of wood was in place adjacent to Fort Fisher, but Lazaretto Battery's iron casemate was the first of its type, one that would grow in popularity with some engineers. The river duty seemed to agree with more than just a few of McGoogan's fellow soldiers. "We are all enjoying ourselves finely down here at work on the river building a battery and putting up guns to kill the Yankees with," said Private William Scott Conoly. The first two of those guns, with carriages, arrived at Lazaretto Battery on May 22 aboard a lighter operated by Orrell & Hawes of Wilmington.[4]

The line of entrenchments on the east side of the town of Wilmington had advanced from little more than unmanned rifle pits in February to an extensive entrenched camp in May, preordained to mount significant numbers of cannon. The sheer size and scope of the planned defenses called for a garrison not only trained in infantry tactics, but artillery drill as well. Heavy artillery units, as usual, were the only organizations with the necessary skills to perform both artillery and infantry duties, but there weren't nearly enough of those to spread around. No longer able to solve the problem by transfers, General French did the next best thing – he hastened the muster of troops undergoing the organization process during the month of May.[5]

- 10th Battalion North Carolina Heavy Artillery, Major Wilton L. Young - Entrenched Camp at Wilmington.[6]
    Company A, Capt. William B. Lewis[7]
    Company B, Capt. Henry M. Barnes[8]
    Company C, Capt. Chas. M. T. McCauley[9]
- Clark Artillery, Captain Robert G. Rankin - Entrenched Camp at Wilmington[10]
- River Guards, Captain Charles D. Ellis - Light House Battery.[11]
- Lamb Artillery, Captain Francis W. Potter - Fort St. Philip.[12]
- Clarendon Guards, Captain Daniel Patterson - Fort St. Philip.[13]
- Bladen Artillery Guards, Captain George Tait - Fort St. Philip.[14]

- Co. K, 51st Regiment North Carolina Infantry, Captain J. B. Underwood - Camp Holmes.[15]

Transfers into, around, and out of the Cape Fear in May, more numerous than the musters, changed the landscape of the military complex, but did little to strengthen it.

- 2nd Regiment North Carolina Infantry, Colonel Charles C. Tew - Wayne County to Camp Wyatt.[16]
- Staunton Hill Artillery, Captain Andrew B. Paris - Goldsborough and Savannah to Camp Hedrick.[17]
- Gatlin Artillery, Captain James S. Lane - Fort Johnston to Fort Fisher.[18]
- Capt. Alexander McRae's Company Heavy Artillery – Brunswick Point to Fort Fisher.[19]
- Pamlico Artillery, Captain Samuel B. Hunter - Brunswick Point to Fort Caswell.[20]
- 11th Regiment North Carolina Infantry, Colonel Collett Leventhorpe - Camp Mangum near Raleigh to Camp Davis.[21]
- 20th Regiment North Carolina Infantry, Colonel Alfred Iverson - Camp Wyatt to Fort Johnston.[22]
- 30th Regiment North Carolina Infantry, Colonel Frances M. Parker - Onslow County to Camp Lamb.[23]
- 51st Regiment North Carolina Infantry, Colonel John Lucas Paul Cantwell - Camp Morgan to Camp Holmes thence to Camp Davis.[24]
- Company D, 51st Regiment North Carolina Infantry, Captain James R. McDonald - Camp Davis to Lazaretto Battery.[25]
- Company A, 51st Regiment North Carolina Infantry, Captain George F. Walker - Camp Davis to Lazaretto Battery.[26]
- Captain Alexander D. Moore's Battery - Onslow County to Camp Davis.[27]

The 36th Regiment North Carolina Troops (2nd Artillery) had been in existence since 1861, but no regimental officers had ever been elected or commissioned, its existence notable only on paper. On May 12, 1862, General French issued Special Orders No. 247, which officially organized ten companies of heavy artillery within the Cape Fear defenses into the 36th Regiment and directed company officers to meet at Fort Caswell to elect the regimental staff. Two days later, the meeting was held and Major William Lamb was elected Colonel. John Douglas Taylor of the Brunswick Artillery was elected Major of the Regiment and John A. Richardson of the Bladen Artillery was elected as its Lieutenant Colonel. [28]

Colonel Lamb and his fledgling staff assumed command at Brunswick Point and promptly renamed the post Fort St. Philip, honoring the colonial church of that name located within its lines. Despite the formal designations bestowed upon them, the companies of the 36th Regiment continued to function as unattached units, most of them retaining their informal designations, more for brevity and convenience than for any other reason. Lamb's regiment, in spite of the rush to organization, would not undergo official muster until more than two years later. [29]

- ❖ King Artillery, 2nd Co. A
- ❖ Bladen Stars, 3rd Co. B
- ❖ Blocker's Artillery, 2nd Co. C
- ❖ Anderson Artillery, 2nd Co. D
- ❖ Columbus Artillery, Co. E
- ❖ Pamlico Artillery, Co. F
- ❖ Lamb Artillery, 3rd Co. G
- ❖ Clarendon Guards, Co. H
- ❖ Bladen Artillery, 2nd Co. I
- ❖ Brunswick Artillery, Co. K [30]

Colonel William Lamb, PACS. (Courtesy North Carolina Historical Sites – Fort Fisher, North Carolina)

Life wasn't exactly a bed of roses in the Cape Fear forts, at least in Fort Caswell. "The rats got into the cistern in such quantities that the water tastes and smells very strong of the little "devils" which everybody knows is far from being pleasant," complained the Scotch Greys' John B. McNeill. The disgruntled private also offered a disparaging assessment of the drinking water on Oak Island. "Our well water is also of the worst description worse than any mud hole in the cypress ponds about Uncle William's." [31]

The occasional appearance of a U. S. Navy blockader offered a welcome respite from the drudgery of daily drills, often to the amusement of the garrison. "Yesterday morning while our company was drilling on the cannons the blockade [had] the impudence to attempt to scare us down by firing a shell at us but the shell did not come over half way to us and we kept on as if nothing had happened," scoffed McNeill. At about the same time, the Private heard firing in the direction of Captain Galloway's camp below the fort. "The blockade is firing rapidly at the cast [sic] guard about three miles from here." [32]

During Fort Caswell's attempt to prevent the U.S. Navy from boarding the grounded schooner *Emily* on June 26, 1862, Private William W. Lewis of the Brunswick Artillery was "killed by explosion of rifled Columbiad." Fellow Privates Duncan T. Johnson and William T. Padgett of the King Artillery died alongside their battery mate. According to Commander O. S. Glisson, U.S.N., the Federal tars "boarded her under a heavy fire of shell from rifle cannon on Fort Caswell." This unfortunate incident followed similar failures of Tredegar Foundry rifled Columbiads at other notable fortifications, the most significant of which were reported at Yorktown. Those and other instances of bursting led to cessation of production of such pieces in favor of smaller caliber, lighter guns of siege classification. [33]

The high command in Wilmington lost more personnel in June and July of 1862 than it gained. Another round of transfers to the Army of Northern Virginia occasioned a corresponding bout of internal transfers to bolster the depleted Cape Fear garrisons.

- 2nd Regiment North Carolina State Troops, Colonel Charles C. Tew - Camp Wyatt to Richmond. [34]
- 20th Regiment North Carolina Troops, Colonel Alfred Iverson - Fort Johnston to Richmond. [35]
- 30th Regiment North Carolina Troops, Colonel Francis M. Parker - Camp Lamb to Richmond. [36]
- Captain William C. Howard's Local Defense Company of Cavalry mustered out of service at Camp Wyatt. [37]
- Captain Atherton B. Hill's Company of Cavalry - Camp Saunders to Camp Wyatt. [38]
- Captain Elisha A. Perkins' Company of Cavalry - Camp Wyatt to Onslow County. [39]
- 43rd Regiment North Carolina Infantry, Colonel Thomas S. Kenan - Wilmington to Petersburg. [40]
- Company K, 51st North Carolina Infantry, Captain J. B. Underwood - Camp Holmes to Lazaretto Battery. [41]
- Company A, 51st Regiment North Carolina Infantry, Captain George F. Walker - Lazaretto Battery to Camp Davis. [42]
- 51st Regiment North Carolina Infantry, Colonel John Lucas Paul Cantwell - Camp Davis to Camp French thence to Fort Johnston. [43]
- 11th Regiment North Carolina Infantry, Colonel Collett Leventhorpe - Camp Davis to Camp Wyatt thence to Camp Lamb. [44]
- Captain Alexander D. Moore's Battery - from Camp Davis to Rock Spring, thence to Camp Jones. [45]
- Lenoir Braves, Captain William Sutton Wilmington to Fort Fisher. [46]
- Captain E.F. Shaw's Company of Confederate Volunteers - Clinton, N.C. to Camp Wyatt. [47]
- Captain A. B. Hill's Scotland Neck Mounted Rifles - Camp Wyatt to Camp Davis. [48]
- Captain Henry Harding's Company North Carolina Volunteers - Fort Fisher to Wilmington. [49]
- Captain William B. Lanier's Co. (Hill Guards) North Carolina Infantry - Fort Fisher to Wilmington. [50]
- Captain John F. Moore's Company of North Carolina Volunteers - Wilmington to "Camp of Instruction" near Wilmington. [51]

The first six months of 1862 saw great change in the District of the Cape Fear in both ordnance and fortifications, but the single most important change was an influx of personnel that permitted autonomous self-defense to predominate the doctrine of reliance upon infantry supports. A new policy of mustering in numerous unattached companies trained in both infantry and artillery tactics to garrison the various fortifications all but eliminated the rampant conscription of North Carolina's regimental-size units by the Army of Northern Virginia. The vexing lessons learned from the abduction of the 2nd State Troops and the 18th, 20th, 25th, 28th, 30th, and 43rd North Carolina Infantry Regiments were manifest in the words of the departed Brigadier General, Richard C. Gatlin, when he said, "We will have to fight our own battles." [52]

Cognizant of the ongoing inability of the C. S. Ordnance Department to provide guns of long range, General French decided to take matters into his own hands. "My guns are so light that I am now preparing to rifle and band them as far as possible here in the city." One prerequisite for the banding process was a supply of forged bands, four to a gun. Technical work such as this required the services of a large forge, which was apparently not available in Wilmington, thereby compelling their importation. The first twelve of those bands were ordered from the Tredegar Iron Works, but far more pressing matters at that distinguished manufactory would delay their delivery. [53]

Somewhere near noon on the fourth of July, Colonel William Lamb received an unexpected order from General French to report to Fort Fisher and relieve Major John Jackson Hedrick of command, at the latter officer's own request. Presumably leaving Lieutenant Colonel John A. Richardson of the 36th Regiment in command of Fort St. Philip, Colonel Lamb departed for Fort Fisher and before the sun had set on Confederate Point that day, Lamb had inspected the works. He came away with the impression that follows, and it wasn't altogether positive. [54]

They then consisted of, first, a recently erected

work, with two guns, called Shepperd's [sic] Battery. It was on the extreme left and faced the sea, its rear being close to the river shore. Next, towards the sea, came a quadrilateral field work known as Fort Fisher. It was a small work, part of it constructed of perishable sandbags, and its longest face was about one hundred yards. Out of its half dozen large guns, only the two 8-inch Columbiads were suitable for seacoast defence. One of the Federal frigates could have cleaned it out with a few broadsides. Next to this on its right, facing the sea and opposite the bar, came a very handsome and creditable casemated battery of four 8-inch Columbiads, called after Captain Meade. It was constructed of turfed sand over a heavy timber framework, the embrasures of palmetto. Colonel Fremont has informed me since the war, that he designed this work. A one-gun battery stood to the right of this, well out on the seashore. It was called Cumberland Battery and contained a long-ranged rifle-gun, the only piece of modern ordnance on Confederate Point. To the right and rear of this and some two hundred yards apart, were two batteries, each having two barbette guns of modern calibre, one called the Bolles and the other I called Hedrick Battery, after the former gallant commander of the Fort. There was, besides these batteries, a large commissary bomb proof. There were only seventeen guns of respectable calibre, including 32-pounders. There was on Zeke's Island a small two-gun battery . . . [A]s a defence of New Inlet against a Federal fleet, our work amounted to nothing.

It is important to first establish the number of guns in Colonel Lamb's new command before any attempt can be made to precisely define their patterns and calibers. It seems straightforward enough that he deemed seventeen cannon as pieces of respectable caliber, implying that there may have been more guns of inferior caliber. All well and good, except for his later assertion, "Fort Fisher was a small work which, together with adjoining batteries, mounted seventeen guns, only three of heavy calibre. Zeke's [sic] Island had two 32-pounders." The Colonel's choice of words on this later occasion effectively alters the historical perspective on the armament protecting Confederate Point when he assumed command. After all, it may be recollected there were 25 heavy guns and four field pieces in Fort Fisher and its several associated batteries back in January, with the fort reportedly accounting for twelve 32-pounders. Interestingly, eyewitnesses of the U.S. Navy reported the presence of about the same number of guns as Colonel Lamb, but in Fort Fisher only. [55]

While anchored under a flag of truce within 1,000 yards of the works on Confederate Point, Lieutenant Daniel L. Braine of USS *Monticello* had at least an hour to examine them in detail. "The enemy have one open earthwork battery mounting eighteen guns, apparently 32-pounders; also an earth casemate pierced for six guns . . . also two small batteries some distance to the left, of three guns each." Commander O.S. Glisson, U.S.N., more or less corroborated Braine's conclusions. "We have thrown a number of shells into the fort on Federal Point, which has about 20 guns and 1,000 men." [56]

The U.S. Navy's observations, though, were from a distance. Eyewitness accounts from those that served there seem to be the better evidence. According to one soldier that toiled in the forts and batteries on Confederate Point, "We built Fort Fisher with seventeen guns and curtains connecting with some outlying batteries." It seems that Colonel Lamb's original assertion was the more correct. Accepting seventeen as the number of guns in Fort Fisher and then using the Colonel's count in the associated batteries, the most credible inventory of the ordnance on Confederate Point may have been twenty-eight guns, with two 32-pounders mounted in Battery Winder on Zeek's Island. [57]

At this point, identification of the artillery pieces within Lamb's new command can only be derived from an analysis of the terms he used to describe them. The Colonel was an educated man, one who chose his words carefully in his description of the cannon under his jurisdiction. Terms like *modern ordnance, modern caliber, heavy caliber,* and *large guns* are needful of further study in order to understand the nature of Confederate Point's ordnance.

Cumberland Battery was home to a gun of new design and manufacture, the large 4.62-inch Siege Rifle shipped to Colonel Fremont from the Tredegar Iron Works on February 22, 1862. Colonel Lamb referred to it as "the only piece of modern ordnance on Confederate Point," a very specific term used to distinguish a specific piece of ordnance from all the others. It's safe to assume that he regarded modern ordnance to be exclusive of any and all old patterns then in use by the Confederates, in addition to, as it will be amply demonstrated later on, old patterns of new manufacture by the Confederacy. The formidable siege gun was deployed in a very different type of battery, one as yet unseen in the Cape Fear defenses. "Outside the sea front, near the ocean, I sunk a pit, as deep as admissible," said General French of the only true water battery then on Confederate Point. Mounted nearly at sea level, the big gun was in a position to achieve the best prospect for successful ricochet fire on enemy shipping.[58]

To the right of Cumberland Battery and a bit further down the beach was Battery Bolles and about a hundred yards below that was Battery Hedrick, each of which mounted "two barbette guns of modern calibre." Once again, Colonel Lamb used the word *modern*, but instead of using the term *ordnance*, he selected the word *caliber* to describe the guns. All smoothbore calibers within the Cape Fear defenses predated the Civil War, so the Colonel must have been referring to a rifle caliber, of which there were three: 6.4-inch in either old 32-pounder or new 10-inch Columbiad tubes; 5.82-inch cut into either new 8-inch Columbiad or old 24-pounder barrels; and 4.62-inch in old 12-pounder guns or new 24-pounder gun blocks. Significantly, two 32-pounder rifled guns were ordered to Fort Fisher on May 22 by General Robert E. Lee, thereby positively establishing the caliber of two of the rifles in Batteries Hedrick and Bolles. Insofar as the third and fourth rifles in the distant batteries are concerned, surviving map evidence suggests that they too were 32-pounders rifled to 6.4-inch caliber.[59]

In his description of Fort Fisher, the Colonel indicated that the works mounted six large guns, and then, in the same breath, he opined that only the two 8-inch Columbiads had sufficient range to threaten U.S. Navy warships. It would appear he believed anything larger than a 32-pounder to be a large gun. Using that definition, then, Fort Fisher held six cannon of 8-inch bore, that being the only caliber then in the Cape Fear defenses larger than a 32-pounder.[60]

Lamb was specific in his identification of two of the 8-inch guns in Fort Fisher as Columbiads, but he didn't use the words *modern ordnance* with regard to them, an expected term had they been newly designed and manufactured C.S. Pattern 1861 Columbiads. In fact, on 9 April 1901 Colonel Lamb asserted that only three guns in Fort Fisher and its adjoining batteries could be labeled *heavy caliber*, referring, of course, to the two Columbiads and the 4.62-inch Siege Rifle. Exactly which Columbiad pattern rested in Fort Fisher can best be decided by identifying the pattern that was mounted in Battery Meade, since they too were Columbiads, according to Colonel Lamb.[61]

Casemated Battery Meade mounted four 8-inch Columbiads, pieces that were called neither *heavy caliber* nor *modern ordnance* by the Colonel. Seemingly, the opinion was shared by the soldiers that served them. Thaddeus C. Davis of the McMillan Artillery reported to Fort Fisher in April and found "one casemated battery of four or five Columbiad guns of short range, and a square Sand Fort, armed with 32-pounder, smooth bore guns." Thomas F. Wood of the 8th Regiment, recalling September of 1861, later said, "At that time they were just building the casement [sic] guns, those we exercised upon were old Columbia [sic] **en barbette.**" For knowledgeable men to say as much is to imply that the big guns were chambered pieces, capable of short range only using diminished powder charges. By implication, then, the casemate guns in Battery Meade were U.S. Pattern 1844 Columbiads, three from Fort Caswell and a fourth added from outside the Cape Fear, most likely Charleston, South Carolina.[62]

If there is a distinction to be made between an

8-inch Columbiad of heavy caliber and one of light caliber, the chambered Pattern 1844 would be the top qualifier for the latter category. It was a decidedly fragile cannon that was relegated to the role of a shell gun shortly after the New Columbiad was introduced in 1857. Capable of safely firing reduced loads only, the gun couldn't propel a solid shot far enough to be effective in a seacoast defense role. If the Columbiads in Fort Fisher were of heavy caliber but not modern ordnance, then they were of neither the new C.S. Pattern 1861 nor the chambered Pattern 1844. Such an assumption narrows the possibilities to just one – the unchambered U.S. Pattern 1857 Columbiad, a conclusion supported by surviving photographic evidence. [63]

Two 8-inch Siege Howitzers shipped by the Tredegar Iron Works to Colonel Fremont on February 22 were probably still at Fort Fisher as part of Lamb's half dozen large guns. Mindful that Fort Caswell had divested itself of its U.S. Pattern 1839 or 1840 Seacoast Howitzers and its 8-inch Navy Shell Guns by April past, the other two large guns in Fisher were of the latter type. Once again, photographic evidence exists to support these conclusions. [64]

According to General French, there were only eight Columbiads in the Cape Fear defenses at the time of Lamb's ascent to command. With two U.S. Pattern 1857 Columbiads in Fort Fisher and four Columbiads in the casemate battery, only two then remained to defend Fort Caswell's gorge, both of them undoubtedly Confederate Columbiads. [65]

Mysterious can hardly describe the placement and orientation of Shepherd's Battery in 1862. Engineering intent cannot be divined, but it appears the purpose was flank defense of the land face of Fort Fisher. From Lamb's account, the battery would have been about 500 to 600 yards distant from the west flank of the fort, well outside the effective range of canister yet near enough for everything else in the Confederate magazines. Unsaid by Colonel Lamb, the two guns in Shepherd's battery were undoubtedly either Navy 32-pounders or ancient 24-pounders, survivors of the early 1800's.

Whitworth 2.75-inch (12-pounder) breechloading rifle. (Library of Congress, Prints and Photographs Division)

On the night of June 26, 1862, the British steamer *Modern Greece* grounded about ¾ mile off Fort Fisher. Sunk by the guns of the fort to prevent her capture, the coveted cargo consisted of liquor, medicine, powder, 7,000 stand of small arms, and, to the great delight of all concerned, "four 12-pounder Whitworth rifle-guns." If only temporarily, the liquor was saved first, but the heavy lifting was left for Colonel Lamb and his troops. He was rewarded by the assignment of two of the breech-loading British rifles to Fort Fisher. The other two rifles, in the company of a detachment from "Starr's Light Battery," were sent to Fort Caswell in defense of the entrance to the river. [66]

Already capable of hurling a twelve pound projectile out to an average range of 4,000 yards using a powder charge of 1¾ pounds and muzzle elevation of 10 degrees, the Whitworth's range of lethality could be increased to about five miles by elevating the muzzle to 25° and leaving the powder charge unchanged. This, the homeliest of cannon, would soon provide the motivation for the blockading fleet to maintain a respectable distance from the North Carolina coastline. [67]

Colonel Collett Leventhorpe, PACS
(*Confederate Military History*, Volume IV)

Brigadier General Samuel G. French's tenure of command in Wilmington was a busy one and his accomplishments many. He presided over the muster and/or transfer into his District of untold unattached heavy artillery companies, one heavy artillery battalion, and several infantry regiments. He was responsible for advancing the works at Fort St. Philip, Fort French, Light House Battery, and Lazaretto Battery, not to mention improving Wilmington's land defenses from a long line of entrenchments to a series of artillery batteries interconnected by breastworks. Under General French's supervision and direction, Fort Fisher was enlarged, with part of its construction effected in a very inventive way:

Commencing at the right of the casemate battery, I caused a line of revetment to be put up, extending parallel with the ocean, a distance of perhaps half a mile; knowing the winds would blow the sands up and make a glacis in front; and so the windstorms blew thousands of tons of sand, forming a smooth slope to the seashore.

Photographic evidence suggests that those early revetments may have been erected by stacking hardened marsh sod, a material easily harvested from adjacent marshes on the Cape Fear River. [68]

Unluckily for the District of the Cape Fear, Brigadier General Samuel Gibbs French was called to Petersburg, Virginia by General Holmes on July 15 to "assume command of the department." In June, Holmes' Department of North Carolina had been "extended to the south bank of the James River, including Drewry's Bluff." It's clear the order's intent was for General French to assume command of the Petersburg defenses, since Major General Daniel Harvey Hill was "assigned to the command of the division and district lately commanded by Major-General Holmes" on 17 July. Holmes, as it turned out, had been reassigned to command the troubled Trans-Mississippi Department. [69]

Colonel Collett Leventhorpe of the Eleventh Regiment North Carolina Infantry, by virtue of his date of rank, assumed command of the troops in Wilmington. Colonel Leventhorpe was senior to Colonel Cunningham at Fort Caswell, but there is some indication that the latter officer was officially in command of the Cape Fear defenses during the last three days of July. [70]

With the transfer of General French, and for reasons known only to the Confederate high command in Richmond, the District of the Cape Fear ceased to be referred to as such. Loss of District status brought with it a time of confusion and inattention to the details of fortifying the river defenses. It was also a time of uncertainty of command, featuring a revolving door for generals utterly unfamiliar with the defensive scheme devised by Whiting and Gatlin, and then later refined and improved upon by Generals Anderson and French. Given the intricacy and extent of the burgeoning defensive complex, the learning curve was just too steep.

Brigadier General Thomas Lanier Clingman, PACS (*Confederate Military History*, Volume IV, p. 296)

On August 18, Brigadier General Thomas Lanier Clingman received orders "to assume command of the troops at Wilmington." The multi-faceted order was issued by Major General D. H. Hill, commanding the "District of North Carolina." Included in Hill's directive was an unusual order. He actually relieved himself of the district's command and went on to name Brigadier General James Green Martin as his replacement. This is the first official indication that the Old North State had been downgraded from a department to a district, the limits of which "extended from the right banks of the Roanoke to the South Carolina line." [71]

General Clingman, apparently recuperating from foot surgery in Goldsboro, didn't report to Wilmington immediately. The truth of the matter is that it wasn't much before his successor was named on September 3 that he took the reins, having had the luxury of calling upon the very considerable military talents of Colonel Collett Leventhorpe. Brigadier General Gabriel J. Rains was the man ordered to assume command in Wilmington, but he didn't arrive until September 19, just in time to discover that an epidemic might be brewing in the headquarters city. All things considered, General Clingman probably had little, if anything, to do with advancing the defenses of the Cape Fear River. [72]

The outbreak of yellow fever in Wilmington in the summer of 1862 has been attributed to its importation from Nassau on board the steamer *Kate*. Even though the ship arrived in the port city on August 6, evidence suggests that cases had appeared among civilians and the soldiery as early as July, but wasn't immediately recognized as yellow fever. The topic of the epidemic's onset has been discussed among physicians since that time, as has the question of whether or not the spread of the disease could have been an interpersonal event. The common beliefs were that the illness was spread by contact and that the steamer *Kate* began it all, but the scientific study of the epidemic since then suggests that neither premise is accurate. From a strictly historical perspective, it's important to know that the yellow fever probably assailed the Cape Fear region well before the *Kate* made her appearance at the Wilmington docks. [73]

With the introduction of the Whitworth guns into the Cape Fear defenses, military strategy soon evolved into one that would come to define Wilmington's role in the Civil War. The long-range capabilities of the Whitworth afforded military authorities the luxury of offensive action against the blockading fleet, thus establishing the Cape Fear River as a haven for blockade runners.

It all began on August 5, 1862. 1st Lieutenant Thomas C. Fuller led a detachment of Starr's battery to a point about three miles north of Fort Fisher, where they attacked two unsuspecting blockading vessels of the U.S. Navy, engaging them for about 30 minutes. A precipitous retreat by the Federal vessels was reported to be the result of the action. Then, on August 9, it was Captain Starr's turn to lead a detachment up the beach to attack a solitary enemy steamer with two Whitworths. The outcome on this occasion was uncertain, it being early dawn and the effect of the nine shots taken by the Confederates not visible. Those two seemingly inconsequential actions led one U.S. Navy officer to issue a warning of things to come. "The rebels are very active in strengthening their fortifications, and have on the New Inlet side, and probably on this, rifle guns of great range." [74]

Brigadier General Gabriel James Rains, PACS
(*Confederate Military History*, Volume IV, p. 296)

Aside from the very considerable marching and countermarching of infantry regiments, there were but few troop movements in the Cape Fear defenses from July 1862 through the end of the year. To understate the case, more troops left the district that entered it. The intra-district transfers were more of a rotational nature than strategic and served only to garrison vacated duty stations critical to the defenses, leaving the rest bereft of manpower.

- 11th Regiment North Carolina Troops, Colonel Collett Leventhorpe - Wilmington to Franklin, Virginia. [75]
- 51st Regiment North Carolina Troops, Colonel John Lucas Paul Cantwell - Fort Johnston to Kinston. [76]
- 56th Regiment North Carolina Infantry, Colonel Paul F. Faison - Camp Mangum near Raleigh to Camp Badger (near Camp Wyatt), thence to Goldsborough. [77]
- 61st Regiment North Carolina Infantry, Colonel James D. Radcliffe - Camp Lamb to Kinston. [78]
- Starr's Light Battery, Captain Joseph B. Starr Fort Fisher to Kinston. [79]
- Captain Alexander D. Moore's Battery - Camp Jones to Northeastern North Carolina. [80]
- Cumming's Battery, Captain James D. Cumming - Camp Hedrick to Eastern North Carolina. [81]
- Captain E.F. Shaw's Company of Confederate Cavalry - Camp Wyatt to Garysburg. [82]
- Captain Elisha A. Perkins' Company of Cavalry - Onslow County to Garysburg. [83]
- Lamb Artillery, Captain Francis W. Potter - Fort St. Philip to Fort Caswell. [84]
- Columbus Artillery, Captain Oliver H. Powell Fort Caswell to Fort St. Philip. [85]
- Captain Benjamin Smith's Company of Cavalry - Camp Davis to Camp Badger (near Camp Wyatt). [86]
- Bladen Artillery Guards, Captain George Tait Fort St. Philip to Camp Wyatt, thence to Fort Fisher. [87]
- Company A, 10th Battalion North Carolina Heavy Artillery, Captain William B. Lewis Wilmington Defenses to Camp French. [88]
- Gatlin Artillery, Captain James S. Lane - Fort Fisher to Zeek's Island. [89]
- Anderson Artillery, Captain Edward B. Dudley Zeek's Island to Fort Fisher. [90]
- Andrews' Battery, Captain William S. G. Andrews - Exchanged Fort Macon Prisoners of War to Wilmington City Garrison. [91]
- Adams' Battery, Captain Zachariah T. Adams Camp Johnston (near Kinston) to Camp Holmes Landing. [92]

After more than a year of service for many of its companies, the 41st Regiment, North Carolina State Troops mustered into Confederate service on September 3, 1862. Also known as the 3rd

North Carolina Cavalry, the companies would continue to serve in a detached status with a variety of commands. Of greatest importance to the Cape Fear were the companies commanded by Captains Abram W. Newkirk, Benjamin G. Smith (vice Captain Atherton B. Hill), and Edward W. Ward. Those units had served the district since their organization and were well acquainted with the duties required of them. [93]

As the yellow fever continued its lethal march through the streets of Wilmington, work came to a halt in the defenses. The Wilmington Iron Works stopped production of a pile driver it was building for the government in mid-August. Begun in late May, the equipment's intended use was the installation of permanent obstructions in the Cape Fear River, commanded by Light House Battery and Fort French. [94]

The yellow fever scourge was also culpable in the curtailment of construction on a pair of C.S. Navy ironclad rams at Wilmington's docks. The ironclads were intended to operate against the blockading fleet, as well as within the confines of the river, should the Federals manage to pass the fortifications at Old and New Inlets. When completed, the hope was that *C.S.S. Raleigh* and *C.S.S. North Carolina* would offer a significant threat to the blockaders, one that Washington could ill afford to ignore. [95]

Although Wilmington sustained 1,505 cases resulting in 680 deaths from the epidemic's inception through November 17, 1862, it seems that no such statistic exists for deaths within the military establishment, per se. Whatever the reason, the specific attributions to death from yellow fever in the official records are far less prevalent than those attributed to "fever," "typhoid," or even the less definitive "disease." The lack of specific references to yellow fever as the cause of death in soldier fatalities may be due to the quarantine of Wilmington by Colonel Leventhorpe. However misguided it may have been, limiting access to human contact saved the lives of a good number of the region's fighting men by keeping them away from the true source of the pestilence - the tainted ecosystem. [96]

Their betterment restrained by the tiniest of organisms on one hand, and lately by leadership unfamiliar with fortifications on the other, the defenses lay in stasis, awaiting a savior. They wouldn't have much longer to wait. The yellow fever epidemic had not yet abated when the Adjutant and Inspector General's Office issued this order:

> Brig. Gen. W. H. C. Whiting is assigned specially to the defense of the Cape Fear River. He will proceed to Wilmington, N. C., and enter upon that duty.

It's difficult to imagine just how pleased the denizens of Wilmington must have been with the news. Whiting was, by marriage, one of their own – a respected engineer who served them first in a uniform of blue, left them for a time, and then returned clad in gray to be the architect of the city's defenses. The blueprint was his, one that was refined and prosecuted by a long line of successors after he was called to the sanguinary battlefields of Virginia. [97]

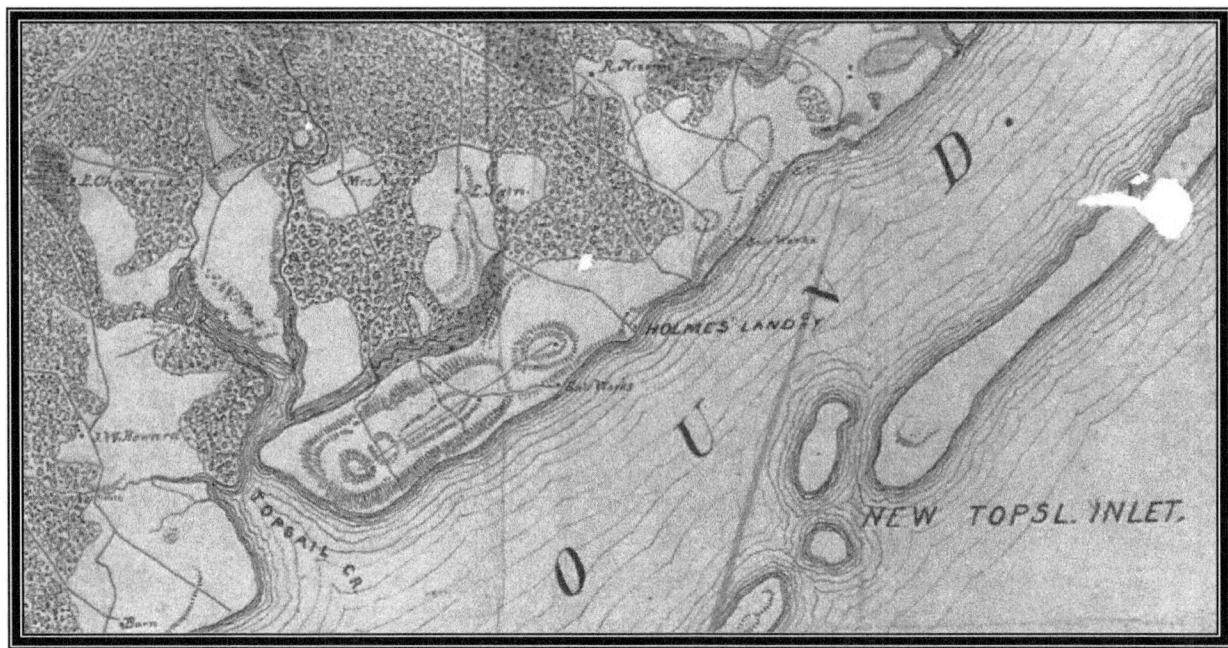

Camp Holmes Landing on Topsail Sound across from New Topsail Inlet., the duty station of Adams' Battery. This, the northernmost outpost in the immediate Cape Fear defenses, provided an early warning capability for Fort Fisher and Wilmington. (*Map of country between N. E. Cape Fear River and Topsail Sound*, Gilmer Papers, SHC, UNC-CH)

Camp Jones on Collins Creek, Myrtle Sound. On or adjacent to the Jones property is believed to have been the camp of Moore's Battery, even if for a short time. Located in a position to respond to emergencies in any direction, this camp was seldom used after Captain Moore and his men left the Cape Fear for eastern North Carolina. (*Map of Confederate Point, New Hanover Co., N.C.*, Gilmer Papers, SHC, UNC-CH)

Land defenses of Wilmington. The batteries and entrenchments are seen as an irregular line extending from Green's Old Mill Pond on the south side of the town to a point a little above Dam No. 4 on the east side. (*Map of parts of Brunswick and New Hanover Counties showing the approaches to Wilmington, N.C.*, Gilmer Papers, SHC, UNC-CH)

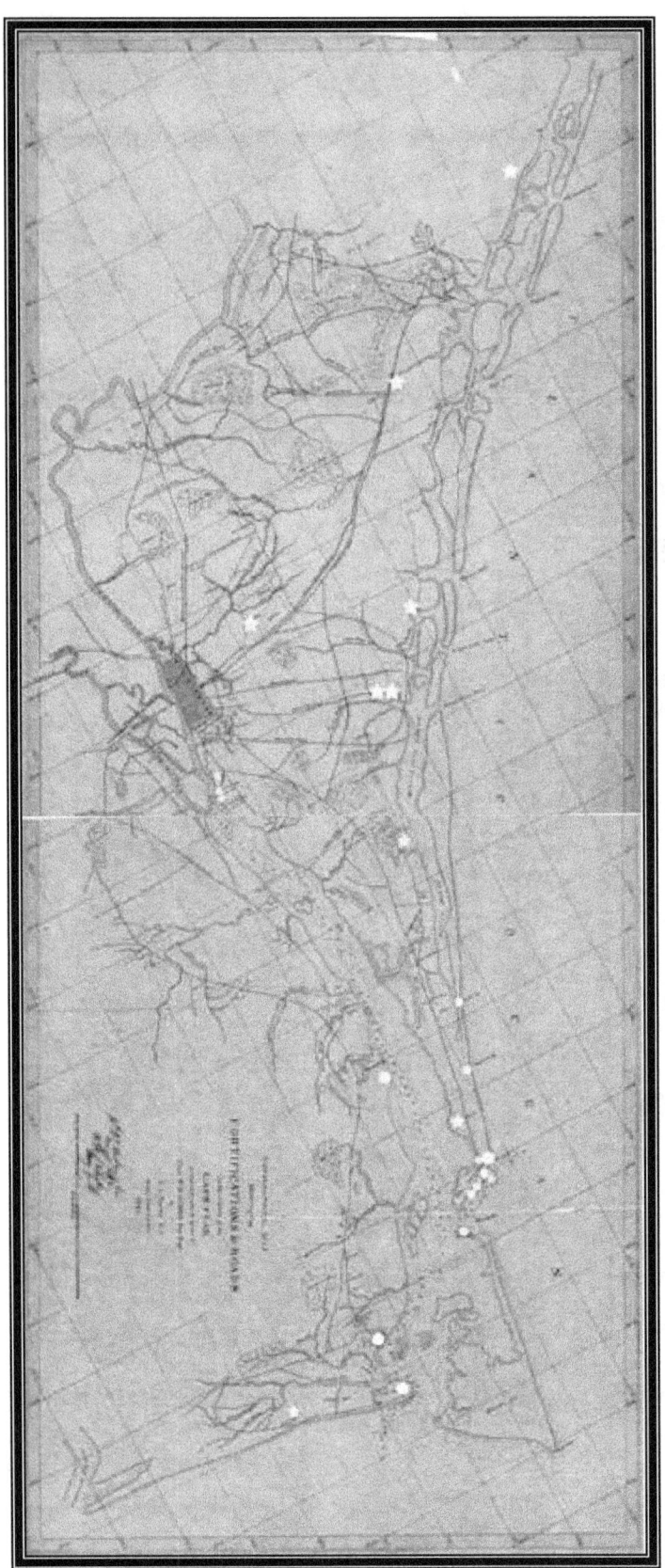

Cape Fear defenses in November, 1862. The three small emplacements below Wilmington were the Light House Battery, Fort French, and Lazaretto Battery. Further downriver on the west side was the site of Fort St. Philip, then consisting of perhaps two batteries and a line of entrenchments extending from water's edge to Orton Pond. Below that lay the ancient Fort Johnston, followed by Fort Caswell and Captain Galloway's Coast Guard camp. On the right side of the river, beginning at the bottom of the map was Battery Winder on Zeek's Island, followed by the batteries of Confederate Point – Battery Hedrick, Battery Bolles, Battery Meade, Cumberland Battery, Fort Fisher, and Shepherd's Battery. Camp Wyatt (star) came next, followed by Batteries Anderson and Gatlin on the beach. Continuing up the beach were found Camp Jones, Camps Davis and Holmes, and then Camp Grant, followed by Camp Heath at Scott's Hill. The new camp furthest north was Camp Holmes Landing, occupied by Adams' Battery. The camp on the plank road to Wilmington is thought to be the site of Camp Hopkins. By this time, the entrenchments on the east side of the city had transitioned to a series of batteries mounting cannon, connected by curtain walls and rifle pits. (*Topographic Map Showing the Fortifications and Roads in the Vicinity of the Cape Fear*, Gilmer Papers, SHC, UNC-CH)

Nine

*"Assigned to take charge of defense of Wilmington,
I arrived here November 17, 1862."*

Brigadier General William Henry Chase Whiting

As chief of staff to General Joseph Eggleston Johnston, commanding Virginia forces at the seizure of the U.S. Arsenal at Harper's Ferry, Major William H. C. Whiting first planned and then carried out its demolition before conducting the withdrawal of the army to reinforce General Beauregard at Manassas Junction. His actions at the Battle of First Manassas earned for him a battlefield promotion to Brigadier General by none other than President Jefferson Davis. In command of Bee's Brigade at Yorktown, he, in consort with General John Bell Hood's Brigade facilitated the Confederate withdrawal by routing an entire Federal Division. Then, at the Battle of Seven Pines, when in command of General Gustavus W. Smith's Division, he prevented the junction of two Federal Divisions that, if successful, might have spelled disaster for the Confederate cause. The service of his small division, consisting of the brigades of Evander Law and John Bell Hood, is credited with the victory at the Battle of Gaines Mill. Such a man comes along rarely, and this one was going home to rejuvenate a defensive system utterly adrift. [1]

By order of the Secretary of War, three of General Whiting's staff officers were directed to accompany him to Wilmington: his brother-in-law, Major James H. Hill, Assistant Adjutant General (AAG) and Chief of Staff; Captain Robert Tansill, Inspector General (IG); and Captain William Chase Strong, Aide-de-camp (ADC) and, when necessary, assistant to Major Hill. [2]

A return for the month of September 1862 listed the Quartermaster of the District of the Cape Fear as Major John W. Cameron, reporting to Brigadier General Gabriel James Rains. There would be no change in that staff position, for, insofar as General Whiting was concerned, the Major's capabilities spoke for themselves. His service began in August of 1861 as an Assistant Quartermaster (AQM), with the rank of Captain, in the Quartermaster General's Office of the State of North Carolina. That assignment was followed by service as Chief Quartermaster for the Department of North Carolina under General Richard C. Gatlin and his successors. [3]

General Whiting had two subsistence officers. When General Rains came to the Cape Fear in September, he brought with him Major Allan B. Magruder, at that time serving as his Brigade Commissary of Subsistence. Major Magruder, by virtue of his rank and previous association with Rains, became the Cape Fear's Commissary of Subsistence (CS). As it was on the September 1862 return for Rains' command, Captain Henry M. Drane was serving as Assistant Commissary of Subsistence (ACS) for the Cape Fear. Captain Drane began his service about May 6, 1861 as Acting Commissary of North Carolina Troops. After the Confederacy ascended to power, he was appointed to Captain and ACS in the Provisional Army and assigned to General Gatlin on July 19, 1861. On November 21, 1861, a return of General Joseph R. Anderson's District of the Cape Fear listed Drane as Captain and Commissary, but he was rendered subordinate by the appearance of Major Magruder.[4]

Upon assuming command of the deceased General Barnard Bee's brigade, General Whiting inherited Volunteer Aide-de-camp (VADC) A. Vanderhorst as part of his staff. Vanderhorst followed Whiting to Wilmington as a volunteer, but styled with the rank of Captain, "by courtesy only." Whether by choice or by chance, it seems as if the volunteer had never been recommended for appointment in the Provisional Army, an oversight the General would soon rectify.[5]

General Whiting's Chief of Artillery (CA) was no stranger to him. Major Bushrod W. Frobel served on his staff on the peninsula and was General John Bell Hood's divisional Chief of Artillery when he received orders to report for duty in Wilmington on November 8, 1862.[6]

Possibly the most important staff position in Wilmington was that of Ordnance Officer (OO). Captain James W. Archer was transferred to the port city soon after General French replaced the departed General Anderson. Of proven value to Anderson's command, Captain Archer's mandate to continue the uninterrupted flow of munitions and ordnance supplies to the Cape Fear forts and batteries remained unchanged.[7]

With a capable staff in place and certain confidence in his many engineering abilities, General Whiting was eager to bring the Cape Fear to a higher state of readiness. But he would have to begin with a sadly depleted command, one that had been bogged down by discontinuity of leadership and stripped of all infantry support.

Cape Fear River Defenses, Brigadier General W. H. C. Whiting, commanding

Command Staff:
    Major James H. Hill, AAG and Chief of Staff
    Major Bushrod W. Frobel, CA
    Major John W. Cameron, QM
    Major Allan B. Magruder, CS
    Captain Henry M. Drane, ACS
    Captain Robert Tansill, IG
    Captain William Chase Strong, ADC
    A. Vanderhorst, Volunteer ADC
    Captain James W. Archer, OO

Fort Johnston:
    Co. B, 61st N.C. Infantry, Captain Henry Harding
    Herring Artillery, Captain William A. Herring
Fort Caswell, Colonel George A. Cunningham
    Scotch Greys (Unattached), Capt. Malcom H. McBryde
    King Artillery, Captain James Martin Stevenson
    Brunswick Artillery, Captain Daniel K. Bennett[8]
    Pamlico Artillery, Captain Samuel B. Hunter
    Lamb Artillery, Captain Francis W. Potter
Beach West of Fort Caswell:
    Captain John Galloway's Company, Coast Guards
Zeek's Island (Winder Battery):
    Gatlin Artillery, Captain James S. Lane
Fort Fisher, Colonel William Lamb
    Bladen Stars, Captain Daniel Munn
    Bladen Artillery, Captain John T. Melvin
    Braddy's Battery, Captain Kinchen J. Braddy[9]
    McMillan Artillery, Captain William H. Tripp
    Lenoir Braves, Captain William Sutton[10]
    Captain Charles C. Whitehurst's Company
    Captain Alexander McRae's Company
    Anderson Artillery, Captain Edward B. Dudley
    Bladen Artillery Guards, Captain George Tait
Camp Badger:
    Capt. Benjamin G. Smith's Company of Cavalry
    Staunton Hill Artillery, Captain Andrew B. Paris[11]
Camp Heath:
    Captain A. F. Newkirk's Company of Cavalry
Camp Holmes Landing:
    Adams' Battery, Captain Zachariah T. Adams
Fort St. Philip, Lt. Col. John A. Richardson
    Bridgers' Artillery, Captain John E. Leggett
    Captain Calvin Barnes' Company (Unattached)
    Clarendon Guards, Captain Daniel Patterson
    Columbus Artillery, Captain Oliver H. Powell[12]
Camp French:
    Co. A, 10th Bn. N.C. Hvy. Arty., Capt. Wm. B. Lewis

Fort French:
    Washington Grays, Captain Thomas Sparrow
Light House Battery
    River Guards, Captain John William Taylor [13]
Wilmington City Garrison and Land Defenses
    10th Bn. N.C. Heavy Artillery, Major Wilton Young
        Co. B, Captain Henry M. Barnes
        Co. C, Captain Charles M.T. McCauley
    Clark Artillery, Captain Robert G. Rankin
    Andrews' Battery, Captain William S.G. Andrews

For the first time, a good glimpse of the land and river defenses of Wilmington is available, and by none other than General Whiting himself.

> Assigned to take charge of defense of Wilmington, I arrived here November 17, 1862. The yellow fever, which had desolated the city and stopped all work, had not yet ceased. The condition, importance, and necessities of the place were immediately set forth and have since been repeatedly urged to the department. I found the defensive works generally imperfect and many important points neglected; a partial line of earthworks, well constructed but weak in profile, had been thrown up between the two mill-ponds on the east and south of the city 1½ miles in extent. They had twelve pieces of artillery mounted, mostly naval 24s and 32s, of the old pattern. These [*sic*, should read Three] batteries, mounting eight guns, had been placed just below the upper jetty lights, and two to command an imperfect obstruction, composed of logs and chains, near Mount Tirza. An attempt had been made to build an iron battery for this purpose, but so defective in design and position that I directed it to be stopped. On the opposite side of the river, 14 miles from the city, Battery Saint Philip had been erected, well constructed, mounting eleven guns, but defective in the quality and caliber of its ordnance and in the location of proper protecting traverses from enfilade and even reverse fire. [14]

The Wilmington defenses had graduated from mere rifle pits to a chain of batteries mounting twelve pieces of artillery in all, most of them Navy 24 and 32-pounders of the oldest pattern. Batteries were only occasionally connected by breast height curtain walls, only by rifle pits in others, but more often than not, there was no connection at all. Roughly 330 yards apart, the batteries stretched from Green's Millpond on the north side of the city to the Greenfield Millpond on the south.

The term *old pattern* once again crept into the artillery vernacular, hinting that Wilmington's land defenses may have mounted aged pieces from the War of 1812 or even earlier. There is, however, sufficient evidence to surmise that they weren't quite that old. In fact, there is every reason to believe that almost all of the Navy cannon in the Wilmington defenses were short, the length of which is generally assumed to be about seven feet or thereabouts. That being the case, the relatively large number (thirty-nine) of 32-pounder Shubrick Guns of 41 cwt. shipped to North Carolina from the Gosport Navy Yard sets them far apart from the paltry number (four) of 27 hundredweight 32-pounders shipped in June of 1861. Sheer numbers notwithstanding, the presence of a ringknob on the first pattern Shubrick Gun may have been a key factor in General Whiting's decision to refer to them as old pattern guns. [15]

U.S. Navy 24-pounder medium gun of 31 hundredweight mounted on a siege carriage. (Library of Congress, Prints and Photographs Division)

Early Navy 24-pounder medium guns of 31 hundredweight also came with ringknobs, more likely than not General Whiting's sole criterion for identifying a piece of artillery as one of an older pattern. After all, the general's very first use of the term was in reference to the 32-pounder Carronades he requisitioned from Gosport during his first tour in secession-minded Wilmington. Those diminutive pieces were also manufactured with ringknobs.[16]

The batteries below Wilmington, known to be Light House Battery, Fort French and Lazaretto Battery, were described by General Whiting as mounting eight guns. Ironclad Lazaretto Battery, having received two cannon and carriages on May 22 past, fell into the general's disfavor at first sight and its construction was terminated. The others went on to serve as the defenders of what became known as "The Obstructions," a man-made obstacle to navigation of the Cape Fear River.

It's probably not too far-fetched to say that those batteries mounted guns from Fort Caswell, unceremoniously cast off just as soon as more modern ordnance became available. Designed to mount five guns, Light House Battery received one cannon on May 22 and a 24-pounder on May 23, but indications are there were not more than two others there at the time Whiting assumed command. Fort French, it seems, never mounted more than two guns, but the types and calibers at this point in the war are purely conjectural.[17]

Fort St. Philip, with eleven guns, was well on its way to becoming the final obstacle to an enemy land advance on Wilmington. Outwardly not very impressed with St. Philip's armament, General Whiting was even less dazzled by the fort's defensive profile and lack of protective traverses. It was a given that the 31 guns in the Wilmington land and river defenses were mostly old pattern Navy smoothbore cannon of 24 and 32-pounder caliber, but the Confederates could ill afford to lose any of them for lack of attention to detail in constructing the fortifications that they served.

With the dispersal of guns from Forts Caswell and Fisher to points upriver and the ever increasing influx of guns into the Cape Fear, an accurate reconstruction of the armament in the district at the time of General Whiting's arrival is simply not possible. What is possible is to estimate the total number of guns and summarize the patterns represented in the Cape Fear defenses.

Thirty-one guns in the upper river defenses is considered completely accurate, as inspected by General Whiting when he assumed command in November 1862. Winder Battery on Zeek's Island probably retained its two guns and Fort Fisher's July armament of twenty-eight cannon was augmented by four Whitworth guns courtesy of the wrecked *Modern Greece*. Fort Caswell mounted 36 guns in April past, but later transfers to the upper river and Fort Fisher reduced the armament to an unknown level, replenished only partially by new arrivals from Richmond. It's probably safe to assume that the number of big guns in the Cape Fear defenses at the time of Whiting's arrival was a little over ninety.

A mixed bag of patterns and calibers were present in the defenses, a summary of which is presented below.

- ❖ U.S. Pattern 1844 8" Columbiad
- ❖ U.S. Pattern 1857 8" Columbiad
- ❖ C.S. Pattern 1861 8" Columbiad (Rodman)
- ❖ U.S. Pattern 1839/1840 8" Seacoast Howitzer
- ❖ U.S. Navy 8" Shell Gun
- ❖ C.S. 8" Siege Howitzer
- ❖ U.S. Navy 32-pounder smoothbore (long)
- ❖ C.S. 6.4" Rifled Navy 32-pounder (banded)
- ❖ C.S. 6.4" Rifled Navy 32-pounder (unbanded)
- ❖ U.S. Navy 32-pounder Shubrick gun (short)
- ❖ U.S. Navy 32-pounder Carronade
- ❖ U.S. 24-pounder Siege Gun (old pattern)
- ❖ U.S. Navy 24-pounder of 31 cwt. (short)
- ❖ C.S. 5.82" Rifled 24-pounder (unbanded)
- ❖ C.S. 4.62" Siege Rifle
- ❖ Whitworth 2.75-inch Breechloading Rifle

Thus equipped, fortified and manned, the Cape Fear defenses were prepared to begin a journey under new leadership. It was to be an odyssey that blended energy with skill, determination with innovation, and courage with dedication to earn the time-honored appellation – *Lifeline of the Confederacy*.

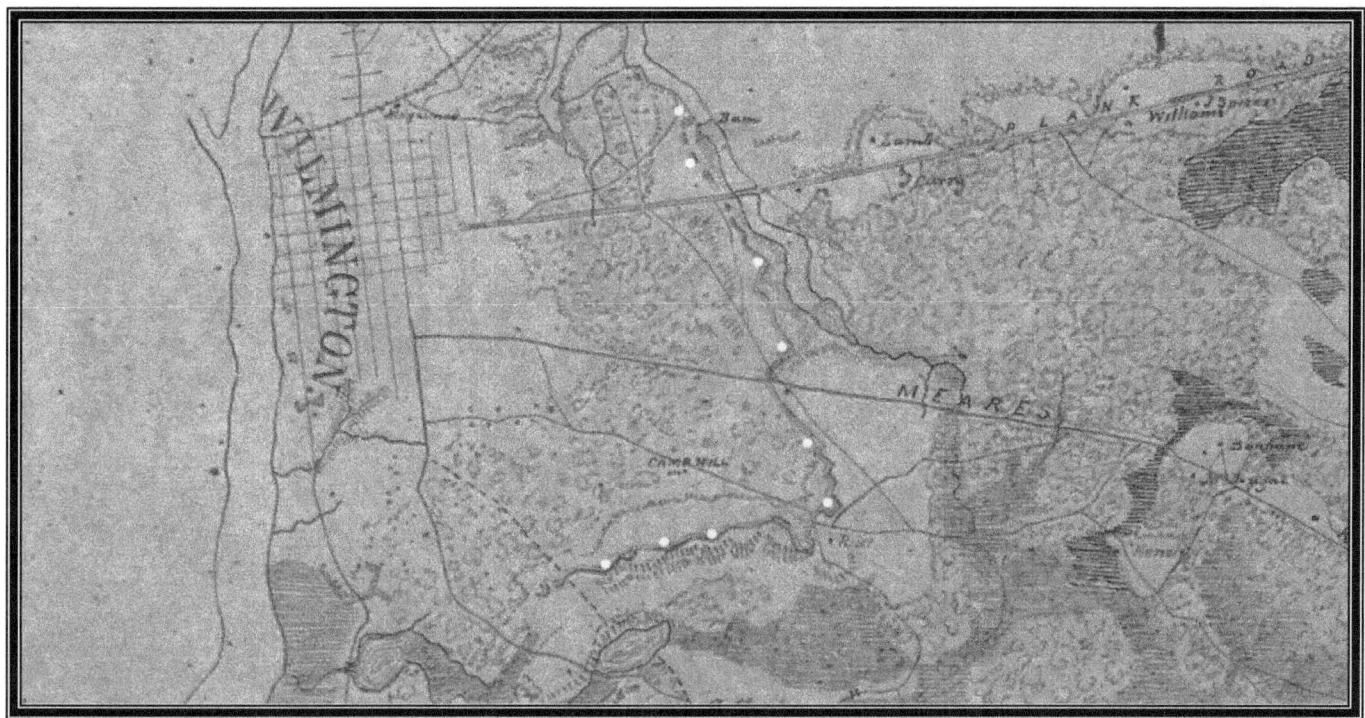

The approximate positions of the batteries in the line of entrenchments in the land defenses of Wilmington, at about the time of Brigadier General William Henry Chase Whiting's assumption of command of the Cape Fear River defenses. From north to south are Batteries Green, Andrew, Smith, Hobson, and Moore's Bastion; and then, from east to west, Batteries Dawson, McRee, Wright and Bellamy. The open area surrounding the Lamb residence may well have been the site of Camp Lamb and the bivouac shown as Camp Hill was first known only as "The Entrenched Camp." (*Map of the vicinity of Wilmington*, Gilmer Papers, SHC, UNC-CH)

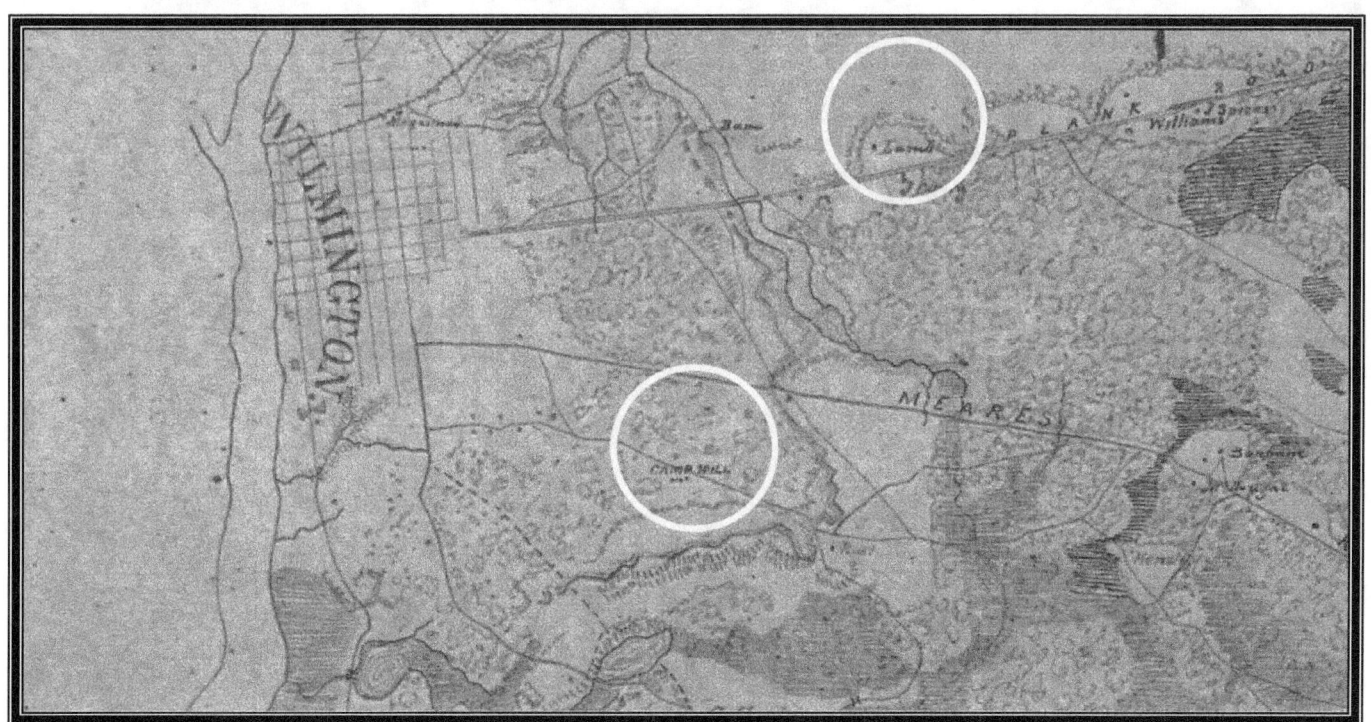

U.S. Navy 24-pounder medium gun of 31 hundredweight, length 79 inches. The presence of this very pattern in the Cape Fear defenses is of the highest probability, the ringknob effectively rendering its pattern to be old. Most often mounted on siege carriages, these small bore cannon were widely used in the defenses of Richmond. (Photography courtesy of Eric B. Ramey)

U.S. Navy 32-pounder chambered cannon of 41 hundredweight, 1st Pattern, length 84 inches – the Shubrick Gun. Forty guns of this pattern were manufactured in 1837 for *USS Cyane*, formerly *HMS Cyane*, and *USS Levant*, namesake of the sloop captured and lost by *USS Constitution* in February, 1815. Thirty-nine cannon of this weight were shipped from the Gosport Navy Yard to North Carolina. Of those 39 guns, ten were earmarked for Fort Macon. As for the rest, the presence of at least some in the land defenses of Wilmington is highly likely, if not certain. (Photography courtesy of W. J. Corey and Kim Davenport, Brown Library, Washington, North Carolina)

U.S. Navy 32-pounder chambered cannon of 41 hundredweight, 2nd Pattern, length 82.17 inches. Twenty-four guns of this pattern were cast for the sloop of war *USS Saratoga* in 1842. It remains possible that this pattern may have been present in the Wilmington land defenses in late 1862, but its newer gusset jaws and larger lockpiece give it a different profile than the Navy 24 and 32-pounders with ringknobs and small lockpieces. For that reason alone, the first pattern guns seem the more likely to have captured General Whiting's attention as "old pattern" pieces. NOTE: This photograph has been altered from a U.S. Navy 32-pounder of 42 hundredweight to produce a faithful facsimile of the shorter 41 hundredweight gun. (Photography courtesy of Eric B. Ramey, altered by the author)

Glossary

Abatis [**ab**-*uh*-tee]: an obstacle or barricade of trees with bent or sharpened branches directed toward an enemy, the purpose of which is to impede an enemy's progress and bring them under close musket fire.

Advanced Work: any fortification lying outside the enceinte, and beyond the range of its cannon.

Artillery: cannon, singly and collectively.

Banded Gun: an artillery piece that has been reinforced by wrapping an additional layer of iron around the breech to prevent bursting from the use of large powder charges. Many pieces were manufactured this way initially, but it was also found desirable to band older smoothbore cannon after they had been rifled. The Confederates did not always have the luxury of banding every smoothbore they rifled, and numerous failures resulted.

Banquette: a step that allowed a defender to rise above the parapet to fire a musket then step down to safely reload.

Barbette: See Carriage, Barbette

Barbette Tier: the upper level of a fort upon which en barbette cannon are deployed.

Barrack(s): a building used to house military personnel, very often used in the plural.

Base of the Breech: the rearmost surface of the breech of a cannon.

Base Ring: a raised band of metal between the base of the breech and the cannon tube.

Bastion [**bas**-ch*uh*n]: an angular work projecting outward from the face of a fortification, allowing enfilade fire to be directed along the front of an adjacent curtain or scarp wall. A bastion consisted of four parts: two faces forming a salient angle oriented towards the enemy, and two reentering flanks that connected the salient angle to the wall of the fortification.

Battering Cannon: see siege gun.

Battery: (1) a tactical unit of artillery. In fortifications, a battery may be a cluster of cannon if they are grouped together on the parapet; or it may be just one cannon, if it is alone on the parapet and separated from other batteries. Normally commanded by a captain, the field artillery battery is a unit of two or more sections of at least two field pieces each, as well as its associated equipments, men and horses. (2) cannon that have been placed in firing position are said to be "in battery."

Berm: the horizontal plane of earth that connects the exterior slope of the parapet or the face of a fortification to the ditch.

Blockhouse: a fortified building that is loopholed to allow riflemen to fire through its walls, with a projecting upper story that allows defenders to direct plunging musket fire on assaulting forces attempting to breach the structure at the ground level.

Bolt: a cylindrical solid projectile, used in rifled cannon to engage hard targets with direct fire.

Bomb-proof: a reinforced structure built to absorb the impact of artillery fire without penetration to the protected space below. Normally, heavy supporting timbers and thick timber decking surmounted by a thick layer of soil or sand were employed to protect personnel, ammunition, and powder during enemy bombardment.

Breastwork: a breast-height mound of earth thrown up under battlefield conditions for the protection of troops.

Breech: the mass of metal behind the bore of a cannon.

Breeching Ring: a ring of metal at the base of the breech of a navy cannon, through which a rope is passed to restrain the cannon's recoil to its maximum allowable travel aboard ship. Almost always seen in conjunction with an army knob. See also ringknob.

Breeching Jaws: an open-ended breeching ring, closeable with a pinned block or a bolt. The necks of the jaws were thin and therefore subject to breakage. Later patterns had reinforced gussets, closeable by a pin only. This was a revision that produced stronger breeching, an absolute necessity for restraining the recoil of navy rifled cannon.

Canister [**can**-iss-tur]: a metal cylinder packed with spherical solid shot and employed by artillery against infantry.

Cannon: artillery piece(s).

Caponiere [**cap**-oh-neer]: A work projecting outward from the scarp of a fortification into the ditch, often spanning it entirely. Sometimes resembling a low blockhouse, it may be constructed on, or partially below the floor of the ditch, but its purpose is to achieve enfilade fire along its length. Access is gained from the main fortress via a postern through the rampart, and the structure is built as a bomb-proof to protect its interior from artillery and small arms fire.

Carriage:

> *Barbette*: an artillery carriage that travels into battery and absorbs recoil atop a chassis, all of which raises a cannon sufficiently to allow it to be fired over the parapet.
>
> *Deck*: a naval carriage of any type.
>
> *Field*: a carriage for transporting a field piece or a piece of field artillery.
>
> *Four-truck*: a naval four-wheel ship's carriage.
>
> *Siege*: a very heavy four-wheeled carriage mounting a siege gun. Very much larger than a field carriage, these unwieldy devices made siege operations somewhat more mobile, but only over short distances and with great difficulty.

Cartridge: the combination of a cartridge bag and a cartridge block, pre-assembled to conserve time in battle conditions.

Cartridge Bag: a bag containing cannon powder that constitutes the charge for firing a projectile from a cannon.

Cartridge Block: a circular block of wood, to which a cartridge bag is tied preparatory to loading large caliber chambered cannon using reduced charges. The block is sized so as to completely fill the chamber with the charge.

Cascabel: every part of the cannon behind the base ring.

Case Shot: a thin-walled hollow projectile, either spherical or cylindrical, containing lead or iron balls or bullets that are deployed on target using an internal powder charge actuated by a time fuze. Case shot produces virtually the same effect on infantry as canister, only at far greater distances.

Casemate: an enclosed artillery position having a roof and an embrasure for the cannon to fire through.

Casemated: cannon in a casemate is said to be casemated.

Chamber: (1) the tapered portion of a howitzer tube into which the powder charge is introduced prior to loading the projectile.

Charge: the amount of cannon powder required to fire a projectile from a cannon to achieve maximum range and effect.

Chase Ring: the raised band around the neck of a cannon.

Chassis: the wheeled railway upon which the cannon and carriage rest and by means of which the entire assembly may be moved horizontally and upon which the carriage moves to and from battery.

Chevaux-de-frise [she-**voh**-*duh*-**freeze**]: an obstacle consisting of two or more chained-together logs having a diameter of about one foot, into which diagonal holes have been drilled to allow for the placement of sharpened stakes. In profile, the obstacle rests on the ground in the shape of an X. One of these obstacles is a cheval-de-frise.

Citadel: a fortified place within a larger fortification from which a final defense may be conducted, often also used as a barrack for the garrison.

Columbiad [koh-**lum**-bee-add]: a large smoothbore heavy artillery piece. The first patterns were characterized by the presence of a firing chamber while the later patterns were unchambered.

Columbiad Block: a cartridge block for a chambered Columbiad.

Cordon: a continuous outward protrusion of brick from near the top of the masonry scarp of a fortification that provides a barrier to rainwater running down the face of the wall and degrading its structural integrity. It can also be a minor impediment to an attack by escalade.

Counterscarp: the inner slope of a ditch that is furthest from the outer face of the scarp of a fortification.

Covered Way: in permanent fortifications, a walkway extending around the outside of the moat or ditch of the main works. It was not "covered," in the sense of being roofed over, but instead provided cover from horizontal gunfire. Alternatively, a road around a fortification between the ditch and the glacis. It was protected from enemy fire by a parapet, at the foot of which was generally a banquette enabling coverage of the glacis with musketry. In addition to its function as an outer line of defense, it served as a place for sorties to assemble.

Cunette [kyew-**net**]: a narrow drainage ditch running along the bottom of a trench or a main ditch.

Curtain: a wall of earth or masonry that connects two bastions or batteries. Often, the curtain is topped by a parapet and may therefore be termed a rampart.

Defilade [**def**-*uh*-layd]: a fortification or attacking force that is hidden from view or enemy fire.

Demilune [**deh**-mee-loon]: a semi-circular outwork that protrudes from the face of a fortification, capable of directing enfilade fire along its length.

Detached Works: *fortifications* constructed in advance of the enceinte and its outworks to delay an enemy's approach.

Ditch: an excavation at least five to eight feet deep and 12 or more feet wide in front of the face of a fortification that provided material to build up the protective ramparts. Of equal importance, it served as an impediment to attacking troops attempting to surmount the ramparts.

Drawbridge: a bridge across the ditch which may be raised to isolate the enceinte from the covered way or other approach.

Embrasure [em-**bray**-zher]: an angled opening built into a wall or parapet to allow artillery to fire through it. The opening is angled so that it is larger on the inside than on the outside. Such an opening to accommodate musket fire is termed a loophole.

En Barbette: said of cannon that are in a position and of sufficient elevation to fire over a parapet, instead of through an embrasure.

Enceinte [en-**saint**; ahn-**sahnt**]: everything located within the parapet of a fortification, whether it be a fort, a castle, or a city. As used in military terms, it is the entirety of the **enclosed** fortification, but does not include an outwork or an advanced work.

Enfilade [**en**-*fuh*-layd]: said of a fortification or body of troops taken under fire along its entire length. A fortification may only be in enfilade when taking fire from its right or left. Troops, however, may be in enfilade from their front or rear when marching in column, or from the left or right when deployed in a skirmish line or final assault formation.

Entrenchment: loosely applied term for any earthen fortification, whether it be a simple field breastwork or a more substantial curtain.

Epaulement [ee-**pawl**-ment]: a short protective wall or barrier angling rearward from the flank of a parapet to protect the men and cannon from enfilade artillery or small arms fire.

Eprouvette: a short mortar used only to test the explosive force of gunpowder by measuring the range of a projectile and comparing the result to the expected range under battlefield conditions.

Escalade: the assault of a fortification by ascending its face in an attempt to gain the parapet and drive the defenders from the ramparts. Usually attempted with ladders, such a tactic often culminated in catastrophic results to the attacking force.

Face: (1) the front of a curtain or scarp facing the enemy; (2) when used in the plural, the term commonly refers to the two exterior fronts of a salient angle.

Field Artillery: (1) cannon or artillery units that are easily moved and deployed in the field.

Field Gun: a cannon that is easily moved and deployed in the field, usually not larger than a 24-pounder howitzer or a 20-pounder Parrott.

Field Piece: see field gun.

Fixed Ammunition: an artillery projectile and its required powder charge that have been affixed to a sabot, eliminating the need for loading powder and projectile separately.

Flank: the side of a military unit or a fortification.

Flanked: passed around a military unit, defensive feature, or fortification and got behind it.

Fort: an enclosed fortification defended by artillery.

Fortification: structures, whether of earth, wood, masonry or other materials, that enable a place to be defended from an attacking force.

Fuze: An ignition device used to detonate a fragmentary projectile. In Civil War artillery, it was activated in the projectile by firing the cannon, then burning for a designated time during flight, and finally reaching the internal powder charge, whereupon it burst over or near the target, spreading shell fragments over a wide area. See also case shot and shell.

Fuze Plug: an adapter hammered or screwed into a case shot or shell projectile, the function of which is to accept the fuze.

Garrison: a body of troops serving in a fortification.

Glacis [**gla**-sis; **glay**-see]: gently sloping ground at the edge of a fortification that conceals the scarp from artillery fire.

Gorge: the rear of a work, whether it be a fort, a bastion, a lunette, a ravelin, or a salient angle.

Grapeshot: usually, three tiers of three metal spherical shot, held in place by rings of iron between two slabs of wood that are bolted together. By the time of the Civil War, U.S. forces used grapeshot only in naval warfare. Since grapeshot was larger in diameter than canister shot, the Army abandoned it in favor of the far more lethal canister round.

Gun: (1) a smoothbore or rifled artillery piece characterized by the absence of a firing chamber that attains a flat trajectory of fire using a relatively heavy powder charge. (2) any cannon, except when used with an adjective to further describe the type of gun (i.e. **siege** gun; **rifled** gun; **banded** gun).

Gussets: reinforcements above and below the breeching jaws of a cannon.

Heavy Artillery: said of artillery that is too heavy for field use. Normally it is artillery that is fixed in a permanent fortification or on a ship, and mounted on carriages that are not adapted for mobility. Usually a cannon that is not mounted on a field carriage.

Howitzer [**how**-its-ur]: a smoothbore light or heavy artillery piece characterized by the presence of a firing chamber that achieves a high trajectory of fire using a relatively small powder charge.

Knob: the protrusion from the base of the breech of a cannon. Normally seen on army cannon.

Light Artillery: See field artillery.

Longarm: a shoulder-fired long gun; a musket or a rifle.

Long Gun: unchambered Navy 32-pounder cannon of 96 inches or more in length, with weights of 42, 46, 51, 57, and 61 hundredweight.

Loophole [**loop**-hohl]: an angled opening built into a wall or parapet to allow muskets to fire through it. The opening is angled so that it is larger on the inside than on the outside. Such an opening to accommodate artillery fire is termed an embrasure.

Loopholed: pierced with loopholes.

Lunette [loo-**net**]: a detached earthwork, open to the rear, composed of two faces forming a salient angle and two flanks, flanks and faces being of approximately equal length. When two or more are connected by a curtain wall, they become bastions.

Machicoulis [**match**-i-co*h*l-iss]: special loopholes along the cantilevered outer edge of the second story of a blockhouse or other fortified structure that permits fire to be delivered downward from cover.

Magazine: any structure where gunpowder and artillery projectiles are stored.

Main Work: see enceinte

Moat: ditch in front of a fortification that was purposely filled with water.

Mortar: a muzzle-loading cannon with a very short barrel that lobs low-velocity shells in high trajectories to engage troops behind fortifications.

Muzzle: The forward end of the barrel of a cannon or a firearm, from which the projectile is expelled.

Muzzle Swell: the thickest part of the cannon ahead of the neck.

Neck: the narrowest part of the cannon ahead of the reinforce(s).

Obstacle: a device to impede or deny passage of a point by men, vehicles or animals.

Obstruction: an obstacle placed in a waterway to inhibit passage of a point by ships.

Ordnance: (1) specifically, artillery or cannon; (2) loosely, all military materiel used in waging war.

Ordnance Stores: those items necessary to serve the artillery.

Outwork: any fortification lying outside the enceinte, but within musket range of it.

Palisade [pal-*uh*-**sayd**]: a wall or high fence of sharpened stakes placed in front of a defensive fortification to impede an enemy's progress.

Parade: a centrally located area within a permanent fortification where troops assembled for drill and inspection.

Parapet: a protective wall atop the rampart behind which the defenders were protected and over which they delivered their fire.

Pintle: An upright cylinder of iron, around which the chassis traverses. It is inserted in and firmly fastened to a block of stone called the pintle block.

Front Pintle: the chassis is attached to the pintle by its front transom and traverses around it in a semicircle, thereby limiting the cannon's field of fire to 180 degrees. Most commonly found with closed fortifications where the parapets command the entire field.

Center Pintle: the chassis is attached to the pintle at its center, and traverses around it through the entire circumference of the traverse circle, thus allowing a 360 degree field of fire. Most commonly seen in use with Columbiads and large rifled guns and in fortifications with an open gorge that can be covered by reversing the *cannon.*

Pintle Block: a block of stone used to secure the pintle.

Place of Arms: an enlargement in the covered way at a salient angle to secure regular approaches to a fortification and in which troops could be assembled for a sortie against a besieging enemy.

Portcullis [port-**cull**-iss]- A heavy gate of timber or iron grating sliding within vertical channels in a portal that can be quickly lowered to deny entry to the fortified place. Such gates are often studded with spikes on the underside and may be employed as a counterweight to assist in raising a drawbridge.

Postern [**post**-urn]: a passage leading from the interior of a fortification to the ditch.

Rampart: the walls surrounding a fortification, which includes the scarp. Usually made of mounded earth or masonry or a combination of the two, it presented the principal obstacle to an attacking enemy.

Ravelin [**rav**-linn]: a detached work, open to the rear with two long faces forming a salient angle and two short flanks.

Redoubt: an enclosed fortification without bastions, designed to be defended from all sides. Most often, it was a detached work that stood alone as part of a larger defensive system.

Reinforce: The thickest part of the cannon tube. If more than one reinforce is present, the thickest is termed the first reinforce, the next thickest is the second reinforce, etc.

Revetment: a retaining wall constructed to support the interior slope of a parapet, ditch, rampart, or traverse.

Revetted: earth retained with a revetment; a retaining wall.

Ricochet: the practice of firing an artillery projectile at a waterborne target so that it strikes the water at an angle of four or five degrees, causing it to skip one or more times with the object of striking the target at or below its waterline. This practice reduces the need for accuracy of range estimation and increases the chances of striking the target if pointing of the cannon is reasonably accurate.

Rifle: (1) a cannon that has rifling; (2) an infantry longarm that has rifling.

Rifled Gun: a cannon or other firearm that has rifling.

Rifling: spiral grooves cut into the bore of a cannon, into which a projectile or its sabot expands, thereby imparting a spin to the projectile.

> *Hook-slant Rifling*: a hybrid type of rifling that combines the single-shouldered groove of the Blakely pattern and the equidistant lands and grooves of the Scott's pattern.

> *Parrott Rifling*: rectangular rifling wherein the lands are wider than the grooves, therefore not equidistant.

> *Rectangular Rifling*: typically, rifling with equidistant lands and grooves, the shape of both appearing to be rectangular in cross-section.

Rimbase: a shoulder at the base of the trunnion that reinforces them and serves to center the cannon in its carriage,

Ringknob: an army knob integrated with the base of the breech of a cannon by a navy breeching ring.

Round Shot Gun: U.S. Navy unchambered cannon deemed capable of firing spherical solid shot, namely the 57 and 61 hundredweight cannon. The latter cannon was further identified as being heavy.

Sabot: (1) as used in smoothbore cannon, a wooden platform to which an artillery projectile and its powder charge were affixed to speed up the loading process; (2) as used in rifled cannon, a thin soft-metal base affixed to an artillery projectile that is superheated at firing, causing it to expand into the rifling, thereby imparting a spin to the projectile. See also rifling.

Salient Angle: an angle in the trace of a fortification facing outward toward the direction from which an attack was likely to come. An angle so formed was never less than 60 degrees to allow unrestricted movement of the defenders of the parapet.

Sally Port: (1) a passage, either open or covered, from the covered way to the country; or a passage under the rampart, usually vaulted, from the interior of a fortification to the exterior, primarily to provide for sorties. (2) the main entrance to a fortification through its rampart.

Scarp: technically, the inner slope of the ditch that is closest to the face of a fortification. Since the faces of many masonry forts were also the inner slopes of their ditches, they were therefore scarps in the truest sense of the word. Some masonry forts, however, employed a ditch with scarp, counterscarp and berm, which connected the face of the fort with the scarp of the ditch. In this last case, engineers ignored the technical aspect of the scarp as part of the ditch, choosing instead to refer to the face of the fort as the scarp. Fort Caswell falls into the latter category.

Section: a subdivision of the *field artillery battery*. Normally consisting of two cannon commanded by a Lieutenant, it may be employed as a separate tactical unit or in concert with the battery of which it is a part.

Shell: a hollow artillery projectile, either spherical or cylindrical, with thicker walls than case shot, to which was added an internal powder charge that was detonated by a timed fuze after penetrating structures or earthworks. The thicker shell allowed the projectile to penetrate objects without being destroyed by the impact, and the larger powder charge exploded it with great force. Normally employed to reduce fortifications and against personnel within them.

Shell Gun: U.S. Navy chambered cannon deemed safe to fire shell projectiles only.

Short Gun: U.S. Navy chambered cannon of lengths 84 inches and less, weighing 27, 33, or 41 hundredweight.

Shot: a solid iron spherical projectile used in smoothbore cannon to engage hard targets.

Shrapnel: see case shot

Shubrick Gun: U.S. Navy cannon of 41 hundredweight, either 1st Pattern or 2nd Pattern, perhaps both.

Siege Gun: see Siege and Garrison Gun.

Siege and Garrison Gun: a classification for a type of artillery too heavy for use as field artillery and designated specifically for attacking a fortification or for defending it. Beginning in 1819, there was only a 24-pounder gun within this classification, and its production was confined to the Models 1819, 1840, and 1845. In 1839, 12-pounder and 18-pounder guns were introduced into this classification with the Models 1840 and 1845.

Smoothbore: (1) a cannon without rifling. (2) an infantry longarm without rifling.

Solid Shot: see shot.

Sortie: a sudden and unexpected attack on attackers by troops from a defensive work. The main objective was to destroy siege works that had been erected by the aggressors.

Spherical Projectile: a round projectile, whether shot, shell, or case shot.

Stockade: (1) a fort made of logs or planks; (2) a fence of logs or planks to close the gorge of a work that is open in the rear.

Sub-Terra Battery: a random series of underground explosive devices employed against infantry. In modern terminology, such an array of devices is called a minefield.

Tabby Work: See Tapia.

Tapia [**tap**-ee-*uh*]: slurry or paste made from water, lime and ash from live oyster shells that was poured into forms and left to harden into the ramparts of a fortification. A primitive and often ineffective form of concrete.

Terreplein [**tare**-*uh*-plane]: in permanent fortifications, the flat surface of the rampart behind the parapet where the gunners ply their trade.

The Heavy Gun: U.S. Navy 32-pounder heavy (round shot) gun of 62 hundredweight.

The Long Gun: U.S. Navy 32-pounder (round shot) gun of 57 hundredweight.

Time Fuze: see fuze.

Torpedo: An underwater explosive device employed against ships. In modern terminology, such a device is called a mine.

Traverse: (1) a mound of protective earth that is higher than the guns and men at the parapet of a fortification, shielding them from enfilade fire; (2) to rotate a heavy cannon on its carriage to change its point of aim.

Traverse Circle: arced segments of iron, continuously arranged to form a circle or part of a circle, all resting on a bed of masonry or wood, upon which the traverse wheels of a chassis roll.

Traverse Wheels: the chassis is supported by wheels that roll on a traverse circle, allowing horizontal movement of a cannon mounted *en barbette*.

Truck: traditionally, one wheel of a naval carriage.

Trunnions: the cylindrical protrusions from near the center of a cannon tube that carry its weight while mounted on the carriage.

Wood Circle: traverse circle made of wood, instead of iron.

Works: a generic term used to describe fortifications, and even components thereof at times. It may be used to describe a bastion or the entire fortification of which it is a part. Exactly which part or entirety must be taken from the context in which it is used. For example, the commander of a bastion within a fortification may report "the works sustained severe damage during the bombardment." Such a report would have reflected his perception of the event within his sphere of influence, but more would be the disaster if the same report were to be made by the overall commander of the fort.

Notes

Chapter One: Fort Johnston

[1] Report Of Col. John L. Cantwell, April 17, 1861, *The War of the Rebellion: a Compilation of the Official Records of the Union and Confederate Armies*, Washington, D.C.: U.S. Government Printing Office, 1880-1901 (hereinafter cited as *OR*), Series 1, Volume 51, Part 2, pp. 1-3; Noble J. Tolbert, Editor, *The Papers of John Willis Ellis*, Volume Two, Raleigh: State Department of Archives and History, 1964 (hereinafter cited as Tolbert, Ed., *The Papers of John Willis Ellis*), p. 609.

[2] Ibid.; Report of John L. Cantwell, April 17, 1861, *OR* Series 1, Volume 51, Part 2, pp. 1-3.

[3] Walter Clark, ed., *Histories of the Several Regiments and Battalions From North Carolina in the Great War 1861-'65*, Goldsboro, North Carolina: Nash Brothers, 1901 (hereinafter cited as Clark, *North Carolina Regiments*), Vol. 5, pp. 23-24.

[4] Ibid., pp. 24-25; Reports of Ordnance Sergeant James Reilly, January 9 & 10, 1861, *OR*, Series 1, Volume 1, pp. 474-475.

[5] James Sprunt, *Chronicles of the Cape Fear River, 1660-1916*, Raleigh, North Carolina: Edwards & Broughton Printing Co., 1916 (hereinafter cited as Sprunt, *Chronicles*), p. 277; Reports of Ordnance Sergeant Frederick Dardingkiller, January 10 & 11, 1861, *OR* Series 1, Vol. 1, p. 476.

[6] Clark, *North Carolina Regiments*, Vol. 5, p. 25; Daves to Cantwell, January 11, 1861, *OR*, Series 1, Volume 51, Part 2, p. 4.

[7] Clark, *North Carolina Regiments*, Vol. 5, p. 25-27; Cantwell to Hedrick, January 12, 1861, *OR*, Series 1, Volume 51, Part 2, p. 5; Hedrick to Cantwell, January 13, 1861, *OR*, Series 1, Volume 51, Part 2, p. 6.

[8] Wilson Angley, *A History of Fort Johnston on the Lower Cape Fear*, Southport, NC: Southport Historical Society, Inc., 1996 (hereinafter cited as Angley, *A History of Fort Johnston*), pp. 1-3.

[9] Sprunt, *Chronicles*, pp. 53; Department of the Army, Military Traffic Management Command, Headquarters, Military Ocean Terminal, Sunny Point, Southport, North Carolina, *Chronology – Fort Johnston, Southport, North Carolina*, n.d.

[10] Angley, *A History of Fort Johnston*, pp. 7, 8, 10, 11, 15.

[11] Ibid., pp. 23, 25-27.

[12] Ibid., pp. 27-28; Sprunt, *Chronicles*, pp. 55.

[13] Ibid., pp. 134-135.

[14] Ibid. In his memoirs, Joseph G. Swift perhaps had a faulty recollection that the date of his arrival in Wilmington was June 17, 1805. His military biography indicates that he was assigned to Fort Johnston in 1804, and cemetery records indicate he was married on June 6, 1805. Brevet Major General George W. Cullum, *Biographical Register of the Officers and Graduates of the U. S. Military Academy at West Point, N. Y. From Its Establishment, March 16, 1802, to the Army Reorganization of 1866-1867*, Second Edition, Volume 1, New York: D. Van Nostrand, 192 Broadway, 1868 (hereinafter cited as Cullum, *Biographical Register of the Officers and Graduates of the U. S. Military Academy*), pp. 89-90; Washington Street Cemetery, Geneva, New York.

[15] Sprunt, *Chronicles*, pp. 134-135.

[16] Cullum, *Biographical Register of the Officers and Graduates of the U. S. Military Academy*, pp. 89-90; *Letter*, Swift to Burbeck, October 4, 1811, Rudy Spurling Papers, North Carolina Maritime Museum, Southport, North Carolina; United States Congress, *American State Papers: Military Affairs*, Washington: Gales and Seaton (hereinafter cited as *ASP: Military Affairs*), 1st Congress, 1st Session, Military Affairs: Volume 1, p. 246, From Library of Congress, *A Century of Lawmaking for a New Nation: U.S. Congressional Documents and Debates, 1774-1875*, <http://memory.loc.gov/ammem/amlaw/lwsp.html>, (accessed October 3, 2007).

[17] James Sprunt, *Tales and Traditions of the Lower Cape Fear, 1661-1896*, Wilmington, North Carolina: Legwin Brothers, Printers, 1896 (hereinafter cited as Sprunt, *Tales and Traditions*), pp. 138-139.

[18] Ibid.

[19] Angley, *A History of Fort Johnston*, p. 50; *ASP*, 1st Congress, 1st Session, Military Affairs: Volume 1, pp. 310, 821.

[20] *ASP*, 16th Congress, 1st Session, Military Affairs: Volume 2, pp. 348, 472; *ASP, Military Affairs*, 22nd Congress, 1st Session, Military Affairs: Volume 5, p. 854.

[21] Sprunt, *Tales and Traditions*, p. 134; *ASP: Military Affairs*, Vol. 5, p. 854.
[22] Sprunt, *Chronicles*, p. 55; House of Representatives, 37th Congress, 2nd Session, Report No. 86, *Permanent Fortifications and Sea-Coast Defence*, (hereinafter cited as House Report No. 86, 37th Congress, 2nd Session), pp. 203, 342-343; W.H.C. Whiting, *Sketch of Fort Johnston*, 1856, City of Southport, North Carolina.
[23] Sprunt, *Tales and Traditions*, p. 134; *Extract from annual report, dated October 1, 1861*, OR Series 1, Volume 1, p. 478.
[24] Report of Col. John L. Cantwell, April 17, 1861, OR Series 1, Volume 51, Part l, pp. 1-3; Tolbert, Ed., *The Papers of John Willis Ellis*, pp. 631, 640; House of Representatives, 37th Congress, 2nd Session, Report No. 86, *Permanent Fortifications and Sea-Coast Defence*, (hereinafter cited as House Report No. 86, 37th Congress, 2nd Session), pp. 342-343.
[25] The Civil War Artillery Page, <http://www.cwartillery.org/ve/6gun1.html>, (accessed March 6, 2009); Edwin Olmstead, et al, *The Big Guns: Civil War Siege, Seacoast, and Naval Cannon*, Alexandria Bay, NY: Museum Restoration Service, 1997 (hereinafter cited as Olmstead, et al, *The Big Guns*), pp. 285-297.
[26] John Gibbon, *The Artillerist's Manual*, Compiled from Various Sources, and Adapted to the Service of the United States, Second Edition, West Point, New York: 1863 (hereinafter cited as Gibbon, *The Artillerist's Manual*), Appendix, pp. 27, 40.

Chapter Two: Fort Caswell

[1] George M. Vickers, Ed., *Under Battle Flags: A Panorama of the Great Civil War, as represented in Story, Anecdote, Adventure, and the Romance of Reality*, Veteran Publishing Company, 1896 (hereinafter cited as Vickers, *Under Battle Flags*), James Eastus Price, "What a North Carolina Boy Saw During the War," pp. 339 & 343; Jim McNeil, *Masters of the Shoals, Tales of the Cape Fear Pilots Who Ran the Union Blockade*, Cambridge, MA: Da Capo Press, 2003 (hereinafter cited as McNeil, *Masters of the Shoals*), p. 130.
[2] See Glossary.
[3] House Report No. 86, 37th Congress, 2nd Session, pp. 2-4; Wikipedia, The Free Encyclopedia, <http://en.wikipedia.org/wiki/Seacoast_Defense_(US)>, (accessed January 23, 2008).
[4] Ibid.
[5] Ibid.
[6] See Glossary.
[7] Profiles and Sections of the *Fort projected for Oak Island, Mouth of Cape Fear River, N.C.*, Drawer 63, Sheets 2 & 2 1/2, National Archives and Records Administration, Cartographic Division; College Park, MD (hereinafter cited as *Fort projected for Oak Island*, NARA); See Glossary.
[8] *Fort projected for Oak Island*, NARA; See Glossary.
[9] *Fort projected for Oak Island*, NARA; See Glossary.
[10] *ASP: Military Affairs*, Vol. 3, p. 359; Cullum, Biographical Register of the Officers and Graduates of the U. S. Military Academy, p. 141; James Grant Wilson, Editor, *The Memorial History of the City of New-York From Its First Settlement to the Year 1892*, Volume IV, New York: New-York History Company, 1893, p. 48.
[11] U.S. House of Representatives, *Reports From The Court of Claims Submitted to the House of Representatives, The First Session of the Thirty-Fourth Congress, 1855-'56*, Volume 2, No. 38, Washington: Cornelius Wendell, Printer, 1856 (hereinafter cited as House of Representatives, *Reports From The Court of Claims*), p. 2.
[12] Ibid., pp. 6-7.
[13] Ibid., pp. 33-34.
[14] Ibid., pp. 47, 38-39, 34.
[15] Ibid., p. 9.
[16] Ibid., pp. 30-32.
[17] Sprunt, *Tales and Traditions*, p. 112; House of Representatives, *Reports From The Court of Claims*, pp. 39, 29-30.
[18] Ibid., pp. 38, 39.
[19] Ibid., pp. 130, 153, 130-131.
[20] Ibid., pp. 130-131, 36-37, 34. Three decades after the incident, the U.S. Government awarded Thomas Crown the princely sum of $3,500.00 for "gross and oppressive breach of contract on the part of Capt. Blaney." House of Representatives, *Reports From The Court of Claims*, pp. 159, 153.
[21] *ASP: Military Affairs*, Vol. 3, pp. 359.
[22] Ibid., p. 628.
[23] Ibid., Volume 4, pp. 13 & 164; Ibid., Vol. 5, p. 43.
[24] Cullum, *Biographical Register of the Officers and Graduates of the U. S. Military Academy*, pp. 51-52 & 448.

[25] *ASP: Military Affairs*, Vol. 5, p. 185; Ibid., p. 387; Cullum, *Biographical Register of the Officers and Graduates of the U.S. Military Academy*, p. 141.
[26] *ASP: Military Affairs*, Vol. 5, p. 656; Ibid., Vol. 6, p. 848.
[27] *ASP: Military Affairs*, Washington: Gales and Seaton, Vol. 7, pp. 632-633; Ibid., p. 900.
[28] The Buffalo Barracks Historical Website, (accessed October 29, 2008) <http://www.buffalonet.org/army/1002.htm>; Report Of Col. John L. Cantwell, April 17, 1861, *OR*, Series 1, Volume 51, Part 2, pp. 1-3.
[29] Ibid.; Tolbert, Ed., *The Papers of John Willis Ellis*, pp. 624, 617, 665.
[30] Report Of Col. John L. Cantwell, April 17, 1861, *OR*, Series 1, Volume 51, Part 2, pp. 1-3; Winslow to Davis, April 16, 1861, *OR* Series 1, Volume 51, Part 2, p. 13; Ellis to Davis; Davis to Ellis, April 19, 1861, ibid., p. 17.

Chapter Three: Siege Pieces

[1] Tolbert, Ed., *The Papers of John Willis Ellis*, pp. 638, 640; Olmstead, et al, *The Big Guns*, pp. 195-199.
[2] Walter Clark, Editor, *Histories of the Several Regiments and Battalions From North Carolina in the Great War 1861-'65*, Goldsboro, NC: Nash Brothers, Book and Job Printers, 1901 (hereinafter cited as Clark, *North Carolina Regiments*), Volume 4, p. 343; C.B. Comstock, Lt. Col. A.D.C. & Brvt. Brig. Gen. & c., *Plan and Sections of Fort Fisher Carried by assault by the U.S. Forces Maj. Gen. A.H. Terry Commanding Jan. 15th 1865 Head Qurtrs [sic], U.S. Forces Fort Fisher, Jan. 27th 1865 Forwarded to Engineer Dep't. with letter of this date*, Engineer Department, Library of Congress, Geography and Map Division, Washington, D.C. (hereinafter cited as Comstock, *Plan and Sections of Fort Fisher*).
[3] Olmstead, et al, *The Big Guns*, pp. 25, 28, 29, 34.
[4] Commander Tyrone G. Martin, U.S. Navy (Retired), "*Constitution*'s Wartime Gun Batteries," *The War of 1812 Magazine*, Issue 3, June 2006; *ASP: Military Affairs*, Volume 2, p. 511; Ibid., Volume 5, p. 594.
[5] William E. Birkhimer, *Historical Sketch of the Organization, Administration, Materiel and Tactics of the Artillery, United States Army*, Washington, DC: James J. Chapman, Agent, 1884 (hereinafter cited as Birkhimer, *Historical Sketch*), p. 278; Olmstead, et al, *The Big Guns*, pp. 25, 195; *ASP: Military Affairs*, Volume 2, p. 511; Ibid., Volume 7, p. 515.
[6] William Angley, *A History of Fort Johnston on the Lower Cape Fear*, Southport, NC: Southport Historical Society, 1996, p. 50; *ASP: Military Affairs*, Vol. 1, p. 821; ibid., Vol. 2, pp. 338, 487, 667; ibid., Vol. 5, pp. 854, 855.
[7] House Report No. 86, 37th Congress, 2nd Session, pp. 203, 342-343.
[8] Serviceable arms at the U.S. forts and arsenals, n.d., *OR* Series 3, Volume 1, p. 43.
[9] Confederate States of America War Department, *Regulations for the Army of the Confederate States, 1862*, Richmond, Virginia: J.W. Randolph, 1862, p. 313; United States War Department, *Regulations for the Army of the United States, 1857*, New York: Harper & Brothers, Publishers, p. 342; United States War Department, *Revised United States Army Regulations of 1861*, Washington: Government Printing Office, 1863, p. 407.
[10] Gibbon, *The Artillerist's Manual*, Appendix, pp. 27, 43.
[11] Tolbert, Ed., *The Papers of John Willis Ellis*, pp. 616.
[12] Ibid., pp. 622, 627.
[13] Ibid., p. 628; Orrell & Hawes, *Citizens File*, Voucher, State of North Carolina Ordnance Department To Orrell & Hawes, April 20, 1861, "For Transportation by order of D.K. McRae of the following articles from Depot of W & M R R to depot of W & W R R for shipment to Fort Macon – Viz. . . 4 cannon . . ." NARA.
[14] Ibid., pp. 619, 581; Tredegar Iron Works, Foundry Sales Book, 1860-1867 Library of Virginia, Richmond, Virginia (hereinafter cited as *Tredegar Sales Book*), April, 1861, p. 63.
[15] Tolbert, Ed., *The Papers of John Willis Ellis*, p. 629; *Tredegar Sales Book*, April, 1861, p. 64.
[16] Tolbert, Ed., *The Papers of John Willis Ellis*, pp. 619, 630, 721; Charles B. Dew, *Ironmaker to the Confederacy*, Richmond, VA: The Library of Virginia, 1999, p. 47. The Bellona Foundry never made a Pattern 1844 Columbiad. Olmstead, et al, *The Big Guns*, pp. 237-238. "4 – 8 in Columbiads – 36,980 [lbs];" Pattern 1861 8-inch Confederate Columbiads weighed in at about 8,750 lbs. and the Pattern 1857 8-inch Columbiad weighed, on average, 9200 lbs. *Tredegar Sales Book*, April, 1861, p. 68; Olmstead, et al, *The Big Guns*, pp. 64, 66, 67.
[17] Tolbert, Ed., *The Papers of John Willis Ellis*, pp. 636, 721, 653.
[18] *Tredegar Sales Book*, April, 1861, p. 68; Tolbert, Ed., *The Papers of John Willis Ellis*, p. 721; UNC Library, *Convention/Docsouth*, p. 39. "I have sent to Fort Macon one 10-inch columbiad, with its carriage, chassis, & c., complete, and four 8-inch columbiads . . ." "We [Fort Caswell] now have one 8-inch columbiad, mounted, two 8-inch sea-coast howitzers, and nine 24-pounders. In a few days two more columbiads, six 24-pounders, and some flank-defense 32-pounder carronades

will be in position." Whiting to Cooper, May 11, 1861, *OR* Series 1, Volume 51, Part 2, p. 84. The Cape Fear defenses mounted no 10-inch Columbiads until 1863. Whiting to Smith, December 22, 1862, *OR* Series 1, Volume 18, p. 808; Smith to Seddon, January 26, 1863, ibid., p. 859.

[19] Foster to Totten, March 28, 1861, *OR* Series 1, Volume 1, p. 225; *Interior view of Fort Sumter on the 14th April 1861, after its evacuation by Major Robert Anderson, 1st Artillery. U.S.A. Commanding: 1857 - 1942*, Still Picture Records Section, Special Media Archives Services Division (NWCS-S), National Archives and Records Administration (hereinafter cited as *Interior View of Fort Sumter on the 14th April 1861*, NWCS-S, NARA); Olmstead, et al, *The Big Guns*, p. 70.

[20] Gibbon, *The Artillerist's Manual*, Appendix, pp. 27, 44.

[21] Engineer Journal of the Bombardment of Fort Sumter, By Capt. J. G. Foster, Corps of Engineers, U.S. Army, October 1, 1861, *OR* Series 1, Volume 1, p. 19; Whiting to Beauregard, April 16, 1861, *OR* Series 1, Volume 51, Part 2, p. 13; *Interior View of Fort Sumter on the 14th April 1861*, NWCS-S, NARA.

[22] Range data for the Pattern 1844 Columbiad is taken from an older manual. *Ordnance Manual for the Use of the Officers of the United States Army*, Second Edition, Washington: Gideon & Co., Printers, 1850 (hereinafter cited as *U.S. Ordnance Manual*, 1850), pp. 362-363.

[23] Gibbon, *The Artillerist's Manual*, p. 159.

[24] Ibid., pp. 278, 405, 163-164.

[25] Ibid., p. 164-165, 405.

[26] Ibid., pp. 160, 269, Appendix, p. 29.

[27] Ibid., pp. 62, 65; Olmstead, et al, *The Big Guns*, pp. 227-228, 237-238.

[28] Gibbon, *The Artillerist's Manual*, pp. 66, 405.

[29] Ibid., pp. 62-63, 405.

[30] Ibid., pp. 68-69.

[31] Olmstead, et al, *The Big Guns*, p. 63; Gibbon, *The Artillerist's Manual*, pp. 68, 70, 462; Olmstead, et al, *The Big Guns*, p. 66.

[32] Gibbon, *The Artillerist's Manual*, p. 350; *The Ordnance Manual for the Use of the Officers of the United States Army*, Third Edition, Philadelphia: J.B. Lippincott & Co., 1862 (hereinafter cited as *U.S. Ordnance Manual*, 1862), p. 282.

[33] Gibbon, *The Artillerist's Manual*, pp. 350-351.

[34] Ibid., pp. 350-352, 70.

[35] Ibid., pp. 259, 350.

[36] Ibid., pp. 340-349.

Chapter Four: Inspector General Whiting

[1] Tolbert, Ed., *The Papers of John Willis Ellis*, p. 654; General Orders No. 13, Headquarters Provisional Forces, Charleston, S.C., April 11, 1861, *OR* Series 1, Volume 1, p. 305; Whiting to Beauregard, April 22, 1861, ibid., pp. 486-487.

[2] Francis B. Heitman, *Historical Register and Dictionary of the United States Army*, Volume I, Washington: Government Printing Office, 1903 (hereinafter cited as Heitman, *Historical Register*), page 1030; *Handbook of Texas Online*, http://www.tshaonline.org/handbook/online/articles/WW/fwhew.html (hereinafter cited as *Handbook of Texas Online*), (accessed October 24, 2007).

[3] Ibid.; *Register of Appointments, Confederate States Army*, Compiled Military Service Records of William Henry Chase Whiting, Textual Archives Services Division, National Archives and Records Administration, Washington, DC (hereinafter cited as NARA).

[4] *Handbook of Texas Online*; Whiting to Totten, January 7, 1861, *OR* Series 1, Volume 1, pp. 318-319; Report of Capt. Wm. H. C. Whiting, January 28, 1861, ibid., pp. 323-324.

[5] Heitman, *Historical Register*, p. 1030; Compiled Military Service Records of W.H.C. Whiting, *Register of Appointments, Confederate States Army*, NARA. The Army of the Confederate States (ACSA) was established by an act of the Confederate States Congress on March 6, 1861, thereby "providing for the military establishment of the Confederacy," in essence the Confederate Regular Army. Jefferson Davis, *The Rise and Fall of the Confederate Government*, Volume I, New York: D. Appleton and Company, 1881 (hereinafter cited as Davis, *The Rise and Fall of the Confederate Government*), p. 306. Davis to Whiting, February 23, 1861, *OR* Series 1, Volume 1, p. 258; Reports of Brig. Gen. G.T. Beauregard, March 6, 1861, ibid., p. 26; Beauregard to Walker, March 15, 1861, ibid., p. 275.

[6] General Orders No. 13, Headquarters Provisional Forces, Charleston, S.C., April 11, 1861, *OR* Series 1, Volume 1, p. 305.

[7] Whiting to Beauregard, April 22, 1861, *OR* Series 1, Volume 1, pp. 486-487.

[8] Sprunt, *Chronicles*, p. 281.
[9] Charles B. Hall, Compiler, *General Officers of the Confederate States of America*, New York: Lockwood Press, 1898, p. 13; Special Orders No. 32, Adj. and Insp. General's Office, Montgomery, April 22, 1861, *OR* Series 1, Volume 51, Chapter 2, p. 23; Ellis to Walker, April 26, 1861, *OR* Series 1, Volume 1, p. 488.
[10] *North Carolina. Convention (1861-1862). North Carolina. Military Board.* 70 pages, [Raleigh] Syme & Hall, Printers to the Convention 1861 Call number VC342.2 1861d v. 1, (North Carolina Collection, University of North Carolina at Chapel Hill), From the University Library, *Documenting the American South*, <http://docsouth.unc.edu/imls/troops/troops.html> (accessed October 31, 2007), (hereinafter cited as UNC Library, *Convention/Docsouth*), Holmes to Riddick, May 13, 1861, pp. 54 & 55. Brackets by author.
[11] Whiting to Beauregard, April 22, 1861, *OR* Series 1, Volume 1, pp. 486-487.
[12] Hart & Bailey, *Order*, April 28, 1861, *Confederate Papers Relating to Citizens or Business Firms, 1861-1865*, National Archives and Records Administration Publication No. M346, Washington, DC (hereinafter cited as *Citizens File*).
[13] Hart & Bailey, Voucher, State of North Carolina to Hart & Bailey, April 26, 1861, *Citizens File*, NARA; Whiting to Cooper, May 11, 1861, *OR* Series 1, Volume 51, Part 2, p. 84.
[14] Whiting to Walker, April 29, 1861, *OR* Series 1, Volume 1, p. 488; UNC Library, *Convention/Docsouth*, p. 51. "For transportation of 12 Carronades . . . from Portsmouth to Weldon" [and] "For transportation of 12 Carronades . . . from Portsmouth to Weldon," appears on first of three pages under date of May 6, 1861; *Commonwealth of North Carolina to Seaboard & Roanoke R. Rd. Co.* [3 pages], May 6, 1861, Seaboard R.R. Co., *Citizens File* (hereinafter cited as Seaboard R.R. Co.), NARA. Proceedings of the Advisory Council to the State of Virginia, May 7, 1861, *OR* Series 1, Volume 51, Part 2, p. 72. Brackets by author.
[15] Clement A. Evans, Editor, *Confederate Military History: A Library of Confederate States History Written by Distinguished Men of the South*, Atlanta, GA: The Confederate Publishing Company, 1899 (hereinafter cited as Evans, Ed., *Confederate Military History*), Volume III, pp. 124-126; *Journals and Papers of the Virginia State Convention of 1861*, Volume III, Documents, Doc. No. 40, Richmond, VA: Virginia State Library, 1966.
[16] Hart & Bailey, *Citizens File*.
[17] Ibid. "Columbiad Blocks" refer to cartridge blocks for a chambered Columbiad. Gibbon, *The Artillerist's Manual*, p. 350: Whiting to Beauregard, April 22, 1861, *OR* Series 1, Volume 1, pp. 486-487.
[18] Extract from annual report, dated October 1, 1861, *OR* Series 1, Volume 1, p. 478; Gibbon, *The Artillerist's Manual*, p. 206.
[19] Hart & Bailey, *Citizens File*.
[20] Voucher, North Carolina Ordnance Department To Thomas E. Roberts, June 29, 1861, Thomas E. Roberts, *Citizens File*, NARA; Voucher, North Carolina Ordnance Department To Orrell & Hawes, May 20, 1861, "For Transportation for Fort Caswell of 13 32 pdr. Carronades from depot . . . to Clarendon Iron Works," Orrell & Hawes, *Citizens File*, NARA.
[21] Whiting to Beauregard, April 22, 1861, *OR* Series 1, Volume 1, p. 486; Whiting to Cooper, May 11, 1861, *OR* Series 1, Volume 51, Part 2, p. 85.
[22] Sprunt, *Chronicles*, p. 135.
[23] Tolbert, Ed., *The Papers of John Willis Ellis*, p. 638; Telegram, McRee to Cantwell, April 16, 1861, John L. Cantwell Collection, Division of Archives and History, Raleigh, NC.
[24] Sprunt, *Chronicles*, pp. 281, 311; UNC Library, *Convention/Docsouth*, Schedule C, May 27, 1861, p. 20; Chris E. Fonvielle, Jr., *The Wilmington Campaign – Last Rays of Departing Hope*, Mechanicsburg, PA: Stackpole Books, 1997 (hereinafter cited as Fonvielle, Jr., *The Wilmington Campaign*), p. 36.
[25] Ibid.; Whiting to Cooper, May 11, 1861, *OR* Series 1, Volume 51, Part 2, p. 84.
[26] Fonvielle, Jr., *The Wilmington Campaign*, p. 36; Compiled Military Service Records of William Lord DeRosset and Henry Savage, NARA.
[27] Tolbert, Ed., *The Papers of John Willis Ellis*, p. 639; Fonvielle, Jr., *The Wilmington Campaign*, p. 36; Whiting to Cooper, May 11, 1861, *OR* Series 1, Volume 51, Part 2, p. 84; Tolbert, Ed., *The Papers of John Willis Ellis*, pp. 814, 823, 751.
[28] Whiting to Cooper, May 11, 1861, *OR* Series 1, Volume 51, Part 2, p. 84.
[29] UNC Library, *Convention/Docsouth*, pp. 29-31.
[30] Captain Simonton and his company were mustered into the 4th North Carolina State Troops on May 16, 1861 at Garysburg, and were therefore not in the Cape Fear on May 27, 1861. Clark, *North Carolina* Regiments, Volume 1, pp. 230-231.
[31] Captain Jones identified as Joseph P. Jones. Tolbert, Ed., *The Papers of John Willis Ellis*, p. 683.
[32] "The true title of the Company is Cabarrus Black Boys Riflemen." Tolbert, Ed., *The Papers of John Willis Ellis*, p. 775.
[33] Captain McNeely and his company were mustered into the 4th North Carolina State Troops on May 16, 1861 at Garysburg, and were therefore not in the Cape Fear on May 27, 1861. Clark, *North Carolina* Regiments, Volume 1, p. 231.
[34] Capt. Claudius B. Denson and his "Confederate Grays" identified. Clark, *North Carolina Regiments*, Vol. 4, p. 420.
[35] Bladen Guards, Capt. George Tait identified. *Hillsborough Recorder*, July 3, 1861.

[36] Bladen Infantry, Capt. Robert Tait identified. *Hillsborough Recorder*, July 3, 1861.
[37] Whiting to Cooper, May 11, 1861, *OR* Series 1, Volume 51, Part 2, p. 84.
[38] Ibid.
[39] Tolbert, Ed., *The Papers of John Willis Ellis*, p. 743; UNC Library, *Convention/Docsouth*, p. 54; Tolbert, Ed., *The Papers of John Willis Ellis*, p. 769.
[40] Orders, May 24, 1861, *OR* Series 1, Volume 2, p. 871; Tolbert, Ed., *The Papers of John Willis Ellis*, p. 751.
[41] Gwynn to Smith, May 23, 1861, *OR* Series 1, Volume 51, Part 2, p. 102; General Orders No.2, State of North Carolina Adjutant General's Office, May 27, 1861, ibid., p. 116. The Provisional Army of the Confederate States (PACS) was authorized by an act of the Confederate Congress on February 28, 1861, "to receive into the service . . . such forces now in the service of said States (Confederate States) as may be tendered, or who may volunteer by consent of their State . . . for any time not less than twelve months, unless sooner discharged." The intent being that such a force would be disbanded after the crisis was ended. Davis, *The Rise and Fall of the Confederate Government*, p. 304. Special Orders No. 8, State Troops of North Carolina, Adjutant General's Office, June 1, 1861, *OR* Series 1, Volume 51, Part 2, p. 125.

Chapter Five: General Gatlin

[1] Special Orders No. 8, State Troops of North Carolina, Adjutant General's Office, June 1, 1861, *OR* Series 1, Volume 51, Part 2, p. 125; Clark, *North Carolina Regiments*, Volume 1, p. 215; General Orders No. 4, State of North Carolina Adjutant General's Office, June 18, 1861, *OR* Series 1, Volume 51, Part 2, p. 146.
[2] Wikipedia, <http://en.wikipedia.org>, (accessed March 28, 2009).
[3] Cullum, *Biographical Register of the Officers and Graduates of the U. S. Military Academy*, p. 414.
[4] Ibid., pp. 414-415.
[5] Ibid., p. 415.
[6] Report of Maj. Richard C. Gatlin, April 24, 1861, *OR* Series 1, Volume 1, p. 650; Cullum, *Biographical Register of the Officers and Graduates of the U. S. Military Academy*, p. 415.
[7] Tolbert, Ed., *The Papers of John Willis Ellis*, p. 638; Company Muster Roll, June 12 to Aug. 31, 1861, Co. C, 2 Regiment North Carolina Artillery (36 State Troops), known as Capt. John J. Hedrick's Co. C, 36 Regt. N.C. Artillery, NARA; Louis Manarin, Compiler, *North Carolina Troops, 1861-1865, A Roster*, Raleigh, North Carolina: North Carolina Office of Archives and History, 2004 (hereinafter cited as Manarin, *North Carolina Troops*), Volume 1, p. 218; Statement of artillery subject to the order of the Ordnance Department, and their places of deposit, on the 30th day of June, 1861, *OR* Series 4, Volume 1, p. 621.
[8] Manarin, *North Carolina Troops*, Volume 1, p. 174. Bunting stationed "near Camp 'Davis' New Hanover County" from muster into service until October 31, 1861. Company Muster Roll, ____, 1861 to Oct. 31, 1861, Co. A, 2 Regiment North Carolina Artillery (36 State Troops), NARA. Sprunt, *Chronicles*, p. 312.
[9] Clark, *North Carolina Regiments*, Volume 2, pp. 111-113.
[10] Sprunt, *Chronicles*, p. 356; Devane's Company, as part of the "Sampson Rangers," was at Fort Johnston in May of 1861. UNC Library, *Convention/Docsouth*, p. 31. After forming a new company in July, Devane's Independent Company "remained at the fort." Confederate Veteran, *Maj. John R. Paddison*, Vol. XXVIII, No. 1, January, 1920, p. 27.
[11] Company Muster Roll, April 23 to Aug 31, 1861, Co. G, 3 Reg't North Carolina Cavalry (41 State Troops), NARA; *North Carolina Standard*, June 26, 1861.
[12] General Orders No. 10, Hdqrs. Southern Department, Coast defenses, June 22, 1861, *OR* Series 1, Volume 51, Part 2, pp. 146, 193; Gatlin to Winslow, July 17, 1861, ibid., p. 193.
[13] Statement of artillery subject to the order of the Ordnance Department, and their places of deposit, on the 30th day of June, 1861, *OR* Series 4, Volume 1, p. 621.
[14] Fort Sumter counted a total of four Seacoast Howitzers on its barbette tier after it was surrendered by Union forces in April of 1861. Foster to Totten, March 28, 1861, *OR* Series 1, Volume 1, P. 225. All twenty carronades requisitioned by Inspector General Whiting were shipped from Portsmouth to Weldon on 6 May. "May 6 – Transportation of 12 cannonades [sic] wgt 25200 lbs from Portsmouth to Weldon [and] 8 cannonades [sic] wgts 16800 lbs from Portsmouth to Weldon," Invoice, Commonwealth of North Carolina to Seaboard & Roanoke R. Rd. Co., page 1 of 3 pages, Seaboard R.R. Co., *Citizens File*, NARA. Then, on 6 May, the carronades were divided with one car to go to Wilmington and 2 cars to go to New Berne, but the greater number of carronades ended up in Wilmington. "May 6 - Mileage on 2 cars of cannonades [sic] from Weldon to Newbern [and] mileage on 1 car of cannonades [sic] to Wilmington," page 3 of 3 pages, ibid. Of the fifty cannon approved for

distribution from the State of Virginia to the State of North Carolina, twenty-six were dispatched to Hatteras and Ocracoke Inlets aboard the steamer *Fairfield* on 22 May. UNC Library, *Convention/Docsouth*, p. 39, 56. The remaining 24 guns, exclusive of the carronades, were shipped by rail to Weldon: "May 27 For transportation of 24 cannon shot shell & c. [etc.] wgts 86 tons from Portsmouth to Weldon at $2.50 per ton." Invoice, Commonwealth of North Carolina to Seaboard & Roanoke R. Rd. Co. page 1 of 3 pages, Seaboard R.R. Co., *Citizens File*, NARA. By virtue of the presence of eleven 32-pounders (obviously exclusive of the carronades) and two Navy shell guns in the Cape Fear defenses on June 30, it must be presumed that they were shipped soon after, leaving eleven in depot at Weldon. "I shall be glad to receive the eleven 32-pounders . . ." Gatlin to Winslow, July 17, 1861, *OR* Series 1, Volume 51, Part 2, p. 193. Brackets by author.

[15] *Journals and Papers of the Virginia State Convention of 1861*, Volume III, Documents, Richmond, Virginia: Virginia State Library, 1966 (hereinafter cited as *Virginia State Convention*, VSL), Doc. No. 40, pp. 82-83; Lieutenant Edward Simpson, Compiler, *A Treatise on Ordnance and Naval Gunnery*, New York: D. Van Nostrand, 192 Broadway, 1862 (hereinafter cited as Simpson, Comp., *A Treatise on Ordnance and Naval Gunnery*), pp. 122-128; Hart & Bailey, *Citizens File*; Proceedings of the Advisory Council of the State of Virginia, May 1, 1861, *OR* Series 1, Volume 51, Part 2, p. 60.

[16] Olmstead, et at, *The Big Guns*, pp. 33-34, 148-149.

[17] Inventory of cannon at Gosport stated: ". . . 235 61 cwt. old style, fifty 70 cwt. old style . . . ;" *Virginia State Convention*, VSL, Volume III, Doc. No. 40, p. 32.

[18] Olmstead, et al, *The Big Guns*, pp. 33-37; *Virginia State Convention*, VSL, Volume III, Doc. No. 40, p. 32. "I am moving some of the 32-pounders to the land side, but short guns of that caliber and carronades on siege carriages would be much more effective. Five 32s of twenty-seven hundredweight or thirty-three hundredweight and two carronades would, I think, be sufficient." Maury to Randolph, April 26, 1862, *OR* Series 1, Volume 11, Part 3, p. 497.

[19] Olmstead, et al, *The Big Guns*, pp. 37-40.

[20] Ibid., p. 43. "Steamer Yorktown . . . will mount 1 Sixty-four pounder pivot gun of 106 cwt." United States Government Printing Office, *Official Records of the Union and Confederate Navies in the War of the Rebellion*, Washington, D.C.: 1894-1922 (hereinafter cited as *ORN*), Series 1, Volume 5, p. 804. "Are there any 68-pounders (ship guns) mounted at the navy yard? Walker to Forney, March 2, 1861, *OR* Series 1, Volume 52, Part 2, p. 23. Please to have the columbiads (or navy 68-pounders) . . . sent to this place." R.E. Lee to Huger, May 7, 1862, *OR* Series 1, Volume 11, Part 3, p. 497.

[21] Olmstead, et al, *The Big Guns*, pp. 33-40, 59-66; U.S. Navy, Ordnance Instructions, Appendix B, No. VI, p. xvi.

[22] Report of Captain Barron, Virginia navy, June 10, 1861, "List of guns sent from the Norfolk navy yard to North Carolina, Tennessee, Louisiana, and Georgia," *ORN*, Series 1, Volume 5, pp. 803, 806.

[23] A 32-pounder projectile is 6.25 inches in diameter. The base of the pile of shot to the right of the image contains six shot, totaling 37.25 inches. The distance from the rear of the chase ring (muzzle ring) to the end of the muzzle is 9.75 inches. Applying these rudimentary measurements to the visible length of the gun in the first image very closely approximates the nominal length of this pattern and weight, but does not approach the length of those weights above and below it. Olmstead, et al, *The Big Guns*, p. 39.

[24] Ibid., p. 41.

[25] Clark, *North Carolina Regiments*, Volume 2, pp. 16-17; Letter, William H. Best to James High, September 3, 1861, *High Family Papers, 1861-1865*, Manuscripts Collection, Special Collections Department, William Madison Randall Library, University of North Carolina at Wilmington, Wilmington, NC (hereinafter cited as High Family Papers, Randall Library, UNC, Wilmington).

[26] Military Notices, *The Daily Journal*, July 19, 1861; Tolbert, Ed., *The Papers of John Willis Ellis*, pp. 886-887.

[27] Samuel A. Ashe, et al, Editors, *Biographical History of North Carolina From Colonial Times to the Present*, Volume VII, Greensboro, NC: Charles L. Van Noppen, 1908 (hereinafter cited as Ashe, et al, Eds., *Biographical History of North Carolina*), p. 62; Clark, *North Carolina Regiments*, Volume IV, p. 421; *Abstract*, Childs, Frederick L., Capt., AAAG and Lt. Col. Comdg. Arsenal, July 11, 1861, Compiled Military Service Records of Frederick L. Childs NARA; Gatlin to Winslow, July 17, 1861, *OR* Series I, Volume 51, Part 2, p. 193.

[28] Report of Flag Officer Pendergrast, July 14, 1861, U. S. Government Printing Office, *Official Records of the Union and Confederate Navies in the War of the Rebellion*, 30 Volumes in Two Series, Washington, D.C.: 1894-1922 (hereinafter cited as *ORN*), Series 1, Vol. 5, p. 792.

[29] Hart & Bailey, *Citizens File*.

[30] *Preliminary Chart of the Entrances to Cape Fear River and New Inlet*, Survey of the Coast of the United States, 1853.

[31] Ibid.; John Lucas Paul Cantwell Papers, Collection #3027, *Memo*, November 6, 1889, Southern Historical Collection, Wilson Library, University of North Carolina at Chapel Hill (hereinafter cited as *Cantwell Papers*, SHC, UNC-CH); Abstract log of the USS Daylight, July 17, 1861, *ORN*, Series 1, Volume 6, p. 691.

[32] Gatlin to Winslow, July 17, 1861, *OR* Series 1, Volume 51, Part 2, p. 193. See Note 14 on pages 168 and 169 for discussion of the number and types of guns sent to North Carolina from the Gosport Navy Yard in June 1861, particularly the 24 sent to Weldon and the subsequent partial shipment of 13 from there to Wilmington.

[33] Gatlin to Messrs. John McRae, William A. Wright, and John Bellamy, Members of the Committee of Safety of the Town of Wilmington, July 23, 1861, Ibid., pp. 201-202; Gatlin to Winslow, July 17, 1861, *OR* Series 1, Volume 51, Part 2, p. 193.

[34] Ibid.; Gatlin to Messrs. John McRae, William A. Wright, and John Bellamy, Members of the Committee of Safety of the Town of Wilmington, July 23, 1861, Ibid., pp. 201-202.

[35] Gatlin to Winslow, July 17, 1861, *OR* Series I, Volume 51, Part 2, p. 193; Gatlin to McRae, et al. July 23, 1861, ibid., pp. 201-202; Winslow to The President, July 22, 1861, ibid., pp. 192-193.

[36] Company Muster-In and Descriptive Roll, August 14, 1861, Capt. Galloway's Co., Coast Guards, N.C.; Company Muster Roll, August 14 to December 31, 1861, Capt. Galloway's Co., Coast Guards, North Carolina, NARA. "The blockade is firing rapidly at the cast [coast] guard about three miles from here." Letter, John B. McNeill to Miss Mollie, May 30, 1862, McNeill Papers, Duke University; Clark, *North Carolina Regiments*, Volume 5, p. 678. Brackets by author.

[37] Special Orders No. 64, Adjutant and Inspector General's Office, June 5, 1861, *OR* Series 1, Volume 2, p. 907; Cooper to Gatlin, August 19, 1861, *OR* Series 1, Volume 51, Part 2, p. 240.

[38] Gatlin to Cooper, August 25, 1861, ibid., p. 251; Gatlin to Cooper, August 26, 1861, ibid., p. 255.

[39] Francis B. Heitman, Compiler, *Historical Register and Dictionary of the United States Army From Its Organization, September 29, 1789, to March 2, 1903*, Volume 1, Washington: Government Printing Office, 1903 (hereinafter cited as Heitman, *Historical Register and Dictionary of the United States Army*), p. 436; Gatlin to Cooper, August 26, 1861, *OR* Series I, Volume 51, Part 2, p. 255; Ashe to Walker, September 7, 1861, Ibid., p. 277. "Captain Winder's plan of defence for Federal Point consisted in a strong fort at the Point; a redoubt at the head of the sound, and an intermediate one, with a heavy covered-way striking from the head of the Sound to Fort Fisher, and commanding the beach." Clark, *North Carolina Regiments*, Vol. 4, p. 422.

[40] Register containing Rosters of Commissioned Officers, Provisional Army Confederate States, Compiled Military Service Records of Franklin J. Faison, NARA. Lieutenant Colonel Faison's command of Fort Caswell is noted by his relief from that command. Special Orders No. 143, District of the Cape Fear, December 17, 1861, ibid.; J.G. Martin, Travel Pass, August 28, 1861, *Cantwell Papers*, SHC, UNC-CH.

[41] *Report of the Joint Committee on the Conduct of the War*. In Three Parts, Washington: Government Printing Office, 1863, Part III, p. 282; Report of Lieut. F.U. Farquhar, September 7, 1861, *OR* Series 1, Volume 4, pp. 590-592; Maxwell to Rowan, September 18, 1861, *ORN* Series 1, Volume 6, p. 223.

[42] Invoice, State of North Carolina To W. & W. R. R. Co. for Transportation, Augt. 31, 1861, Wilmington & Weldon Rail Road Co., *Citizens File*, NARA; Invoice, Confederate States of America, To Thomas E. Roberts of Wilmington, N.C., August 29 (1861), Thomas E. Roberts, *Citizens* File, NARA. "I found in the yard of the Clarendon Iron Works thirteen 32 pounder Carronades mounted on carriages just completed at that establishment. I took them for the flank defences at Fort Caswell and for land front defences at Fort Fisher." Certification by S.L. Fremont, Col & Chf Engineer, District Cape Fear, December 31, 1861, ibid.

[43] Holmes to His Excellency the President, August 31, 1861, *OR* Series I, Volume 51, Part 2, pp. 263-264.

Chapter Six: General Anderson

[1] Cooper to Anderson, September 3, 1861, *OR* Series I, Volume 4, p. 639.

[2] Cullum, *Biographical Register of the Officers and Graduates of the U. S. Military Academy*, p. 631.

[3] Gatlin Papers, UNC at Chapel Hill, "*Report of Opperations* [sic] *in the Department of North Carolina from the 20th August 1861 to 19th March 1862* (hereinafter cited as *Report of Opperations*, Gatlin Papers, UNC-CH); Gatlin to Cooper, September 4, 1861, *OR* Series I, Volume 51, Part 2, p. 270; Clark to Walker, September 7, 1861, ibid., p. 643.

[4] Special Orders No. 151, Adjutant and Inspector General's Office, September 12, 1861, Compiled Military Service Records of John A. Brown, NARA; Clark, *North Carolina Regiments*, Vol. 4, pp. 421-422.

[5] Ashe to His Excellency, Jefferson Davis, September 20, 1861, *OR* Series I, Volume 51, Part 2, pp. 304-305; *Regimental Return*, September, 1861, Compiled Military Service Records of Franklin J. Faison, NARA.

[6] Gatlin to Adjutant-General C.C. Army, September 21, 1861, *OR* Series I, Volume 51, Part 2, pp. 307-308; Special orders No. 166, Adjutant and Inspector General's Office, September 29, 1861, *OR* Series I, Volume 4, p. 662.

[7] Clark, *North Carolina Regiments*, Volume 4, pp. 421-422.

[8] Letter, Colin Shaw to "My Dear," September 22, 1861, *Colin Shaw Papers*, Division of Archives and History, Raleigh, NC; North Carolina Historical Sites, Fort Fisher, <http://www.nchistoricsites.org/fisher/fort-fisher.htm> (accessed April 24, 2009); Anderson to Cooper, September 24, 1861, *OR* Series I, Volume 4, p. 654.

[9] William Lamb, "Defence of Fort Fisher, North Carolina," *Papers of the Military Historical Society of Massachusetts*, Vol. 9, Boston: By the Society, 1912 (hereinafter cited as Lamb, "Defence of Fort Fisher, North Carolina,") p. 349; Ashe to His Excellency, Jefferson Davis, September 20, 1861, *OR* Series I, Volume 51, Part 2, pp. 304-305.

[10] Abstract from return of the Confederate Department of North Carolina, Brig. Gen. Richard C. Gatlin, commanding, for the month of September, 1861, *OR* Series 1, Volume 4, p. 662.

[11] Regimental Return, September 1861, Companies A, C, G, H, I, and K, 10th Reg't N.C. Inf., shows station of each company as Fort Johnson [sic], NARA.

[12] Devane's Company, as part of the "Sampson Rangers," was at Fort Johnston in May of 1861. UNC Library, *Convention/Docsouth*, p. 31. After forming a new company in July, Devane's Independent Company "remained at the fort." Confederate Veteran, *Maj. John R. Paddison*, Vol. XXVIII, No. 1, January, 1920, p. 27.

[13] Regimental Return for September 1861, Companies B, D, and F, 10th Reg't N.C. Inf., NARA, shows station of each company as Fort Caswell, NARA.

[14] Captain Slough's Company was recalled to Fort Johnston and Captain Denson's Company took its place at the Radcliffe Battery sometime before September. Regimental Return for September 1861, Co. A, 20 Regiment North Carolina Infantry, shows station of company as Fort Johnston, NARA; Regimental Return for September 1861, Co. E, 20 Regiment North Carolina Infantry shows station of company as Radcliffe Battery, NARA.

[15] "About the middle of September, Companies F and I were sent to Fort Fisher . . ." Clark, *North Carolina Regiments*, Volume. 2, p. 17.

[16] Company Muster Roll, for September and October 1861, Capt. John J. Hedrick's Detached Co. of Artillery, NARA.

[17] "About the middle of September . . . Company K from its vicinity, was sent across New Inlet channel to a battery on Zeke's Island." Clark, *North Carolina Regiments*, Volume. 2, p. 17. Captain Purdie's company received a Columbiad carriage at Fort Fisher about September 20, 1861 – "carriage in position at Fort Fisher under command of Capt. Purdie." Voucher, n. d., Confederate States of America To Wilmington & Weldon R. R., Wilmington & Weldon Rail Road Co., *Citizens File*, NARA.

[18] Field & Staff Muster Roll for September 1861, shows station of Field & Staff, Camp Wyatt, 18th Reg't N.C. Inf., NARA.

[19] From the 18th Regiment, "three companies detached to work the guns at Fort Fisher . . . and Bolles Battery." Company A Muster Roll, Record of Events for June 15 to August 31, 1861, 18th Regiment North Carolina Infantry, NARA. "About the middle of September, Companies F and I were sent to Fort Fisher . . ." Clark, *North Carolina Regiments*, Volume. 2, p. 17. Captain Savage's Company is therefore assumed to have been the third company and to have remained at Bolles Battery, where they began their service on Confederate Point.

[20] Moore's Battery returned to the Cape Fear and occupied Camp Hopkins in early September, soon after its muster into State service on August 30 at Camp Boylan near Raleigh. Gatlin Papers, UNC at Chapel Hill, "*Report of Opperations [sic] in the Department of North Carolina from the 20th August 1861 to 19th March 1862*; Company Muster Rolls, August 23 to 31, 1861 and August 23, 1861, Co. E, 1 Regiment North Carolina Artillery (10 State Troops), NARA.

[21] Company Muster Roll for ___ 1861 to Oct. 31, 1861, Capt. Samuel R. Bunting's Co., Wilmington Horse Arty., NARA.

[22] The 15th Regiment, led by Colonel Thomas Lanier Clingman was only partially armed and, upon its arrival in Wilmington, was assigned to Camp Davis on Masonborough Sound. Clark, *North Carolina Regiments*, Vol. 2, p. 293.

[23] Incidental to Captain Edmondston's resignation in September, 2nd Lieutenant Atherton B. Hill assumed command of the Scotland Neck Mounted Rifles. Hill wasn't promoted to Captain until 9 October 1861. Company Muster Roll for Sept. & Oct. 1861, (New) Co. G, 3 N.C. Cavalry (41 State Troops), formerly Capt. Atherton B. Hill's Co. Cav., Scotland Neck Rifles, NARA.

[24] Colonel James Henry Lane's 28th Regiment had no weapons at all when it arrived in Wilmington. In order to better furnish their subsistence and equipment, the 28th Volunteers were encamped on the "Goldsboro Rail Road" near Wilmington. Clark, *North Carolina Regiments*, Vol. 2, pp. 467-469; Roll of Honor, Historical Memoranda, p. 2, n.d., 28 Reg't North Carolina Troops, NARA.

[25] Colonel Frances Marion Parker's 30th Regiment was the only one that was fully armed, so it was ordered to Smithville, encamping at Camp Walker the evening of 29 September. Report of Brig. Gen. Richard C. Gatlin, October 1, 1862, *OR* Series 1, Volume 4, p. 575; Abstract from return of the Confederate Department of North Carolina, Brig. Gen. Richard C. Gatlin, commanding, for the month of September, 1861, *OR* Series I, Volume 4, p. 662; Gatlin to Hill, October 2, 1861, *OR* Series 1, Volume 51, Part 2, p. 332; Roll of Honor, Historical Memoranda, p. 2, n.d., 30 Reg't North Carolina Troops, NARA.

[26] Company Muster Roll, Aug 14 to Dec. 31, 1861, Capt. Galloway's Co., Coast Guards, North Carolina also known as Lt. Galloway's Detachment Coast Guards, NARA.

[27] Clark, *North Carolina Regiments*, Vol. 2, pp. 467-469.

[28] Clark, *North Carolina Regiments*, Vol. 1, p. 581; Anderson to Cooper, September 24, 1861, *OR* Series 1, Volume 4, pp. 656-657; J. R. Anderson and Co., *Citizens File*, Invoices, September 11-30, 1861; Gibbon, *Artillerist's Manual*, Appendix, p. 41.

[29] Report of Flag-Officer Forrest, September 2, 1861, *ORN* Series 1, Vol. 6, p. 150; Report of Captain Hull, August 31, 1861, ibid., p. 149; George M. Brooke, Jr., Editor, *Ironclads and Big Guns of the Confederacy, The Journals and Letters of John M. Brooke*, Columbia, SC: University of South Carolina Press, 2002 (hereinafter cited as Brooke, Jr., Ed., *Ironclads and Big Guns of the Confederacy*), pp. 40, 43; Cooper to Hill, October 3, 1861, *OR* Series 1, Volume 4, p. 674.

[30] Report of Lieut. Daniel W. Flagler, February 20, 1862, *OR* Series I, Volume 9, p. 81.

[31] Brooke, Jr., Ed., *Ironclads and Big Guns of the Confederacy*, pp. 45, 47; Olmstead, et al, *The Big Guns*, pp. 113, 125, 157.

[32] Mallory to Hon. Secretary of War, October 23, 1861, *OR* Series 1, Volume 4, p. 687.

[33] *South Carolina, 1670. 1783. The Centennial of Incorporation, 1883*, Charleston, S. C.: The News and Courier Book Press, 1884, p. 235; *Charleston Mercury*, July 20, 1861; *Columbus Times*, September 9, 1861.

[34] Bell, *Civil War Heavy Explosive Ordnance*, pp. 173, 267, 389; Olmstead, et al, *The Big Guns*, pp. 197-199; Leadbetter to Lockett, August 22, 1861, *OR* Series 1, Volume 52, Part 2, p. 131.

[35] *Letter*, Clark to Drane, September 11, 1861, Governors' Papers, *Governor Henry T. Clark's Letter Book*, North Carolina State Archives, Raleigh, NC.

[36] Clark, *North Carolina Regiments*, Volume 4, p. 422; *Letter*, Clark to Eason, September 26, 1861, Governors' Papers, *Governor Henry T. Clark's Letter Book*, North Carolina State Archives, Raleigh, NC; Anderson to Davis, September 28, 1861, *OR* Series 1, Volume 51, Part 2, p. 322.

[37] Anonymous 1864 Cape Fear inspection: three 24-pounder and four 32-pounder rifles, all unbanded. This inspection did not include the batteries at the obstructions. Anonymous, *List of Ordnance at the Forts & Batteries & Light Batteries in the Command Defcs Mth of Cape Fear River*, August, 1864, Record Group 109, Microfilm M935, Roll 18, National Archives (hereinafter cited as *List of Ordnance*, RG 109, Microfilm M935, Roll 18, National Archives). Inspection of the obstructions in February, 1865 found two unbanded 24-pounders. Hebert to Anderson, February 4, 1865, *OR* Series 1, Volume 47, Part 2, p. 1115. The presence of four unbanded 32-pounders in 1865 is contradicted by the presence of five rifled 32-pounders mounted at Fort Caswell's gorge on April 27, 1862. The greater number must be accepted as the actual number of that caliber initially rifled by the Easons. "On the S.W. side of fort there are 6 rifle guns, 1 large 64-pounder, and 5 32-pounders . . ." Abstract Log of the USS Monticello, April 27, 1862, *ORN* Series 1, Volume 7, pp. 718-719.

[38] Voucher No. 41, Oct. 3, 1861, Confederate States of America To: Richmond and Petersburg R. R. Co., p. 2 of 12 pp., Richmond & Petersburg Rail Road Co., *Citizens* File, NARA; *Tredegar Sales Book*, October 4, 1861, p. 144; Charles B. Dew, *Ironmaker to the Confederacy – Joseph R. Anderson and the Tredegar Iron Works*, Richmond: The Library of Virginia, 1999, p. 112; Invoice of Ordnance and Ordnance Stores turned over to Capt. John A. Brown CS Arty – comdg Fort Caswell NC, Oct 26th 1861, pp. 1-2, Compiled Military Service Records of Ravenscroft Burr, NARA.

[39] *Abstract*, October 3, 1861; *Pay Voucher*, Nov. 13, 1861, Compiled Military Service Records of John A. Brown, NARA.

[40] This cavalry company from New Hanover County mustered into Confederate service on 10 October under the provisions of a Confederate act of Congress to provide for local defense and special service. Company Muster-in Roll, October 10, 1861, Capt. Howard's Co. Cav., N.C. (Local Defense), NARA; An Act to Provide for Local Defense and Special Service, August 21, 1861, *OR* Series 4, Volume 1, p. 579. Considered to be made up of "men too old for service in the field," Howard's Company was sent to Swansborough soon after its muster and ordered to submit to the orders of Brigadier General D. H. Hill instead of General Anderson, in whose district the hamlet on the sounds was situated. Apparently, neither Hill nor Gatlin realized that Howard's men had enlisted "to be employed for the defense of the City of Wilmington and its vicinity, extending to the sea coast." While it might be argued that Swansborough was in the vicinity of Wilmington, Captain Howard must have believed otherwise. Within weeks of its arrival in Swansborough, the local defense cavalry company was ready to go home. When D.H. Hill reported the situation to Gatlin, the General seemed to acquiesce to the conditions of Howard's service in his reply. "I am surprised to hear that Captain Howard intends to return to Wilmington." Sprunt, *Chronicles*, p. 226; Gatlin to Hill, October 30, 1861, *OR* Series 1, Volume 51, Part 2, p. 365.

[41] Abram Francis Newkirk's cavalry company was mustered into Confederate service on 18 October at Camp Heath near Scott's Hill in New Hanover County under provisions of the Confederate States local defense law. Newkirk's Company, unlike Howard's Company before it, was simply ordered to serve in local defense and special service for twelve months, without special conditions. Company Muster-in Roll, October 18, 1861, New Co. A, 3 Cav., N.C. (41 State Troops), known as Capt. A.F. Newkirk's Co. of Cav., NARA; Company Muster Roll, Oct. 10 to Dec. 31, 1861, New Co. A, 3 Reg't North Carolina Cavalry (41 State Troops), NARA.

[42] On October 7, after three weeks of waiting in Richmond for assignment, Captain John O. Grisham's "Confederate Guards Artillery" from Pontotoc County, Mississippi finally received the orders they had been expecting, but their destination was altogether unexpected. "We were having a good time, when, to our surprise and disappointment, we were ordered to Wilmington, N.C. Northern Virginia had been our objective point," lamented Lieutenant Patrick C. Hoy. Special Orders, No.

173, Adjt. And Insp. General's Office, Richmond, October 7, 1861, *OR* Series 1, Volume 51, Part 2, p. 336; Patrick C. Hoy, *A Brief History of Bradford's Battery, Confederate Guards Artillery of Pontotoc County, Miss., Personal Recollections of Lieut. P.C. Hoy*, Petersburg, VA: July 1, 1903 (hereinafter cited as Hoy, *A Brief History of Bradford's Battery*).

[43] Richardson's Company was organized and mustered into State service on 19 October 1861, whereupon it was assigned to Fort Fisher. Manarin, *North Carolina Troops*, Volume 1, p. 313; Company Muster Roll for Oct. 19 to Dec. 31, 1861, Captain John A. Richardson's Co, (Bladen Artillery), North Carolina Volunteers, NARA.

[44] McNair's Company from Robeson County was mustered into State service on September 25, 1861 and into Confederate service soon thereafter. Orders to report to Raleigh were countermanded en route and the company was retained in Wilmington, where it encamped until late October, at which time orders were received to report to Fort Caswell. The "Scotch Greys" posted their first-ever Muster Roll from that duty station on October 31, 1861. Manarin, *North Carolina Troops*, Volume 1, pp. 236; Company Muster Roll, Sept. 25 to Oct. 31, 1861, Co. E, 3 Regiment North Carolina Artillery (40 State Troops), known as Capt. M. McNair's Co. (Scotch Greys Artillery) N.C. Vols., NARA.

[45] Henry Harding's unattached company mustered into Confederate service at Wilmington on 6 November 1861. Company Muster-in Roll, November 7, 1861, Captain Henry Harding's Company of North Carolina Volunteers, NARA.

[46] Captain Stevenson's unattached company was mustered into Confederate service at Fort Caswell on November 15, 1861, where it remained on permanent duty. Company Muster-in Roll, Nov. 15, 1861, Co. A, 2 Reg't N.C. Art'y (36 State Troops), known as Captain Jas. M. Stevenson's Co. of Art'y., N.C. Vols., NARA.

[47] Captain Walton's "Davis Dragoons" mustered into State service on November 23 subsequently transferring to Confederate service on December 1. Not long after muster, the cavalrymen pitched their tents at Camp Anderson in the town limits of Wilmington. Company Muster-in Roll, December 17, 1861, Co. F, 3 Reg't. N.C. Cav (41 Regt. State Troops), known as Captain Thos. G. Walton's Company of North Carolina Volunteers, NARA.

[48] Just three days before year's end, Captain Ward's Company of Cavalry was mustered into State service and assigned to the same coast guard duty at Swansborough that Captain Howard's Company not so subtly rejected. Company Muster-in Roll, December 28, 1861, Co. "New B", 3 Reg't N.C. Cav., known as Captain Edward W. Ward's Company of Cavalry of North Carolina Volunteers, NARA; Company Muster Roll, Jan. & Feb., 1861, ibid.

[49] Hoy, *A Brief History of Bradford's Battery*; Gibbon, *Artillerist's Manual*, Appendix, p. 40.

[50] Letter, J. M. Stevenson to Miss M. J. Beatty, President, Lisbon Soldiers Aid Society, November 17, 1861, *G. H. Beatty Papers, 1861-1862*, Special Collections Library, Duke University, Durham, NC (hereinafter cited as *Beatty Papers*, Special Collections Library, Duke University).

[51] Clark, *North Carolina Regiments*, Volume 2, p. 293; Ibid., Vol. 1, p. 581; Ibid., Volume 2, p. 18.

[52] Ibid., p. 497. "We were encamped near Craig's on Federal Point which you will see on my map. From this camp we marched out every morning to practice with the heavy guns at Fort Fisher, about half a mile or more away. At that time they were just building the casement [sic] guns, those we exercised upon were old Columbia [sic] en barbette." Dr. Thomas Fanning Wood – Journal, *"Some Recollections of My Life Written for My Children During My Confinement With Aneurysm Beginning 25th April, 1886,"* Wood Family Papers #172 in the Special Collections Department, Randall Library, University of North Carolina-Wilmington. "Three companies detached to work the guns at Fort Fisher – Anderson Battery, Gatlin Battery and Bolles' Battery." Company Muster Roll, June 15 to Aug 31, 1861, Co. A, 18 Regiment North Carolina Infantry (State Troops), NARA.

[53] Special Orders, No. 222, Adjutant And Inspector General's Office, November 14, 1861, *OR* Series I, Volume 51, Part 2, p. 377.

[54] The unattached "Confederates" were transferred from Fort Johnston to Fort Caswell on 27 October 1861. Company Muster Roll for Enrollment to October 31, 1861, Co. A, 61 Regiment North Carolina Infantry, known as Capt. Wm. S. Devane's Co. (Confederates) N.C. Vols., NARA.

[55] On the last day of October, Captain Thomas J. Purdie's Company K of the 18th Regiment was officially detached from its regiment and re-designated Company B of the 36th Regiment North Carolina Troops. Manarin, *North Carolina Troops*, Volume 1, p. 198. Transferred from Zeek's Island (Winder Battery) to Fort Fisher on or before 14 November 1861. Letter, G.H. Beatty to his Mother, November 14, 1861, *Beatty Papers*, 1861-1862, Special Collections Library, Duke University. The apprehension felt by the men of Purdie's Battery that their stay at Fort Fisher might be an extended one was erased on December 12, when they were ordered to trade places with Captain John J. Hedrick's "Cape Fear Light Artillery" on Zeek's Island. Manarin, *North Carolina Troops*, Volume 1, p. 218.

[56] Within a week of the departure of Radcliffe's command, Colonel Parker's 30th Regiment was transferred from Camp Walker near Smithville to Camp Wyatt, where two of his men died of disease in mid-November 1861. Compiled Military Service Records of Obed Carr [November 16] and William W. Cox [November 17], NARA. Brackets by author.

[57] Howard's Company hadn't returned to Wilmington as of October 30, 1861, but duty station shown as Wilmington on a company muster roll for November and December. Gatlin to Hill, October 30, 1861, *OR* Series I, Volume 51, Part 2, p. 365;

Muster Roll for Oct. 10 to Dec. 31, 1861, Capt. Howard's Co. Cavy. (Local Defense), N.C., NARA. Duty station shown as Fort Fisher for January and February, 1862. Muster Roll for Jan. and Feby., 1861, Capt. Howard's Co. Cav. (Local Defense), N.C., NARA. It should be noted that General Anderson counted no cavalry at Fort Fisher on February 13, 1862, but did indicate the presence of one company at Camp Hopkins on that date. All other companies and their duty stations have been otherwise accounted for, therefore indicating that Captain Howard's company was at Camp Hopkins until sometime in February, when it was transferred to Fort Fisher and mustered its troops for the period January and February, 1861. Anderson to Cooper, February 13, 1862, *OR* Series 1, Volume 9, p. 432.

[58] Bunting's Battery transferred from Camp Davis to Camp Anderson in Wilmington in early November, probably to receive its ordnance and begin the metamorphosis from coast guard to light artillery. Manarin, *North Carolina Troops*, Volume 1, p. 174. Bunting's Battery was transferred from Wilmington back to Camp Davis on January 11, 1862. Company Muster Roll, Jan. and Feb., 1862, Capt. S.R. Bunting's Co. Wilmington Horse Artillery, NARA.

[59] Atherton B. Hill was promoted to Captain on 9 October 1861. Company Muster Roll for Sept. and Oct., 1861 shows date of commission as "Oct 9, 1861," Co. H (Atherton B. Hill), 3 Cav. (41 State Troops), N.C., known as Capt. Atherton B. Hill's Co., (Scotland Neck Rifles), North Carolina Cavalry, NARA. Sometime in the last two months of the year, the cavalry company from Halifax County moved from Camp Winslow to Camp Grant, supposed to be situated on land owned by Grant's Salt Works about a mile north of Wrightsville, on the Sound. Company Muster Roll for Nov. & Dec. 1861, (New) Co. G, 3 N.C. Cavalry (41 State Troops), formerly Capt. Atherton B. Hill's Co. (Scotland Neck Rifles), North Carolina Cav., NARA.

[60] The "Scotch Greys" were transferred to Fort Caswell in mid-November 1861. Manarin, *North Carolina Troops*, Volume 1, p. 417. Company Muster Roll for Nov. and Dec. 1861, Co. E, 3 Regiment North Carolina Artillery, formerly Capt. McNair's Co., (Scotch Greys Artillery) N.C. Vols., NARA.

[61] Patrick C. Hoy, *A Brief History of Bradford's Battery, Confederate Guards Artillery of Pontotoc County, Miss., Personal Recollections of Lieut. P.C. Hoy*, Petersburg, VA: July 1, 1903 (hereinafter cited as Hoy, *A Brief History of Bradford's Battery*).

[62] "This company changed station from Zeke's [sic] Island to Fort Fisher December 12, 1861." Company Muster Roll for Nov. and Dec., 1861, Capt. Cummings' Co. C, 2 Regiment North Carolina Artillery (36 State Troops), formerly Capt. John J. Hedrick's Co. (Cape Fear Artillery) N.C. Vols., NARA.

[63] Gatlin to Anderson, December 4, 1861, *OR* Series 1, Volume 51, Part 2, p. 405; Gatlin to Martin, December 6, 1861, *OR* Series 1, Volume 51, Part 2, p. 406.

[64] Company Muster-in Roll, January 1, 1862, Captain Daniel Munn's Company of Artillery, North Carolina Volunteers, NARA; Company Muster Roll for Jan. and Feb. 1862, Capt. Munn's Co. B, 2 Regiment North Carolina Artillery (36 State Troops), NARA.

[65] Special Orders No. 143, December 17, 1861, Compiled Military Records, Franklin J. Faison, NARA. "Joined Post from sick leave of absence Oct. 28, 1861." Regimental Return of the Post of Fort Caswell (20th North Carolina) for the month of October, 1861, ibid.; Brown to Heath, January 1, 1862, *OR* Series 1, Volume 51, Part 2, p. 430.

[66] William and Mary College, *Letters of Major Thomas Rowland, C.S.A.*, Quarterly Historical Magazine, Volume XXVI, No. 4, April 1917 (hereinafter cited as William and Mary College, *Letters of Major Thomas Rowland, C.S.A.*), pp. 226, 227.

[67] Ibid., pp. 233, 225; Manarin, *North Carolina Troops*, Vol. 1, p. 158.

[68] Abstract from return of District of the Cape Fear, commanded by Brig. Gen. Joseph R. Anderson, for January, 1862, *OR* Series 1, Volume 9, p. 424.

[69] "Fort Caswell is supported by the remaining nine companies of the Twentieth Regiment North Carolina Volunteers, stationed at Smithville or Fort Johnston, numbering in the aggregate 765 men." Anderson to Cooper, February 13, 1862, *OR* Series 1, Volume 9, p. 432.

[70] "Fort Caswell, on the south side of the Cape Fear River, about 30 miles from Wilmington, is manned by three unattached companies and one company of the Twentieth Regiment North Carolina Volunteers . . ." While Company H is still most likely to have been that one company of the 20th Volunteers, no evidence can be located to confirm it. Anderson to Cooper, February 13, 1862, *OR* Series 1, Volume 9, p. 432.

[71] "At the Northern or New Inlet of the Cape Fear River the defenses consist of a battery on Zeeke's Island, manned by one company, of the aggregate strength 99, and Fort Fisher, manned by two unattached companies and one company of the Thirtieth Regiment North Carolina Volunteers, aggregate 250, supported by nine companies of the Thirtieth Regiment, aggregate of which is 770, and a battery of light artillery of four 12-pounders." Anderson to Cooper, February 13, 1862, *OR* Series 1, Volume 9, p. 432.

[72] See Note 71.

[73] See Note 71.

[74] "I have at Wilmington the Twenty-eighth Regiment North Carolina Volunteers, aggregate 933, and one battery of light artillery of six 6-pounders." Anderson to Cooper, February 13, 1862, *OR* Series 1, Volume 9, p. 432. General Anderson may

have forgotten that Bunting's Battery was transferred from Wilmington to Camp Davis on January 11, 1862. In any event, Anderson's statement confirms that the reason for bringing Bunting to Wilmington was to arm his battery and it also positively fixes the Captain's armament at six 6-pounder guns. See Note 58.

[75] See Note 57.

[76] After five months on the beach west of Fort Caswell, the detachment of coast guardsmen finally recruited enough men by January 29 to be mustered into Confederate service as "Captain John W. Galloway's Company of North Carolina Volunteers, known as Coast Guards." Company Muster-in and Descriptive Roll, January 29, 1862, Captain John W. Galloway's Company of North Carolina Volunteers, known as Coast Guards, NARA.

[77] *Tredegar Sales Book*, October 4, 1861, p. 186; Invoice No. 258, Jany. 1861, p. 9 of 13 pp., Confederate States of America To: Richmond & Petg. R. R. Co., Richmond & Petersburg Rail Road, *Citizens File*, NARA.

[78] "We were encamped near Craig's on Federal Point which you will see on my map. From this camp we marched out every morning to practice with the heavy guns at Fort Fisher, about half a mile or more away. At that time they were just building the casement [sic] guns, those we exercised upon were old Columbia [sic] en barbette." Dr. Thomas Fanning Wood, *Journal, Book 2, Some Recollections of My Life Written for My Children During My Confinement With Aneurysm Beginning 25th April, 1886*, Wood Family Papers, Special Collections, William Madison Randall Library, University of North Carolina at Wilmington, Wilmington, NC. One Columbiad carriage and platform was manufactured by Ettenger & Edmond of Richmond and transported to Wilmington via the Wilmington & Weldon Rail Road Co. on September 19. "One 8-in. Columbiad Carriage, complete with . . . platform" was "in position at Fort Fisher under command of Capt. Purdie" later in the month. Receipt, Sept. 19th, 1861, Ettenger & Edmond, *Citizens File*, NARA; Voucher for columbiad carriage, n.d., Confederate States of America To Wilmington Weldon R. R., Wilmington & Weldon Rail Road Co., *Citizens File*, NARA.

[79] Report of Lieutenant Braine, January 5, 1862, *ORN* Series 1, Volume 6, p. 499.

Chapter Seven: General French

[1] Shaw to Wise, January 8, 1862, *OR* Series 1, Volume 9, p. 418; Report of the Investigating Committee Confederate House of Representatives, ibid., p. 184; Report of Lieut. Daniel W. Flagler, February 29, 1862, ibid., p. 81.

[2] The Federal capture of Roanoke Island left the six gun battery on Huggins' Island without means of communication or support, causing orders to be issued for its withdrawal to Morehead City. Special Orders No. 36, Head Quarters, Department of N. C., Goldsboro, Feb'y 19th 1862, Compiled Military Service Records of Daniel Munn, NARA. From there, Captain Munn's guns were to be transported by rail to either New Berne or Wilmington, depending upon greatest need. A week passed with no word from Munn, a source of agitation for General Gatlin. Gatlin to Branch, February 26, 1862, *OR* Series 1, Volume 51, Part 2, p. 480-481. When Munn's "Bladen Stars" reported to General Anderson, they were ordered into Fort Fisher. Manarin, *North Carolina Troops*, Vol. 1, p. 207.

[3] Mustered February 19, 1862. Soon after enlistment the battery was stationed at Fort Caswell. Ibid., p. 325.

[4] Ibid., p. 225-226; "Date of entry or muster into Confederate service, Feb. 15, 1862," Roster, Jan. 1864, 36th Regiment of North Carolina Volunteers, Compiled Military Service Records of Octavious H. Blocker, NARA.

[5] "Starr's Light Battery," commanded by Captain Joseph B. Starr, entered Confederate service soon after mustering into State service on 1 March, but was stated by Lieutenant Myrover to have been at Fort Fisher since 22 January 1862. Without field guns, however, the neophyte battery drew heavy artillery duty at Fort Fisher. Clark, *North Carolina* Regiments, Volume 4, p. 342; Company Muster Roll for March & April 1862, shows station of company, Fort Fisher, Capt. Starr's Co. B, 2 Regiment North Carolina Artillery (36 State Troops), NARA.

[6] Captain Henry Harding's Company North Carolina Volunteers was mustered as an independent company on November 9, 1861, well before being assigned as Company B of the 61st North Carolina Infantry and mustered into Confederate service on 5 September 1862. Company Muster-in Roll, November 9, 1861, Capt. Henry Harding's Co., 61 Reg't. N.C. Inft., Subsequently Co. B, 61 N.C. Inf., NARA; Company Muster Roll, for Feb 28 to July 1, 1862, Co. B, 61 Regiment North Carolina Infantry, shows station of company, Fort Fisher, N.C., NARA.

[7] "Muster Roll of Captain John R. Lanier's (Infantry) Company . . . of North Carolina Volunteers." Company Muster-in Roll, November 6, 1861, 1st Co. B, 42 Reg't N.C. Inf., NARA. Exact date of transfer to Fort Fisher is uncertain, but occurred not later than the end of February 1862. Company Muster Roll, Jany and Feby, 1862, 1st Co. B, 42 Regiment North Carolina Infantry shows station of company, Ft. Fisher, NARA.

[8] The former Hatteras prisoners of war, fresh from their parole and exchange on 3 February, reformed at Wilmington in time to report for duty at Fort French by February 28. Company Muster Roll, Feb. 28 to June 30, 1862, Co. K, 1 Regiment North Carolina Artillery (10 State Troops), NARA.

[9] William and Mary College, *Letters of Major Thomas Rowland, C.S.A.*, pp. 227, 228; Roll of Honor, Historical Memoranda, March 17, 1864, 1st Battalion [N.C.] Heavy Artillery, NARA. Brackets inserted by the author.

[10] Clark to Benjamin, February 22, 1862, *OR* Series 1, Volume 9, p. 438. On the east side are three batteries: First, Lazaretto Battery . . . ; second, Fort French, a bomb-proof . . . ; third, Fort Ellis [Lighthouse Battery] . . . The first battery is about 7 miles from Wilmington; the second is within 500 yards of the first, and the third 3 miles from the first, and are all open gorge." Foster to Halleck, October 3, 1862, *OR* Series 1, Volume 18, p. 415. The location of Fort Ellis [Lighthouse Battery] is established by Foster as being closest to Wilmington. A Confederate map establishes Fort Strong as being the nearest battery to Wilmington and also the only battery next to a lighthouse. Fort Strong, aka Fort Ellis, was therefore known first as the Light House Battery. The map also shows Foster's locations to be accurate, but not his distances from Wilmington. *Topographic Map Showing the Fortifications and Roads in the Vicinity of the Cape Fear*, Gilmer Papers, SHC, UNC-CH. Brackets by the author.

[11] Special Orders No. 46, Adjutant and Inspector General's Office, February 26, 1862, Compiled Military Service Records of John A. Brown, NARA.

[12] "Captain Edward B. Dudley's Company North Carolina Volunteers Artillery" was mustered into service at Wilmington on March 12 and ordered to relieve Purdie's Company on Zeek's Island, a directive that was carried into effect at 2:30 in the afternoon of the following day. Company Muster Roll, March 3 to April 30, 1862, Capt. E.B. Dudley's Co. (Anderson Art'y) attached to 20th Reg't N.C. Troops, NARA; Manarin, *North Carolina* Troops, Vol. 1, pp. 236.

[13] Manarin, *North Carolina Troops*, p. 198.

[14] Company Muster-in Roll, March 12, 1862, Captain Nathan L. Williamson's Company (Columbus Art'y) N C Vol's, NARA.

[15] Clark, *North Carolina Regiments*, Vol. 2, p. 468.

[16] Manarin, *North Carolina Troops*, p. 174.

[17] Hoy, *A Brief History of Bradford's Battery*.

[18] Purdie's Battery, lately withdrawn from Zeek's Island, rejoined the 18th Regiment North Carolina Infantry as it passed through Wilmington en route from South Carolina to New Berne. At that time, the company was officially transferred back into Colonel Radcliffe's regiment as Company K. Clark, *North Carolina Regiments*, Vol. 2, p. 20.

[19] Captain Thomas G. Walton was not re-elected to command by the officers of his company at its reorganization, in favor of Captain Elisha A. Perkins. Company Muster Roll, Mch & Apr, 1862, Co. F, 3 Reg't North Carolina Cavalry (41 State Troops), NARA.

[20] Muster Roll, Mch & Apr., 1862, Capt. Howard's Co. Cav., N.C. (Local Defense), NARA.

[21] Lest communications with New Berne be cut following the loss of the city, Captain Edward W. Ward's Company of Cavalry was withdrawn from Swansborough and assigned to picket duty in Onslow County. Company Muster Roll, Mch & Apr., 1862, Co. New B, 3 Reg't North Carolina Cavalry (41 State Troops), NARA.

[22] Confederate commanders thought Onslow County important enough to transfer Captain Atherton B. Hill's Company of Cavalry from Camp Grant in New Hanover County to a new base of operations called Camp Saunders. Company Muster Roll, Mch & Apl, 1862, (New) Co. G, 3 Reg't North Carolina Cavalry (41 State Troops), NARA; Compiled Military Service Records of Private Henry A. Moore, NARA.

[23] Anderson to Cooper, March 25, 1862, *OR* Series 1, Volume 9, p. 451. ". . . ordered to Watson's Branch, New Hanover County." Regimental Return for Mar., 1862, No. 2, Apl. 23 1862, 1 Reg't N.C. Artillery (10 State Troops), NARA.

[24] Captain Moore reported his station as Camp Holmes on April 30, 1862. Company Muster Roll, Dec. 31 to April 30, 1862, Co. E, 1 Regiment North Carolina Artillery, NARA. One of Captain Moore's men died at Camp Holmes on April 12. Compiled Military Service Records of Pvt. Caswell Bailey, NARA. ". . . Camp Holmes, seven miles from Wilmington . . ." Craig S. Chapman, *More Terrible Than Victory*, Dulles, VA: Brassey's, 1998 (hereinafter cited as Chapman, *More Terrible Than Victory*), p. 54. "Left Camp Wyatt March 14, 1862 for Camp Lamb near Wilmington, a distance of twenty-two miles, from there we took up the line of march for a new camp which was called Camp French, which place we reached March 26 a distance of three miles. Left Camp French March 30 for a place near Masonboro Sound, a distance of five miles, which camp was called Camp Holmes." Company Muster Roll, Mch & Apr., 1862, Co. A, 30 Regiment North Carolina Infantry, NARA.

[25] Roll of Honor, Card No. 2, obverse, Historical memoranda continued, n.d., 30 Reg't North Carolina Troops, NARA.

[26] *Abstract*, Compiled Military Service Records of John J. Hedrick, NARA; Manarin, *North Carolina* Troops, Vol. 1, p. 218. Cumming's Battery was ordered to report to Wilmington on April 19, presumably for muster into Confederate service for the war's duration and to receive the light artillery battery that had eluded it for more than a year. Two days later, they arrived at their destination somewhere in New Hanover County, where they established their own camp of instruction, aptly named Camp Hedrick. The exact location of this camp of instruction is unknown. Clark, *North Carolina Regiments*, Vol. 4, p. 361.

[27] "6-inch rifles" refers to a rifled 32-pounder of 6.4-inch caliber, an arm with which most Navy personnel were completely unfamiliar. *List of fortifications on the Neuse River, near New Berne . . .* March 13 and 14, 1862, *ORN* Series 1, Volume 7, p. 109. "Ranging from 32-pounders to 80-pounders rifled." Detailed Report of Commander Rowan, March 20, 1862, ibid., pp. 110-112; Clark to Benjamin, March 15, 1862, *OR* Series 1, Volume 9, pp. 444-445; Report of Brig. Gen. Richard C. Gatlin, October 1, 1862, *OR* Series 1, Volume 4, p. 579.

[28] Special Orders No. 60, Adjutant and Inspector General's Office (AIGO), March 15, 1862, *OR* Series 1, Volume 9, p. 445; William and Mary College, *Letters of Major Thomas Rowland, C.S.A.*, p. 230.

[29] "The undersigned, by virtue of Special Orders, No. 60, Adjutant and Inspector Generals Office, Richmond, dated March 15, 1862, hereby assumes command of the District of the Cape Fear . . ." General Orders No. 13, Headquarters, District of the Cape Fear, March 22, 1862, *OR* Series 1, Volume 9, p. 450. Special Orders No. 53, Headquarters, Department of North Carolina, March 17, 1862, *OR* Series 1, Volume 9, p. 447; General Orders No.1, Headquarters, Kinston, March 18, 1862, *OR* Series 1, Volume 9, p. 448.

[30] Special Orders No. 56, AIGO, March 11, 1862, Compiled Military Service Records of George A. Cunningham, NARA.

[31] General Orders No. 13, Headquarters, District of the Cape Fear, March 22, 1862, *OR* Series 1, Volume 9, p. 450; "Commander of the Post since Mar. 25, 1862." Special Orders No. 58, Department of North Carolina, March 22, 1862, Compiled Military Service Records of George A. Cunningham, NARA; Return of Post of Fort Caswell, N.C., May, 1862, ibid. Special Orders No. 67, AIGO, March 24, 1862, *OR* Series 1, Volume 9, p. 450-452; General Orders No. 6, Hdqrs., Dept. Of North Carolina, March 25, 1862, *OR* Series 1, Volume 9, p. 452.

[32] Compiled Military Service Records of Brigadier General Samuel Gibbs French, NARA; French, *Two Wars*, pp. 1-135.

[33] Company Muster Roll, March & April 1862, shows "station of Company, Camp Wyatt," Co. B & C, 20 Regiment North Carolina Infantry, NARA; Holmes to Lee, March 27, 1862, *OR* Series 1, Volume 9, pp. 452, 453; Samuel G. French, *Two Wars: An Autobiography of Gen. Samuel G. French*, Nashville, Tennessee: Confederate Veteran, 1901 (hereinafter cited as French, *Two Wars*), pp. 359-360.

[34] Ibid., p. 144; William and Mary College, *Letters of Major Thomas Rowland, C.S.A.*, Quarterly Historical Magazine, Volume XXVI, No. 4, April 1917, p. 230.

[35] William and Mary College, *Letters of Major Thomas Rowland, C.S.A.*, Quarterly Historical Magazine, Volume XXVI, No. 4, April 1917, p. 230.

[36] Holmes to Lee, March 27, 1862, *OR* Series 1, Volume 9, p. 453.

[37] ". . . ordered to Wilmington, NC & from thence down to old Brunswick Point Battery where they arrived March 29 1862." Regimental Return for Mar., 1862, No. 3 reverse, 1 Regiment North Carolina Artillery (10 State Troops), NARA.

[38] "On the 28th, it was ordered to Wilmington, where it remained until 1 April, at which time it was transported with six other heavy artillery companies from the Pamlico and Neuse rivers, and landed at the different fortifications on the Cape Fear river. This company was sent to Fort Johnston, at Smithville." Clark, *North Carolina Regiments*, Vol. 2, p. 752.

[39] ". . . it was ordered to Wilmington, where it arrived about the last of March, and the next day (1 April) it was sent down the Cape Fear river, with other Artillery companies from the Pamlico and Neuse rivers. This company with Company G, was sent to Fort Johnson at Smithville." Clark, *North Carolina Regiments*, Vol. 2, p. 749.

[40] Manarin, *North Carolina Troops*, Vol. 1, p. 500.

[41] "We remained in and Near Kinston until 27 [March] when we were ordered to Wilmington to report to Genl. French and were sent by him to this place at night on the 29th." Company Muster Roll, reverse, for Mch & Apr 1862, shows station of company, Fort Fisher, Co. B, 3 Regiment North Carolina Artillery (40 State Troops), NARA. Bracketed words inserted by the author.

[42] "From Kinston it went in camp at Falling Creek, where it remained until about the first of April, 1862, when it was ordered to Fort St. Philip, on the Cape Fear river." Clark, *North Carolina Regiments*, Vol. 2, p. 749.

[43] "Capt. MacRae's [sic] Company was mustered into the service of the State of N.C. by Col. J. L. Cantwell on the 9th day of April, 1862." Roll of Honor, March 17, 1864, Card No. 1, reverse, 1st Battalion Heavy Artillery (North Carolina Troops) NARA. "Capt. MacRae [sic] was assigned . . . to Fort St. Phillip at Old Brunswick on the Cape Fear River." Ibid.

[44] "Arriving at Wilmington early in April, it was detailed on provost guard duty." Manarin, *North Carolina Troops*, p. 375.

[45] "It did not reach there in time, so it went in camp at Kinston, where it remained until ordered to Fort Fisher, where it arrived about 1 April, 1862, and became a part of its garrison." Clark, *North Carolina Regiments*, Vol. 2, p. 754.

[46] Colonel Thomas S. Kenan was paid for his period of service in the Cape Fear defenses by Major J.B. Morey, General French's Chief Quartermaster. Pay Voucher, 1862 Apl 21 to 1862 May 31, paid on 3 June 1862, The Confederate States of America to Col. Thos. S. Kenan, Compiled Military Service Records of Colonel Thomas S. Kenan, 43rd Regiment North Carolina Infantry, NARA.

[47] "The regiment was organized at Wilmington, N. C., 13 April, 1862," Clark, *North Carolina Regiments*, Vol. 3, p. 205. "Changes of Station: Camp Morgan to Camp Holmes May 3, 1862, near Wilmington, N.C." Regimental Return for the month

of May, 1862, Record of Events, 51 Reg't N.C. Inft., NARA. Company B was still stationed at Fort Fisher. See Note 6. Company K had not yet been mustered into service. Company Muster-in and Descriptive Roll, May 10, 1862, Co. K, 51 Reg't N.C. Inf., NARA.

[48] Company A was detached from its regiment in mid-April and dispatched to Wilmington. ". . . on leaving 2 Reg't. N.C. S. Troops to which my Company ("A") belonged our tents were left by order of Col. C.C. Tew therefore we are without them and it is very necessary for us to have them." Special Requisition for 12 Tents & fixtures, April 22, 1862, Compiled Military Service Records of Calvin Barnes, NARA.

[49] Company Muster Roll for Mch. & Apl., 1862, Co. B, 1 Reg't Maryland Inf., shows station of company, Brunswick Point, N.C., NARA. Company stationed in Kinston on March 31. Ordnance Receipt, March 31, 1862, Compiled Military Service Records of Captain Charles C. Edelin, NARA. Company stationed in the Cape Fear by April 12, 1862. Ordnance Receipt, April 12, 1862, ibid.

[50] The 60th Virginia was in Wilmington on April 19 and in Virginia by April 23. Organization of the troops serving in the Department of North Carolina, April 19, 1862, *OR* Series 1, Volume 9, p. 460; Lee to Johnston, April 23, 1862, *OR* Series 1, Volume 11, Part 3, p. 458. Taylor to Holmes, April 20, 1862, *OR* Series 1, Volume 9, pp. 461-462.

[51] Regimental Return for April, 1862, Card No. 2, 1 Regiment North Carolina Artillery (10 State Troops), NARA.

[52] Roll of Honor, n.d., Card No. 2, Historical memoranda continued, 30 Reg't North Carolina Troops, NARA; Clark, *North Carolina Regiments*, Vol. 2, p. 497.

[53] Abstract Log of the USS Monticello, April 27, 1862, *ORN* Series 1, Volume 7, pp. 718-719.

[54] Report of Lieutenant Braine, May 5, 1862, ibid., p. 323.

[55] Ibid.

[56] Olmstead, et al, *The Big Guns*, pp. 219, 66; *Tredegar Sales Book*, October, 1861, p. 144; Bell, *Civil War Heavy Explosive Ordnance*, p. 435.

[57] "By Special Orders No. 144, Adjutant General's Office, 1860, a board of artillery and ordnance officers was appointed to make more elaborate trials of the rifled cannon and projectiles. The report of this board was submitted November 1st, 1860. Regarding the method of rifling and of constructing projectiles to be used therewith presented to it for trial, the board remarked: It is admirably adapted to the various calibres of guns now in use, requiring only that they be rifled (which can be done at the forts and arsenals where they now are) and supplied with proper proportions of rifled projectiles. Another advantage is that these same guns, and without increase of charge, will be enabled to throw a weight of metal about double what they have heretofore fired, [accentuation by the author] with more accuracy, effectiveness, and greater range. The board, therefore, recommends the rifling of all, or at least fifty per cent, of the guns at forts and arsenals." Birkhimer, *Historical Sketch*, p. 284; Olmstead, et al, *The Big Guns*, p. 147.

[58] At that time they were just building the casement [sic] guns, those we exercised upon were old Columbia [sic] en barbette." Dr. Thomas Fanning Wood, *Journal, Book 2, Some Recollections of My Life Written for My Children During My Confinement With Aneurysm Beginning 25th April, 1886,* Wood Family Papers, Special Collections, William Madison Randall Library, University of North Carolina Wilmington, Wilmington, NC; *Tredegar Sales Book*, January 13, 1862, p. 186; Olmstead, et al, *The Big Guns*, p. 147.

[59] *Tredegar Sales Book*, February, 1862, p. 198; O'Sullivan, Timothy H., 1840-1882, photographer, *Fort Fisher, North Carolina. Panoramic view of front. (Part 2)*, Library of Congress Prints and Photographs Division, Washington, D.C. 20540 USA.

[60] Olmstead, et al, *The Big Guns*, p. 53; Bell, *Civil War Heavy Explosive Ordnance*, p. 434.

[61] Edward Manigault, Warren Ripley, Ed., *Siege Train: The Journal of a Confederate Artilleryman in the Defense of Charleston*, Columbia, SC: University of South Carolina Press, 1986, p. 35. Identifies the range of a rifled Columbiad. "The 5.82-inch rifled Columbiad in the Fort was fired at a Union gunboat in the mouth of North River near Harker's Island (range about 4 miles) and hit within six feet of the ship on the second shot." Paul Branch, Fort Macon Ranger/Historian, *Armament of Fort Macon*. < http://www.crystalcoast.com/fortmacon/fortmaconarmament.shtml> (accessed 26 August 2010)

[62] Olmstead, et al, *The Big Guns*, p. 16.

[63] Confederate *Instruction for Heavy Artillery*, p. 269.

[64] Voucher, Confederate States of America to Orrell & Hawes, April 11, 1862, Orrell & Hawes, *Citizens File*, NARA.

Chapter Eight: Colonel Lamb

[1] *The Greensborough Patriot*, p. 4, September 11, 1862, "From the Raleigh Standard – Fort Macon – Its Defence, etc."; Report of Col. Moses J. White, *OR* Series 1, Volume 9, p. 293.

[2] Report of Commander Armstrong, May 14, 1862, *ORN* Series 1, Volume 7, p. 354; Letter, John B. McNeill to Miss Mollie, May 30, 1862, *Mary Margaret McNeill Papers*, Rare Book, Manuscript, and Special Collections Library, Perkins Library, Duke University, Durham North Carolina (hereinafter cited as McNeill Papers, Duke University).

[3] Voucher, May 14, 1862, Confederate States of America to E.A. Keith, E.A. Keith, *Citizens* File, NARA; 1860 United States Census for Wilmington, New Hanover County, North Carolina, NARA; William and Mary College, *Letters of Major Thomas Rowland, C.S.A.*, Quarterly Historical Magazine, Volume XXVI, No. 4, April 1917, pp. 231, 232.

[4] Letters, Hugh McGoogan to Dear cousin, June 24, 1862 and W.S. Conoly to Miss Mary M. McNeill, June 1, 1862, *McNeill Papers*. Duke University; Voucher, May 22, 1862, Confederate States of America to Orrell & Hawes, Orrell & Hawes, *Citizens File*, NARA.

[5] "The city is defended by intrenched [sic] works on the east, but I have no men to man them." Anderson to Cooper, February 13, 1862, *OR* Series 1, Volume 9, p. 433.

[6] Manarin, *North Carolina Troops*, Vol. 1, p. 512.

[7] Company Muster Roll for April 23 to June 30, 1862, shows station of company, Entrench [sic] Camp near Wilmington NC, Co. A, 10 Batt'n North Carolina H, Arty., NARA.

[8] Company Muster Roll for May 9 to June 30, 1862, shows station of company, Entrench [sic] Camp, Wilmington, NC, Co. B, 10 Batt'n North Carolina H, Arty., NARA.

[9] Company Muster Roll for May 19 to June 30, 1862, shows station of company, Entrenched Camp near Wilmington, NC, Co. C, 10 Batt'n North Carolina H, Arty., NARA.

[10] "Captain Rankin's Company was assigned to the fortifications around Wilmington where it remained until the 8th of September, 1863." Roll of Honor, n.d., Card No.2, reverse, Historical Memoranda, 1st Battalion [North Carolina] Heavy Artillery, NARA. Brackets by author.

[11] "Captain Ellis' Company was assigned to Fort Strong [Light House Battery] near Wilmington . . ." Roll of Honor, n.d., Card No.2, Historical Memoranda, 1st Battalion [North Carolina] Heavy Artillery, NARA. Brackets by author.

[12] Company Muster-in Roll, Muster Roll, May 5, 1862, Captain Francis W. Potter's Company, Station Fort St. Philip, [erroneously filed under head of Capt. Russell's Co. G, 2 Regt. Arty. N.C. (36 State Troops)], NARA. Brackets by author.

[13] Company Muster Roll, May 10, 1862, shows station of company, Fort St. Philip, Patterson's Co. H, 2 Regiment North Carolina Artillery (36 State Troops), NARA.

[14] Its organization completed on 15 May, Captain George Tait's unattached "Bladen Artillery Guards" became the first unit to muster into service at Fort St. Philip. Company Muster-in and Descriptive Roll, May 15, 1862, shows station of company, Fort St. Philip, New Co. K, 3 Reg't. N.C. Arty . . . Captain George Tait's Company of North Carolina Volunteers, known as Bladen Artillery Guards, NARA.

[15] Company Muster-in and Descriptive Roll, May 10, 1862, station Camp Holmes near Wilmington, Co. K, 51 Reg't N.C. Inf., also known as Captain J.B. Underwood [sic] Company of North Carolina Volunteers, known as Confederate Stars, NARA.

[16] "On the 3rd of April, 1862 . . . we were ordered to report to Brig. Gen'l. French at Wilmington and were assigned to duty at Confederate Point." Roll of Honor, n.d., Historical memoranda continued, Card No. 3, 2nd Reg't North Carolina Troops, NARA.

[17] For the first time in the short history of the Cape Fear defenses, a Virginia light artillery battery appeared on the scene. Known as the "Staunton Hill Artillery," the men of the battery were seasoned veterans of the march, but not of battle. One section of two guns had served at Hamilton, North Carolina and then at Goldsborough, but the other two sections comprised of four guns had been serving in Savannah since late March. When the sections were brought together at Camp Hedrick about May 20, the battery reorganized under the terms of the conscription laws and Andrew Bailey Paris was elected its captain. Jeffrey C. Weaver, *Branch, Harrington and Staunton Hill Artillery*, Lynchburg, VA: H.E. Howard, Inc., 1997 (hereinafter cited as Weaver, *Branch, Harrington and Staunton Hill Artillery*), p. 85.

[18] Clark, *North Carolina Regiments*, Vol. 1, p. 405.

[19] Ibid., p. 21.

[20] Captain S.B. Hunter listed as sick, but posted at Fort Caswell at the end of May, 1862. Return of Post of Fort Caswell, N.C., May, 1862, Compiled Military Service Records of Samuel B. Hunter, NARA.

[21] Colonel Collett Leventhorpe's 11th Regiment North Carolina Infantry transferred from Camp Mangum near Raleigh to Wilmington in early May. Clark, *North Carolina Regiments*, Vol. 1, p. 583. From Wilmington it was ordered to Camp Holmes to check a feared Union incursion into Masonboro Sound. Craig S. Chapman, *More Terrible Than Victory – North Carolina's Bloody Bethel Regiment 1861-1865*, Dulles, VA: Brassey's, 1999 (hereinafter cited as Chapman, *More Terrible Than Victory*), p. 54. The threat didn't materialize, so the 11th was sent instead to the sand flea-infested Camp Davis on May 14. Regimental Return for the month of May, 1862, shows Field and Staff and companies stationed at Camp Davis, 11 Reg't N. Car. Inf., NARA.

[22] "The 20th, my old confreres, have been ordered back to Fort Johnson [sic]." William and Mary College, *Letters of Major Thomas Rowland, C.S.A.*, Quarterly Historical Magazine, Volume XXVI, No. 4, April 1917, p. 232.

[23] "[O]n the morning of the 9th the Colonel received orders to return with his regiment to Wilmington . . . The Colonel took up a line for Wilmington on the evening of the 12th. May 15th were ordered to Wrightsvill [sic] Sound eight miles where we remained until the 21st when we moved to Masonboro Sound and remained at Camp until the 27th when we left this camp and went to Wilmington were [sic] we received orders to await orders and quietly went into camp at Camp Lamb." Roll of Honor, n.d., Card No. 3, 30 Reg't North Carolina Troops, NARA. Brackets by author.

[24] "Changes of Station: Camp Morgan to Camp Holmes May 3, 1862, near Wilmington, N.C. Camp Holmes to Camp Davis May 17, 1862, near Wilmington, N.C." Regimental Return for May, 1862, shows Field and Staff and companies stationed at Camp Davis, near Wilmington, N.C., 51 Reg't N.C. Inft., NARA.

[25] "Company D on detached service building Batteries on Cape Fear River, commencing on May 21, 1862." Ibid.

[26] "Company "A" was detached from the regiment from May 19, 1862 to May 31, 1862 down the Cape Fear River building battery known as the Lazaretto Battery." Ibid.

[27] Moore's Battery is assumed to have been recalled from Onslow County at about the same time its infantry support, the 30th Regiment, was recalled on May 9th (See Note 23). When the 30th left Masonboro Sound, the battery was probably left at Camp Davis. "The Company was moved from Camp Davis June 24, 1862." Company Muster Roll for May & June, 1862, shows station of company, Camp Jones, Co. E, 1 Regiment North Carolina Artillery (10 State Troops), NARA.

[28] Manarin, *North Carolina Troops*, p. 172.

[29] Ibid.; William and Mary College, *Letters of Major Thomas Rowland, C.S.A.*, Quarterly Historical Magazine, Volume XXVI, No. 4, April 1917, p. 232.

[30] Manarin, *North Carolina Troops*, Vol. 1, pp. 500, 172.

[31] Clark, *North Carolina Regiments*, Vol. 5, p. 678; Letter, John B. McNeill to Miss Molle, May 30, 1862, *McNeill Papers*, Duke University.

[32] Ibid.

[33] Report of Commander Glisson, U.S. Navy, June 26, 1862, *ORN* Series 1, Volume 7, p. 504; Compiled Military Service Records of Private William W. Lewis, 51st Regiment, NCST, NARA. "Another 24-pounder rifle burst to-day [sic] and one of Piersons [sic] 6.4-inch guns." Hill to Randolph, April 24, 1862, *OR* Series 1, Volume 11, Part 3, p. 461.

[34] "The enemy having concentrated his forces under McClellan around Richmond, we were ordered to that place where we arrived on the 17th of June." Roll of Honor, n.d., February 2, 1864, Card No. 3, 2nd Reg't. North Carolina Troops, NARA.

[35] "The Regiment numbering 1012 men was ordered to Va, June 14 1862." Roll of Honor, January 8, 1864, n.d., Card No. 1 (reverse), 20th Reg't. North Carolina Troops, NARA.

[36] "Left Wilmington 13th June with orders to report to Gen'l R.E. Lee and arrived at Richmond Va. on the 16th." Roll of Honor, n.d., Card No. 3 (reverse), 30 Reg't. North Carolina Troops, NARA.

[37] While stationed at Camp Wyatt in early to mid-May, Captain William C. Howard's Local Defense Company of Cavalry experienced forty-three personnel transfers to other cavalry companies, enough to render it unfit for service. Then commanded by First Lieutenant David J. Southerland, the company was mustered out of the service on June 7, 1862 and its men discharged. Muster Roll, Apr. 30 to June 7, 1862, Capt. Howard's Co. Cav., N.C. (Local Defense), NARA.

[38] Company Muster Roll for May & June, 1862, shows station of company, Camp Wyatt, N.C., (New) Co. G, 3 Reg't North Carolina Cavalry (41 State Troops), NARA.

[39] Company Muster Roll for May & June, 1862, shows station of company, Onslow County, Co. F, 3 Reg't North Carolina Cavalry (41 State Troops), NARA.

[40] Clark, *North Carolina Regiments*, Vol. 2, p. 4; Report Of Col. Junius Daniel, July 16, 1862, *OR* Series 1, Volume 11, Part 2, pp. 913-914.

[41] "Co. K, 51Regt. N.C. Troops left Camp Davis on the morning of the 2nd June and arrived the same day at Lazaretto Battery: distance 10 miles." Company Muster Roll for May 10 through June 30, 1862, Co. K, 51 Regiment North Carolina Infantry, NARA.

[42] "Company "A" was detached from the regiment from May 19, 1862 to May 31, 1862 down the Cape Fear River building battery known as the Lazaretto Battery." Company A assumed to have returned to camp with its regiment after May 31, 1862 since no return to the contrary has been found. Regimental Return for May, 1862, shows Field and Staff and companies stationed at Camp Davis, near Wilmington, N.C., 51 Reg't N.C. Inft., NARA.

[43] "Two moves during the month: 1st from Camp Davis to Camp French in the vicinity of Rock Spring between Camp Wayatt [sic] & Davis near Wilmington, N.C. 23 June, 1862. 2nd move from Camp French to Fort Johnson [sic] June 26, 1862." Regimental Return for the month of June, 1862, shows Field and Staff and companies stationed at Fort Johnson N.C., 51 Reg't N.C. Inft., NARA.

44 The 11th Regiment was ordered from Camp Davis to Camp Wyatt on June 14, and from there to Wilmington a week later under orders to entrain for Richmond. The order was countermanded and the 11th encamped near Wilmington. Chapman, *More Terrible Than Victory*, pp. 56-57; Regimental Return for the month of May, 1862, shows Field and Staff and companies stationed at Camp Lamb, 11 Reg't N.C. Inf. (Bethel Regiment), NARA.

45 "The Company was moved from Camp Davis June 24, 1862 by order of Gen. French Comdg. to Rock Spring, from which on account of unfavorable locality it was moved July 1 to Camp Jones, near Jones Mill Pond, on Sound Road to Confederate Point." Company Muster Roll for May & June, 1862, shows station of company, Camp Jones, Co. E, 1 Regiment North Carolina Artillery (10 State Troops), NARA. "Rock Spring between Camp Wayatt [sic] & Davis." Regimental Return for the month of June, 1862, shows Field and Staff and companies stationed at Fort Johnson N.C., 51 Reg't N.C. Inft., NARA.

46 Return for May shows Captain William Sutton at Fort Fisher in May, but the entry is marked with an X that is annotated at the bottom of the Return "Brief shows June, 1862." June is therefore accepted as the month of the company's move from Wilmington to Fort Fisher. Return of Post of Fort Fisher, N.C. for the month of May [June] 1862, Compiled Military Service Records of William Sutton, NARA. Brackets by author.

47 Company Muster-in Roll, July 19, 1862, Co. C, 5 Reg't. N.C. Cav. NARA; Company Muster Roll for July to Sept. 1, 1862, shows station of company, Camp Wyatt, Co. C, 5 Regiment North Carolina Cavalry (63 State Troops), NARA.

48 While an exact date of transfer for this company is not available, it is believed that it was transferred out of Camp Wyatt when Captain Shaw's company was transferred there in early to mid-July 1862. Company Muster Roll for July & Aug, 1862, shows station of Company, Camp Davis, (New) Co. G, 3 Reg't North Carolina Cavalry (41 State Troops), NARA.

49 Transfer from Fort Fisher to Fort Johnston occurred after 1 July 1862 and before 1 October 1862. Company Muster Roll for Feb 28 to July 1, 1862, shows station of company, Fort Fisher, N.C., Compiled Military Service Records of Henry Harding, NARA; Company Muster and Descriptive Roll, Oct 1, 1862, shows station of company, Smithville, NC, Co. B, 61 Reg't., N.C., NARA.

50 "This company was formerly (1st) Company B, 42nd Regiment North Carolina Infantry (State Troops). Some of the rolls show 59th Regiment North Carolina Infantry (State Troops), which was probably due to a misunderstanding of the line number the regiment was to receive." Company Muster and Descriptive Roll for May & June, 1862, Capt. William B. Lanier's Co. (Hill Guards), 59 Reg't North Carolina Infantry (State Troops), Compiled Military Service Records of William B. Lanier, NARA. Captain William B. Lanier succeeded Captain John R. Lanier who was not re-elected to captaincy of the company. "Elected Capt 1st May 1862 upon reorganization of Company and commencement [of] service." "This company subsequently became Company H, 61st Regiment North Carolina Infantry (State Troops)." Company Muster Roll of Capt. William B. Lanier's Co. (Hill Guards), North Carolina Infantry for May & June, 1862, ibid. Company Muster Roll for July & Aug., 1862, shows station of company, Wilmington N.C., Co. H, 61 Regiment North Carolina Infantry, NARA. Captain William B. Lanier was paid for May and June, 1862 on July 10 by Major John B. Morey in Wilmington, further indicating the reassignment of the company to that location in anticipation of the imminent mustering in of the 61st Regiment. Pay Voucher, July 10, 1862, Compiled Military Service Records of William B. Lanier, NARA. Brackets by author.

51 Moore's Company mustered "in the 59 Regiment . . . at Wilmington." "This company subsequently became Company G, 61st Regiment North Carolina Infantry (State Troops). Some of the rolls show 59th Regiment North Carolina Infantry (State Troops), which was probably due to a misunderstanding of the line number the regiment was to receive." Company Muster-in and Descriptive Roll, May 12, 1862, Captain John F. Moore's Company of North Carolina Volunteers, found in Compiled Service Records of Co. G, 61 Reg't N.C. Inf., NARA. Issued tents at Wilmington on July 22, 1862. Special Requisition, July 22, 1861, Compiled Military Service Records of John F. Moore, NARA. "70 men Company infantry in Camp of instruction, commanded by Capt. J.F. Moore," Requisition for Straw, August, 1862, ibid. The company's duty stations are unknown from May 12, 1862 to the date of muster into the 61st Regiment, hence Wilmington is selected as the default duty station.

52 Gatlin to Branch, February 4, *OR* Series 1, Volume 51, Part 2, 1862, p. 463.

53 French to Randolph, June 26, 1862, *OR* Series 1, Volume 14, p. 573; *Tredegar Sales Book*, VSL, September 15 & 23, 1862, p. 257.

54 Ibid.; Lamb, "Defence of Fort Fisher, North Carolina," pp. 349-350.

55 Clark, *North Carolina Regiments*, Volume 2, p. 631; Abstract from return of District of the Cape Fear for January, 1862, commanded by Brig. Gen. Joseph R. Anderson, *OR* Series 1, Volume 9, p. 424.

56 Report of Lieutenant Braine, U.S. Navy, June 22, 1862, *ORN* Series 1, Volume 7, p. 497; Report of Commander Glisson, U.S. Navy, June 3, 1862, *ORN* Series 1, Volume 7, p. 451.

57 Clark, *North Carolina Regiments*, Volume 2, p. 755.

58 *Tredegar Sales Book*, VSL, February 22, 1862, p. 108; French, *Two Wars*, p. 144; Lamb, "Defence of Fort Fisher, North Carolina," p. 349.

59 Lamb, "Defence of Fort Fisher, North Carolina," pp. 349, 350; Lee to French, May 22, 1862, *OR* Series 1, Volume 9, p. 472. One year after Colonel Lamb assumed command of Fort Fisher, a map of the fort by L.C. Turner dated 3 July 1863 shows two

unbanded 32-pounder rifles in Battery Bolles and two 32-pounder rifles in Battery Hedrick, one banded and one unbanded. Gilmer, Jeremy Francis, 1818-1883, *Fort and adjoining fortifications, with note, 3 July 1863*, Gilmer Maps, University of North Carolina at Chapel Hill Library, Southern Historical Collection, University of North Carolina at Chapel Hill.

[60] Lamb, "Defence of Fort Fisher, North Carolina," p. 349.

[61] Clark, *North Carolina Regiments*, Vol. 2, p. 631.

[62] Ibid., pp. 631, 748; Dr. Thomas Fanning Wood, *Journal, Book 2, Some Recollections of My Life Written for My Children During My Confinement With Aneurysm Beginning 25th April, 1886,* Wood Family Papers, Special Collections, William Madison Randall Library, University of North Carolina at Wilmington, Wilmington, NC.

[63] A definition of pre-Civil War Columbiads: "U.S. Columbiads were U.S. 8-, 10-, and one 12-inch, **shell-guns** . . .". Olmstead, et al, *The Big Guns*, p. 63. Timothy H. O'Sullivan, 1840-1882, photographer, *Fort Fisher, North Carolina, View on land face*, Reproduction Number: LC-DIG-cwpb-04094, Library of Congress Prints and Photographs Division Washington, D.C. 20540 USA. Emphasis by author.

[64] *Tredegar Sales Book*, VSL, February 22, 1862, p. 108; Timothy H. O'Sullivan, 1840-1882, photographer, *Fort Fisher, North Carolina. Panoramic view of front. (Part 2)*, Reproduction Number: LC-DIG-cwpb-03907, Library of Congress Prints and Photographs Division Washington, D.C. 20540 USA; Timothy H. O'Sullivan, 1840-1882, photographer, *Fort Fisher, North Carolina. Interior view*, Reproduction Number: LC-DIG-cwpb-00561, Library of Congress Prints and Photographs Division Washington, D.C. 20540 USA.

[65] Lamb, "Defence of Fort Fisher, North Carolina," p. 349; Clark, *North Carolina Regiments*, Volume 2, p. 748. "I have no Dahlgrens and only eight columbiads." French to Randolph, June 26, 1862, *OR* Series 1, Volume 14, p. 573.

[66] French to Cooper, June 27, 1862, *OR* Series 1, Volume 51, Part 2, pp. 584-585; Lamb, "Defence of Fort Fisher, North Carolina," p. 354; Clark, *North Carolina Regiments*, Volume 4, p. 343.

[67] Scott, *Military Dictionary*, New York: D. Van Nostrand, 1864, p.526; Lamb, "Defence of Fort Fisher, North Carolina," p. 354.

[68] French, *Two Wars*, p. 144.

[69] Holmes to French, July 15, 1862, *OR* Series 1, Volume 11, p. 643; Special Orders No. 140, Hdqrs., Dept. of Northern Virginia, June 21, 1862, *OR* Series 1, Volume 11, p. 611; Special Orders No. 165, July 17, 1862, *OR* Series 1, Volume 9, p. 476.

[70] Chapman, *More Terrible Than Victory*, pp. 54, 57. Cunningham was absent from his post commanding Fort Caswell while "[i]n command of the Dist. Cape Fear since July 29, 1862." Return of Post of Forts Caswell and Johnson [*sic*], N.C., July, 1862, Compiled Military Service Records of Geo. A. Cunningham, NARA. Cunningham was, however, present "commanding post" of Fort Caswell in the month of August. Field and Staff Muster Roll of Post of Fort Caswell, August 31, 1862, ibid. Brackets by author.

[71] Special Orders, No. 180, Hdgrs. District of North Carolina, Petersburg, Va., August 18, 1862, *OR* Series 1, Volume 9, p. 480.

[72] J. Timothy Cole and Bradley R. Foley, *Collett Leventhorpe, the English Confederate: The Life of a Civil War General, 1815-1889*, Jefferson, N.C.: McFarland & Co., 2007, pp. 75, 76; Special Orders, No. 206, Adjt. And Insp. General's Office, Richmond, September 3, 1862, *OR* Series 1, Volume 51, Part 2, p. 615.

[73] William T. Lusk, M.D. and James B. Hunter, M.D., Editors, The New York Medical Journal, Volume XVI, New York: D. Appleton & Company, 1872, pp. 225-259.

[74] Company Muster Roll for July & August, 1862, shows station of company, Fort Fisher, Capt. Starr's Co. (B), 1 Regiment North Carolina Artillery (36 State Troops), NARA; Report of Commander Armstrong, U.S. Navy, of affairs off Wilmington, N.C., August 13, 1862, *ORN* Series 1, Volume 7, pp. 644, 645.

[75] "We served around Wilmington and at various points on the coast until the 1st of October, when we were ordered to Franklin, Va." Clark, *North Carolina Regiments*, Vol. 1, p. 587.

[76] "Sept. 17 Regt marched from Camp Campbell [Wilmington] to Kinston, N.C." Muster Roll for Sept. & Oct., 1862, Field and Staff, 51 Reg't NC Inf, NARA. Withdrawal of the 51st from Wilmington also occasioned the withdrawal of Companies D and K from Lazaretto Battery. They were replaced by Company B, 56th Regiment on 19 September, which in turn was withdrawn from Lazaretto Battery when the parent Regiment was transferred to Northeast Station near Wilmington on the Wilmington & Weldon Rail Road on 6 October 1862. Regimental Return for the month of Oct., 1862, shows Field and Staff and companies stationed at Camp Clingman, near Goldsboro, N.C., 56 Reg't. N.C. Inf., NARA. Brackets by author.

[77] Regimental Return for the month of Aug., 1862, shows Field and Staff and companies stationed at Camp Badger, near old Camp Wyatt, N.C., 56 Reg't, N.C. Inf., NARA. The 56th Regiment was transferred to Northeast Station on 6 October, and from there to Goldsboro on 17 October 1862. Regimental Return for the month of Oct., 1862, shows Field and Staff and companies stationed at Camp Clingman, near Goldsboro, N.C., 56 Reg't, N.C. Inf., NARA.

[78] "After the organization of the regiment as above stated, it was assigned to Clingman's Brigade, which was composed of the Eighth, Thirty-first, Fifty-first and Sixty-first North Carolina Regiments, and remained at Camp Lamb, near Wilmington, until 16 September, when it took a move on itself and went to Smithville and remained there till the 25th when, on account of yellow fever outbreak it moved to Camp Radcliff [sic], three miles out, returning to Smithville on 4 October, en route to North East bridge, above Wilmington, which was reached on the 5th. From North East bridge we went to Camp Collier near Goldsboro on the 14th; to Tarboro on the 19th; left Tarboro for the country around Plymouth on the 24th . . ." Clark, *North Carolina Regiments*, Volume 3, pp. 505, 506. Colonel Radcliffe, however may have left the Cape Fear somewhat later than 4 October: "On the 20th, Radcliffe's regiment was ordered up in place of Cantwell's, and Colonel Radcliffe has been directed to move with his regiment and Martin's on Plymouth. I presume Radcliffe will move the last of this week, or early next week, on Plymouth, and I hope with successful results." French to Vance, October 22, 1862, *OR* Series 1, Volume 18, p. 760. The following five independent companies mustered into the 61st North Carolina and left their respective duty stations in the Cape Fear with the regiment: Confederates, Captain William S. Devane – Fort Caswell; Captain William B. Lanier's Co. (Hill Guards) North Carolina Infantry – Wilmington Camp; Captain Henry Harding's Company of North Carolina Volunteers – Wilmington Camp; Captain John F. Moore's Company of North Carolina Volunteers – Wilmington Camp; Captain Edward Mallett's Robinson Artillery – Fort Fisher. Ibid., pp. 503, 504.

[79] "On the 13th Oct received orders to report at Kinston, N.C. Left Fort Fisher at 1 o'clock p.m., on the 14th, marched 13 miles, encamped for the night. Arrived at Kinston, N.C., at 4 o'clock, p.m., 18th." Company Muster Roll for Sept. & Oct., 1862, Co. B, 2 Regiment North Carolina Artillery (36 State Troops), NARA.

[80] "The Company was in service in North Eastern N. Carolina most of the month of October and moved their camp almost daily." Company Muster Roll for June 30 to Oct. 31, 1862, Co. E, 1 Regiment North Carolina Artillery (10 State Troops), NARA.

[81] "After remaining in the camp of instruction [Camp Hedrick] until November, 1862, it was ordered to Eastern North Carolina where it remained until the Spring of 1863." Clark, *North Carolina Regiments*, Volume 4, p. 361. Brackets by author.

[82] "The Company marched from Camp Wyatt to this (Camp Long) distance about 200 miles in ten days starting on the 20th Oct 1862." Company Muster Roll for Sept and Oct, 1862, shows station of company, Camp Long near Garysburg, Co. C, 5 Regiment North Carolina Cavalry (63 State Troops), NARA.

[83] "There were some complaints came to me respecting the withdrawal of forces from Onslow County. The same cavalry force is there under Captain Ward that has been there since the fall of New Berne except two companies of Partisan Rangers. When these rangers are disciplined in the camps of instruction at Garysburg we will have a force for the position that can move rapidly from point to point." French to Vance, October 22, 1862, *OR* Series 1, Volume 18, p. 760. Of the five cavalry companies stationed in the Cape Fear in April, 1862, Captain Shaw's company was in Garysburg (see Note 77); the companies of Captains Smith, Newkirk, and Ward were still in the Cape Fear district. Company Muster Roll for Nov & Dec, 1862, shows station of company, Camp Badger, (New) Co. G, 3 Reg't North Carolina Cavalry (41 State Troops), NARA; Company Muster Rolls for Sept and Oct and Nov & Dec, 1862, shows station of company, Camp Heath, (New) Co. A, 3 Reg't North Carolina Cavalry (41 State Troops), NARA; French to Vance, October 22, 1862, *OR* Series 1, Volume 18, p. 760. Captain Perkins' company must therefore have been the other "Partisan Ranger" company sent to the Camp of Instruction in Garysburg.

[84] "The Company was ordered to Fort Caswell from Fort St. Philip on the 22nd day of August, 1862 – arrived on the 24th of August, 1862." Company Muster Roll for May 5 to Aug. 31, 1862, Co. G, 2 Regiment North Carolina Artillery (36 State Troops), NARA.

[85] This company was at Fort St. Philip in September and at Fort Caswell in July. With no August muster roll surviving, the company's transfer from Caswell to St. Philip must have occurred soon after the Lamb Artillery arrived at Caswell in late August. Therefore, very early September is the logical choice for the transfer to have occurred. Return of Post of Forts Caswell and Johnson [sic], N.C., for the month of July, 1862; Return of Troops stationed at Fort St. Philip, N.C., for the month of Sept., 1862, NARA.

[86] Formerly Captain A. B. Hill's Scotland Neck Mounted Rifles. Company Muster Roll for July & Aug, 1862, shows station of company, Camp Davis, (New) Co. G, 3 Reg't North Carolina Cavalry (41 State Troops), NARA; Company Muster Roll for Nov & Dec, 1862, shows station of company, Camp Badger, (New) Co. G, 3 Reg't North Carolina Cavalry (41 State Troops), NARA.

[87] Transfer of this company from Fort St. Philip to Camp Wyatt came after 30 August 1862. Company Muster Roll for May 15 to Aug 31, 1862, shows station of company, Fort St. Philip, NC, (New) Co. K, 3 Regiment North Carolina Artillery (40 State Troops), NARA. Furthermore, the transfer is believed to have occurred soon after Captain Shaw's company vacated Camp Wyatt on 22 August (see Note 77). "This company was organized in Bladen County, 1 May, 1862, and mustered in service at Wilmington, N. C., and ordered to duty at Fort St. Philip (afterwards known as Fort Anderson), where it remained a short time, and was ordered to Camp Wyatt, about two miles above Fort Fisher, where it remained four or five weeks; afterwards ordered to, and became a part of the garrison of Fort Fisher." Clark, *North Carolina Regiments*, Vol. 2, p. 754.

[88] Company Muster Roll for July & Aug, 1862, shows station of company, Camp French, Wilmington NC, Co. A, 10 Batt'n North Carolina H, Arty., NARA.

[89] Manarin, *North Carolina Troops*, p. 405.

[90] Based solely upon the transfer of the Gatlin Artillery from Fort Fisher to Zeek's Island in October, it is assumed that the transfer of the Anderson Artillery from Zeek's Island to Fort Fisher occurred at the same time. Ibid., p. 237.

[91] Manarin, *North Carolina Troops*, p. 101.

[92] Company Muster Roll for July & Aug, 1862, dated Dec 6, 1862, shows station of company, Camp Holmes Landing, Capt. Adam's [sic] Co. (G), 2 Regiment North Carolina Artillery+ (36 State Troops), NARA. "With the rest of the army it retired to Kinston where it remained until transferred to Wilmington in the fall of 1862. Manarin, *North Carolina Troops*, p. 272. Previous duty station of Camp Johnston must therefore have been in or near Kinston. Company Muster Roll for May & June, 1862, dated July 4, 1862, shows station of company, Camp Johnston, Capt. Adam's [sic] Co. (G), 2 Regiment North Carolina Artillery, (36 State Troops), NARA.

[93] Clark, *North Carolina Regiments*, Volume 2, pp. 767, 770, 771.

[94] "I may add that the danger of its reduction is more imminent from the disorders consequent on the pestilence which has desolated the unfortunate city. Preparations have been suspended, the garrison reduced and withdrawn, the workshops deserted, transportation rendered irregular and uncertain, provisions, forage, and supplies exhausted." Whiting to Randolph, November 14, 1862, *OR* Series 1, Volume 18, p. 776.

[95] "On the gunboats the pestilence had stopped labor; both were on the stocks and no provision whatever had been made or even projected for saving them in case of disaster or providing for them during attack." Whiting to Cooper, January 15, 1863 *OR* Series 1, Volume 18, p. 849.

[96] *Wilmington Journal*, November 20, 1862.

[97] Special Orders, No. 262, Adjt. And Inspector General's Office, Richmond, Va., November 8, 1862, *OR* Series 1, Volume 18, p. 770.

Chapter Nine: Major General Whiting

[1] Confederate Military History, Vol. V, p. 352.

[2] Special Orders No. 262, Paragraph VI, [with endorsement by the Secretary of War], Adjutant and Inspector General's Office, Richmond, November 8, 1862, Compiled Military Service Records of William Henry Chase Whiting, NARA. William Chase Strong was, in truth, a 1st Lieutenant at this point in the war. He had not as yet been promoted to Captain except on this document, which seems to have been an error by the War Department. Compiled Military Service Records of William Chase Strong, NARA. Brackets by author.

[3] Abstract of assignments, Compiled Military Service Records of John W. Cameron, NARA.

[4] Abstract of assignments, Compiled Military Service Records of Allan B. Magruder, NARA; Abstract of assignments, Compiled Military Service Records of Henry M. Drane, NARA.

[5] Abstract of assignments, Compiled Military Service Records of A. Vander Horst, NARA.

[6] Special Orders No. 262, Paragraph VII, Adjutant and Inspector General's Office, Richmond, November 8, 1862, *OR* Series 1, Volume 51, Part 2, p. 642.

[7] Abstract of assignments, Compiled Military Service Records of James W. Archer, NARA.

[8] "1st Lieutenant Daniel K. Bennett, commanding Company since May 14, 1862 promoted to Captain 10 October 1862." Company Muster Roll for July & Aug., 1862, Lieut. D.K. Bennett's Co, (K), Cape Fear Regiment of Artillery; Roster of the Thirty-sixth Regiment of North Carolina Volunteers, Roster dated Jan, 1864, Compiled Military Service Records of Daniel K. Bennett, NARA.

[9] Captain Octavious H. Blocker resigned on 18 July 1862, accepted by Secretary of War after 29 July 1862 [actual date cut off of original document]. Letter of Resignation [and endorsements thereon], August 22, 1862, Compiled Military Service Records of Octavious H. Blocker, NARA. 1st Lieutenant Kinchen J. Braddy promoted to Captain 1 August 1862 and assumed command of Company, thereby changing the local designation from Blocker's Artillery to Braddy's Battery. Roster of the Thirty-sixth Regiment of North Carolina Volunteers, Roster dated Jan, 1864, Compiled Military Service Records of Kinchen J. Braddy, NARA. Brackets by author.

[10] Captain William Sutton resigned 25 September 1862, accepted by Secretary of War after 9 October 1862. Letter of Resignation [and endorsements thereon], 25 September 1862, Compiled Military Service Records of William Sutton, NARA.

1st Lieutenant Ancram W. Ezzell promoted to Captain 15 October 1862 and assumed command of Company. Manarin, *North Carolina Troops*, p. 375. Brackets by author.

11 Captain Paris' Company moved from Camp Hedrick to Camp Wyatt and then to Camp Badger, all in the space of less than three months, between 31 July and sometime in October 1862. Battery was at Camp Hedrick on 31 July. Requisition for Forage, July 31, 1862, Compiled Military Service Records of Andrew B. Paris, NARA. Battery was at Camp Wyatt on 1 September. Requisition for Forage, September 1, 1862, Compiled Military Service Records of Andrew B. Paris, NARA. Battery was at Camp Badger in October. Requisition for Medicines, Hospital Stores & c., October, 1862, "required at Camp Badger for the Staunton Hill Artillery Virginia Volunteers, Capt. A.B. Paris, one hundred & fifty men (150)," Compiled Military Service Records of Andrew B. Paris, NARA.

12 Captain Nathan L. Williamson resigned 22 August 1862, accepted by Secretary of War on 5 September 1862. Letter of Resignation [and endorsements thereon], August 22, 1862, Compiled Military Service Records of Nathan L. Williamson, NARA. 1st Lieutenant Oliver H. Powell promoted to Captain on 13 September 1862 and given command of the Company. Roster of the Thirty-sixth Regiment of North Carolina Volunteers, Roster dated Jan, 1864, Compiled Military Service Records of Oliver H. Powell, NARA. Brackets by author.

13 Captain Charles D. Ellis' resignation was effective on October 11, 1862, whereupon 1st Lieutenant John William Taylor was promoted to Captain and assumed command of the company. Manarin, *North Carolina Troops*, p. 11.

14 Whiting to Cooper, January 15, 1863, *OR* Series 1, Volume 18, p. 848.

15 Thomas Sparrow (1819-1884), Ordnance Inspection, various dates, *Thomas Sparrow Papers, 1835-1871*, Collection Number 01878, The Southern Historical Collection at the Louis Round Wilson Special Collections Library, University of North Carolina at Chapel Hill, North Carolina (hereinafter cited as *Sparrow Papers*, UNC-CH); List of guns sent from the Norfolk navy yard to North Carolina, Tennessee, Louisiana, and Georgia, *ORN*, Series 1, Volume 5, p. 806.

16 Ibid.

17 Map dated 1 May 1863 shows Fort Strong [Light House Battery] mounting five guns. Jeremy Francis Gilmer, *Chart of the obstructions in the Cape Fear and Brunswick Rivers and the batteries commanding them*, in the Jeremy Francis Gilmer Papers #276, Southern Historical Collection, Wilson Library, University of North Carolina at Chapel Hill. An ordnance inspection by Major Thomas Sparrow dated 17 October 1863, however, shows Fort Davis (vice Fort Strong) mounting the six guns stated in the narrative. *Sparrow Papers*, UNC-CH. Brackets by author.

32-pounder Navy Gun, banded and presumed rifled. Note the "renewed trunnions." Some of the Gosport Navy Yard cannon had their trunnions broken off by the Federals before they abandoned the yard, hence the use of this innovative technique. A forged assembly, the banded trunnions were heat-shrunk onto the tube in the same manner as the breech bands., and, in this case, most likely at the same time. In all, the labor to produce this piece probably consumed four to five days, not to mention the cost to manufacture the parts. (Library of Congress, Prints and Photographs Division)

Bibliography

Manuscripts

Anonymous. List of Ordnance at the Forts & Batteries & Light Batteries in the Command Defcs Mth of Cape Fear River, August, 1864. Record Group 109, Microfilm M935, Roll 18, National Archives.

Beatty, G.H. Papers, 1861-1862. Duke University, Rare Book, Manuscript, and Special Collections Library, Perkins Library, Durham, North Carolina.

Cantwell, John L. Collection. North Carolina Office of Archives and History. Raleigh, NC.

Cantwell, John Lucas Paul, 1828-1909. Papers, 1830-1925, Collection #3027. Southern Historical Collection at the Wilson Library. University of North Carolina at Chapel Hill.

Clark, Governor Henry T. Letter Book. North Carolina Office of Archives and History. Raleigh, NC.

Leventhorpe, Collett, Letters. North Carolina Office of Archives and History. Raleigh, NC.

Gatlin, R.C. Papers, 1744-1967, Collection #3868. Southern Historical Collection at the Wilson Library. University of North Carolina at Chapel Hill.

Gilmer, Jeremy Francis, 1818-1883. Papers, 1839-1894, Collection #276. Southern Historical Collection at the Wilson Library. University of North Carolina at Chapel Hill.

High Family. Papers, 1861-1865. Manuscripts Collection. Special Collections Department, William Madison Randall Library. University of North Carolina at Wilmington.

Library of Congress, Washington, D. C. Geography and Map Division.

Library of Congress, Washington, D. C. Prints and Photographs Division.

McGimsey, Laura Cornelia. Papers. Collection #2680-z. Southern Historical Collection at the Wilson Library. University of North Carolina at Chapel Hill.

McNeill, Mary Margaret, Papers. Duke University, Rare Book, Manuscript, and Special Collections Library, Perkins Library, Durham, North Carolina.

National Archives and Records Administration (NARA). Washington, D.C.

Record Group 77. Fort File. National Archives at College Park. Cartographic Division. 8601 Adelphi Road, College Park, Maryland 20740-6001

Record Group 109. War Department Collection of Confederate Records, 1825 – 1927. Compiled Service Records of Confederate Soldiers Who Served in Organizations from the State of North Carolina. Archives I Reference Section, Textual Archives Services Division (NWCT1R), National Archives Building, 7th and Pennsylvania Avenue NW, Washington, DC, 20408.

Record Group 109. War Department Collection of Confederate Records, 1825 – 1927. Papers Relating to Citizens or Business Firms. Archives I Reference Section, Textual Archives Services Division (NWCT1R), National Archives Building, 7th and Pennsylvania Avenue NW, Washington, DC, 20408.

Still Picture Reference. Special Media Archives Services Division. National Archives at College Park. 8601 Adelphi Road, College Park, Maryland 20740-6001.

National Oceanographic and Atmospheric Administration, Washington, D. C. Preliminary Chart of the Entrances to Cape Fear River and New Inlet. Survey of the Coast of the United States, 1853.

North Carolina. Military Board. Convention (1861-1862). 70 p. [Raleigh] Syme & Hall, Printers to the Convention 1861 Call number VC342.2 1861d v. 1. North Carolina Collection at the Wilson Library. University of North Carolina at Chapel Hill. (See also Electronic Sources)

North Carolina Collection. Prints and Photographs. Wilson Library. University of North Carolina at Chapel Hill. (See also Electronic Sources)

Shaw, Colin. Papers. North Carolina Office of Archives and History. Raleigh, NC.

Sparrow, Thomas. Papers, 1819-1872. East Carolina University. Special Collections Department, J. Y. Joyner Library, Greenville, North Carolina.

Sparrow, Thomas, 1819-1884. Papers, 1835-1871, Collection #1878. Southern Historical Collection at the Wilson Library. University of North Carolina at Chapel Hill.

Spurling, Rudy. Papers. North Carolina Maritime Museum, Southport, North Carolina.

Tredegar Iron Works. Accession #23881. Foundry, Sales Book, 1860-1867. Library of Virginia, Richmond, Virginia.

Weston, R.D. Plan of Fort Johnston (ca. 1836). Southport, North Carolina

Whiting, W.H.C. Sketch of Fort Johnston (ca. 1856).

Whiting, William Henry Chase. Image. South Carolina Historical Society, Charleston, South Carolina.

Wood, Dr. Thomas Fanning. Wood Family Papers. "Journal, Book 2, Some Recollections of My Life Written for My Children During My Confinement With Aneurysm Beginning 25th April, 1886." Special Collections, William Madison Randall Library, University of North Carolina Wilmington, Wilmington, NC.

Published Primary Sources

Ashe, Samuel A, Stephen B. Weeks, and Charles L. Van Noppen, Editors. Biographical History of North Carolina From Colonial Times to the Present, Volume VII, Greensboro, NC: Charles L. Van Noppen, 1908.

Brooke, George M., Jr., Editor. Ironclads and Big Guns of the Confederacy: The Journal and Letters of John M. Brooke, Columbia, SC: University of South Carolina Press, 2002

Clark, Walter, Editor. Histories of the Several Regiments and Battalions From North Carolina in the Great War 1861-'65. 5 Volumes. Goldsboro, North Carolina: Nash Brothers, 1901.
Davis, Jefferson. The Rise and Fall of the Confederate Government, Volume I, New York: D. Appleton and Company, 1881.

Evans, Clement A., Editor. Confederate Military History: A Library of Confederate States History Written by Distinguished Men of the South. In 12 Volumes. Atlanta, GA: The Confederate Publishing Company, 1899.

French, Samuel G. Two Wars: An Autobiography of Gen. Samuel G. French. Nashville, Tennessee: Confederate Veteran, 1901.

Hayes, John D. and Lillian O'Brien. "The Early Blockade and the Capture of the Hatteras Forts: From the Journal of John Sanford Barnes, July 19 to September 1, 1861." *New York Historical Society Quarterly*, by the Society: 1962, Volume 46, pp. 60-85.

Hoy, Patrick C. A Brief History of Bradford's Battery, Confederate Guards Artillery of Pontotoc County, Miss., Personal Recollections of Lieut. P.C. Hoy. Petersburg, VA: July 1, 1903.

Lamb, William. "Defence of Fort Fisher, North Carolina", Papers of the Military Historical Society of Massachusetts, Volume 9. Boston: By the Society, 1912.

Manigault, Edward, Warren Ripley, Editor. Siege Train: The Journal of a Confederate Artilleryman in the Defense of Charleston, Columbia, SC: University of South Carolina Press, 1986.

Simpson, Lieutenant Edward, Compiler, A Treatise on Ordnance and Naval Gunnery, New York: D. Van Nostrand, 192 Broadway, 1862.

Stevens, John Austin, Editor. The Union Defence Committee of the City of New York, Minutes, Reports, and Correspondence, New York: The Union Defence Committee, 1885.

Tolbert, Noble J., Editor. The Papers of John Willis Ellis, Two Volumes. Raleigh, NC: State Department of Archives and History, 1964.

Vickers, George M., Editor. Under Battle Flags: A Panorama of the Great Civil War, as represented in Story, Anecdote, Adventure, and the Romance of Reality. Veteran Publishing Company, 1896.

Virginia House of Delegates, Documents of the, 1861-1862. Report of Ordnance and Ordnance Stores on Hand at the Gosport Navy yard on the 21st of April, 1861. Richmond, Virginia: Virginia State Library, 1966. Volume III, Document No. 25.

Virginia State Convention of 1861. Journals and Papers. Richmond, Virginia: Virginia State Library, 1966. Volume III, Document No. 40.

William and Mary College, Quarterly Historical Magazine. Letters of Major Thomas Rowland, C.S.A. Volume XXVI, No. 4, April 1917.

Published Secondary Sources

Allardice, Bruce S. Confederate Colonels, a Biographical Register. Columbia, MO: University of Missouri Press, 2008

Angley, Wilson. A History of Fort Johnston On The Lower Cape Fear. Southport, NC: Southport Historical Society, Inc., 1996.

Bell, Jack. Civil War Heavy Explosive Ordnance, A Guide to Large Artillery Projectiles, Torpedoes, and Mines, Denton, TX: University of North Texas Press, 2003.

Birkhimer, William E. Historical Sketch of the Organization, Administration, Materiel and Tactics of the Artillery, United States Army, Washington, DC: James J. Chapman, Agent, 1884.

Chapman, Craig S. More Terrible Than Victory, North Carolina's Bloody Bethel Regiment, 1861-1865. Dulles, VA: Brassey's, Inc., 1998.

Cole, J. Timothy and Bradley R. Foley. Collett Leventhorpe, the English Confederate: The Life of a Civil War General, 1815-1889. Jefferson, N.C.: McFarland & Co., 2007

Cullum, Brevet Major General George W. Biographical Register of the Officers and Graduates of the U. S. Military Academy at West Point, N. Y. From Its Establishment, in 1802, to 1890 With the Early History of the United States Military Academy, Volume 1. Boston and New York: Houghton, Mifflin and Company and printed by The Riverside Press, 1891.

Denson, C. B. An Address delivered in Raleigh, N. C., on Memorial Day (May 10), 1895. Containing a Memoir of the late Major-General William Henry Chase Whiting of the Confederate Army. Raleigh, NC: Edwards and Broughton, 1895. Reprinted Pikeville, KY & Saltville, VA: Twin Commonwealth Press, LLC, 2005.

Dew, Charles B. Ironmaker to the Confederacy, Richmond, VA: Library of Virginia, 1999.

Fonvielle, Jr., Chris E. The Wilmington Campaign. Last Rays of Departing Hope. Mechanicsburg, PA: Stackpole Books, 2001.

Hall, Charles B., Compiler, General Officers of the Confederate States of America, New York: Lockwood Press, 1898

Heitman, Francis B., Compiler. Historical Register and Dictionary of the United States Army From Its Organization, September 29, 1789, to March 2, 1903, Volume 1. Washington: Government Printing Office, 1903.

Holley, Alexander L. A Treatise on Ordnance and Armor, New York: D. Van Nostrand, 192 Broadway, 1865)

Lusk, M.D., William T. and James B. Hunter, M.D., Editors. The New York Medical Journal, Volume XVI. New York: D. Appleton & Company, 1872.

Manarin, Louis, Compiler. North Carolina Troops, 1861-1865, A Roster, 5 Volumes. Raleigh, North Carolina: North Carolina Office of Archives and History, Third Printing, 2004.

Martin, Tyrone G. "*Constitution*'s Wartime Gun Batteries," The War of 1812 Magazine, Issue 3, June 2006.

McNeil, Jim. Masters of the Shoals, Tales of the Cape Fear Pilots Who Ran the Union Blockade, Cambridge, MA: Da Capo Press, 2003.

Olmstead, Edwin, Wayne E. Stark, and Spencer C. Tucker. The Big Guns: Civil War Siege, Seacoast, and Naval Cannon. Alexandria Bay, NY: Museum Restoration Service, 1997.

Porter, John W. H. A Record of Events in Norfolk County, Virginia, from April 19th, 1861 to May 10th, 1862, With a History of the Soldiers and Sailors of Norfolk County, Norfolk City and Portsmouth Who Served in the Confederate States Army or Navy. Portsmouth, VA: W. A. Fiske, Printer and Bookbinder, 1892.

Ripley, George and Charles A. Dana, Editors. The American Cyclopaedia, A Popular Dictionary Of General Knowledge, with supplement, Volume XV. Shomer – Trollope, New York: D. Appleton & Company, 1, 3, and 5 Bond Street, 1883.

Roosevelt, Theodore. The Naval War of 1812, Part II, New York and London: G.P. Putnam's Sons, 1900.

South Carolina. 1670. 1783. The Centennial of Incorporation, 1883. Charleston, S. C.: The News and Courier Book Press, 1884.

Sprunt, James. Tales and Traditions of the Lower Cape Fear, 1661-1896. Wilmington, North Carolina: Legwin Brothers, Printers, 1896.

Sprunt, James. Chronicles of the Cape Fear River, 1660-1916. Raleigh, North Carolina: Edwards & Broughton Printing Co., 1916.

Stewart, Colonel William H. History Of Norfolk Co., Virginia, and Representative Citizens. Chicago, IL: Biographical Publishing Co., 1902.

Weaver, Jeffrey C. Branch, Harrington and Staunton Hill Artillery, Lynchburg, VA: H.E. Howard, Inc., 1997.

Wilson, James Grant, Editor. The Memorial History of the City of New-York From Its First Settlement to the Year 1892, Volume IV, New York: New-York History Company, 1893.

Official Publications

Aide-Mémoire to the Military Sciences. Framed From Contributions Of Officers Of The Different Services, And Edited By A Committee Of The Corps Of Royal Engineers In Dublin, 1845. Part A. B. C. Sketch Of The Art And Science Of War. Abattis – Contours. With Eighty-Nine Plates And Numerous Woodcuts. Volume I, Part I. London: John Weale, High Holborn and printed By W. Hughes, King's Head Court, Gough Square, 1845.

Confederate States of America. War Department. Ordnance Manual for the Use of the Officers of the Confederate States Army: Prepared Under the Direction of Col. J. Gorgas, Chief of Ordnance, and Approved by the Secretary of War, First Edition, Richmond, VA: West and Johnston, 1862.

Confederate States of America. War Department. Regulations for the Army of the Confederate States, 1862, Richmond, Virginia: J.W. Randolph, 1862.

Confederate States of America. War Department. Instruction for Heavy Artillery, Prepared by a Board of Officers for the Use of the Army of the United States. First Confederate Edition. Charleston: Steam-Power Presses of Evans & Cogswell, No. 3 Broad and 103 East Bay Streets, 1861.

Gibbon, John. Artillerist's Manual, Compiled from Various Sources, and Adapted to the Service of the United States, Second Edition, West Point, New York: 1863.

Scott, Colonel H.L. Military Dictionary: Comprising Technical Definitions; Information on Keeping and Raising Troops; Actual Service, Including Makeshifts and Improved Materiel; and Law, Government, Regulation, and Administration Relating to Land Forces, New York: D. Van Nostrand, 1864.

United States of America. Congress. American State Papers: Military Affairs, 7 Volumes. Washington: Gales and Seaton, 1832-61. From Library of Congress: A Century of Lawmaking for a New Nation: U.S. Congressional Documents and Debates, 1774-1875 (see Electronic Sources).

United States of America. Congress. Documents and Debates, 1774-1875, Statutes at Large. 27th Congress, 1st Session. Washington, D. C.: United States Government Printing Office.

United States of America. Congress. Report of the Joint Committee on the Conduct of the War. In Three Parts. Washington: Government Printing Office, 1863, Part III.

United States of America. House of Representatives. 37th Congress, 2nd Session, Report No. 86, Permanent Fortifications and Sea-Coast Defence. Washington, D. C.: United States Government Printing Office.

United States of America. House of Representatives. Reports From The Court of Claims Submitted to the House of Representatives, The First Session of the Thirty-Fourth Congress, 1855-'56, Two Volumes. Washington: Cornelius Wendell, Printer, 1856.

United States of America. Naval War Records Office. Official Records of the Union and Confederate Navies in the War of the Rebellion. 30 Volumes in Two Series. Washington, D. C.: United States Government Printing Office, 1894-1922.

United States of America. War Department. Atlas to Accompany the Official Records of the Union and Confederate Armies. United States War Department. Washington, D.C.: U.S. Government Printing Office, 1891-1895.

United States of America. War Department. Instruction for Heavy Artillery, Prepared by a Board of Officers for the Use of the Army of the United States. Washington: Government Printing Office, 1862.

United States of America. War Department, Regulations for the Army of the United States, 1857, New York: Harper & Brothers, Publishers.

United States of America. War Department, Revised United States Army Regulations of 1861, Washington: Government Printing Office, 1863

United States of America. War Department. The War of the Rebellion: a Compilation of the Official Records of the Union and Confederate Armies. 70 Volumes in 128 Parts. Washington, D.C.: United States Government Printing Office, 1880-1901.

United States Army, Military Traffic Management Command Headquarters. Chronology – Fort Johnston, Southport, North Carolina, n.d. Military Ocean Terminal, Sunny Point, Southport, North Carolina.

United States Army. Ordnance Department. Ordnance Manual For The Use Of The Officers Of The United States Army, Second Edition. Washington: Gideon & Co., Printers, 1850.

United States Army. Ordnance Department. Ordnance Manual for the Use of the Officers of the United States Army, Third Edition, Philadelphia: J.B. Lippincott & Co., 1862

United States Navy. Bureau of Ordnance. Ordnance Instructions for the United States Navy. Washington, D. C.: United States Government Printing Office, 1866.

Electronic Sources

American Civil War Research Database, <http://www.civilwardata.com>

Branch, Paul. Fort Macon Ranger/Historian. Armament of Fort Macon.
< http://www.crystalcoast.com/fortmacon/fortmaconarmament.shtml>

Fort Fisher State Historical Site, <http://www.nchistoricsites.org/fisher/fort-fisher.htm>

Library of Congress. A Century of Lawmaking for a New Nation: U.S. Congressional Documents and Debates, 1774-1875. <http://memory.loc.gov/ammem/amlaw/lwsp.html>

Message From The Execttive [*sic*] Of The Commonwealth, With Accompanying Documents, Showing The Military And Naval Preparations For The Defence Of The State Of Virginia, &c. &c.: Electronic Edition, Virginia. Executive Dept. "LIST OF GUNS Sent From The Norfolk Navy Yard to North Carolina, Tennessee, Louisiana and Georgia". Academic Affairs Library, UNC-CH, University of North Carolina at Chapel Hill, 1999.

North Carolina. Convention (1861-1862). North Carolina. Military Board. 70 pp. [Raleigh] Syme & Hall, Printers to the Convention 1861 Call number VC342.2 1861d v. 1, (North Carolina Collection, University of North Carolina at Chapel Hill), From the University Library, The University of North Carolina at Chapel Hill, Documenting the American South. <http://docsouth.unc.edu/imls/troops/troops.html>

Texas State Historical Association. Handbook of Texas Online, http://www.tsha.utexas.edu/handbook/online/

The Buffalo Barracks Historical Website. <http://www.buffalonet.org/army/1002.htm>

The Civil War Artillery Page. <http://www.cwartillery.org>

United States Army. Center of Military History. Accessed March 9, 2008.
<http://www.history.army.mil/StaffRide/1st%20Bull%20Run/Artillery.htm>

United States Navy, Naval Historical Center.
<http://www.history.navy.mil/danfs/s12/shubrick-ii.htm>

Wikipedia, The Free Encyclopedia, <http://en.wikipedia.org/wiki/Seacoast_Defense_(US)>

Periodicals

Charleston Mercury

Columbus Times

Confederate Veteran, Vol. XXVIII, No. 1, January, 1920

Daily Journal (Wilmington)

Frank Leslie's Illustrated Newspaper

Greensborough Patriot

Hillsborough Recorder

North Carolina Standard

Index

Adams, Zachariah T., Captain, Adams' Battery, 140, 146
Adams' Battery, 140, 142, 144, 146
Advisory Council to the State of Virginia, 68
Alabama, State of, 99
Anderson, Joseph Reid, *biography*, 93-94
   2nd Lieutenant, 3rd Artillery, U. S. A; Brevet 2nd Lieutenant, Corps of Engineers, U. S. A., 93
   Assistant Engineer, City of Richmond, VA, 93
   Chief Engineer, Valley Turnpike Company, VA, 93
   Member, Virginia House of Delegates, 93-94
   Superintendent and Partner, Tredegar Iron Works, 52, 93
   Brigadier General, PACS, *image*, 93; 93-96, 99-102, 118-120, 123, 138, 146, (*n*172), (*n*174)
Anderson, Robert, Major, 1st Artillery, U. S. A., 54
Anderson Artillery, 125, 133, 140, 146, (*n*176), (*n*184)
Andrews, William S. G., Captain, Andrews' Battery, 140, 147
Andrews' Battery, 140, 147
Archer, James W., Captain, PACS, Ordnance Officer, Whiting's Command, Cape Fear River Defenses, 146
Arkansas, State of, 78
Arkansas River, 78
Armstrong, James F., Commander, U.S. N., 131
Army of Northern Virginia, 6, 121, 133, 134
Army of the Confederate States of America (ACSA), 66, (*n*166)
Artillery,
  Ammunition,
    Canister, 53, 55, 57-59, 69, 83, 124, 137, 154, 155, 157; *images*, 55, 59, 63, 64
    Conical (Rifle) Projectiles, 99, 109, 115, 123, 124, 154, 155, 160; *images*, 98, 108, 109, 115

Artillery (continued),
  Ammunition (continued),
    Grapeshot, 3, 53, 55, 56, 57, 59, 83, 124, 157, *images*, 56, 59, 63, 64
    Spherical Projectiles, 6, 15, 53, 55-58, 63, 68, 69, 82, 96, 99, 100, 154, 155, 158, 160, 161, *images*, 55, 57
  Ballistics, 6, 51, 53, 81-81, 96, 100, 124, 137, (*n*178)
  Banding by Confederates, 97; *images*, 97
  Implements, *images*, 63, 64, 68
  Rifling, *general discussion*, 96-98
    Blakely, 98; *images*, 108
    Hook-Slant, 97, 98, 99; *images*, 98
    Parrott, 160
    Rectangular, 99, 123, 124, 160
    Scott's, 98; *images*, 108
Ashe, Samuel A'Court, 2nd Lieutenant, 67, 83, 94, 99
Ashe, William S., 93, 94
Atwell, James B.,
   Captain, Cabarrus Black Boys Riflemen, 71
   Captain, Company B, 10th Regiment North Carolina Volunteers, 79, 95

Badham, William, Captain, Company B, 3rd Battalion North Carolina Light Artillery, 96
Bailey, John C., 68; see also Hart & Bailey
Bald Head Island, 95
Bald Head Point, 122
Barnes, Calvin, Captain, 1st Company A, 2nd Regiment North Carolina State Troops, 121, 146
Barnes, Henry M., Captain, Company B, 10th Battalion North Carolina Heavy Artillery, 132, 147
Baton Rouge, LA, 78
Battery Anderson, 100; *maps*, 107, 126, 144
Battery Andrew, *map*, 149

Battery Bellamy, *map*, 149
Battery Bolles, 70, 71, 80, 84, 95, 103, 135, 136, (*n*171), (*n*181); *maps*, 73, 88, 107, 126, 144
Battery Dawson, *map*, 149
Battery Gatlin, 100; *maps*, 107, 126, 144
Battery Green, *map*, 149
Battery Hedrick, 135, 136, (*n*181); *map*, 144
Battery Hobson, *map*, 149
Battery McRee, *map*, 149
Battery Meade, 135, 136; *map*, 144
Battery Smith, *map*, 149
Battery Wright, *map*, 149
Beacon Island, NC, 86, see also Ocracoke Inlet
Bee, Barnard Elliott, Brigadier General, PACS, 145, 146
Beauregard, Pierre Gustave Toutant,
  Brigadier General, ACSA, 66, 67
  General, ACSA, 145
Bellona Foundry, James River, VA, 50-52
Bennett, Daniel K.,
  1st Lieutenant, Brunswick Artillery, (*n*184)
  Captain, Brunswick Artillery, 146, (*n*184)
Best, William H., Private, Company H, 8th Regiment North Carolina Volunteers, 83
Biloxi, MS, 65
Bladen Artillery, 100, 102, 125, 133, 146, (*n*173)
Bladen Artillery Guards, 132, 140, 146, (*n*179)
Bladen County, NC, (*n*183)
Bladen Guards, 71
Bladen Infantry, 71, (*n*168)
Bladen Stars, 101, 102, 117, 125, 133, 146, (*n*175)
Blaney, George, U. S. Army Corps of Engineers,
  Captain, 15, 16, 17, 18, 30; (*n*164)
  Brevet Major, 18
Blocker, Octavious H., Captain, Blocker's Artillery, 117, 125, (*n*184)
Blocker's Artillery, 117, 125, 133
Blockhouse, *plan*, 12
Bogue Inlet, 101
Bogue Sound, 86
Bolles, Charles Pattison, Captain, 9, 69, 70
Bolles Battery, see Battery Bolles
Bomford, George, Lieutenant Colonel, Chief of U.S. Army Ordnance, 16
Boston, MA, 65
Braddock, Edward, General, Colonial British Army, 3
Braddy, Kinchen J.,
  1st Lieutenant, Blocker's Artillery, (*n*184)
  Captain, Braddy's Battery, 146, (*n*184)
Braddy's Battery, 146, (*n*184)

Bradford, James A. J., Colonel, North Carolina Corps of Artillery, Ordnance and Engineers, 83
Braine, Daniel L., Lieutenant, U. S. N., 103, 122, 135
Bridgers' Artillery, 121, 125, 146
Brooks, John S., Captain, Company G, 10th Regiment North Carolina Volunteers, 79, 95
Brown, John A.,
  Captain, Chief of Artillery and Ordnance, Fort Caswell, 94, 95, 99
  Colonel, PACS (Temporary), Commanding Fort Caswell, 99, 101, 102
  Captain, Artillery, 118
Brown, Joseph E., Governor of Georgia, 66
Brunswick, Old, see Old Brunswick
Brunswick Artillery, 117, 125, 133, 146
Brunswick County, NC, *maps*, 87, 105, 143
Brunswick Point, 121, 124, 125, 131-133, (*n*177)
Brunswick Point Battery, 121, (*n*177)
Buena Vista, Mexico, Battle of, 120
Bunting, Samuel R., Captain, 79, 95, 102, 118
Bunting's Battery, 95, 101, 102, 107, 118, (*n*168), (*n*174), (*n*175)
Burlington Academy, NJ, 119
Burrington, George, 1st Royal Governor of North Carolina, 2

Cabarrus Black Boys Riflemen, 71, (*n*167)
Cabarrus Guards, 70, 71
Cameron, John W., Major, PACS, Quartermaster, Whiting's Command, Cape Fear River Defenses, 145, 146
Camp, Entrenched, Wilmington, NC, 132; *map*, 149
Camp, Galloway's, 85, 95, 102, 107, 125, 133, 146, (*n*175); *maps*, 87, 88, 107, 126, 144
Camp, Montfort's Mill, Onslow County, NC, 118, 125
Camp, Rock Spring, 134, (*n*180), (*n*181)
Camp, Watson's Branch, 118, (*n*176); *map*, 128
Camp Anderson, 100, 101,102, 118, (*n*173), (*n*174)
Camp Badger, 140, 146, (*n*182), (*n*185)
Camp Boylan, Raleigh, NC, 83, (*n*171)
Camp Campbell, (*n*182)
Camp Clingman, Goldsborough, NC, (*n*182)
Camp Collier, Goldsborough, NC, (*n*183)
Camp Davis, 79, 95, 100, 101, 102, 118, 132, 134, 140, (*n*171), (*n*174), (*n*175), (*n*179), (*n*180), (*n*181); *maps*, 87, 88, 107, 126, 128, 144
Camp French, 102, 118, 119, 134, 140, 146, (*n*176), (*n*180)

Index | 197

Camp Grant, 101, 102, 118, (*n*174), (*n*176); *maps*, 105, 107, 126, 144
Camp Heath, 100, 102, 132, 146, (*n*172); *maps*, 104, 107, 126, 144
Camp Hedrick, 125, 140, (*n*176), (*n*179), (*n*183), (*n*185)
Camp Hill, *map*, 149
Camp Holmes, 118, 119, 122, 132, 134, (*n*176), (*n*179), (*n*180); *maps*, 126, 128, 144
Camp Holmes Landing, 140, 146; *maps*, 142, 144
Camp Hopkins, 95, 100, 102; *maps*, 106, 107, 126, 144, (*n*171), (*n*174)
Camp of Instruction, Wilmington, 134
Camp Johnston, Kinston, NC, 140, (*n*184)
Camp Jones, 134, 140, (*n*181); *maps*, 142, 144
Camp Lamb, 119, 132, 134, 140, (*n*176) (*n*180), (*n*183); *map*, 149
Camp Long, Garysburg, NC, (*n*183)
Camp Mangum, Raleigh, NC, 132, 140, (*n*179)
Camp Morgan, 121, 125, 132, (*n*180)
Camp Nacogdoches, TX, 78
Camp Radcliff[e], (*n*183)
Camp Saunders, Onslow County, NC, 118, 122, 125, 134, (*n*176)
Camp Walker, 95, 101, (*n*171), (*n*173)
Camp Winslow, 79, 95, 101, 128, (*n*174); *maps*, 88, 107, 128; *military notice*, 78
Camp Wyatt, 80, 85, 94, 95, 101, 102, 118, 120, 125, 132, 134, 140, (*n*176), (*n*177), (*n*180), (*n*181), (*n*182), (*n*183), (*n*185); *maps*, 88, 107, 126, 144
Campbell, Reuben, Colonel, 7th Regiment North Carolina State Troops, 86
Cannon
  2.75-inch Whitworth Breechloading Rifle, 137-138, 139-140, 148; *image*, 137
  4.62-inch C.S. Siege Rifle, 123, 124, 136, 148; *image*, 130; *plan*, 124
  5.82-inch Rifle, see 24-pounder, rifled
  5.82-inch C.S. Rifled Columbiad, 99, 102, 122, 123, 124, 133, 136, (*n*178)
  6-pounder, smoothbore, 5, 6, 52, 53, 55, 56, 80, 96, 102, (*n*174), (*n*175); *images*, 7, 8, 48; *plan*, 6
  6-pounder, rifled, 52
  6.4-inch Rifle, see 32-pounder, U.S. Navy Cannon, rifled
  8-inch Columbiad, U.S. Pattern 1844, 53, 54, 56, 57, 63, 67, 69, 74, 75, 80, 81, 84, 103, 122, 123, 136, 148, (*n*175), (*n*182); *images*, 53, 61; *plan*, 62
  8-inch New Columbiad, U.S. Pattern 1857, 52, 137, 148; *image*, 53
  8-inch Columbiad, C.S. Pattern 1861, 102, 137, 148; i*mage*, 109, 122
  8-inch Seacoast Howitzer, U.S. Pattern 1839 or 1840, 52, 53, 54, 56, 57, 63, 67, 69, 80, 84, 103, 123, 148, (*n*168); *images*, 53, 59; *plan*, 60
  8-inch Shell Gun, U.S. Navy, smoothbore, 80, 81, 82, 103, 123, 137, 148; *image*, 84
  8-inch Shot Gun, U.S. Navy, smoothbore, 81
  8-inch U.S. Siege Howitzer, 56, 57, 124
  8-inch C.S. Siege Howitzer, 123, 137, 148; *image*, 124
  10-inch New Columbiad, U.S. Pattern 1857, 52, 54
  12-pounder Battering Cannon, smoothbore, 5, 55
  12-pounder Heavy Field Gun, smoothbore, 52, 55, 102; *image*, 113; *plan*, 114
  12-pounder Howitzer, smoothbore, 55, 96; *images*, 96, 111; *plan*, 112
  12-pounder Siege and Garrison Gun, 123, 136, 161
  12-pounder Whitworth Rifle, see 2.75-inch Whitworth Breechloading Rifle
  18-pounder Battering Cannon, smoothbore, 5
  18-pounder Siege and Garrison Gun, 161
  24-pounder Battering Cannon, 5
  24-pounder, rifled, 98, 99, 103, 148
  24-pounder Siege Gun, U.S. Pattern 1816, 49-51, 68, 69, 70, 80, 84, 94, 99, 103, 137; *images*, 49, 50
  24-pounder Siege and Garrison Gun, U.S. Pattern 1819, 49-51, 68, 69, 70, 80, 84, 94, 98, 99, 103, 137, 161; i*mages*, 51, 58
  24-pounder Siege and Garrison Gun, U.S. Pattern 1840/1845, 98, 161; *image*, 76
  24-pounder U.S. Navy Cannon, medium gun, 82, 147, 148; *images*, 147, 150
  24-pounder U.S. Navy Cannon, Pattern 1807, 50, 148; *plan*, 50
  32-pounder Carronade, smoothbore, 41, 68, 69, 70, 80, 82, 86, 103, 148, (*n*170); *image*, 89
  32-pounder, U.S. Army Patterns, smoothbore, 56, 98, 136
  32-pounder, U.S. Navy, smoothbore, 68, 69, 80, 81, 82, 84, 98, 103, 119, 122, 124, 135, 136, 137, 147, 148, 158, 161; *images*, 89, 90
  32-pounder, U.S. Navy, rifled, 97, 99, 117, 122, 123, 136, 148, (*n*177), (*n*181)
  Shubrick Gun, 81, 147, 148, 161; *images*, 151, 152
  64-pounder, rifled, 122, 123
Cannon (continued on page 198)

Cannon (continued from page 197),
  64-pounder, smoothbore 53, 56, 81, 123
  128-pounder, rifled, *image*, 123
  128-pounder, smoothbore, 53, 56
Cantwell, John Lucas Paul,
  Colonel, 30th North Carolina State Militia, 1, 2, 5, 11, 18, 19, 69, 70, 71, 84, 86
  Colonel, PACS, 51st Regiment North Carolina Infantry, 121, 125, 132, 134, 140, (n177)
Cape Fear, 1, 2, 3, 4, 6, 17, 50, 52, 66, 68, 69, 79, 80, 83, 85, 90, 93, 94, 96, 97, 98, 99, 100, 101, 103, 113, 118, 119, 121, 123, 124, 132, 134, 136, 139, 141, 139, 146, 148, (n183); *maps*, 2, 88, 106, 107, 142
Cape Fear Defenses, 6, 52, 53, 67, 68, 69, 70, 71, 79, 80, 82, 83, 85, 89, 91, 94, 95, 96, 99, 102, 103, 117, 118, 119, 123, 132, 133, 134, 136, 137, 138, 139, 140, 146, 147, 148, 150, (n183); *maps*, 88, 107, 126, 142, 144
Cape Fear, District of the, see District of the Cape Fear
Cape Fear, Lower, 1, 2, 15, 18, 70, 120; *map*, 9
Cape Fear Light Artillery, 5, 70, 79, 95, 101, 102, 119, (n173); *military notice*, 5; see also Cumming's Battery
Cape Fear Minute Men (Local Militia), 1-2
Cape Fear Rifles, 71
Cape Fear River, 1, 2, 15, 17, 19, 26, 52, 69, 84, 102, 117, 120, 122, 138, 139, 141, 148, (n174), (n177), (n180); *maps*, 104, 142
Captain William S. Devane's Independent Company (Confederates), North Carolina State Troops, 79, 95, 101, 102, 125, (n168), (n171), (n183)
Carpenter, Nathan S., 52
Casemate Battery, Confederate Point, 100, 103, 121, 137, 138; *maps*, 107, 126; see also Battery Meade
Caswell, Richard, First Governor of the State of North Carolina, 77
Cecil Iron Works, Havre de Grace, MD, 50, 51
Charleston, SC, 1, 17, 51, 65, 66, 83, 89. 98, 99, 136
Charleston Arsenal, 83
Charleston Mercury, 98-99
Chesnutt, Owen F., Captain, Company F, 10th Regiment North Carolina Volunteers, 79, 95
Childs, Frederick Lynn, Captain, ACSA, Chief of Artillery and Ordnance, Fort Caswell, 66, 67, 68, 69, 71, 83, 94
Clarendon Guards, 132, 133, 146
Clarendon Iron Works, 69, 86, (n170)
Clark, Henry Toole, Governor of North Carolina, 83, 85, 86, 94, 99, 117-118

Clark Artillery, 132, 147
Clarksville, NC, 79
Clarke, John, see Bellona Foundry
Clarke, William J., Major, Mustering Officer, North Carolina State Troops, 79
Clingman, Thomas Lanier,
  Colonel, PACS, 15th Regiment North Carolina Volunteers, 100, (n171)
  Colonel, PACS, 25th Regiment North Carolina Infantry, 101
  Brigadier General, PACS, Clingman's Brigade, 139, (n182); *image*, 139
Clinton, NC, 134
Collett, James Abraham, Captain, Colonial British Army, 3
Collins Creek, NC, *map*, 142
Columbus Artillery, 125, 133, 140, 146, (n185)
Columbus Guards No. 2, 71
Columbus Guards No. 3, 71
Columbus Guards No, 4, 71
Confederacy, see Confederate States of America
Confederate(s), see Confederate States of America
Confederates (Captain William S. Devane's Independent Company North Carolina Troops), 102, 125, (n168), (n171), (n173), (n183);
Confederate Greys, 71, (n167)
Confederate Guards Artillery, 100, 101, 102, 113, 118, (n172)
Confederate Point, 70, 71, 80, 84, 85, 86, 94, 95, 103, 123, 134, 135, 136, (n179), (n181); *maps*, 73, 107, 126; see also Federal Point
Confederate States of America (CSA), 6, 48, 78, 80, 84, 85, 86, 88, 89, 90, 94, 96, 97, 98, 102, 109, 111, 112, 113, 114, 115, 118, 119, 120, 123, 124, 136, 137, 140, 148, 153
  Army, 49, 51, 58, 72, 81, 83, 85, 86, 91, 92, 101, 121, 122, 131, 136, 137, 140, 145; see also North Carolina Regiments
  Adjutant and Inspector General's Office, 119, 141, (n177)
  Ordnance Department, 55, 57, 80, 92, 98, 99, 115, 134
  Regular Army, see Army of the Confederate States of America
  Reserve Army, see Provisional Army of the Confederate States of America
  Government, 101, 102, 119, 131, 138, (n166), (n168), (n172)
  Secretary of War, 94, 145, (n184), (n185)
  Navy, 97, 98, 141
  Warrington Navy Yard, FL, 58

USS Constitution, 81, 151
Cornehlsen, Christian,
  Captain, German Volunteers, 18, 19, 71
  Captain, Company A, 8th Regiment North Carolina Volunteers, 83, 95
Council of Three, see Advisory Council to the State of Virginia
Cox, Uzz, Captain, Company H, 10th Regiment North Carolina Volunteers, 79, 95
Craig's Wharf, Confederate Point, (n173), (n175)
Craney Island, VA, 97
Craven County, NC, 121
Crown, Thomas, 15, 16, 17, (n164)
HMS Cruizer, 3
Cumberland Battery, 135, 136; *map*, 144
Cumming, James D.,
  Lieutenant, Cape Fear Light Artillery, 119
  Captain, Cumming's Battery, 119, 125, 140,
Cumming's Battery, 119, 125, 140, (n176)
Cunningham, George A., Colonel, Fort Caswell, 119, 125, 138, 146, (n182)
HMS Cyane, 81
USS Cyane, 81, 151

Dalrymple, John, Captain, Colonial British Army, 3
Dardingkiller, Frederick, Ordnance Sergeant, United States Army, 2, 18
Daves, Graham, 2
Davis, Jefferson, President, Confederate States of America, 19, 65, 66, 85, 86, 94, 120, 145
Davis, Thaddeus C., Private, McMillan Artillery, 136
Davis, Thomas, Charleston, SC, 17
Davis Dragoons, 100, (n173)
USS Daylight, 84
Denson, Claudius B.,
  Captain, Confederate Greys, 71, (n167)
  Captain, Company E, 10th Regiment North Carolina Volunteers, 79, 95, (n171)
  Captain, Confederate Corps of Engineers, 99
Department of Fredericksburg, VA 72, 85
Department of North Carolina 85, 86, 94, 95, 119, 138, 145
DeRosset, William Lord,
  Captain, Wilmington Light Infantry, 19, 70
  Major, PACS, 3rd Regiment North Carolina State Troops, 70, 77
Devane, William Stewart,
  Private, Sampson Rangers, 79, (n168)
  Captain William S. Devane's Independent Company (Confederates), North Carolina State Troops, 95, 101; see next *Confederates* (continued)

Devane, William Stewart (continued),
  Captain, Company A, 61st Regiment North Carolina Infantry, (n183)
District of the Cape Fear, 95, 119, 120, 124, 125, 131, 134, 138, 145, 146, 149, (n177), (n182); *maps*, 107, 127, 134
District of North Carolina, 139
District of the Pamlico, 94, 119
Dobbs, George, 6th Royal Governor of North Carolina, 3
Dolphin, schooner, 1
Drane, Henry M., Captain, PACS, Assistant Commissary of Subsistence, Whiting's Command, Cape Fear River Defenses, 146
Drewry's Bluff, VA, 138
Dudley, Edward B., Captain, Edward B. Dudley's Company North Carolina Volunteers Artillery, 118; see next Anderson Artillery
Dudley & Dickinson, New York, NY, 17

Eason, James M., see James M. Eason and Brother
Edelin, Charles C., Captain, Company B, 1st Regiment Maryland Infantry, 121, 125
Edmondston, Patrick M., Captain, Scotland Neck Mounted Rifles, 79, (n171)
El Paso, TX, 65
Ellis, Charles D., Captain, River Guards, (n179), (n185)
Ellis, John Willis, Governor of North Carolina, 1, 2, 19, 51, 52, 65, 67, 68, 72, 77, 79, 83, 84
Emily, schooner, 133
Entrenched Camp, Wilmington, NC, 132; *map*, 149
Ettenger & Edmond, Richmond, VA, (n175)
Evansport, VA, 120
Ezzell, Ancram W.,
  1st Lieutenant, Lenoir Braves, (n184-n185)
  Captain, Lenoir Braves, (n184-n185)

Fair Bluff Volunteers, 70
Faison, Franklin J.,
  Captain, Sampson Rangers, 71
  Lieutenant Colonel, 10th Regiment North Carolina Volunteers, 79, 86, 94, 99, 101
Faison, James A., Captain, Company I, 10th Regiment North Carolina Volunteers, 79, 95
Faison, Paul F., Colonel, 56th Regiment North Carolina Infantry, 140
Falling Creek, NC, (n177)
Fayetteville Arsenal, see North Carolina Arsenal
Federal Government, see United States Government

Federal Point, NC, 4, 69, 70, 135 (*n*170), (*n*173), (*n*175)
Fish, Sewall L., see Fremont, Sewall L.
Fisher, Charles Frederick, Colonel, 6th North Carolina State Troops, 94
Florida, State of, 58, 65, 66, 78
Florida War, see Seminole War
Fort Adams, RI, 18
Fort Branch, NC, 8
Fort Brown, Mexico, 78
Fort Caswell, NC, 1, 2, 5, 9, 13, 14, 15, 17, 18, 19, 49, 50, 51, 52, 53, 62, 65, 66-67, 68, 69 70-71, 72,, 73, 74, 75, 76, 79, 80, 82, 83, 84, 85, 86, 94, 95, 98, 99, 101, 102, 103, 117, 118, 119, 120, 122, 123, 125, 131, 132, 133, 136, 137, 138, 140, 146, 148, (*n*170), (*n*173), (*n*174), (*n*175), (*n*179), (*n*182), (*n*183); *images*, 33-37, 41; *maps*, 2, 9, 73, 88, 107, 126, 144; *plans*, 21-32, 38-40, 42- 47; *plat*, 20
Fort Clark, Hatteras Inlet, NC, 86
Fort Clinch, FL, 66
Fort Craig, New Mexico Territory, U. S., 78
Fort Davis, see Fort Strong
Fort Delaware, DE, 15
Fort Ellis, see Light House Battery, Wilmington
Fort Fisher, NC, 49, 50, 51, 53, 82, 86, 94, 95, 100, 101, 102, 103, 117, 118, 119, 121, 123, 124, 125, 131, 132, 133, 134, 135, 136, 137, 138, 139, 140, 142, 146, 148, (*n*170), (*n*171), (*n*173), (*n*174), (*n*175), (*n*177), (*n*178), (*n*181), (*n*183), (*n*184); *maps*, 107, 126, 144
Fort French, NC, 102, 117, 118, 125, 138, 141, 147, 148, (*n*176); *maps*, 126, 129, 138, 144
Fort Gibson, Indian Territory, U. S., 78
Fort Hamilton, NY, 15
Fort Hatteras, 86; see also Hatteras Inlet, NC
Fort Johnston, NC, 1, 2 3, 4, 5, 6, 9, 17, 18, 50, 51, 65, 69, 70, 71, 79, 80, 85, 86, 95, 98, 101, 102, 103, 117, 118, 121, 125, 132, 134, 140, 146, (*n*173), (*n*174), (*n*177), (*n*179), (*n*180), (*n*181), (*n*183); *maps*, 2, 9, 73, 88, 107, 126, 144; *site plans*, 10, 11
Fort Laramie, Missouri Territory
Fort Leavenworth, Missouri Territory, 78
Fort Lee, see Fort French
Fort Macon, NC, 51, 52, 68, 77, 80, 86, 131, 140, 151
Fort Pulaski, GA, 66, 93
Fort St. Philip, 131, 132, 133, 134, 138, 140, 146, 147, 148, (*n*177), (*n*179), (*n*183); *maps*, 126, 127, 144
Fort Smith, Indian Territory, 78
Fort Strong, see Light House Battery, Wilmington

Fort Sumter, SC, 1, 2, 51, 52, 53, 62, 65, 66, 80, 98; *image*, 54; *schematic*, 54
Fort Washington, MD, 51
Fortress Monroe, VA, 15, 17
Forts, American System of, 14
Foster, John Gray, Captain, U.S. Army Corps of Engineers, 1, (*n*176)
Franklin, VA, 140, (*n*182)
Fredericksburg, VA, Department of, see Department of Fredericksburg, VA
Fremont, Sewall L.,
   Superintendent, Wilmington & Weldon Rail Road Company, 85
   Colonel, 1st Artillery Regiment North Carolina State Militia, 85, 94. 95, 102, 103, 123, 135, 136, 137, (*n*170)
French, Samuel Gibbs, *biography*, 119-120
   2nd Lieutenant and 1st Lieutenant, 3rd Artillery, U.S.A.; Captain, Quartermaster Corps, U.S.A., 119
   Lieutenant Colonel, Chief of Ordnance, Army of Mississippi, 120
   Major, Corps of Artillery, ACSA, 120
   Brigadier General, PACS, 118, 119, 120, 121, 125, 132, 134, 136, 137, 138, 146, (*n*177), (*n*179), (*n*181); *image*, 120
Frobel, Bushrod W., Major, PACS, Chief of Artillery, Whiting's Command, Cape Fear River Defenses, 146
Fuller, Thomas C., 1st Lieutenant, Starr's Battery, 139
Fulton, James, 51

Gaines Mill, VA, Battle of, 145
Galloway, John W., see also Camp, Galloway's
   2nd Lieutenant J. W. Galloway's Detachment of North Carolina Volunteers, aka Coast Guard Detachment, 85, 95, 107
   Captain John Galloway's Company, Coast Guards, 102, 125, 133, 146, (*n*175)
Garwood, Henry, Private, King Artillery, 122
Garysburg, NC, 140, (*n*167), (*n*183)
Gatlin, Richard C., *biography*, 77-78
Gatlin, Richard C. [
   Brevet 2nd Lieutenant; 2nd Lieutenant, 1st Lieutenant, Adjutant, Captain, 7th Infantry; Major, 5th Infantry, U. S. A., 78
   Brigadier General, PACS, 85, 86, 93, 94, 99, 100, 101, 119, 134, 138, 145, 146, (*n*172), (*n*175)
Gatlin, John Slade, 77
Gatlin, Susannah Caswell, 77

Gatlin Artillery, 121, 125, 132, 140, 146, (*n*184)
George, Forney,
  Captain, Columbus Guards No. 3, 71
  Captain, Company C, 8th Regiment North Carolina Volunteers, 83, 95
Georgetown College (Georgetown University), 65
Georgia, State of, 66
German Volunteers, 19, 71; *military notice*, 18
Glisson, O. S., Commander, U. S. N., 133, 135
Goldsborough, NC, 52, 94, 100, 119, 132, 139, 140, (*n*171), (*n*179), (*n*182), (*n*183)
Gomez, see Gonzalez, Ambrosio Jose
Gonzalez, Ambrosio Jose, Volunteer Aide-de-Camp, South Carolina Forces, 67
Gorgas, Josiah, Colonel and Chief of Ordnance, Confederate States of America, 92
Gosport Rifle, 97, 98, 99, 108
Gosport U.S. Navy Yard, Norfolk, VA, 68, 72, 80, 81, 82, 86, 89, 90, 97, 98, 117, 147, 148, 151
Gradual Increase Guns, 81
Grant's Salt Works, Wrightsville Sound, NC, (*n*174)
Gratiot, Charles, Brevet Brigadier General, Chief of the U. S. Army Corps of Engineers, 16
Greenfield Millpond, 147
Green's Old Mill Pond, Wilmington Land Defenses, 143, 147
Grisham, John O., Captain, Confederate Guards Artillery, 100, 102, 103, 110, 113, 118, (*n*172)
Gwynn, Walter,
  Brigadier General, Virginia Forces, Norfolk, VA, 72
  Brigadier General, North Carolina Troops, 72

Halifax County, NC, 79, (*n*174)
Hall, Edward Dudley,
  Captain, Rifle Rangers, 70
  Captain, Company H, 8th Regiment North Carolina Volunteers, 83, 95
Hamilton, NC, (*n*179)
Hankins, M. M., Captain, Cape Fear Rifles, 71
Harding, Henry,
  Captain Henry Harding's Company of North Carolina Volunteers, 100, 117, 125, 134, (*n*173), (*n*175), (*n*181)
  Captain, Company B, 61st Regiment North Carolina Infantry, 146, (*n*183)
Harker's Island, NC, (*n*178)
W.W. Harllee, steamer, 1
Harpers Ferry Arsenal, see United States Arsenal
Hart & Bailey, 68, 69, 74, 75, 76, 80, 84, 94, 141; *newspaper advertisement*, 67

Hart, Levi A., 68; see also Hart & Bailey
Hatteras Inlet, NC, 86, 96, 117, (*n*176)
Hawes, John R., Captain, Company E, 8th Regiment, North Carolina Volunteers, 83, 95
Hedrick, John Jackson,
  Captain, Cape Fear Light Artillery, 70, 79, 95, 102, (*n*171), (*n*173); *military notice*, 5
  Major, Cape Fear Minute Men (Local Militia), 2
  Major, PACS, 119, 125, 134
Henry, George, Private, King Artillery, 122
Herring, William A., Captain, Herring Artillery, 121, 125, 146
Herring Artillery, 121, 125, 146
Hewlitt's Creek, NC, 118
Hill, Atherton B.,
  2nd Lieutenant Atherton B. Hill's Company of North Carolina Volunteers, 95, (*n*171)
  Captain Atherton B. Hill's Company of Cavalry, 101, 102, 107, 118, 122, 125, 134, 141, (*n*174), (*n*176)
Hill, Daniel Harvey,
  Brigadier General, PACS, 94, (*n*172)
  Major General, PACS, 138, 139
Hill, James H., Major, PACS, Assistant Adjutant General and Chief of Staff, Whiting's Command, Cape Fear River Defenses, 145, 146
Hill Guards, 134, (*n*181), (*n*183)
Hoke, John F., Adjutant General, North Carolina State Troops, 52, 65
Holmes, James C., Captain, Sampson Rangers, 79
Holmes, Theophilus Hunter,
  Colonel, ACSA/Brigadier General, North Carolina Volunteers, 67, 69, 71, 72; *image*, 67
  Brigadier General, PACS, 72, 77, 85, 86
  Major General, PACS, 119, 121, 138
Hood, John Bell, Brigadier General, PACS, 145, 146
Hook-Slant Rifling
Howard, William C., Captain William C. Howard's Company of Cavalry, North Carolina Volunteers, 100, 101, 102, 118, 125, 134, (*n*172), (*n*173), (*n*174), (*n*180)
Howe, Robert, Revolutionary Patriot, 3
Hoy, Patrick C., Lieutenant, Confederate Guards Artillery, 100, (*n*172), (*n*173)
Huggins Island, NC, 101, 117, (*n*175)
Hughes, Samuel, see Cecil Iron Works
Hunter, Samuel Benjamin, Captain, Pamlico Artillery, 132, 146, (*n*179)

Indian Territory, U. S., 78
Iredell Blues, 71, (*n*167)

Iverson, Alfred,
  Colonel, 10th Regiment North Carolina Volunteers, 79, 86, 95,
  Colonel, 20th Regiment North Carolina Infantry, 101, 102, 119, 120, 125, 132, 134

James M. Eason and Brother, 98, 99, 123
James River, VA, 138
Jefferson Barracks, Missouri, 78
Johnson, Duncan T., Private, King Artillery, 133
Johnston, Gabriel, 3rd Royal Governor of North Carolina, 3
Johnston, Joseph Eggleston, Brigadier General, ACSA, 145
Jones, Joseph P., Captain, 71, (n167)
Jones, John Meredith, 1st Lieutenant, Company B, 3rd Battalion North Carolina Light Artillery, 96
Jones Mill Pond, NC, (n181)

Kate, blockade runner, 139
Keith, E. A., 131
Kenan, Thomas S., Colonel, 43rd Regiment North Carolina Infantry, 121, 125, 134, (n177)
King Artillery, 100, 102, 122, 125, 133, 146, (n173)
Kinston, NC, 77, 121, 140, (n177), (n178), (n182), (n183), (n184)

Lamb, William,
  Major and Assistant Quartermaster, 120, 133
  Colonel, 36th Regiment North Carolina Troops (2nd Artillery), 131, 133, 134, 135, 136, 137, 146, 149, (n181); *image*, 133
Lamb Artillery, 132, 133, 140, 146, (n183)
Lane, James Henry, Colonel, 28th Regiment North Carolina Infantry, 95, 96, 102, 118
Lane, James S., Captain, Gatlin Artillery, 121, 125, 132, 140, 146
Lanier, John R., Captain John R. Lanier's Company North Carolina Volunteers, 117, 125, (n175), (n181)
Lanier, William B.,
  Captain William B. Lanier's Company North Carolina Infantry, 134, (n181), (n183); see also Hill Guards
  Captain, Company H, 61st Regiment North Carolina Infantry, (n183)
Laura, steamer, 84
Law, Evander McIver, Colonel, PACS, 145
Lazaretto Battery, 118, 132, 134, 138, 148, (n176), (n180), (n182); *maps*, 126, 129, 144

Lee, Robert Edward, General, ACSA, 121, 136, (n180)
Leggett, John E., Captain, Bridgers' Artillery, 146
Lenoir Braves, 121, 125, 134, 146
Lenoir County, NC, 77
Letcher, John, Governor, State of Virginia, 52, 68, 80
H.M.S. Levant, 81
USS Levant, 81, 151
Leventhorpe, Collett, Colonel, 11th Regiment North Carolina Infantry, 132, 134, 138, 139, 140, 141, (n179); *image*, 138
Lewis, William B., Captain, Company A, 10th Battalion North Carolina Heavy Artillery, 132, 140, 146
Lewis, William W., Private, Brunswick Artillery, 133
Light House Battery, Wilmington, 117, 118, 125, 132, 138, 141, 147, 148, (n176), (n179), (n185); *maps*, 126, 129, 144
Lighthouse Battery, Confederate Point, 84, 94-95, 100; *maps*, 88, 107
Lisbon Soldiers Aid Society, 100
Louisiana, State of, 78

Magruder, Allan B., Major, PACS, Commissary of Subsistence, Whiting's Command, Cape Fear River Defenses, 145-146
Mallett, Edward,
  Captain, Robinson Artillery, 121, 125, (n183)
  Captain, Company C, 61st Regiment North Carolina Infantry, (n183)
Malloy, Charles, Captain, Company F, 8th Regiment North Carolina Volunteers, 83, 94, 95
Manassas, VA, 1st Battle of, 145
Martin, James Green, Brigadier General, District of North Carolina, 139
Martin, Josiah, Last Royal Governor of North Carolina, 3
Maryland Regiments,
  1st Regiment Maryland Infantry, 121, 125, (n178)
Masonborough Inlet, *maps*, 87, 88, 126
Masonborough Sound, 78, 79, 118, 119, (n171), (n176), (n179), (n180); *map*, 107
Massachusetts, State of, 65
McArthur, John S., 1st Lieutenant, Scotch Greys, 125
McBryde, Malcom H., Captain, Scotch Greys, 146
McCauley, Charles, M. T., Captain, 10th Battalion North Carolina Heavy Artillery, 132, 147
McClellan, George Brinton, Major General, USA, (n180)
McDonald, Ann, 4
McDonald, James R., Captain, Company D, 51st North Carolina Infantry, 132

McGoogan, Hugh, Private, Company D, 51st North Carolina Infantry, 131
McLaurin, William H., 1st Lieutenant, 100
McLean, A.B., 17
McMillan, John Cornelious, Captain, Company E, 30th Regiment North Carolina Infantry, 125
McMillan Artillery, 121, 125, 136, 146
McNair, Malcom, Captain Malcom McNair's Company, North Carolina Volunteers, 100; see next Scotch Greys
McNeely, Francis M. Y., Captain, Rowan Rifle Guards, 71, (n167)
McNeill, John B., Private, Scotch Greys, 131, 133
McRae, Alexander, Captain Alexander McRae's Company Heavy Artillery, 121, 125, 132, 146, (n177)
McRae, Duncan K., 51, 52
McRae, John J., Governor of Mississippi, 120
Meade, Richard Kidder, Captain, C. S. Corps of Engineers, 135
Meares, Oliver Pendleton,
  Captain, Wilmington Rifle Guards, 18, 19, 71
  Lieutenant Colonel, PACS, 8th Regiment North Carolina Volunteers, 83
Meares, Thomas D., 51
Melvin, John T., Captain, Bladen Artillery, 146
Mexican War, 78, 119, 120
Mississippi, State of, 65, 78, 120, (n172)
  Army of Mississippi, 120
Missouri, State of, 78
Missouri, U. S. Territory of, 78
Mobile, AL, 99, 123
Modern Greece, blockade runner, 137, 148
Monterey, Mexico, Battle of, 78, 120
USS Monticello, 103, 122, 135
Moore, Alexander D., Captain, Company E, 10th Regiment North Carolina State Troops (1st Artillery Regiment), 78, 83, 95, 96, 100, 118, 125, 132, 134, 140, 142; *military notice*, 78; see also Moore's Battery
Moore, James, Captain, Colonial British Army, 3
Moore, John F.,
  Captain John F. Moore's Company of North Carolina Volunteers, 134, (n181), (n183)
  Captain, Company G, 61st Regiment North Carolina Infantry, (n183)
Moore's Bastion, *map*, 149
Moore's Battery, 83, 95, 96, 100, 118, 122, 125, 132, 134, 140, 142, (n171), (n176), (n180)
Morehead City, NC, (n175)

Morey, John B., Major and Chief Quartermaster, 120, (n177), (n181)
Morris Island, SC, 65, 66, *image*, 89
Mount Tirza, NC, 147
Munn, Daniel,
  Captain Daniel Munn's Company of Artillery, North Carolina Volunteers, 101; see next Bladen Stars
Myrover, James H., 1st Lieutenant, Starr's Battery, 49, (n175)
Myrtle Sound, NC, *map*, 142

Nassau, Bahamas, 139
National Intelligencer, Washington, 15
Neuse River, NC, 101, (n177)
New Berne, NC, 3, 67, 80, 86, 99, 118, 119, (n168), (n175), (n176), (n183)
New Hanover County, NC, (n172); *maps*, 87, 105, 142, 143, (n176)
New Inlet, Cape Fear River, 4, 69, 70, 79, 80, 103, 135, 140, 141, (n174); *maps*, 88, 107
New Jersey, State of, 119
New Mexico, U. S. Territory of, 78
New Orleans Barracks, LA, 78
New Topsail Inlet, *map*, 142
Newkirk, Abram Francis, Captain A. F. Newkirk's Company of Cavalry, 100, 102, 104, 107, 122, 125, 141, 146, (n172), (n183)
Norfolk, VA, 68, 86, 97, 100, 118, (n
Norment, William Stokes, Captain, Company D, 8th Regiment North Carolina Volunteers, 83, 95
CSS North Carolina, 141
North Carolina, Department of, see Department of North Carolina
North Carolina, District of, 139
North Carolina, Royal Colony of, 2, 3
  General Assembly, 3
North Carolina, State of, 1, 3, 18, 19, 51, 52, 53, 67, 68, 69-70, 72, 77, 78, 79, 80, 82, 85, 86, 89, 90, 91, 96, 97, 101, 117, 120, 131, 139, 142, 145, 147, 151
  Arsenal at Fayetteville, 83
  Coast Defenses, 67, 72, 85, 86, 93, 94
    Northern Department, 72, 94
    Southern Department, 72, 77, 79
  Convention, see North Carolina Convention
  Defenses, 65, 66, 67
  Government, 83
North Carolina, State of (continued on page 204),

North Carolina, State of (continued from page 203),
  Military Board, 77
  Militia,
    1st Artillery Regiment, 85
    30th Infantry, 1, 2
    Corps of Artillery, Ordnance and Engineers, 83
    Quartermaster General's Office, 145
  Volunteers, see North Carolina Regiments
North Carolina Convention, 52, 117
North Carolina Regiments,
  2nd North Carolina State Troops, 121, 125, 132, 134, (n178)
  3rd Battalion, North Carolina Light Artillery, 96
  3rd North Carolina State Troops, 70, 77
  6th North Carolina State Troops, 94
  7th North Carolina State Troops, 86
North Carolina Regiments (continued),
  8th North Carolina State Troops, (n183)
  8th Volunteers, 83, 85, 94, 95, 100, 136, (n171)
  10th Battalion North Carolina Heavy Artillery, 132, 140, 146, 147
  10th North Carolina State Troops (1st Artillery)
    Company E, see Moore's Battery
    Company I, see Whitford's Battery
    Company K, see Washington Grays
  10th Volunteers, 79, 86, 95, 102, 121
  11th Infantry, 132, 134, 138, 140, (n179), (n180)
  15th Volunteers, 95, 100, (n171)
  18th Infantry (vice 8th Volunteers), 101, 134, (n173) (n176)
  20th Infantry (vice 10th Volunteers), 101, 102, 107, 118, 119, 120, 125, 132, 134, (n174), (n179)
  25th Infantry (vice 15th Volunteers), 101, 134
  28th Infantry, 95, 96, 101, 102, 118, 134, (n174)
  30th Infantry, 95, 101, 102, 107, 118, 119, 122, 125, 132, 134, (n171), (n173), (n174), (n180)
  31st Infantry, (n183)
  36th North Carolina Troops (2nd Artillery), 101, 102, 118, 132, 133, 134, (n173)
  41st Regiment North Carolina State Troops (3rd Cavalry), 139-140
  42nd Infantry, (n181)
  43rd Infantry, 121, 125, 134, (n177)
  51st Infantry, 121, 125, 131, 132, 134, 140, (n180), (n182), (n183)
  56th Regiment North Carolina Infantry, 140, (n182)
  59th Infantry, (n181)
  61st Infantry, 140, 146, (n175), (n181), (n183)
North River, NC, (n178)
Northeast Station [Bridge], NC, (n182), (n183)

Oak Island, NC, 2, 4, 15, 16, 18, 70, 71, 79, 80, 84, 95, 120, 131, 133; *maps*, 9, 73, 107
Obstructions, The, 148
Ocracoke Inlet, (n169)
Oglethorpe Barracks, Savannah, GA, 66
Old Brunswick, 3, 84, 121
Old Inlet, Cape Fear River, 122, 141
Onslow County, NC, 118, 122, 125, 132, 134, 140, (n176), (n180), (n183)
Orrell, James, see Orrell & Hawes
Orrell & Hawes, 69, 124, 132
Orton Plantation, 121
Orton Pond, *maps*, 126, 144

Padgett, William T, Private, King Artillery, 133
HMS Palliser, 3
Palo Alto, Mexico, Battle of, 120
Pamlico, District of the, see District of the Pamlico
Pamlico Artillery, 132, 133, 146
Pamlico River, NC, 101, 117, (n177)
Paris, Andrew Bailey, Captain, Staunton Hill Artillery, 132, 146, (n179), (n185)
Parker, Frances Marion, Colonel, 28th Regiment North Carolina Infantry, 95, 102, 122, 125, 132, 134, (n171), (n173)
Partisan Rangers, (n183)
Pass Christian, Mississippi, 78
Patterson, Daniel, Captain, Clarendon Guards, 132, 146
Pendergrast, G. J., Flag Officer, U. S. N., 84
Pensacola, FL, 65
Perkins, Elisha A., Captain Elisha A. Perkins' Company of Cavalry, 118, 125, 134, 140, (n176), (n183)
Peters, William H., Navy Agent, State of Virginia, 68
Petersburg, VA, 52, 134, 138
Pickens, Francis, Governor, State of South Carolina, 51, 53
Piney Point, NC, 85; *map*, 87
Plymouth, NC, (n183)
Pontotoc County, MS, (n172)
Port Royal, SC, 100
Portsmouth, VA, 68, 100, (n167), (n168), (n169)
Portsmouth, NC, 86
Potter, Francis W., Captain, Lamb Artillery, 132, 140, 146
Potter, Samuel, 16, 17
Powder Charges, Propellant, 92
Powell, Oliver H.,
  1st Lieutenant, Columbus Artillery, (n185)
  Captain, Columbus Artillery, 140, 146, (n185)

Preston, John Thomas Lewis, Lieutenant Colonel, 97
Price, James Eastus, 13
Price's Creek, 84
Projectiles, Spherical, see Artillery Ammunition
Projectiles, Conical, see Artillery Ammunition
Provisional Army of the Confederate States (PACS), 72, 85, 86, 99, 120, 146, (n168), (n170)
Purdie, Thomas James,
   Captain, Company K, 8th Regiment North Carolina Volunteers, 83, 95, (n171), (n173)
   Captain, Company B, 36th Regiment North Carolina Troops, see Purdie's Battery]
   Captain, Company K, 18th Regiment North Carolina Infantry, (n171), (n176)
Purdie's Battery, 101, 102, 118, (n173), (n175), (n176)

Radcliffe, James D.,
   Captain, Sampson Rangers, 71, 79
   Colonel, PACS, 8th Regiment North Carolina Volunteers, 83, 95, 100
   Colonel, PACS, 18th Regiment North Carolina Infantry, 101, (n173)
   Colonel, PACS, 61st North Carolina Infantry, 140, (n183)
Radcliffe Battery, 70, 79, 95, (n171); *maps*, 73, 88
Rains, Gabriel James, Brigadier General, Cape Fear River Defenses, 139, 145, 146; *image*, 140
CSS Raleigh, 141
Raleigh, NC, 19, 83, 84, 96, 132, 140, (n173), (n179)
Raleigh and Gaston Rail Road, 52
Raleigh Standard, (n178)
Rankin, Robert G.,
   Member, Wilmington Committee of Safety, 1
   Captain, Clark Artillery, 132, 147
Reeves' Point, 84
Reilly, James
   Ordnance Sergeant, United States Army, 1, 2
Resaca de la Palma, Mexico, Battle of, 120
Richardson, John A.,
   Captain, John A. Richardson's Co., North Carolina Volunteers, 100; see next Bladen Artillery
   Lieutenant Colonel, 36th Regiment North Carolina Troops (2nd Artillery), 133, 134, 146
Richmond, VA, 52, 85, 93, 98, 116, 117, 119, 121, 134, 138, 141, 148, 150, (n175), (n180)
USS Roanoke, 84
Richmond & Petersburg Rail Road Company, 99
River Guards, 147, (n179), (n185)
Roanoke Island, 117, 118, (n175)
Roanoke River, 139

Roberts, Thomas E., see Clarendon Iron Works
Robinson Artillery, 121, 125, (n183)
Rodgers, John, Commodore, U.S. Navy, President of the Board of Naval Commissioners, 16
Rodman, William B., Captain, Bridgers' Artillery, 121, 125
Rowan Rifle Guards, 71, (n167)
Rowland, Thomas, Cadet, C.S. Corps of Engineers, 101, 102, 117, 120, 121, 131
Russell, John, Civilian Fort Keeper, Fort Caswell, 18

St. Philip's Parish, NC, *church*, 131, 133
Sampson Rangers, 71, 79, (n168), (n171)
San Antonio, TX, 65
USS Saratoga, 81
Savage, Henry,
   3rd Lieutenant, Wilmington Light Infantry, 70, 71
   Captain, Company G, 8th Regiment North Carolina Volunteers, 83, 95
USS Savannah, 97
Savannah, GA, 66, 93, 132, (n179)
Savannah River. GA, 93
Scotch Greys, 101, 102, 125, 131, 133, 146, (n173), (n174)
Scotland Neck Mounted Rifles, 79, 95, 107, 134, (n171), (n174), (n183)
Scott's Hill, NC, (n172); *maps*, 104, 126, 144
Seaboard & Roanoke Rail Road, 68, 80
Seawell, J., Fayetteville, NC, 17
Seminole War, 78
Seven Pines, VA, Battle of, 145
Shaw, Elias F., Captain E. F. Shaw's Company of Confederate Volunteers, 134, 140, (n181), (n183)
Shepherd's Battery, 135, 137; *map*, 144
Shubrick Gun, 81, 147, 148, 161; *images*, 151, 152
Simons, James, Brigadier General, South Carolina Volunteers, 66
Simonton, Absalom K., Captain, Iredell Blues, 71, (n167)
Skates and Company, 99
Slough, Nelson,
   Captain, Cabarrus Guards, 70, 71
   Captain, Company A, 10th Regiment North Carolina Volunteers, 79, 95, (n171)
Smith, Benjamin, contractor at Fort Johnston, 3
Smith, Benjamin G., Captain, Benjamin Smith's Company of Cavalry, 140, 141, 146, (n183)
Smith, Burrell,
   Captain, Fair Bluff Volunteers, 70
   Captain, Company C, 10th Regiment North Carolina Volunteers, 79, 95

Smith, Gustavus Woodson, Major General, PACS, 145
Smith, John L., Captain, United States Army Corps of Engineers, 16
Smith Battery, see Battery Smith, 149
Smith's Island, NC, see Bald Head Island
Smithville, NC, 1, 2, 4, 13, 15, 16, 18 84, 95, 101, (n171), (n173), (n174), (n177), (n183); *map*, 9
Smithville Guards, 2
South Carolina, State of, 1, 17, 51, 65, 66, 83, 89. 98, 99, 100, 136, 139
Southerland, David J., First Lieutenant, Captain William C. Howard's Company of Cavalry, North Carolina Volunteers, (n180)
Spanish Navy, 3
Sparrow, Thomas, Captain, Company K, 10th Regiment North Carolina State Troops (1st Artillery), 102, 117, 125, 147; see Washington Grays
USS State of Georgia, 131
Stanly, John Bunn,
   Captain, Columbus Guards No. 4, 71
   Captain, Company D, 10th Regiment North Carolina Volunteers, 79, 95
Starke, William E., Colonel, 60th Virginia Infantry Regiment, 118
Starr, Joseph B., Captain, Starr's Light Battery, 117, 125, 137, 139, 140, (n175)
USS State of Georgia, 131
Staunton Hill Artillery, 132, 146, (n179), (n185)
Stevenson, James Martin,
   1st Lieutenant, Cape Fear Light Artillery, 5
   Captain James M. Stevenson's Company of Artillery, North Carolina Volunteers, 100, (n173); see next King Artillery
Strong, William Chase, First Lieutenant, Aide-de-camp, Whiting's Command, Cape Fear River Defenses, 145, 146, (n184)
Sugar Loaf Landing, Confederate Point, NC, 100
Sutton, William, Captain, Lenoir Braves, 121, 125, 134, 146, (n181), (n184)
Swansborough, NC, 100, 101, 102, 118, (n172), (n173), (n176)
Swift, Alexander J., 2nd Lieutenant, United States Army Corps of Engineers, 17, 18, 30
Swift, Joseph Gardner, United States Army Corps of Engineers,
   2nd Lieutenant, 3-4,
   Captain, 5, 17, 18, 69, (n14); *image*, 4
   Brigadier General, 17
Swift Creek Bridge, Craven County, NC, 121

Tait, George,
   Captain, Bladen Guards, 71
   Major, 8th Regiment North Carolina Volunteers, 83
   Captain, Bladen Artillery Guards, 132, 140, 146, (n179)
Tait, Robert,
   Captain, Bladen Infantry, 71, (n168)
   Captain, Company B, 8th Regiment North Carolina Volunteers, 83, 95
Taliaferro, William Booth, Major General, Virginia Militia, 68
Tansill, Robert, Captain, PACS, Inspector General, Whiting's Command, Cape Fear River Defenses, 145, 146
Tarboro, NC, (n183)
Taylor, John Douglas,
   Captain, Brunswick Artillery, 117, 125
   Major, 36th Regiment North Carolina Troops (2nd Artillery), 133
Taylor, John William,
   1st Lieutenant, River Guards, (n185)
   Captain, River Guards, 147, (n185)
Taylor, Walter H., Assistant Adjutant General on the staff of General Robert E. Lee, 121
Tew, Charles Courtenay, Colonel, 2nd North Carolina State Troops, 77, 132, 134. (n178)
Texas, Republic of, 78
Texas, State of, 65
Thurston, Stephen D., Captain, Smithville Guards, 2
Toon, William H.,
   Captain, Columbus Guards No. 2, 71
   Captain, Co. K, 10th Regiment North Carolina Volunteers, 79
Toon, Thomas Fentress, Captain, Company K, 10th Regiment North Carolina Volunteers, 95
Topsail Sound, *maps*, 104, 142
Trans-Mississippi Department, 138
Tredegar Foundry, see Tredegar Iron Works
Tredegar Iron Works, 52, 53, 56, 93, 96, 99, 102, 109, 112, 123, 124, 133, 134, 136, 137; *image*, 116
Trenton, NJ, 119
Tripp, William H., Captain, McMillan Artillery, 121, 125, 146
Turner, L. C., Civil Engineer, (n181)

Underwood, Joseph B., Captain, Company K, 51st North Carolina Infantry, 132, 134
United States of America, 2, 3, 5, 6, 7, 13, 14, 18, 19, 50, 51, 52, 53, 56, 58, 59, 60, 61, 62, 98, 99, 103, (continued on page 207)

United States of America (continued from page 206) 112, 113, 114, 123, 124, 136, 137, 141
   Army, 1, 2, 5, 5, 11, 14, 18, 49, 50, 51, 53, 55, 57, 66, 67, 77, 78, 83, 86, 94, 97, 118, 120, 123, 131, 145, 148
      1st Artillery, U. S. A., 54, 65
      3rd Artillery, U. S. A., 93, 120
      5th Infantry, U. S. A., 78
      7th Infantry, U. S. A., 78
      Corps of Engineers, 1, 4, 15, 16, 20, 65
      Ordnance Department, 16
      Ordnance Manual, 57
      Regulations, 50, 51
      System of Land Artillery of 1819, 50
   Arsenal
      Allegheny Arsenal, 16
      Harpers Ferry Arsenal, 145
   Coast Survey, 69
   Government, 1, 3, 69, 78
      Congress, 14, 15, 17, 18, 80
      War Department, 51
         Secretary of War, 4, 50, 69
   Military Academy at West Point, NY, 4, 15, 56, 57, 65, 77, 85, 93, 94, 120
   Navy, 9, 50, 68, 80, 81, 82, 84, 85, 86, 89, 90, 91, 96, 103, 110, 133, 135, 136, 138, 139, 140, 141, 147, 150, 151, 152, 160, 161
      Board of Naval Commissioners, 16
      Warrington Navy Yard, FL, 58
Utah, U. S. Territory of, 78

Vanderhorst, A., Volunteer Aide-de-camp, Whiting's Command, Cape Fear River Defenses, 146
Vicksburg, MS, 120
Virginia Militia, 68, 72
Virginia Regiments,
   60th Infantry, 118, 121, (n178)
Virginia, State of, 15, 17, 50, 52, 68, 71, 72, 82, 83, 84, 85, 93, 94, 97, 116, 120, 121, 141, 145, (n180)

Wade, William, Major, United States Army Corps of Engineers, 16
Walker, _____, Sergeant, United States Army, 18
Walker, George F., Captain, Company A, 51st North Carolina Infantry, 132, 134
Walker, James, 4
Walker, John,
Walker, Louisa Margaret, 4, 17
Walton, Thomas G., Captain Thomas G. Walton's Company of North Carolina Volunteers, 100, 102, (n173), (n176); see also Davis Dragoons

Ward, Edward W., Captain Edward W. Ward's Company of Cavalry of North Carolina Volunteers, 100, 102, 118, 125, 141, (n173), (n176), (n183)
Washington, D. C., 1, 4, 14, 15, 16, 17, 65, 93, 141
Washington Grays, 102, 125, 147
Watson's Branch, 118; see Camp, Watson's Branch
Wayne County, NC, 132
Weldon, NC, 52, 68, 80, 84, n167), (n168), (n169)
White Oak River, NC, 101
Whitehurst, Charles C., Captain Charles C. Whitehurst's Company, 121, 125, 146
Whitford, John Dalton, North Carolina Convention Delegate, 52
Whitford, John N., Captain, Company I, 10th Regiment North Carolina State Troops (1st Artillery), 121,
Whitford's Battery, 121
Whiting, Levi, Lt. Colonel, 1st U. S. Artillery, 65
Whiting, Mary A., 65
Whiting, William Henry Chase, *biography*, 65-66; *image*, 66
   U. S. Army Corps of Engineers, 65, 66
   Major, ACSA/Assistant Adjutant and Inspector General, South Carolina Forces, Morris Island, SC, 66
   Major, ACSA/Inspector General, North Carolina Defenses, 65, 66, 67, 68, 69, 70, 71, 77, 80, 84, 86, 138
   Major, ACSA/Chief of Staff to General Joseph Eggleston Johnston, 145
   Brigadier General, PACS, 141, 145, 146, 147, 148, 149, 152
Williams, Lewis S., Captain, Hornet's Nest Riflemen, 19
Williams, Robert D., Captain, Company I, 8th Regiment North Carolina Volunteers, 83, 94, 95
Williamson, Nathan L., Captain Nathan L. Williamson's Company of North Carolina Volunteers, 118, (n185); see Columbus Artillery
Wilmington, NC, 1, 2, 4, 15, 18, 19, 51, 52, 65, 66, 67, 69, 70, 71, 72, 79, 80, 85, 86, 94, 95, 9, 98, 99, 100, 101, 102, 103, 109, 117, 118, 119, 120, 121, 122, 125, 131, 132, 133, 134, 138, 139, 140, 141, 142, 145, 146, 147, 148, (n173), (n174), (n175), (n176), (n177), (n178), (n179), (n180), (n181), (n182), (n183), (n184); *maps*, 87, 105, 106, 107, 126, 128, 129, 143, 144, 149
Wilmington and Manchester Rail Road, 52
Wilmington and Weldon Rail Road, 52, 69, 80, 85, 86, 96, (n175), (n182)
Wilmington City Garrison, 140, 147

Wilmington Committee of Safety, 1, 49, 69, 70, 79, 85, 94

Wilmington Horse Artillery, 79; see also Bunting's Battery

Wilmington Iron and Copper Works, see Hart & Bailey

Wilmington Journal, 96

Wilmington Land Defenses, 132, 138, 140, 142, 147, 148, 151, 152; *maps*, 143, 147, 149

Wilmington Horse Artillery, 79; see also Bunting's Battery, 79

Wilmington Journal, 96

Wilmington Light Artillery, 78, 83; see also Moore's Battery

Wilmington Light Infantry, 19, 70; *military notice*, 70

Wilmington Rifle Guards, 19, 71; *military notice*, 18

Winder, John H., Colonel, U.S. Army, 71

Winder, John C., Captain, North Carolina Corps of Artillery, Ordnance and Engineers, Chief Engineer, Cape Fear Defenses, 67, 79, 83, 86, 94, (n170)

Winder Battery, 79, 80, 82, 95, 102, 103, 125, 135, 146, 148, (n173); *maps*, 88, 107, 126, 144

Winslow, Warren, Military Secretary to the Governor of North Carolina, 19, 84, 85

Wood, Thomas F., Private, 8th Regiment North Carolina Volunteers, 136

Woolley, Abram R., Colonel, United States Army Corps of Engineers, 16

Wrightsville, NC, (n174)

Wrightsville Sound, (n174), (n180); *map*, 107

Yellow Fever, 139, 141, 147, (n183), (n184)

Yorktown, VA, 123, 133, 145

Young, Wilton L., Major, 10th Battalion North Carolina Heavy Artillery, 132, 147

Zeek's (Zeeke's, Zeke's) Island, 79, 80, 82, 84, 95, 101, 102, 103, 118, 125, 135, 140, 146, 148, (n171), (n173), (n174), (n176), (n184); *maps*, 88, 107, 126, 144

Compendium

Commanders of the Cape Fear

Colonel John Lucas Paul Cantwell, 30th North Carolina State Militia	*16 April 1861 – 21 April 1861*
William Henry Chase Whiting, Inspector General, North Carolina Defenses	*21 April 1861 – 15 May 1861*
Colonel John Lucas Paul Cantwell, 30th North Carolina State Militia	*15 May 1861 – 27 May 1861*
Brigadier General Theophilus Hunter Holmes, North Carolina Troops	*27 May 1861 – 1 June 1861*
Colonel Charles Courtenay Tew, 2nd North Carolina State Troops	*1 June 1861 – 18 June 1861*
Brigadier General Richard C. Gatlin, North Carolina Troops	*18 June 1861 – 18 August 1861*
Brigadier General Richard C. Gatlin, PACS	*18 August 1861 – 20 August 1861*
Colonel Alfred Iverson, PACS, 10th Regiment North Carolina Volunteers	*20 August 1861 – 29 September 1861*
Brigadier General Joseph Reid Anderson, PACS	*29 September 1861 – 15 March 1862*
Colonel Alfred Iverson, PACS, 10th Regiment North Carolina Volunteers	*15 March 1862 – 22 March 1862*
Brigadier General Samuel Gibbs French, PACS	*22 March 1862 – 15 July 1862*
Colonel Collett Leventhorpe, PACS, 11th Regiment North Carolina Infantry	*15 July 1862 – 18 August 1862*
Brigadier General Thomas Lanier Clingman, PACS	*18 August 1862 – 3 September 1862*
Brigadier General Gabriel James Rains, PACS	*3 September 1862 – 8 November 1862*
Brigadier General William Henry Chase Whiting, PACS	*8 November 1862*

www.ingramcontent.com/pod-product-compliance
Lightning Source LLC
Chambersburg PA
CBHW082119230426
43671CB00015B/2736